THE URBAN DWELLER'S
COUNTRY ALMANAC

BERNARD SCHOFIELD

WITH ILLUSTRATIONS AND PICTURES BY

BETTY SWANWICK, ARA., JOHN SHELLEY, JEAN COOKE, RA.,
ROGER KEMLO, REYNOLDS STONE, ALAN FIRTH, AND OTHERS,
INCLUDING THE AUTHOR.

CASSELL
LONDON

CASSELL LTD.
35 Red Lion Square, London WC1R 4SG
and at Sydney, Auckland, Toronto, Johannesburg,
an affiliate of
Macmillan Publishing Co., Inc.,
New York.

First published 1978

ISBN 0 304 30235 X

Designed by Bernard Schofield

Filmset and printed in Great Britain by
BAS Printers Limited, Over Wallop, Hampshire

CONTENTS

ILLUSTRATIONS

ACKNOWLEDGEMENTS

I wish to express my sincerest appreciation to the many contributors to my book; not just those professional people who supplied information, the pictures, illustrations and ideas, but to a host of friends and acquaintances whose invaluable assistance enabled the task of creating *The Urban Dweller's Country Almanac* to be a fulfilling and rewarding experience. Alphabetically, those people are as follows:

Tim and Edna Anderson for train illustrations. Alexandra Artley at the Architectural Press for untold help in preparing the manuscript and photographic material, and especially for permission to reproduce her article on seacoaling. Howard Barker Ltd for permission to reproduce the poem *Sussex Railway* by Philip Burchett. Jo Barry for permission to reproduce her picture *Running Water*. Peter Boyce for his photographs of sea-coaling. The British Bicycle Bureau for permission to reproduce part of their booklet *Before the Traffic Grinds to a Halt*. The British Kite Flyers Association for photographs appearing in the chapter 'Skyworks'. Curtis Brown Ltd for permission to reproduce an illustration by Clare Leighton from her book *Four Hedges: A Garden Chronicle*. Bob and Sarah Bullock for the loan of reference books. Tom Burke and Friends of the Earth for help with the 'Allotment Lib' chapter. Carolyn Canon for allotment photographs. CBS Records for permission to reproduce the lyrics of *London's Burning* by The Clash. Carolyn Chapman for her picture *Hanging Basket*. Collins Ltd for permission to reproduce the illustration by Lennox Paterson taken from the book *The Roadmenders* by Michael Fairless. Jean Cooke, R.A., for permission to reproduce her picture *Persephone*. Ted Cooke for the illustration at the head of the chapter 'Rocks Around the Clock'. The Coo Press for permission to reproduce the photograph by Rostislav Kostal from their book *Creative Camera International Yearbook 1975*. Mike Esau for his photograph of the Bluebell Railway. Alan Firth for providing photographs of his canal paintings. Liz and Gavin Gault – my biggest thank you – for their superb kindness in providing me with a home. Phyllis Hallet for permission to reproduce her photographs of toy theatre sets. Dennis Hawkins for retouching the photographs. The Hunt Saboteurs for providing the information and photographs for the chapter 'Hounds Off Our Wildlife'. The Inland Waterways Association for the use of information about boat hire and navigation in 'Canalways'. Marie and Alan Jenkins for topiary photographs. Keighley and Worth Valley Railway Preservation Society for photographs. Roger Kemlo for jacket illustrations and various illustrations throughout the book. Louise King for supplying original prints and other visual material. Jethro and Jackie Large for the loan of reference books. Gordon and Pam McPherson – a special thank you – for supplying masses of information and visual material. Methuen & Co. for permission to quote from *Wind in the Willows* by Kenneth Grahame (text copyright University Chest, Oxford). Margaret Pemberton for getting the children at the Brook Hospital to draw pictures of bicycles – of which those by David Degan, Sharon Evans, Bernadette Ryan, Dawn Sheldrake and Gary Turner appear in this book. Andy Pittaway, my old mate of *Country Bizarre* fame, for visual material and for the helpful design and photographic services of Walkaway Studios, Banbury. Radio Times Hulton Picture Library for permission to reproduce photographs appearing in the chapters 'The Strange World of Topiary' and 'The Art of Dowsing'. The Arthur Ransome Estate for permission to reproduce the illustration from *Peter Duck* by Arthur Ransome and to quote from that book and from *Pigeon Post*. Romney, Hythe and Dymchurch Light Railway Co. for photographs. Charli and Mick Sanderson – a special thank you – for the loan of many beautiful books and other visual material, and especially for negotiating permission to reproduce engravings by Charli's uncle, Reynolds Stone. John Shelley for supplying photographs of his paintings. Dave Smith for photographic services. Denis and Denny Smith for topiary photographs. Keith Smith for railway photographs. The Smithsonian Institution for permission to reproduce the illustration at the head of the chapter 'A Gourmet Guide to Wild Eating'. Reynolds Stone for the title page engraving and that appearing on page 8. Betty Swanwick, A.R.A. – a special thank you – for permission to reproduce four of her paintings, for much of the information appearing in the chapter 'The Juvenile Theatre', and for her much-valued friendship and support. *Time Out* magazine for permission to reproduce the illustration by Bill Sanderson. Mary Van Riemsdyk for permission to reproduce her drawing *Wild Plants*. Nicholas Verrall for his picture *Harvest Mice*. Mark Wilkins for the photographs of the Torbay Railway.

I would especially like to thank Simon Scott my editor, Simon Bell my designer, and Stanley Mitchell my production manager at Cassell for all their help and assistance. Finally I wish to thank JC for letting it all happen.

INTRODUCTION

When we come to look back on the sophisticated seventies as an historical exercise, or nostalgically in much the same way as we are now viewing the forties, fifties and sixties, I am certain that, contrary to the general opinion, there will be much to admire amongst the current trends in life. Exactly what will be regarded as good may be open to discussion but I am sure a strong contender will be the ecological/self sufficiency/crafts revival movement which so many people have embraced in one way or another. And here I am thinking not so much of those adventurers who, in feeling the call of the wild, have uprooted themselves and sought solace in the country as part of the back-to-nature brigade; I am referring rather to that sizeable majority who live and work in the cities and suburbs.

As someone, strange as it may be, who passionately loves the city and all it has to offer, I find it heartening to see so much evidence of this 'new awareness' of the environment among urban people in what is basically a more human approach to life. Whether it be working an allotment, travelling by bicycle, baking home-made bread, or making a stand against bureaucratic vandalism of buildings or communities, the changing attitudes towards what has for long been an entrenched way of life can only be for the good. The sickness in our society may be attributed to many complex factors but there can be no doubt that the vast process of dehumanization in one form or another that affects everybody, but especially the urban dweller, has contributed greatly to society's ills. We can be thankful that there are signs that ordinary people have had enough. From the grassroots movements just mentioned to the more fundamental issues of human rights there are signs that urban man is undergoing a period of considerable change, and some of it is for the good.

The *Urban Dweller's Country Almanac*, then, is not just a colourful book of rustic allsorts for urban people but a serious reflection of the new awareness. It presents in a seasonal format a breath of clean air to those of us who, through accident or design, have little time on our hands to get out of town; a rural sampler for those to whom the countryside is at the other end of a day excursion or the annual holiday, where 'back to the soil' and its related activities are confined to the back garden, and where the crafts revival is simply an after-dinner substitute for the television.

The book should work on two levels. On the one hand the sheer weight of information within its pages should be enough to keep the reader engrossed for hours, with as condensed and comprehensive a guide to the twenty-odd subjects featured as can ever be found, including an all-embracing reference section. On the other hand, dear reader, the book should visually blow your mind. Among the many illustrations, photographs, paintings and engravings that are to be found inside, there is a wealth of talent from contemporary artists as well as the unquestionable 'greats' from the past.

I hope, then, that you enjoy this book. Although it took a lot of hard work to complete I derived immense pleasure from seeing it all come together. If some of this pleasure rubs off on others then at least the effort will not have been in vain.

Bernard Schofield

Spring
Section

THE SUBURBAN BUTTERFLY FARM

Everyone may confirm his belief in the Divine when he considers those insects which, impelled by the craving of a sort of love, ardently seek for a change from their earth-bound state to one like that of heaven. For this purpose they creep into suitable places, weave round themselves a cocoon and thus, as it were, return into the womb to be born again, becoming pupae and finally butterflies. When they have passed through these changes and put on their beautiful wings after their kind, they fly into the air as into a heaven of their own, where they sport in happy mood, choose mates, lay their eggs, and provide for themselves a posterity. In this state they feed upon a sweet and pleasant nectar drawn from the flowers. Anyone who confirms his belief in the Divine from the visible things of nature sees an image of man's earthly state in them as insects, and of his heavenly state in them as butterflies.

EMMANUEL SWEDENBORG, FROM
'THE TRUE CHRISTIAN RELIGION'

ONE of the strangest and truly exciting events in my life goes back to early childhood days when I was holidaying with my parents on the Isle of Wight. On this particular day we were on one of those holiday camp mystery tour coach rides going round the island. It was a gloriously sunny day, I remember, with the deepest of blue skies and not a cloud in sight. Suddenly as we came round a sharp bend in the road the coach became enveloped in what at first appeared to be a snow storm. The 'snow' turned out to be white butterflies – cabbage white most probably – millions of them. I remember the coach driver stopped and everyone gasped with wonder and delight at what we might now call a freak of nature. In those days, though, clouds of butterflies were not uncommon. In our garden at home I can always remember the blue scabious and phlox flowers being smothered with Red Admirals and Tortoiseshells and how impossible it was to walk down the garden path for fear of treading on dozens of butterflies sunning themselves.

Sadly, many once common species such as the Swallowtail, Glanville Fritillary and Large Blue are now tragically rare and a few are on the verge of extinction. As usual, man is the root cause of the severe drop in the butterfly population. Collecting, pollution, and environmental disruption of natural habitats have all taken their toll. So it is not without special significance that this chapter is devoted to the breeding and subsequent releasing of butterflies back into the wild. Apart from the benefit to the local ecosystem (even though it be an urban one) there will be the added joy of observing at close quarters the astonishing life cycle of the butterfly, surely one of the wonders of nature.

Collecting and Buying Livestock

Some books advocate collecting the eggs and larvae of some of the more common species from the wild but this seems wholly irresponsible. Even removing eggs from the confines of a private garden is to be discouraged unless the habitat or foodstuff is under threat of destruction. The golden rule is to obtain livestock from a reputable butterfly farm. Stock from a farm will not have endangered the population in the wild and there is the added advantage of a wide range of species from which to choose.

Which Species to Breed?

If the motive behind breeding is the eventual release of adults into the wild, then careful consideration must be given to the species reared. Most butterflies (except Red Admiral, Clouded Yellow and Painted Lady) remain in the locality where they were born provided there is sufficient food. Therefore the choice of species should be governed by the types of flowers, shrubs and trees growing in your own particular area. A check at the local natural history museum or nature centre should provide details of butterflies native to the district and a thorough survey of the neighbourhood flora will give a guide to the species which might survive. Here is a list of British butterflies, their habitat and the foods on which their larvae feed:

ADONIS BLUE (*Lysandra bellargus*). Chalk and limestone areas in southern England. Vetches.

BATH WHITE (*Pontia daplidice*). Very rare in the south of England. Wild mignonette, weld, various cruciferae.

BLACK-VEINED WHITE (*Aporia crataegi*). Kent. Whitethorn, cherry, fruit trees.

BRIMSTONE (*Gonepteryx rhamni*). England, south and west Ireland. Buckthorn, alder buckthorn.

BROWN ARGUS (*Aricia agestis*). Local in south England and Wales. Storksbill, rock rose.

BROWN HAIRSTREAK (*Thecla betulae*). Local in south and west England and southern Ireland. Blackthorn, birch.

CAMBERWELL BEAUTY (*Nymphalis antiopa*). Rare in Great Britain. Birch, willow, poplar.

CHALK-HILL BLUE (*Lysandra coridon*). Chalk and limestone areas in England. Vetches.

CHEQUERED SKIPPER (*Carterocephalus palaemon*). Rare in open places and woods in the Midlands and southern English counties. Plantain, grasses.

CLOUDED YELLOW (*Colias croceus*). Great Britain generally. Clover, vetch.

COMMA (*Polygonia c-album*). Lanes, hedges and waste ground in England. Wild currant, raspberry, hop, hazel, honeysuckle, nettle, thistle, sloe, elm, willow.

COMMON BLUE (*Polyommatus icarus*). Great Britain generally. Clover, broom, yarrow, plantain, wild strawberry.

DARK GREEN FRITILLARY (*Argynnis aglaia*). Great Britain generally. Heaths, meadows, woods and downs. Dog violet.

DINGY SKIPPER (*Erynnis tages*). Railway embankments, heaths, woody pastures in Great Britain.

DUKE OF BURGUNDY FRITILLARY (*Hamearis lucina*). Sunny woods, bushes and hilly places in southern English counties and southern Scotland. Primrose, dock.

GATEKEEPER (*Pyronia tithonus*). Bushes and woodland paths in Great Britain, except Scotland. Brambles, wood sage, marjoram, meadow grass.

GLANVILLE FRITILLARY (*Melitaea cinxia*). Rare in the Isle of Wight. Hawkweed, plantain, germander, speedwell.

GRAYLING (*Hipparchia semele*). Local in Great Britain on heaths, dry stone places and on chalk. Couchgrass and other dry grasses.

GREEN HAIRSTREAK (*Callophrys rubi*). Shrubland and bramble. Broom, blackberry.

GREEN-VEINED WHITE (*Pieris napi*). Widespread in Great Britain, except Scotland.

GRIZZLED SKIPPER (*Pyrgus malvae*). Local in Great Britain. Blackberry, raspberry, bilberry, teazle.

HIGH BROWN FRITILLARY (*Argynnis adippe*). Heaths in England. Sweet violet, heartsease, bramble.

HOLLY BLUE (*Celastrina argiolus*). Open woods, gardens and hedgerows in England, Wales and Ireland. Flowers of buckthorn, ivy, holly.

LARGE BLUE (*Maculinea arion*). Very rare in the south. Thyme.

LARGE COPPER (*Lycaena dispar*). Very rare in the fens. Great water dock.

LARGE GARDEN OR CABBAGE WHITE (*Pieris brassicae*). Widespread in Great Britain. Cabbage, radish, mustard, cress.

LARGE HEATH (*Coenonympha tullia*). Scotland, Ireland, North Wales and the Midlands. Meadow grass, beak sedge.

LARGE SKIPPER (*Ochlodes venata*). Lanes and bushy areas throughout Great Britain. Couchgrass and meadow grasses.

LARGE TORTOISESHELL (*Vanessa polychloros*). Southern England, Wales and Scotland. Elm, willow, poplar, cherry, pear, apple.

LONG-TAILED BLUE (*Lampides boeticus*). Very rare in southern England. Pea-pods.

LULWORTH SKIPPER (*Thymelicus acteon*). Very rare in southern England. Grasses.

MARBLED WHITE (*Melanargia galathea*). Damp meadows and open woodland. Couchgrass and meadow grasses.

MARSH FRITILLARY (*Euphydryas aurinia*). Damp places and swamps, except in Scotland. Scabious, germander, speedwell, plantain.

MEADOW BROWN (*Maniola jurtina*). Meadows, grassy lanes and hillsides in Great Britain. Meadow grasses.

MONARCH or MILKWEED BUTTERFLY (*Danaus plexippus*). Occasional migrant from North America. Milkweed.

MOUNTAIN RINGLET (*Erebia epiphron*). Scotland, southern and western Ireland. Grasses in mountainous districts.

ORANGE TIP (*Anthocharis cardamines*). Widespread except north Scotland. Cress, cuckoo-flower, cruciferae.

PAINTED LADY (*Vanessa cardui*). Widespread throughout Great Britain. Nettle, thistle, mallow, artichoke.

PALE CLOUDED YELLOW (*Colias hyale*). Rare in south and east England. Lucerne, trefoil and other leguminous plants.

PEACOCK (*Inachis io*). Woods and lanes throughout Great Britain. Nettle, hop.

PEARL-BORDERED FRITILLARY (*Argynnis euphrosyne*). Woodlands in England and Scotland. Dog violet.

PEARL-BORDERED LIKENESS or HEATH FRITILLARY (*Melitaea athalia*). Heaths and woods in southern England and western Ireland. Plantain, cow wheat.

PURPLE EMPEROR (*Apatura iris*). Large woods in south-east England. Sallow.

PURPLE HAIRSTREAK (*Thecla quercus*). Locally in oak trees throughout Great Britain. Oak leaves.

QUEEN OF SPAIN FRITILLARY (*Argynnis lathonia*). Very rare in woods, gardens, and meadows in southern England and Ireland. Violet, borage.

RED ADMIRAL (*Vanessa atalanta*). Widespread throughout Great Britain in gardens, orchards, hedgerows. Nettle.

RINGLET (*Aphantopus hyperanthus*). Widespread in bushes by woodland paths, lanes and glades throughout Great Britain. Sedges and grasses.

SCOTCH ARGUS (*Erebia aethiops*). Scotland and northern England. Meadow grass.

SHORT-TAILED BLUE (*Everes argiades*). Very rare

in southern England. Lucerne, trefoil.

SILVER-SPOTTED SKIPPER (*Hesperia comma*). Local on meadows and hillsides over chalk in the southern and Midland counties. Couchgrass and meadow grasses.

SILVER-STUDDED BLUE (*Plebejus argus*). England and Wales. Trefoil.

SILVER-WASHED FRITILLARY (*Argynnis paphia*). Woods throughout Great Britain. Dog violet, raspberry, nettle, guelder rose.

SMALL BLUE (*Cupido minimus*). Chalk and limestone areas in southern England. Vetches and other low plants.

SMALL COPPER (*Lycaena phlaeas*). Fields, gardens and heaths in England. Dock and sorrel.

SMALL HEATH (*Coenonympha pamphilus*). Widespread in grassy places, meadows and heaths throughout Great Britain. Meadow grasses.

SMALL SKIPPER (*Thymelicus sylvestris*). Lanes, meadows, outskirts of woods throughout Great Britain. Fescue and other grasses.

SMALL TORTOISESHELL (*Aglais urticae*). Lanes, woods, gardens, and waste ground throughout Great Britain. Nettle.

SMALL WHITE (*Pieris rapae*). Widespread throughout Great Britain. Cabbage hearts, cress, mignonette.

SPECKLED WOOD OR WOOD ARGUS (*Pararge aegeria*). Lanes and woods throughout Great Britain. Couch-grass and meadow grasses.

SWALLOWTAIL (*Papilio machaon*). Norfolk Broads. Fennel, wild carrot, marsh milk parsley.

WALL BROWN (*Lasiommata megera*). Lanes, railway embankments, roadsides and sunny walls in the United Kingdom. Fescue grass.

WHITE ADMIRAL (*Ladoga camilla*). Rare in woods and open spaces in southern England. Honeysuckle.

WHITE LETTER HAIRSTREAK (*Strymonidia w-album*). Elm trees and blackberry blossom in the southern and Midland English counties. Elm.

WOOD WHITE (*Leptidea sinapis*). Local in England and Wales and south-west Ireland. Trefoils, vetches.

However, unless you happen to be lucky enough to live in the country or in close proximity to woods or open spaces, the butterflies released into the wild will inevitably try to make a home in the garden, and this is where positive action can be taken.

A Butterfly Garden

A garden bursting with flowers will not necessarily be a haven for butterflies. Indeed, unless the right type of food is available, they will disappear the moment they are released, and certainly not breed in the garden. Generally, most species are attracted to nectar-bearing flowers and shrubs and in particular the old fashioned, rather simple cottage garden perennials that our grandparents were so fond of. Many of these charming flowers can be bought as seed or even as plants from nurseries. Much the easiest and, incidentally, traditional way is to obtain a root or two from someone who has them growing in their garden (most cottage gardens were created in this way). The following list shows some butterfly-attracting plants:

AGERATUM	MARJORAM
ALYSSUM (white)	MEADOW CRANESBILL
ARABIS (pink and white)	MICHAELMAS DAISY
	MIGNONETTE
AUBRIETIA	MYRRH
BIRDSFOOT TREFOIL	PETUNIA
BLUEBELL	PHLOX
BRAMBLE	PINK THRIFT
BUDDLEIA (the butterfly bush)	POLYANTHUS
	PRIMROSE
CAMPION	RAGWORT
CANDYTUFT	RUBUS
CATNIP	SCARLET GERANIUM (common)
CLOVER	
COMFREY	SEA HOLLY
COWSLIP	SEDUM
DAISY	SENECIO
DANDELION	SOAPWORT
EGLANTINE ROSE	SWEET ROCKET
EVERLASTING PEA	SWEET WILLIAM
FOXGLOVE	THISTLE
FRENCH MARIGOLD (single)	THYME
	VALERIAN
GOLDEN ROD	VERBENA
HEATHERS	WALLFLOWER (purple and yellow)
HEBE	
HELIOTROPE	
HONEYSUCKLE	
KNAPWEED	
LAVENDER	
LILAC	
MALLOW	

Unfortunately, while nectar-bearing flowers may be sufficient to tempt butterflies to feed in the garden, they will not on their own be enough to tempt them to breed. Caterpillars require entirely different food in many cases, most of which falls under the unfortunate heading of 'weeds'. Nettles, thistles and dock, the scourge of most gardens, are the major food source of the Red Admiral, Painted Lady, Peacock, Tortoiseshell, and the Small and Large Copper butterflies. A butterfly garden, then, must have a wild area where nettles and other weeds can flourish undisturbed. This area should be sunny and sheltered and, if possible, lying in a small dip or hollow. An ideal spot is near a shed or some other outside building as certain species such as Peacocks like to hibernate inside for the winter. If possible, provision should be made to leave the door or window of the shed open for the butterflies.

One very important consideration is that of cats and birds. Cats love to chase butterflies and a cat in the house may prove a nuisance. Equally disastrous is a garden full of birds. If you want to encourage butterflies in the garden then don't encourage wild birds. On the positive side, leaving windfall apples on the ground will be beneficial. A number of species will feed from the rotting, fermenting fruit.

BREEDING

Equipment

When the eggs obtained from a butterfly farm hatch into caterpillars, a suitable cage or container will be needed to keep them healthy and under control and safe from pests and diseases. There are various types of containers suitable for this purpose:

CARDBOARD BOXES
An improvised larvae cage can be easily made from a grocer's cardboard box or confectionery carton. A shoe box is ideal. Cut out windows in the top and sides and stick over muslin or fine netting. All edges must be firmly secure to prevent wandering caterpillars from escaping.

PLASTIC BOXES
Plastic breeding boxes can be obtained from the butterfly farms but these are expensive. Exactly the same, but cheaper, are the sandwich boxes obtainable from most departmental stores. Plastic boxes provide a more secure cage and can be washed and sterilized after each breeding session. They must not be left in the sun because of the condensation. As caterpillars breathe very little there need be no concern over lack of air when the lid is on.

CRYSTAL PALACES
These specialized containers are only available from butterfly specialists and farms and consist of either rectangular or cylindrical transparent lids which fit over an opaque plastic bottom. The beauty of this type of cage is that food plants can be grown in them, thus providing a continuous supply of fresh foliage. Plant propagators from a garden centre are just as good but only marginally cheaper than crystal palaces.

WOODEN CAGES
The most suitable type of cage is one made from wood with muslin or netting windows. A cage of this type can be kept outside in the sun or in a greenhouse and is suitable for larvae, pupae or adults. They are expensive to buy but any competent handyman could make one up without too much trouble. A cage one foot square is a good optimum size, but it needs to be much bigger if butterflies are to be housed outside in the garden. For this it should be at least four feet square and bottomless to enable the cage to be positioned over growing plants. The cage must also be secure against wind and predators.

Greenhouses

If a greenhouse can be kept relatively cool (32–37°C) by netting the vents and open windows, then it will be ideal for breeding. Care must be taken to ensure that there are no bugs or spiders and that the place is free of mould or disease.

Hatching

Most eggs will start hatching within three weeks of being laid. They are best placed in a small plastic box lined with absorbent paper such as blotting paper, and a supply of fresh food. The eggs normally darken before hatching and when they do, it is advisable to let the larvae feed on the egg shells before transferring them to the fresh food (the tip of a sable brush is the easiest implement for transporting larvae). Whatever happens, don't put the box in the sun. The ideal position is in a north-facing room. Once the larvae have grown somewhat, transfer them to the rearing cage along with a supply of fresh food.

Feeding
Caterpillars need fresh food every day. For this reason it is easier and more beneficial to use growing plants rather than cut leaves as wilted leaves can be harmful. Healthy plants can be potted from the garden and placed in the cage, or planted straight into the cage itself. If cut food is being used, it is best to stand it in a jar of water to keep it fresh; leaning over to one side to prevent larvae drowning if they fall. It is useful to line the cage with blotting paper which not only soaks up moisture but facilitates cleaning.

When replacing food, the simplest method is to stand the fresh food next to the old and let the caterpillars make their own way to it. They will soon crawl on to the fresh food and the old uneaten food can then be thrown away.

Pupating
Plastic-box-reared larvae must not be left to pupate in the same container but be transferred to another cage or box. A shoe box or similar container makes an adequate pupating house. There they can be left in peace. Cage-reared larvae, on the other hand, are best left where they are and they will pupate hanging from the roof, on the plants, or at the bottom of the cage, depending on the species.

Once the chrysalids or cocoons have formed they must be stored in suitable conditions to prevent them drying out (unless they are going to emerge within a few weeks). In the wild this is effected by the action of rain and dew. In artificial conditions, this is best achieved by keeping them in airtight plastic boxes or tins in the refrigerator or some very cool place in the house or shed. Great care is needed so as not to damage the silk pads by which pupae anchor themselves as this may kill them. On no account put green material in the storing box as this may turn them mouldy and kill them too.

Emerging Butterflies
It is important to know the times of emergence of the species being reared because about three weeks prior to this, the pupae should be brought out from their cold hibernation. Keeping pupae in unnaturally low temperatures beyond their due emergence time will retard them.

Emerging adults will need to be placed in a wooden cage. Plastic boxes are unsuitable as the sides will prove too slippery for them when they try to climb up towards the light to dry their wings. The cage should have a netted top and sides so that the butterflies can secure a firm grip. It is often helpful to place twigs in the cage to assist their climb to the top of the cage. Equally beneficial will be a once-a-day spray of tepid water into the cage. This will help keep the pupae moist.

Once the butterflies have emerged, their immediate need will be for water. The cage and everything in it (including the butterflies) should be sprayed very gently with a very fine spray of water until small droplets appear. Apart from nectar-bearing flowers which need to be provided, it is a good idea to put a saucer of weak honey and sugar soaked into cotton wool in the cage. The solution must not be too strong otherwise the butterflies will gorge themselves to death. An ideal mixture is $\frac{1}{2}$ teaspoon honey, $\frac{1}{2}$ teaspoon sugar, $\frac{1}{4}$ teaspoon salt, dissolved in 1 breakfast cup water.

Newly-emerged adults can be kept in the cage, inside or outside, for about three days before releasing into the wild.

Pairing and Mating Butterflies
Getting hand-reared adults to pair and mate and subsequently lay eggs can be a difficult task as they will more likely be intent on escaping into the sun! However, there are certain rules to follow which will increase the likelihood of success.

Breeding cages should be light and airy. Converted cheese tubs make excellent breeding quarters. The cages with the adults should be placed in the sun while courting takes place. The golden rule with most species is to have the flowers and larval food plants as near to the surface of the cage as possible so that the butterflies have no choice but to be constantly near the egg-bearing plants. It is better to have just a few pairs in the cage. Differentiation between male and female is not immediately obvious but generally the female will either be lighter in colour or less finely marked.

At this stage it will be necessary to know the correct way to handle butterflies as they will need to be transferred to their mating quarters. The correct method of picking them up is to wait until they fold their wings together over their back. Then with thumb and finger they should be held firmly at the base of the wings, making sure that no rubbing occurs which might harm the wing scales.

Always use growing food in the adult mating cage if possible, or make sure that cut plants are perfectly fresh every day. The addition of a cotton wool pad of honey and sugar solution suspended near the roof of the cage is also beneficial. Once the females have laid their eggs (often on the underside of leaves) they should be fed regularly with a constant supply of nectar-bearing flowers and, if necessary, hand feeding using the honey/sugar solution. Pick up the females in the described manner and place gently on the flowers or cotton wool pad. Then gently unroll the proboscis (i.e. tongue) by which they feed, so that the tip is touching the pad. It is very important that their feet are on the pad too as butterflies 'taste' by their feet.

Finally, once the eggs have hatched, ensure the larvae have adequate fresh food, transferred now to the original small plastic boxes in a repeat of the whole amazing life cycle!

Parasites and Diseases
Eggs and larvae can succumb to viruses in captivity if the breeding conditions are unsatisfactory. Dirty cages, overcrowding, wet food, damp conditions and starvation are all adverse to healthy growth. Cages and boxes are best sterilized at the end of every breeding season, using a weak solution of sodium hydroxide.

Certain insects can attack caterpillars, though this is unlikely in sterile breeding conditions. Braconid wasps and dipterous flies are the chief culprits. Always ensure fresh food plants are not harbouring insects and that the soil for potted plants contains no predators such as earwigs. An effective method of eliminating any insect life on food plants is to douse the whole thing for a minute or two in warm water. This will not harm the plant but will kill most insect life.

That blue day, when the white dust paused
in the air as the chisel fissured
granite block – quarried to outlast decay
I remember a blue butterfly
that rose from dry grasses,
lifted airily over granite edge,
over corroded machine, over chasm,
in the beam of the sun – gone

Every moment is goodbye to every moment
but the beam of the mind is butterfly
GEORGE BRUCE

THE NATURAL HEALTH GARDEN

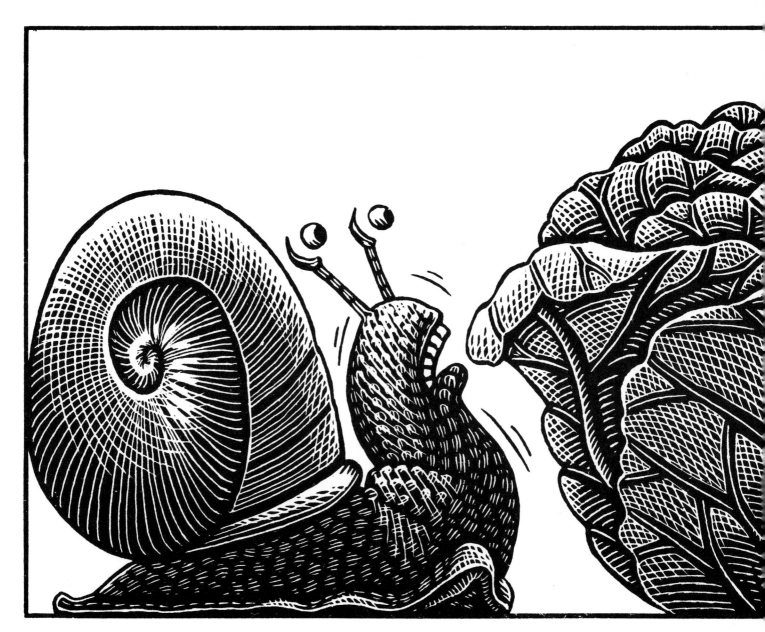

As I sat under a poplar tall
I saw nine pests come over the wall.

I saw nine pests come wandering by
A slug, a snail and a carrot fly.

I saw nine pests descending on me:
Wireworm weevil and radish flea.

I saw nine pests, a depressing sight:
Pear midge, mildew and apple blight.

Nine garden pests came over the wall,
And the woolly aphis was worst of all.
'I SAW NINE PESTS' BY REGINALD ARKELL

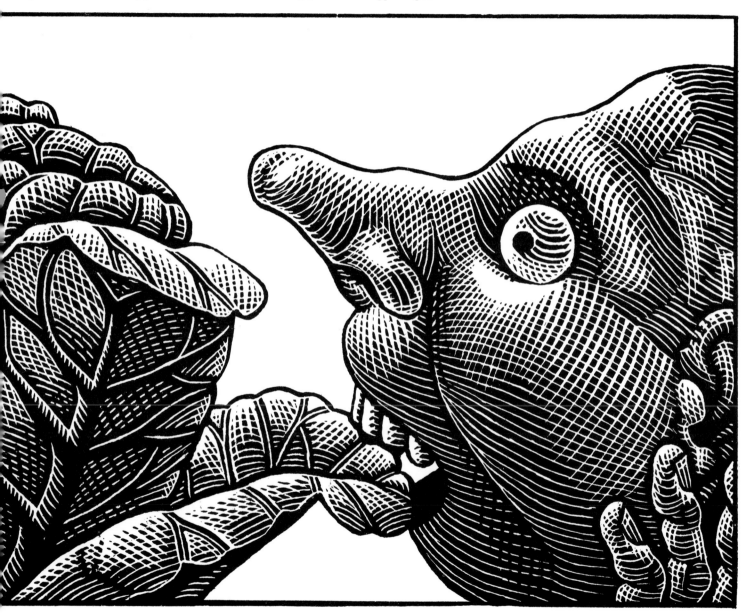

21

IT'S so easy to slip into the local garden centre for a packet of killer dust every time the roses succumb to white fly, or dandelions spring up in the lawn. Unfortunately convenience remedies and eradicators from the big chemical companies, while alleviating one biological problem, will almost certainly trigger off another – in terms of harm to wildlife or even to us humans.

Despite all the ecological doomsdaying that has been levelled at us in the last ten years, we are still basically a nation of chemical fertilizer and puff-pack users. Yet the fact is that while those nasty chemicals may be effective in the short term, in the long term they're downright destructive. And what's more, they're unnecessary too because for practically every pest and disease which scourges the garden there is a natural and non-toxic solution which usually clears up the problem, and at a fraction of the cost of the commercial concoctions.

Natural, or 'biodynamic', gardening consists of numerous radical concepts – companion planting, organic composting, the no-dig method, crop rotation, astrological planting – which fused together aim at natural, ecologically-balanced soil husbandry. Pests and disease are minimalized because as near as is humanly possible, the laws of nature are in control. In a nutshell, the policy of prevention rather than cure. Unfortunately we live in an imperfect world and while you may be doing your biodynamic thing, the next door neighbour isn't – which means you'll probably cop his unwanted slugs, greenfly and the like. In that case, forget about the garden centre and try a natural health cure.

An A–Z Guide to the Natural Health Garden

AMMONIUM SULPHAMATE

A safe non-toxic weed-killer. Within six weeks of use this chemical reverts to ordinary sulphate of ammonia and the ground is safe for crops. Use at the rate of 1 lb (454 g) to 1 gallon (4·5 litres) water and spray from a plastic watering can as it heavily corrodes metal. Only use in the growing season (preferably the spring) on such tenacious weeds as couch grass, dock, thistle, bramble, etc.

ANGLE SHADES MOTH (*Phlogophora meticulosa*)

Attacks chrysanthemums – the grubs feed at night. Treatment: spray with hellebore powder (i.e. dried powdered hellebore leaves). (Eggs laid on leaves in June.) Natural predator: Tachinid flies.

ANTS

A mixture of powdered borax and icing sugar, measure for measure, and sprinkled in the ant-infested area will prove effective indoors and out. Alternatively, derris or liquid pidero is an effective killer (see under separate heading). Otherwise plant ant-hating plants such as lavender, marigolds, tansy and chives.

APHIS BLIGHT

Attacks lettuce. Spray with soap solution or soot dust.

APPLE BLOSSOM WEEVIL (*Anthonomus pomorum*)

A bug that decimates the flowering apple buds. Treatment: tie six-inch bands of sacking or corrugated paper round the trunks or main branches in June. In October remove the bands with the weevils and burn. Natural predators: tits, wagtails and tree pipits.

APPLE CAPSID BUGS (*Plesiocoris rugicollis*)

Affect the fruit and leaves. Treatment: use a combination of the following: spray the tree with warm water to knock the bugs down and then apply grease-bands round the trunk and main branches to prevent their return.

APPLE SAWFLY (*Hoplocampa testudinea*)

The fly lays its eggs in the blossom and the larva tunnels into the fruit. Treatment: spray with quassia (see under separate heading) after the blossom fall and repeat two weeks later. Destroy all contaminated windfall apples, including the shrivelled and infested apples left on the tree. Alternatively, hang flypaper strips in the trees. Natural predator: starlings.

APPLE SUCKER (*Psylla mali*)

This aphis affects the blossom by turning it brown and withered. Treatment: spray in winter with derris or pidero, or with paraffin emulsion after apples are picked. Natural predator: gold crested wren.

APPLE TWIG CUTTER (*Rhychites caeruleus*)

A tenacious weevil that bites through shoot tips. Treatment: systematically pick up all shoots lying on the ground and remove any that are still hanging down on the tree. Burn these tips which contain the weevils.

ASPARAGUS BEETLE (*Crioceris asparagi*)

The grubs feed on the foliage. Treatment: spray the grubs with pidero or liquid derris. Natural predator: ground beetles.

BASIC SLAG

An industrial by-product which is rich in calcium and other nutrients. Ideal as a natural fertilizer.

BATS

Bats eat insects and are therefore friends in any garden. Protect them if you are lucky enough to have them around.

BEES

Bees are essential creatures for the proliferation of the vegetable kingdom which in turn means us. Careless use of chemical fertilizers, pesticides and herbicides kills hundreds and thousands of bees every year. Whenever possible, leave any spraying to be done to the evening when the bees have gone home to the hive as most organic pesticides are rendered harmless by the morning.

BEET AND MANGOLD FLY

Deep dig the bed in winter to destroy the pupae and manure well to encourage rapid growth which enables the plants to resist attack.

BIG BUD MITE

Spray between mid-March and mid-April (when the leaves are no bigger than the size of a thumb) with a weak solution of lime-sulphur, pidero or derris. A yearly spray with a silicon preparation will strengthen the plants' resistance to the pest.

BIOLOGICAL CONTROL

This involves the introduction of another insect or predator to feed off an established outbreak of another pest, usually when there are simply not enough natural predators to do the job. The danger here, of course, is that the newcomers can end up being the pest.

BIRDS

Many species of birds are the natural predator of insects that harm crops. Encourage thrushes, starlings, bullfinches, tits, swallows and others but use birdnets and the good old scarecrow to protect crops from over-zealous visitors.

BLACKFLY

A spray of warm water at 12°C; pyrethrum, derris, quassia; rhubarb; ryania, bracken water, or nettle water eliminates this bug (see under respective headings for individual treatments).

23

The blackfly lays its eggs on euonymus and viburnum plants and so a winter wash of tar oil in December on any nearby hedges of these plants will be greatly beneficial.

BLACKSPOT (*Diplocarpon rosae*)

Affects the leaves and buds on roses with round black patches. Treatment consists primarily of cutting out all affected parts and burning. Secondary treatment should be a heavy mulch of leaf-mould, compost or peat around the base which will prevent secondary infection from the soil. Spraying with an infusion of horsetail (*Equisetum arvense*) is effective, and as a last resort, a spray of liquid copper fungicide solution (see 'Bordeaux mixture').

BONEMEAL

A phosphorus-rich organic fertilizer of long lasting value to the soil. Also a good ant deterrent.

BORDEAUX MIXTURE

A colloidal copper fungicide which is effective in the treatment of various fungal diseases including potato blight. Available ready-to-mix (see list of suppliers).

BRACKEN

Mother Earth (see under Societies at end of book) have experimented with the juice of young bracken as a fungicide with varying results. They say that '. . . under certain conditions, bracken diluted to 1 in 2 (with water) and used regularly, works on certain mildews and fusarium rots although there is much more work that needs to be done before we can determine how valuable it is going to be'.

BROWN ROT

Attacks potatoes and the spores are carried from the foliage to the tubers by means of rainwater. Cut out all infested foliage and burn. Do not harvest for two weeks.

BUFF-TIP MOTH

Attacks roses. The eggs are laid in June. Treatment: gather the eggs or clusters of young caterpillars and destroy, and spray with hellebore. Natural predators: large Ichneumon flies.

BURGUNDY MIXTURE

A concoction comprising two separate mixtures added together. In a plastic bucket mix 3 oz (85 g) copper sulphate with 1 gallon (4·5 litres) water and leave overnight. In another bucket mix 4 oz (113 g) washing soda with 1 gallon water. Mix the two solutions together. Burgundy mixture is an effective treatment for apple and pear tree scab; apple, rose and gooseberry mildew, and peach leaf curl. Must not be sprayed onto foliage.

CABBAGE APHIS (Mealy Cabbage Aphis)

Spraying young crops with derris, pidero or pyrethrum is a good preventative treatment. Otherwise burn all brassica stumps during the winter which is where the aphids hibernate. Spraying with carbolic soap or a dry soot spray is a good preventative treatment. Natural predator: ladybirds.

CABBAGE GALL WEEVIL

Not to be mistaken for club root. In this case the small white larvae of the weevil cause the roots to swell. Systematically burn any infected roots.

CABBAGE MOTH

The eggs are laid in spring. Treatment: spray with a brine solution and gather off and destroy any eggs and larvae.

CABBAGE ROOT FLY (*Delia brassicae*)

Affects cauliflower and cabbages by stunting their growth. The treatment is preventative. Cut out four-inch squares from a length of tarred roofing felt and punch out a hole in the centres (about $\frac{3}{8}$ inch diameter). When planting out the brassica seedlings push the roots through the hole in the felt and plant normally. The growth of the plant makes a firm fit in the felt which thus forms an effective barrier against the fly. For infected plants, a good remedy is to take a handful of washing soda dissolved in a little hot water. Add a wineglass of paraffin and two buckets of cold water. Make a hole alongside each affected plant in a slanting position so as to come in contact with the roots and pour in about one pint of liquid per plant. Alternatively, make a hole beside the affected plants and fill with salt. Natural predator: rove beetles.

CABBAGE WHITE BUTTERFLY (*Pieris brassicae*)

The smell of rotting cabbage attracts this insect so remove all damaged and yellowing foliage. Picking off the caterpillars by hand is the simplest remedy but for severe infestations, spray with nicotine (see under separate heading) up to a month before eating. From then on spray with derris, or 2 oz (57 g) ordinary salt in 1 gallon (4·5 litres) water – on both sides of the leaves. One totally harmless repellent is sour milk. Add a little lemon juice or vinegar to some milk and spoon into the centre of each cabbage.

Effective for up to a week. Natural predators: birds, dragonflies and Ichneumon flies.

CABBAGE WHITEFLY (*Aleyrodes brassicae*)

Remove and burn all the lower leaves once infestation has been detected. Spray the undersides of the leaves with a soap solution (2 oz (57 g) soapflakes to 1 gallon (4·5 litres) water). Alternatively, spray with nicotine up to one month before eating.

CARNATION FLY

The grubs feed in the centre of the shoots. Treatment: spray with carbolic soap solution on the surface at base of plants. Natural predators: rove beetles.

CARPET MOTH

Attacks geraniums. Treatment: shake off the grubs at night and spray the soil with a brine solution.

CARROT FLY (*Psila rosae*)

The carrot fly is strongly attracted by the scent of the carrot's foliage (though it also attacks parsnip and celery) and so the most effective preventative treatment is to interplant the crop with another which has a highly aromatic foliage i.e. onion, garlic, chives, herbs, or shallots (which produce acids lethal to the maggots of the fly). Fresh wood shavings or paraffin-soaked sand or sawdust sprinkled between the rows can work just as well. Alternatively, run creosoted string across the crops. Try sowing a fast-maturing variety (i.e. before the end of April) such as Locki Maincrop which is the least aromatic of carrot varieties. In winter dig over any infested ground to reveal the chrysalids for the birds. Natural predator: rove beetles.

CARROT MOTH

The eggs are laid in the spring tops and the caterpillars spin the leaves up. Treatment: remove and destroy spun leaves and spray with pyrethrum. Natural predators: Ichneumon flies and rove beetles.

CAUSTIC SODA

A good insecticide for red spider, mealy bug, apple sucker, aphis, winter moth, weevils and fungi. Mixture should consist of 12 oz (340 g) soda, 8 oz (227 g) soap, dissolved in 8 gallons (36·5 litres) water (add the soap last). Caution – always wear rubber or protective gloves when mixing and applying, keep away from children, and do not leave in an unmarked container.

25

CELERY FLY (*Philophylla heraclei*)
Causes blistering of the leaves. Treatment: cut out infested leaves and/or spray the plants with soot. The smell of tar wards off the egg-laying females. Natural predators: ground beetles.

CENTIPEDE
Can cause some damage to newly-sewn peas and beans. Overcome this by transplanting the crop at a more mature stage of growth. On the whole, centipedes are beneficial in the garden as they eat many harmful pests.

CHAFER GRUBS
These fat yellow-white grubs munch their way into potatoes and other root crops. Removing by hand is the best treatment.

CHERRY FRUIT MOTH
Affects the fruit. Treatment is the same as for codling moth (see below).

CHOCOLATE SPOT FUNGUS
Caused by a deficiency in potash. The treatment is to dig in a good quantity of wood ash.

CHRYSANTHEMUM LEAF MINER
The grubs tunnel into and disfigure the leaves. Treatment: locate the grub in its leaf-tunnel and put it out of action by squeezing between thumb and finger.

CLOUDED DRAB MOTH (*Orthosia incerta*)
Attacks dahlias. Treatment: dig up the pupae from the surrounding soil in autumn and spray with hellebore solution in the summer. Natural predators: Ichneumon parasites.

CLUBROOT (*Plasmodiophora brassicae*)
This is a common fungoid disease wherever cabbages, cauliflower, broccoli and other brassicas are grown annually. Although there is no perfect remedy there are a number of precautions worth trying. A spring dressing of lime at the rate of 3 lb a square yard helps. Follow this by omitting a brassica crop the following year. Alternatively, dropping three-inch sections of rhubarb or fragments of mothballs into the dibber holes when planting out seedlings also helps. Rhubarb appears to work quite well and this can also be put into the dibber holes in liquid form (boil $1\frac{1}{2}$ lb (595 g) rhubarb leaves in 1 gallon (4·5 litres) water). Remember – rhubarb leaves are poisonous to humans.

CODLING MOTH (*Carpocapsa pomonella*)
The codling moth can have a devastating effect on both the pear and apple harvest. The maggots feed on the fruit and then drop on to the ground, or fall in the windfall fruit. Treatment consists of applying sacking bands (as for apple blossom weevil) and a carefully employed trapping system. The traps should consist of 2 lb containers (i.e. jars or tins) filled 2 inches deep with a brown sugar or black treacle solution (1 lb sugar/treacle to 1 gallon water). Cover tops with wire gauze, perforated zinc, or curtain netting (with a $\frac{3}{16}$ inch mesh) and hang in the tree from early April onwards. The newly emerged moths are attracted to the sweet solution and are trapped inside the jar. This method has been successfully pioneered by the Henry Doubleday Association (see Societies at end of book). Alternatively, give a winter tar wash and burn loose bark, moss, and litter from the trunks. Natural predator: bats.

COLORADO BEETLE
Any outbreak of this virulent pest must immediately be notified to the police. The larva and beetle can devastate the potato crop and a widespread outbreak would be disastrous.

COMMON SOLDIER BEETLE
As a predator, this insect is a friend and should not be killed.

COMPANION PLANTING (Symbiosis)
It is now known that certain plants, especially herbs, have repelling qualities towards certain insects. Also certain plants grow better when planted next to another particular species and together they form a healthy growing relationship. (See bibliography at end of book for books on symbiosis.)

COMPOST
The answer lies in the soil. Sick soils produce sick plants which inevitably fall victim to pests and diseases. Healthy soils strengthen living plants and these have a far higher resistance to pests and disease. By feeding the soil with compost made with rotted-down leaves, lawn cuttings, kitchen waste, etc., goodness is put back into the ground.

CREOSOTE
1 pint creosote dissolved in 1 gallon hot water is a safe and effective path weedkiller.

CROP AND SOIL COMPATIBILITY
Growing plants in unsuitable soil conditions (i.e. lime-loving plants on acid soil, or sand-loving plants in heavy clay) will weaken them and so attract pests and disease. Always check that plants are suited for the soil in your garden.

CROP ROTATION
Growing crops in the same piece of ground year after year is just asking for trouble. It severely depletes the soil and renders the crop susceptible to pests and disease. Alternate crops each year and keep the soil well fed.

CUCKOO SPIT (or Frog Fly)
The flies lay their eggs in the centre of the shoots of chrysanthemums and the grubs feed in the froth. Remove by hand or spray with quassia.

CURRANT APHIDS
There are three types of aphid which attack all of the fruiting currants. To eliminate these pests it is necessary to destroy the plants which harbour the insects during the summer, namely fathen, deadnettle and sow-thistle.

CURRANT CLEARWING MOTH (*Aegeria lipuliformis*)
It is the larvae which do the damage here by tunnelling up young shoots and causing foliage disorders. Removing by hand is the best remedy.

CURRANT GALL MITE (*Eriophyes ribis*) 'Big Bud'
Attacks the buds in spring which causes them to dry up and die. Treatment: burn old and infested bushes. Spray new bushes with sulphur soap solution.

CURRANT SAWFLY (*Nematus ribesii*)
The eggs are laid along the veins of the leaves. Treatment: destroy the eggs and spray with lime water. Natural predator: Ichneumon flies, tits.

CURRANT SHOOT BORER (*Lampronia capitella*)
Another tunnelling larva which attacks the buds and branches of the currant family. A winter wash of tar oil is effective, otherwise cut out all shrivelled and affected buds and shoots and burn them.

CUTTING OUT
A drastic but usually 100 per cent effective treatment for disease or pest-infected plants. Always use a pair of secateurs or a sharp pruning knife.

DANDELIONS AND DAISIES
. . . are a pretty embellishment to any lawn (unless it's used for bowls). Learn to live with them. If they must go, dig them up by hand or apply the traditional lawn sand to the crowns (see under separate heading).

DECAYING HAY
Considered by many to be the finest plant food there is. Use as a compost and/or a mulch.

DERRIS

A safe and really effective pesticide which contains rotenone as its active principle. Absolutely non-poisonous to both humans and wildlife. Available in dust or liquid form (complete with manufacturer's instructions) from any good garden centre. If not, insist they stock it.

DIE-BACK

A fungoid disease which attacks all stone fruit. Sawing off and pruning the dead wood before the spores scatter is the chief remedy. This should be carried out before mid-July, or in the 'snipping season' for all stone fruit. Shoots with brown tips should be cut off down to the healthy wood.

DRIED BLOOD

A nitrogen-rich organic fertilizer and a useful activator in the compost heap.

EARLY AND LATE MATURING CROPS

The use of early or late maturing strains helps reduce peak infestation periods.

EARWIGS (*Forticula auricularia*)

A few earwigs do no real harm and actually eat some pests. Infestations of plants and trees, however, can be eliminated by trapping, or spraying with pidero. An effective trap is a cloth band tied round the branches. Well-tried methods of trapping such as flowerpots suspended upside down on canes really do work for herbaceous plants.

ELDER LEAVES

A half-hour infusion of 3 lb (1·4 kg) elder leaves in 6 pints (3·4 litres) water and mixed with 1 oz (28 g) soap flakes dissolved in 2 pints (1·14 litres) warm water, will make an effective mildew spray for roses.

FARM DISINFECTANT

This solution which contains phenol is ideal for clearing uncultivated land of weeds. Use at the rate of one pint in two gallons water and spray on to the foliage with a fine spray.

FIELD FLY

Sometimes infests spinach and spinach beet. Woodash on and around the crops will prevent this.

FIGURE OF EIGHT MOTH (*Diloba coeruleocephala*)

Eggs are laid on the shoots of pear, plum and cherry trees in September. Treatment: burn dead leaves and twiggy rubbish containing cocoons. Natural predators: starlings and rooks.

FLEA BEETLE

Fond of cabbages and radishes. Spraying the plants with a finely-sieved woodash, soot or flour normally prevents infestations. Otherwise spray with derris dust. Remove any shepherd's purse and charlock growing in the vicinity. Deep dig in the winter.

FLOUR

Ordinary white flour for baking dusted on the leaves (both sides) of crops is an admirable deterrent to most egg-laying insects.

FROGS AND TOADS

These creatures are real chums. They eat all manner of insects from slugs to flies and should positively be encouraged in any garden. If you have a pond, why not introduce a frog or two?

FROST PROTECTION

Both potassium and sodium minerals which are found in organic matter, lower the freezing point of the sap in plants. Keeping crops well nourished with compost, manure and woodash will build up their frost resistance. Extra protection can be ensured by spraying the foliage with liquid seaweed, or an infusion of valerian leaves in water.

FRUIT BARK BEETLE (*Scolytus rugulosus*)

Eggs are laid in the root of apple trees in May and the beetles appear in autumn. Treatment: spray with a weak caustic soda solution and burn prunings.

FRUIT WEEVILS

These cunning creatures infest stone fruit trees as well as soft fruits and cause damage to all parts of the crop. The only real answer is to lay sheets of newspaper underneath the trees or bushes and spread a strip of grease-band mixture (see under separate heading) around the edges. Then at night shine a powerful torch up into the tree which will hoodwink the weevils into thinking it's daytime. This causes them to drop out of the trees where they will find themselves trapped on the newspaper. Dispose of them how you will. (This is another cunning Henry Doubleday invention!)

GARDEN DART MOTH

Attacks sunflowers. Treatment: remove the eggs, and caterpillars at night. Dig up the pupae in the spring.

GARLIC

Both garlic and onions contain insect repellent qualities and interplanting crops with these plants will reduce infestation. Otherwise use a spray made from the following: 2 cloves garlic, 1 large strong onion, 2 hot peppers – minced or blended in two cups of water. Infuse for 2 hours and then strain. The left-over mush can be sprinkled between the rows of crops.

GOOSEBERRY MILDEW

Try spraying with an infusion of tansy. Alternatively, light a small bonfire of damp leaves as near to the bushes as possible and let smoke envelop the leaves and branches. This should kill the spores. Otherwise spray with a mixture of 2 oz (57 g) washing soda and 1 oz (28 g) soap flakes in 1 gallon (4·5 litres) water. In the winter, spray with Burgundy mixture.

GRASSHOPPERS

Another gardener's friend. Grasshoppers devour greenfly and other unwelcome guests so be thankful when you hear their familiar sound.

GREASE BANDS

These are an age-old remedy for checking the upward movement of harmful insects into trees and bushes. Most garden centres will sell them and they are completely harmless to all useful forms of life. Where it is difficult to use bands, for example on old trees with irregular shaped trunks, a grease mixture made from an organic substance can be applied.

GREEN CAPSID BUG (*Lygocoris pabulinus*)

Treat as for apple capsid.

GREENFLY

The finest eliminator of greenfly is the ladybird although there are other predators too. For really bad infestations try one of the following treatments, none of which will harm the natural predators in the process. Spray with warm water (12°C (54°F)). Spray with a soap solution. Spray with an infusion of soap and rhubarb leaves (3 lb (1·4 kg) leaves boiled for half an hour in 6 pints (3·4 litres) water, mixed with 1 oz (28 g) soap flakes in 2 pints (1·14 litres) water). Remember to spray underneath the leaves as well. Pyrethrum and ryania are instant killers but they exterminate predators too.

GREEN LACEWING

The larva of this beautiful insect is a voracious feeder on greenfly.

HAND PICKING
Removing eggs, caterpillars, grubs and adult insects from crops by hand is the finest non-harmful treatment for mildly infested plants.

HEDGEHOGS
A welcome visitor! Hedgehogs feed on all manner of insects as well as slugs and mice.

HELLEBORE SPRAY
An infusion of the leaves, or powdered leaves, of hellebore is a good insecticide for certain pests.

HERBS
You rarely find insect trouble or disease in a herb garden. Many herbs have volatile oils which are highly insect repellent, so by inter-planting among crops insect activity is severely reduced. They also have an effect on fungoid diseases. The most useful herbs are chives, coriander, hyssop, sage, savory, tansy and wormwood. All can be infused in water and used as a spray for infested plants.

HORSETAIL (*Equisetum arvense*)
This wild plant secretes cobalt, silica and calcium. An infusion of the foliage in water makes an effective foliage spray for mildew, black spot and other fungoid diseases.

LACKEY MOTH (*Malacosoma neustria*)
The larvae of the lackey moth feed off the leaves of apple and pear trees. Preventative treatment consists of pruning or rubbing away the brace-lets of eggs around the fruit spurs. Curative treatment involves spraying with derris dust or nicotine in May. Natural predator: the cuckoo.

LADYBIRDS
These delightful insects, beloved of children, are a gardener's best friend. One solitary ladybird can devour anything up to 100 greenfly a day! If your roses are suffering from greenfly, seek out some ladybirds and introduce them to the infested plants.

LAWN SAND AND LAWN WEEDKILLERS
The traditional lawn sand (10 parts of dry sand, 7 parts sulphate of ammonia, 3 parts sulphate of iron) applied at 4 oz per square yard works just as well as the modern chemical equivalent. To eradicate moss first check for poor drainage which is the major cause and generously feed the lawn with liquid organic fertilizer. If this fails, spray with a winter wash of tar oil (1 pint (0·57 litres) in 8 gallons (36·4 litres) water per 32 square yards (26·8 m²)).

LEAF-MINER (*Acidia heraclei*)
Remove the insects by hand and destroy affected foliage by burying deep or burning. Remove all sow-thistles growing in the vicinity as these harbour the leaf-miner insects.

LEAF SPOT (*Gloeosporium ribis*)
This fungoid disease affects currant bushes, mainly due to over-feeding with manure. The fungus spores spread on fallen leaves so remove any from under the bushes and burn. A mulch with lawn clippings or comfrey leaves helps considerably but if all else fails, spray with Bordeaux mixture.

LEATHER-JACKETS
The larvae of cranefly (i.e. Daddy longlegs). Leather-jackets feed on the roots of grass and can produce unpleasant bare patches in lawns. Treatment: thoroughly water the lawn and then immediately cover with sheets of polythene. Leave covered for 4–5 hours and then mow the lawn – which should by then be covered with larvae.

LETTUCE ROOT APHIS
An insect that lives off the roots of lettuce and inevitably kills the plants. Spray the plants with pidero or liquid derris.

LETTUCE ROOT MAGGOT
Causes similar damage to lettuce root aphis. Interplanting with herbs, or garlic/onion will put off any discerning insects, otherwise spray with liquid derris.

LILAC MOTH
Attacks lilac trees, where the caterpillars form leaf rolls in summer. Cut out all infested leaves or spray with pyrethrum in early spring (eggs laid in June).

LIME AND SULPHUR
An effective treatment for big bud mite and rose mildew.

MAGPIE MOTH (*Abraxus grossulariata*)
The yellow and black larva infests currants and other soft fruits. Remove the eggs and larvae by hand and clear away any litter beneath the bushes in winter. Natural predators: parasitic two-winged insects.

MARIGOLDS
Certain varieties of marigolds such as the brown and yellow strain 'Harmony' secrete volatile substances from their roots which are a deterrent to harmful insects and in particular eelworm. Interplant between roses to prevent 'soil sickness'. Other flowers such as chrysan-themum, geranium, calendula and nasturtium (see under separate heading) have similar properties.

MEALY BUG (*Coccus*)
Infests the bark and leaves of vines, figs and tomatoes, feeding on the juices. Treatment: fumigate with tobacco smoke and paint the branches with methylated spirits. Natural pre-dator: tits.

MICE
The harmless fieldmouse and certain other rodents feed on insects.

MILDEW (Rose)
Spray with a solution of horsetail. Spray with a solution of lime and sulphur. Spray with a solution of a dessertspoon of carbolic acid and two ounces of soap flakes dissolved in a gallon of water. In the winter, spray with Burgundy mixture. Spray with onion extract.

MILLIPEDE
The traditional treatment is to punch holes in empty tins (the taller the better), fill with carrot or potato peelings and bury in an upright position in the ground (with a wire handle for access). Empty the contents once a week.

MOLES

A once-and-for-all preventative and curative solution is to break into the moles' main runway (by digging into the biggest molehill) and gas the tunnels with carbon monoxide fumes. A two-stroke lawnmower is ideal for this. Connect a length of rubber tubing to the exhaust and put the other end into the tunnel. Start up the engine and have the revs just ticking over slowly. The stench of the fumes will linger for ages and will prevent any return to the burrows. If this operation is carried out at night the moles will have a chance to escape under the cover of darkness. Alternatively, place pieces of carbide in the tunnels which will eventually react with moisture to form carbide gas. Alternatively, sow the ground with milk spurge (*Euphorbia lactea*) which moles detest. Camphor balls are also a good mole deterrent.

MOTHS

These can be a real pest in fruit trees. Grease bands will effectively stop the wingless females from crawling up the trees to lay their eggs.

MULCHING

There are different reasons for mulching. It can be a reasonably effective method of preventing weeds from germinating between plants. It keeps the soil moist in really dry conditions. It can act medicinally as a repellent to insects and other pests. Or it can be simply a food dressing. Mulches can be organic, such as compost, manure, lawn clippings, straw and seaweed. Alternatively, the mulch can be non-nutritive, such as newspaper, rocks or plastic sheeting such as polythene. Two precautions: (1) don't let the mulch touch the plants; (2) let the soil warm up in the spring before mulching. And remember that surface mulching tends to attract slugs.

MUSSEL SCALE INSECT (*Lepidosaphes ulmi*)

A small mussel-like insect that attacks the bark of apple trees. Treatment: spray with caustic soda solution, or paraffin.

NASTURTIUMS

It is now widely believed that climbing nasturtiums planted around the base of apple trees will sometimes ward off an attack of woolly aphis. Sow one of the strong strains such as *Tropaeolum majus* early in the year to ensure decent sized plants by April when the aphis first appears.

NETTLES

An infusion of nettles in water given to plants is a nutritious feed which in turn builds up immunity to pest and disease. Soak a pound of leaves in a gallon of water for 2–3 days.

NICOTINE

Nicotine is a highly effective pesticide which can be used to eradicate various caterpillars, weevils, leaf miners and aphids. It can be bought in a few places but the easiest way to obtain the poison is by boiling cigarettes in water. Use four ounces of non-filter tips to every gallon water and boil for half-an-hour. When cool, strain through two layers of muslin or a nylon stocking and bottle. Please remember to label very clearly – POISON. Alternatively you can scour the ash trays in pubs and other public places and remove the fag-ends for the same purpose. Nicotine soon breaks down in the soil but do not use indiscriminately and never apply within a month of eating the crops.

NO-DIGGING METHOD

There is still a certain degree of controversy over this natural form of soil management. No-diggers say that nature doesn't turn over the soil every autumn, bring up the subsoil and bury organic topsoil underneath – so neither should the gardener. On the other hand, confirmed diggers say that turning over the soil aerates it and improves drainage. No-digging involves building up the topsoil with a good layer of rich compost so that the soil resembles the richness of a woodland floor. Either way, both compost and fertilizer should always be raked into the surface and not dug in. If digging is preferred, then don't go down further than six inches otherwise undecayed organic matter may go rancid deep down and give off poisonous substances thus endangering plants.

NUT WEEVILS

Attack the fruit of cobs and filberts. To trap them, sacking or tarred boards should be laid on the ground below the bushes and the boughs given a good shake to dislodge the weevils. Burn or destroy the sacking or boards. Burn all 'windfall' nuts during the summer as they may be harbouring a weevil grub.

ONION FLY (*Delia cepetorum*)

This pest devastates the onion bulbs leaving behind a squidgy mess full of maggots. Treatment: earth up to neck, rotate the site for the onion bed each year, and grow onions only from sets. Otherwise grow fly-resisting strains such as 'Giant-Red Rocca', 'Blood Red', 'Long Keeping' and selected strains of 'Bedfordshire Champion'. Natural predator: ground beetles.

OVER-PLANTING

Avoid bunching crops too closely together as this renders them susceptible to pests and disease. Keep to the instructions on the packet and allow a reasonable distance between rows.

PARASITIC INSECTS

There are hundreds of different species and they do immeasurable good in the garden. The adults lay their eggs inside the larvae of a pest species and the parasitic larvae then feed off their host.

PEACH LEAF CURL (*Taphrina deformans*)

A fungoid disease that attacks the leaves causing them to blister and curl. Preventative treatment consists of spraying with Bordeaux mixture when the buds start to swell in February. Curative treatment is uncertain but research into spraying with a foliar feeding liquid manure such as 'Maxicrop', 'Alginure' or 'Sea Majic' has proved encouraging.

PEAR AND CHERRY SLUG WORM (*Eriocampa limacina*)

Attacks the leaves of apples and pears (and other stone fruits). Spray with pidero or derris in June and hoe up soil at the base of the tree. Natural predator: starlings.

PEAR MIDGE (*Contarinia pyrivora*)

Infests the blossom and then feeds off the fruit causing it to swell larger or longer than is normal. Hand pick any infested fruit and burn especially windfalls. Hoe the ground round about the infested trees during the summer to expose the grubs to the birds. Natural predators: swallows and martins.

PERFUME DETERRENTS

The Henry Doubleday Association has been, and is, doing extensive research into the effectiveness of certain powerful scents against pests. The oil of sassafras, heliotrope, aniseed, cumin, geranium, dill, coriander, and oreganum are just some of the perfumes that are being used. The scents are added to a ten per cent solution of Barbados sugar and water, and placed in traps with a bee-excluding grid. The idea is that scent from a flower of the same natural order as the food plant is used in the trap, thus foiling the egg-bearing adult insects.

PERMANGANATE OF POTASH

Use a little in boiling water as an effective path weed-killer and preventative treatment.

PIDERO

A mixture of derris and pyrethrum which is more effective than the individual parts against beetles, weevils, ants, millipedes and other pests.

PITH MOTH (*Blastodacna atra*)

Affects the terminal buds on fruit trees. Prune all the affected parts and burn.

POTATO DISEASE

Causes brown spotting and subsequent shrivelling of the foliage. Preventative action consists of spraying with Bordeaux mixture in mid-June and again in early July. Cut out infected parts.

POTATO FROG FLY

Feeds on the sap of the plant. Treatment: spray with nicotine. Natural predator: ladybirds.

PREDATORS

We have a staggering population of over 1,000,000 different species of insects in the world yet only about 45 are any serious threat to food production. Most of the others do immeasurable good in pollination, aerating the soil, breaking down dead organic matter, and controlling those species which plague our crops. Learn to recognize the goodies in the insect world, such as the ladybird, ground beetle, robber fly, green lacewing, soldier beetle, shieldbug and antlion.

PUG MOTH

Attacks golden rod and campanulas. Shake the grubs off the plants at night and spray the soil with brine. Natural predator: ground beetles eat the pupae.

PYRETHRUM

This safe and non-toxic insecticide is obtained from the blossom of *Chrysanthemum cinerariae-folium*. It has a short-term effectiveness which is useful where bees are very much in evidence.

QUASSIA

A useful insecticide obtained from the wood of a tropical tree. Weaker than either derris or pyrethrum but sparing to many predators. Excellent for eliminating aphis and other soft-skinned insects.

RABBITS

Rabbits will steer clear of foxgloves (*Digitalis purpurea*) which poison them, and also onions.

RASPBERRY BEETLE (*Byturus tormentosus*)

The larvae feed on the raspberry fruit. Turning over the soil in October will expose the pupae to hungry birds. Shake the canes gently over sheets of newspaper when the flowers are out, to remove any harbouring adults. Bad infestations can be eradicated by a spray of liquid derris or pidero ten days after flowering, and again two weeks later.

RASPBERRY CANE SPOT

A fungal disease that affects the canes around the leaf axils causing them to wither. Ensure the rows are airy and light by thinning out the canes. Remove any diseased canes and burn. Light attacks can be cured by spraying with nettle water. Otherwise, cut all the canes to ground level to produce a healthy stock for the following year.

RASPBERRY MOTH (*Lampronia rubiella*)

The larva is a virulent pest that attacks all parts of the raspberry plant. Cut out all infected parts and burn and dig over the soil as deep as possible to bury the larvae. Natural predator: starlings.

RASPBERRY WEEVIL (*Otiorhynchus picipes*)

The weevils feed on the canes, at night and the larvae feed on the roots. Treatment: shake out the weevils at night into a jar of paraffin or strong brine. Natural predators: tits, black-birds, thistles and sand wasps.

RATS

Rats detest *Valeriana officinalis* (cats love it!) and also Euphorbias and *Fritillaria imperialis*.

RED PLUM MAGGOT MOTH (*Cydia funebrana*)

Treat as for codling moth.

RED SPIDER MITE

This creature was once held in check by its natural predator *Anthocoris nemorum*, but since the advent of winter tar washes the predators have been greatly diminished. Red spider mite, which attacks both apples and gooseberries, can be killed without endangering useful predators by spraying with s.m.136 (see separate heading). Natural predator: tits.

RHUBARB

An infusion of rhubarb leaves in water makes a cheap and useful insecticide for aphids, especially greenfly. Three pounds of leaves boiled in six pints of water can be stored in a bottle until needed. (But don't forget to mark the bottle POISON.) The solution is more effective when mixed with a wetting agent such as soapflakes dissolved in water. Mix the soap solution just before spraying and do not bottle mixed with the rhubarb.

ROSE APHIS

First appears in May and feeds on the sap from young shoots. Treatment: use nicotine wash early before the natural predators – ladybirds – are in action.

ROSE BEETLE

The eggs are laid in the soil in spring and the maggots feed throughout the year. Treatment: dig up maggots and spread lime and soot to deter egg laying. Natural predator: starlings.

ROSE SLUG WORM

The eggs are laid in May on the ribs of the leaves and the grubs feed on the top skin. Treatment: remove eggs, shake off caterpillars and destroy.

ROSE TORTRIX MOTH

The eggs are laid in June and the caterpillars spin up in the leaves. Treatment: spray early with pyrethrum and remove and destroy any infested leaves.

ROSY RUSTIC MOTH (*Gortyna micacea*)

Attacks parsnips from which the caterpillars feed. Hand remove the caterpillars and destroy any horsetail and sedges in the vicinity.

RYANIA

An insecticide obtained from the roots of the South American plant *Ryania speciosa*. This weak insecticide is effective for codling moth control and certain other pests.

SALT

Makes a useful path weedkiller. Choose a period when there is little or no rain and scatter on a layer of dry salt until the paths are just white in colour. Leave for a few days and then run a light roller over it. Don't water the paths. The longer the salt stays on the more thoroughly will the grass and weeds be destroyed.

SAPROPHYTE SPRAY

Useful in protecting young fruit trees against disease. It consists of a solution made from an infusion of bark from whatever the particular fruit tree in question. Saprophyte solution contains useful bacterial fungi and yeasts which strengthen the resistance of the growing stocks. To make it, soak $\frac{1}{2}$ oz bark in 2 pints water for 5 days at around 21°C (70°F), aerating every day by pouring from one jar to another. Strain and then spray as needed.

SCAB

A form of fungus that causes blistering and

cracking of young shoots along with blackspots or blotching on fruit. Cut out all affected parts and sweep up infested leaves for burning. Serious attacks must be sprayed with lime-sulphur in February.

SCALE INSECTS
These tiny insects infest fruit trees causing serious damage by sucking out the sap. A harmless treatment is synthetic turpentine or s.m.136 sprayed onto infected parts. For major attacks treat with a winter tar oil wash, followed by lime-sulphur in the spring.

SHOOT AND FRUIT MOTH (*Incurvaria capitella*)
The larvae eat the fruit and shoots of soft fruits. Treatment: handpick and spray with a weak caustic soda solution wash in winter. Natural predator: blue tits.

SILVER LEAF
Treat as for dieback but ensure the pruning is carried out before 15th July – the date given in the Ministry of Agriculture's Silver Leaf order of 1923.

SLOW-WORMS
These very useful creatures sometimes turn up around compost heaps and feed on flies and other pests.

SLUDGE
Human waste in a compost form and highly nutritious for the soil. Available from some local councils via allotment associations.

SLUGS AND SNAILS
The classic non-toxic slug bait is beer mixed with Barbados sugar diluted half and half with water. Pour this into wide, shallow plates or saucers and sink level into the ground. Beer can be obtained for nothing from drip trays at the local pub. The sugar in the solution will also attract other undesirables such as cutworms and yet will not be harmful to pets or wild animals. Alternatively, bait the ground with Fertosan Slug Destroyer, a completely herbal non-toxic killer, or sprinkle the ground with woodash on lime. Or spray the ground with an infusion of fir seeds, or plant with hyssop or thyme.

SMALL ERMINE MOTH
Attacks lilac and other shrubs. The caterpillars spin webs in summer. Treatment: gather and burn web-clusters and spray early with pyrethrum.

S.M.136
A non-toxic insecticide made from polybutene which is more or less a liquid form of polythene. Sprayed on to infected plants it seals up the breathing pores of pests and so eliminates them.

SNOWY FLY (*Aleyrodes proietella*)
Infests the leaves of grapes, figs and tomatoes. Treatment: fumigate with tobacco smoke.

SODA – RESIN WASH
Good for oyster scale, mussel scale, brown currant scale, woolly aphis and mealy bug. The mixture should be 1 oz (28 g) caustic soda and 8 oz (227 g) powdered resin mixed in 1 pint (0·57 litres) boiling water. Then add 1 gallon (4·5 litres) warm water. Harmless to foliage.

SODIUM CHLORATE
A strong effective weedkiller that is harmless to humans and wildlife. Instructions normally come with the tin but the usual strength is a pound of sodium chlorate dissolved in a gallon of water. The one disadvantage is that shrubs and flowers are killed as well so precautions must be taken to limit spraying to weed-stricken areas.

SOIL TESTS FOR POISONS
Test your soil for weedicide damage:
We all know the dangers of chemical fertilizers and weedkillers. If you are about to buy land or have just done so, here is an easy way YOU can test the soil for residues of these poisons. The method is simple. At least five samples of each soil type or each field should be taken. Select the sites at random. If possible a control sample, known to be free of any weedicide, should be run.

All the equipment needed for the sampling is:
1) 5 buckets or containers, clearly labelled with depth intervals of 0–2 ins, 2–4 ins, 4–6 ins, 6–8 ins and 8–10 ins. (1 inch = 25·4 mm)
2) 15 cans or pots with holes for drainage at the bottom.
3) bean and oat seeds.
4) a ruler.

Run the tests as follows:
At each sampling site dig a trench about one foot deep and one or two feet wide. Take a ruler and mark off the depth in two-inch intervals. Take samples from each of the two-inch intervals and place them in the appropriately marked bucket.

Each bucket now contains at least five lots of soil. Mix the soil well. From each bucket fill three pots or cans and mark them with the depth of the sub-sample. Sow bean and oat seeds in these cans and water lightly. Keep the cans moist, but do not over-water as this may leach the chemicals from the soil.

The way in which the seeds germinate indicates the amount of residues.

Results:
(a) If the plants germinate in each sub-sample and then die, this indicates the presence of toxic amounts of weedicide throughout all levels of the soil. The control sample is to ensure that the plants are not dying due to some other factor.
(b) If the plants in the 0–2 ins, 2–4 ins levels only die, this shows the weedicides are still present, but not enough to be fatal to most plants as their roots are deeper.
(c) If all plants in all pots grow – fine. The level of weedicide is low or nil and you are lucky.

SPECTACLE MOTH (*Unca triplasia*)
Attacks dahlias. Remove caterpillars at night and spray with hellebore. (Eggs laid in July.) Natural predator: Tachinid fly parasite.

SPOTTED CRANE FLY
Attacks violas. The grubs or 'leather-jackets' feed on the roots during winter. Treatment: fumigate the soil in winter. Natural predators: starlings and rooks.

SPRAYS
Wherever possible, spray insecticides and weed-killers in the evening when the bees have returned to the hives. Most organic treatments are rendered harmless by the morning.

STEM EELWORM (*Tylanchus devastatrix*)
Bores in the tissues of strawberries. Treatment: put down a 'catch-crop' such as clover and dig up with the eel-worms and destroy.

STONE MEAL
Rich in calcium, potassium, silicon and other elements and an excellent natural fertilizer.

STRAW BELL MOTH
Attacks scabious. The eggs are laid in June and grubs spin in the flowers and leaves. Treatment: spray early with pyrethrum and gather and burn infested leaves. Natural predator: Brachonid egg parasites.

STRAWBERRY BEETLE
An insect which devastates the strawberry buds and blossom. Treat with liquid derris, pyrethrum or pidero.

STRAWBERRY MILDEW

Cut away all the runners and most of the old leaves leaving only a few in the centre to carry on the work of the plant till new leaves are formed. Break up the surface of the soil at regular intervals to prevent mildew settling in.

TAGETES (*Tagetes minuta*) Mexican Marigold

This Mexican wildflower emits powerful volatile secretions from its roots which have a marked effect on soil pests and other weeds in the vicinity. Its qualities have been exploited since ancient times and it is used commercially in countries such as Rhodesia in the cultivation of tobacco. In this country, research has been carried out into pest and weed control with encouraging results. Tagetes has a marked effect on the incidence of potato eelworms, wireworms and keeled slugs. It kills ground elder and greatly affects couchgrass, convolvulus, thistles, and other starch-rooted weeds. To clear an area of elder or some other rampant weed, raise the tagetes plants from seed to a healthy size in pots and then plant a foot apart among the weeds after levelling the area with a sickle or scythe.

THRIPS (Thunder Flies)

This apple and pear thrip infests the blossom of apple, pear and plum trees which results in the russeting of fruit. Try hosing the trees with water to effect an artificial storm. If this fails, spray with pyrethrum in the evening. Other species of thrips can be eliminated with derris or pidero.

TURNIP HOPPER (*Phyllotreta nemorum*)

The adults hide in the soil and leaf litter during winter and eat off the first seed leaves in spring before breeding. Treatment: manure and compost feed to boost plants and dust, when young, with soot.

TURNIP MOTH (*Agrotis segetum*)

The eggs are laid on turnip stems and the larvae feed on the roots. Treatment: thoroughly turn over the soil in winter to expose the pupae. Natural predators: rooks, gulls, starlings.

TURNIP SAWFLY

Attacks the foliage. Treatment: spray soot dust as a preventative measure. Deep-dig the soil in winter where the turnips are to be grown. Treat bad infestations with nicotine spray.

TUSSOCK MOTH

Attacks roses. The eggs are laid in June

Treatment: spray with hellebore and gather off caterpillars and cocoons. Natural predator: Tachinid fly parasites.

VAPOURER MOTH (*Orgyia antiqua*)
Attacks the leaves of apple trees. Treatment: remove larvae webs by hand during August and September. Natural predator: cuckoos.

VINE LOUSE (*Phylloxera vastatrix*)
Attacks vine fruits, figs and tomatoes. The wingless form eats the roots and the winged form infests the branches. Treatment: spray with a weak caustic soda solution. Natural predator: millipedes.

VINE TORTRIX (*Conchylis ambiguella*)
The larvae feed on the flower and fruit of vines, figs and tomatoes. Treatment: gather and destroy the webs in spring. Remove all infected fruit with a blue spot.

VINE WEEVIL (*Otiorhynchus sulcatus*)
Attacks vine fruits, figs and tomatoes. Treatment: shake off grubs into boiling water. Natural predator: sand wasps.

VOLES
These lovely creatures which have a passion for potatoes can be harmlessly controlled by planting peas or broad beans between the rows.

WASPS
Contrary to popular belief, wasps are useful creatures as they affect the presence of flies. Unfortunately they also feed on fruit and really bad infestations can be reduced by baiting them with derris dust mixed in jam, or pidero mixed with brown sugar. Bait near to the nest if possible, otherwise in an area where they gather the most.

WEEDS
All weeds are really legitimate wild flowers growing in the wrong place. Many of them can be eaten, otherwise refer to the compost heap.

WEEVILS
There are numerous species of weevils and pidero is the most effective killer.

WHITE ERMINE MOTH (*Spilosoma lubricipeda*)
Attacks hollyhocks. Treatment: remove egg clusters in June and gather off caterpillars at night.

WINTER MOTH (*Operophtera brumata*)
Attacks apple trees. Treatment: dig up pupae in August, and put on grease bands in October. Natural predators: bullfinches, titmice.

36

WIREWORMS

A pest that lives in turf but infests potatoes and other root crops. A precautionary measure is not to cultivate potatoes where there has recently been grass. Hoe between the plants to expose the larvae for birds, or remove by hand. Alternatively, use the traps as described for millipedes and bait with carrot and potato peelings. Serious infestations may mean burning any turf in the vicinity.

WOOD LEOPARD MOTH (*Zeuzera pyrina*)

The wood-boring larvae make galleries in the trunks of apple trees. Treatment: remove the moths by hand from the trunk. Syringe the tunnels with urine. Natural predators: toads, bats.

WOODLICE

Outside, this creature is rarely a problem but they can be a nuisance indoors, especially in greenhouses. They infest poor soils, so rich compost and other organic matter dug in will usually do the trick. Bad infestations can be eliminated with a bait of pidero mixed with bran. A half-orange or grapefruit skin turned upside down on the shelving will attract a good many woodlice which can then be disposed of at the end of the day.

WOOLLY APHIS (*Eriosoma lanigerum*)

Affects apple trees by covering the branches and stems with a mantle of aphid-infested cotton-wool-like patches. An effective precautionary method is to ensure the ground around the foot of the trees is left undisturbed and to put down a layer of sawdust each autumn. Woolly aphis can be cured by spraying or painting the cotton wool areas with a mixture of $\frac{2}{3}$ paraffin and $\frac{1}{3}$ creosote, or two-stroke petrol mixture or methylated spirits. And try nasturtiums.

WORMS

The humble earthworm is the soil's most beneficial creature. It aerates the soil and pulls down valuable humus and other organic matter. As with bees, under no circumstances should worms be killed. If the soil is severely lacking or devoid of worms, feed with plenty of organic matter and introduce some worms from a friend's garden.

YELLOW UNDERWING MOTH

Attacks lettuce and asters. Cut out any egg infested leaves. Search for caterpillars at night. Dust the soil with soot around every plant.

ALLOTMENT LIB

Happy man, he has an Eden
Blest and brightened by an Eve
Garden – plots that need no weeding
Hoeing, delving, watering, seeding
Ne'er his placid spirit grieve –
Lucky Jonathan!

Wretched I, too, have an Eden,
but it lacks a helpmate Eve
Wearing works this thankless weeding
Hoeing, delving, watering, seeding –
While you chuckle in your sleeve
Lucky Jonathan!

'LUCKY JONATHAN' BY E. J. ARMSTRONG

THE move back to the soil in our towns and cities has put acute pressure on existing allotments to the extent where waiting lists have grown out of all proportion to the plots available. Some councils have designated new land for allotments but nowhere near enough to cope with the demand. As a reaction to this, those stalwart crusaders for the environment, the Friends of the Earth, held a National Allotments Day a few years ago which aimed at turning derelict land into allotments. What follows is a section of their 'Allotments Campaign Manual' which is a guide for converting such land into food-producing allotment plots for the community. And, incidentally, if you can afford the price of this book, you can easily afford to join Friends of the Earth! They desperately need your support.

SECTION ONE

Objectives

The campaign is designed to highlight the fact that vast acreages of land are standing idle in most areas in the U.K. – land which, in the short term, should be used. In the light of the current food shortages and the need for people to be more aware of the role of nature, perhaps the most sensible use of this land would be to use it to meet the growing demand for allotment space. We fully recognize that much of the vacant land in existence today has been earmarked for development. The campaign is designed to promote the short-term use of that land until such time as development commences.

Strategy and Timetable

Your strategy is easily defined. Firstly you need to demonstrate the demand for allotments. Then, if land is unavailable, you need to introduce the argument about short-term use of vacant land. If the authority or land-owner won't offer land on a short-term basis, then borrow it. The food situation in the U.K. and the consequence of isolation from nature is sufficiently serious for us to ignore bureaucratic protocol – or at least to attempt to speed it up. (See Legal section.)

The political lever in this campaign is clearly contesting an authority's claim that allotment space is unavailable. If space is available then your case is obviously weakened – so before you

39

start any detailed investigation, find out about the local situation by means of a phone call to the allotments authority. Then follow up with a letter. It's not worth putting in a lot of preliminary groundwork only to find that you haven't got a case.

JANUARY (END): Send initial letters to authorities.

FEBRUARY (BY 2ND WEEK): Follow up with second letter or phone call.

FEBRUARY (END): By now you ought to have ascertained the attitude of the authority. You've either been offered the use of an allotment or been put on the waiting list. Is the authority keen to see vacant land used in the short term? If so, consider amending your plans accordingly. If official response is negative, start looking for a site and organizing your research programme.

MARCH (BEGINNING): During this month you'll need to continue to dig up all the information you can about vacant land in your area and organize the actual day's event.

MARCH 8TH: Send out press release.

MARCH 15TH: National Allotments Day.

MAY: Reports should now be going to local authorities.

As a precaution it is advisable to start your fact-finding operations as early as possible. If you carry out your research at the same time as you approach the authority, you'll be far better placed to present your case and react to a changing situation. So as far as is possible, carry out the two activities in parallel.

Initial Steps

Before any 'take-over' of land is contemplated it's imperative to allow the legal, democratic process to produce results. Give the authority a month to six weeks in which to offer some positive reaction to your enquiries. After having ascertained (by means of a phone call or letter) the local situation regarding allotment availability, write to the authority asking them if they have considered using vacant or derelict sites as temporary allotment space. Point out that in the light of current and future food shortages all currently wasted land should be utilized for food production. It is important to keep sight of the overall campaign.

Information Gathering

During this period as much background research as possible should be done. The sort of questions to which you will need answers are:

(a) What acreage in the area is currently vacant or derelict? (Most authorities publish these statistics in official documents and a phone call to the surveyor's department could be a useful first step.)

(b) How many people are waiting for allotments? (The authority will give you figures.)

(c) Is this figure a significant increase on last year's figure? Who owns these vacant plots? (Identifying owners is a difficult task, but ask local people or look for evidence of previous occupants and try to trace the owners that way. Ask the authority for a list of land in their ownership and check with community groups who may well have the information you need.)

(d) How many allotments could this amount of land provide? (Take the average allotment size as 300 sq. yds. (250 m²) and calculate the number of potential allotments by dividing this figure into the total area of vacant land – 4,840 sq. yds. (0·405 ha) in an acre.)

(e) Is there public support for the campaign? (The best indicator is the increase in the number of people on the waiting list, but talk to tenants' associations and community groups. Try to get a letter in the local paper raising the issue and try to prolong the correspondence.)

(f) What sort of produce could this land support and in what quantity? (See Section 2.)

It might be an idea to illustrate your argument graphically by drawing up a map or graph which shows clearly the number of allotments in the area, the increases in demand for allotments, and the amount of vacant land in the area. This could form part of your press package and will give you the sort of information you'll need if you intend (as we hope) to produce a report on the subject of vacant land as the next step in the campaign.

This sort of information will be invaluable when presenting your case and justifying your actions. Having prepared your case it's now time to single out one particular site as the focus for your activity, providing of course the authority are clearly not going to be very co-operative. The best course of action is the legal one and if the authority is willing to release land and assist in the campaign then it is advisable to delay any action you might have been contemplating so long as you feel the authority is genuine in its desire to see vacant plots used. If you feel otherwise, it is probably going to be beneficial to take the initiative and prepare for a vacant plot 'take-over'.

Choosing a Site

The ideal site will be somewhere central to local activity – a site which is well-known throughout the district. It should preferably be at least one acre in size (about half the size of a football pitch) and at least half of its area should be suitable for growing crops. Try to choose a site with an abundance of natural vegetation. This will enable you to promote the very important aspect of the campaign concerned with retention of and respect for natural flora and fauna.

A site which has been unused for a long period of time will generally support varied and abundant wildlife. Make a survey of the types of trees, shrubs, insects and birds your site supports and use this information liberally in your campaigning. If the site is biologically rich, try to get the area declared as a nature reserve. There is no need for you to cut everything down in order to start up some vegetable patches.

Try to get as much information about the site as you can. Local people will probably be able to help you here and give you a lead as to where to look for some more information. The local planning register is available for public inspection at the Town Hall and may show applications for planning consent for the site. Old valuation lists, if available (also from the Town Hall) will show who occupied (but not necessarily owned) the site previously. Through these you might be able to trace current owners. The planning authority is generally the borough or district council. A phone call will establish this.

A very important thing to take into consideration when choosing your site is to make sure that no development of the site is liable to take place for at least two years. A phone call to the planning department of the planning authority will answer this point. Although, for obvious reasons, the emphasis of the campaign is on the short-term use of land, a site which has been vacant for a considerable period will take some time to prepare.

In essence, then, you are looking for a piece of vacant or derelict land which has stood unused for many a long year (the longer the better) and one which supports a variety of wildlife and which would lend at least half of its area to the growing of crops. It is of great advantage when it comes to negotiating about the future of the site to have chosen one which is in council ownership. Make sure that no development is liable to take place for at least two years.

Community Involvement

Depending on the circumstances of the campaign (i.e. whether it is a corporate action by a group of people or simply an individual after an allotment) there may arise the need to involve members of community groups or tenants' associations. These people have a direct interest in the use to which vacant land is put and therefore to avoid a conflict of interests, it is wise to ask their opinion of the campaign. They might have their own plans for the site and have been negotiating with the local authority for some time. They wouldn't take kindly to a third party spoiling their work.

As an FOE group, or a group of people who see their role primarily as 'whistleblowers', you may consider that your primary role is that of a catalyst, in which case you will be keen to interest people who are potential allotment owners or who are prepared to manage the site in the long run. Community groups are the best contact points for these people besides which, it is always beneficial to have local community opinion on your side.

The Day

Having undertaken preliminary studies of the site you have chosen, you should now be considering the actual plans for the day of the 'take-over'. In order to maximize the impact of your actions you should aim to carry out the action on a day and at a time which will be suitable for maximum press, radio, and T.V. coverage and when the maximum people are around.

You'll need:
- *A press release* (sent out a week before the event, strictly embargoed until the morning

of the event, especially if you identify the actual site).
- *Hand-outs for passers-by*, giving a brief outline of your reasons for such action and asking for support with letters to the authority.
- *Tools*, especially a pick (if the site is strewn with rubble), a sledge hammer (for breaking up large pieces of concrete) and a scythe (for clearing undergrowth).
- *A banner*, which is always helpful in persuading the press to cover the event.

Make the event as colourful as possible. Try to get hold of bunting with which to decorate the site and lay on a band to herald the 'ceremonial' use of the 'vacant' land. A focus point for the event is always attractive. If the action takes place on a national scale (hopefully) in the spring the time will be right for the planting of many crops. Is there a sympathetic local dignitary or personality who would come along to plant the first seeds?

It's surprising how much work you can get through in a short period of time. One person should be in charge of the actual digging and he/she should have a fair idea of which areas to be dug/cleared and how. Someone should be available at all times to greet the pressmen and escort them via the easiest route to the activities where the 'campaign organizers' or spokesmen should be available for interviews, etc. Be sure to retain an area of vegetation for wildlife and keep an eye on the kids who will (undoubtedly) invade the site. The kids who came to the Waterloo site were employed (willingly) in digging and clearing but soon felt that creating havoc was more in their line, so we had to be constantly alert to their actions.

Make sure that there is a reasonably easy access point to the site. If it involves crossing other people's land or property, contact them prior to the day and make sure you have the necessary permission.

Tactics and Legal Points

Don't let pressure on the authority ease off, either before or after the event. Silence on your behalf will be interpreted as loss of enthusiasm and the authority will be glad to see the whole issue die the death.

Encourage as many people as possible to

write to the press and to the authority to keep the issue 'alive' for as long as possible. If you can leak a story to your local paper on the day before the event, so much the better. Pre-publicity is always helpful so long as it doesn't give the authorities sufficient time to reorganize a defence or to stop the whole thing taking place.

Your initial letter to the allotments authority should be addressed to the Chief Planning Officer, with copies to the Chief Officer, Parks Department and Chief Officer, Valuers Department or equivalent. Make sure that the recipient of your letter is aware that copies have been sent to other people inside the authority.

If you occupy a site without the permission of the owner you are technically trespassing (get permission in writing if possible). The owner can empower the police to evict you, but this is unlikely. The owners are entitled to use 'reasonable force' to evict you but in practice, unless you happen to pick a site which is owned by a particularly aggressive owner, you'll find that no action will be taken. In fact, the owner, should he decide to prosecute, would have to justify the prosecution of 'damage to property' and would have difficulty making the charge stick if the court were to hear that a 'bombed site', lain empty and unused for years, had been turned into a garden.

As has happened on a particular site in London, the owners might welcome such 'take-over' as it deflects criticism over their policy of keeping land empty. Likewise, some authorities may be keen to encourage such action as it alleviates the embarrassment they feel over areas of 'planning blight'. Once you are established on the site, and agreements have been drawn up, the authority is duty-bound to try to find alternative sites when the tenancy is terminated. By taking this sort of action, it could be that the whole bureaucratic system is short-circuited and positive action is forthcoming. Whatever the outcome, the whole issue of derelict and vacant sites will be raised and authority will be forced to provide some kind of policy statement (which will give you something to comment on, criticise or applaud, whatever the case may be).

Letter to Authorities

Here we offer a few pointers to writing an all-embracing letter to your allotments' authority.

The authority might well already be engaged in work on making allotments from vacant land. So don't give them the opportunity to take the wind out of your sails with a glib comeback. Point out that you are aware of the pressures under which they are working and enquire politely if any steps have been taken to answer the lack of allotment space (if there is one) by using vacant land. If so, you would very much like to hear what work they have done and how you can become involved.

Stress your desire to work with the authority and point out that joint action of this sort would bring further pressure to bear on central government to take positive action on land use

policy. Tell them that if they are unable to offer allotment space you would be keen to come to some agreement about temporary use of a vacant site in the area, which you would attempt to reclaim for the purpose of growing food. A possible opening paragraph in your letter which would set the scene could be something like:

'As you are no doubt aware, the U.K.'s vulnerability over availability and soaring prices of foods on world markets is acute; and, in the light of this situation, Friends of the Earth are launching a campaign later this year aimed at encouraging people to grow their own food. This campaign will call on local authorities to provide as many allotment spaces as possible and, where these are in short supply, seriously to consider the temporary use of vacant or derelict land as allotments or community food-growing sites.'

Go on to stress the benefits such a scheme would bring in putting people back in touch with nature and incorporate the points above in your letter.

Report

We have discovered through previous campaigns that those groups who produced well-documented and well-presented reports about the local situation had the most impact. 'The Great Paper Chase', for instance, contains the basic information about how to compile reports and what to do with them when you have them. Although the style and content of a report on allotments will be very different from one on a paper chase the basic approach will be the same. We have outlined below a possible format for such a report on allotment provision to be presented to the council.

Introduction: Outline of food situation and isolation from nature experienced by most urban dwellers.
Allotments: History of local trends and availability of allotments in the area.
Demand for Allotments: Statistical evidence of increase in demand for allotments in last two years, linked to official attitudes about land use and allotments policy. A good place to name a few well-known local sites which have stood idle for years.

Vacant and Derelict Land: Statistical evidence of amount and location of this type of land in the area. How many allotments could this provide?

Ownership: If possible, give a breakdown of land-owners in the area and indicate how much vacant or derelict land each owns.

Conclusions: Obvious.

Recommendations: That the local authority take immediate active steps to offer vacant and derelict sites to people on allotment waiting lists in a positive effort to respond in a constructive way to the growing demand for allotment areas. And that they assist in every practical way to render those sites productive. That the authority takes steps to ensure that in future land being cleared for redevelopment (if it is absolutely necessary) be cleared in such a way that its future short-term use as allotment areas is possible. And that they urge other land-owners to likewise release land for this purpose. That they impress upon Central Government the need to recognize that erosion of agricultural land must stop and that a land use policy, based on the need for the U.K. to ensure as much home food production as possible, must be drawn up.

This outline is clearly just a guide. Depending on the time and manpower you have available, your report could be very detailed and could include a breakdown of the areas from which most of the allotment seekers come, surveys of people's feeling about allotment provision and an analysis of the availability of food growing areas in different parts of the town.

SECTION TWO

Now What?

With regard to press and media coverage, it's important to be clear in your own mind about certain points, such as:

What exactly are you asking the authority to do?

Is the exercise purely a political one, urging authorities to release vacant land for people on allotment waiting lists or do you feel that the site would be an ideal point for your actions locally?

Do you intend to farm the plot yourselves and for how long are you prepared to commit yourselves to farming the plot?

Will you try to involve schools, community groups or people in the area who have been waiting for allotments?

Which areas of the site will you preserve in its natural state?

How will you cope with the possibility of vandalism?

Does the site need fencing?

What will you do with the produce?

The answers to these sorts of questions will largely depend on local conditions. We cannot therefore offer concrete advice but can only point out the importance of demonstrating that your actions are not the result of impetuous skylarking but that they are part of a well thought out campaign to highlight a very serious problem.

Tools

A good look at the site will give you an idea of the sort of tools you will need. If it is heavily overgrown a scythe will come in very handy. A 15 lb. sledge hammer is also useful for breaking up large chunks of concrete which are often found just below the topsoil on many sites. A rake is handy for piling up the cut vegetation and a pick-axe is a must on most sites. It's invaluable for breaking up the soil and loosening tightly packed bricks and earth. You'll obviously need spades and a garden fork for breaking and turning the soil. A wheel-barrow will come in handy if you can lay hands on one.

Tools are expensive but you'll probably find relations or friends will loan them to you for the day. If not, try local allotments owners (if there are any!) or local branches of the Conservation Corps (head office: Zoological Gardens, Regents Park, London N.W.1). It might be worth your while contacting a garden tool manufacturer in the hope that they will loan you tools in return for a 'plug' for their equipment. Alternatively second-hand tools can often be purchased very reasonably in junk shops or next to nothing at jumble sales.

Renovating the Land

(1) *Clearing the Site*

The emphasis at the site itself should be on making the best possible use of available material. Avoid bonfires and use the cut vegetation for compost. The rubble or hard-core can be used for making paths between the vegetable patches and for constructing boxes in which vegetables can be grown on less productive areas of the site. Any wood which may be lying around can be used as pegs for marking out the plots or for making your compost boxes. While you're at it, you could make a display of the tin-cans and bottles you'll doubtless find, for a quick one-off lesson in packaging techniques. If you do make use of discarded bottles for storage purposes, make sure you label the containers clearly.

At the famous Waterloo site some years ago we found two perfectly good steel trolleys on wheels. We haven't a clue why they were there nor whose idea it was to dump them in the first place; but these are ideal containers for collecting rainwater or for growing vegetables. So, be inventive with the 'rubbish' you find and put it to good use wherever possible.

Remember to retain as much of the natural vegetation as possible. The Waterloo site boasts apple, plum and peach trees – trees which have been sown by the casual discarding of stones and pips over the wall running at the side of the site. These clearly must be kept, so you need to be aware of the flora and fauna your site supports.

Soil Fertility and Soil Renovation

The type and quality of the soil on your site will clearly affect the types of crops you grow and what efforts you make in improving the soil. Soil types fall into four main categories:

CHALKY: Usually shallow topsoil, impregnated with lime. Provides good drainage and heats up quickly, but is a poor retainer of moisture and plant nutrients. Good soil for salad vegetables.

Improvement: break up top soil and add compost and manure. In summer months ensure that the soil is frequently fed with a top-dressing of moist material such as garden compost or manure.

LOAM: Basically a mixture of clay, sand and humus. Generally provides good drainage and ventilation and retains plants nutrient well.

Improvement: loam soil is probably the 'ideal' growing soil. Depending on the ratio of sand to clay, a balanced soil can be maintained by adding compost or manure if there is a high lime content, or lime for high acid content.

CLAY: A heavy, sticky soil. Provides poor drainage and ventilation but retains soil nutrients well.

Improvement: turn the soil well from as deep as possible. Break the clods into the smallest possible lumps and, if possible, expose to frost. Add sand, grit or clinker to improve drainage and fork in manure or garden compost regularly. Lime may need to be added as clay soil is often acid.

SAND: Light, open soil providing good drainage and ventilation. Poor retainer of water and allows nutrients to be washed away.

Improvements: apply potash and lime frequently. Dig in compost or manure frequently and, during the summer months, add moisture-retaining compost around plants.

Potassium, nitrogen and phosphorus are all essential elements for a healthy soil. The absence of these can be compensated for by the adding of manure, compost and leafmould. Determining the quality of the soil is clearly problematic but there are organizations and public bodies who will give you advice. Samples of soil from different parts of the plot (about sufficient to fill a pint carton) can be sent to the horticultural adviser of the local authority. Check by phone first to make sure that they provide such a service. The Soil Association (Walnut Tree Manor, Haughley, Stowmarket, Suffolk) is a charitable organization dedicated to furthering the use of organic farming methods. They, together with the Henry Doubleday Research Association (20 Convent Lane, Bocking, Braintree, Essex), produce excellent pamphlets and literature on soil fertility and smallholding management and we would advise you to drop them a line for a list of their publications.

The best thing to do with weeds is to pull them out by hand and add them to your compost pile. As far as possible, stay away from inorganic fertilizers and pesticide sprays as there are ways in which you can concoct your own sprays (*refer to previous chapter*).

Compost boxes can be constructed by driving wooden stakes into the ground and nailing on planks of wood to form a box. Leave a 3-inch (76 mm) gap at the bottom and put a layer of bricks and rubble at the bottom to allow for aeration. Next, lay twigs or coarse vegetable matter over the bricks to prevent blockage of air channels and then pile on all the organic matter you can afford. Make sure you add a layer of manure every 8 inches (203 mm) or so. Human urine is a good activator of compost materials, as is seaweed. Within 6 months your compost will be ready to use.

Guide to Cultivation of Vegetables

Seeds are often germinated in boxes until they are ready to be transplanted to their beds. The alternative is to sow seeds directly into the soil on the site, where you run the risk of losing the crops should a heavy frost be experienced in the coming month or two. You can buy ready-grown young plants from any horticulturalist or garden centre, but, should you decide to take advantage of the mild weather and plant seeds direct into the soil, make sure you sow plenty of seeds to allow for a percentage of non-germination and for thinning at a later stage. Planting seedlings does, however, have the obvious advantage of transforming your site, almost overnight, into a vegetable patch.

A BASIC GROWING GUIDE FOR THE ALLOTMENT

1 oz = 28 gm; 1 square yard = 0·836 m²;
1 in = 25·4 mm; 6 ins = 152·4 mm;
1 ft = 0·3 m; 1 yd = 0·91 m; 50 yds = 45·7 m.

Artichoke (GLOBE)
Propagation: Seed or division
Sowing time: March
Transplanting time: May and September
Distance between rows: 3–4 ft
Distance between plants: 3 ft
Season of use: June–September

Artichoke (JERUSALEM)
Propagation: Tubers
Transplanting time: March
Distance between rows: 2 ft 6 ins
Distance between plants: 20–24 ins
Season of use: November–April

Asparagus
Propagation: Seed
Sowing time: April
Transplanting time: April
Distance between rows: 3 ft 6 ins
Distance between plants: 18–24 ins
Season of use: May–June
Seed quantity: 1 oz per 50 yd row

Bean (BROAD)
Propagation: Seed
Sowing time: February–May
Distance between rows: 2 ft 6 ins
Distance between plants: 8 ins
Season of use: July–September
Seed quantity: 1 qt per 60 yd row

Bean (FRENCH)
Propagation: Seed
Sowing time: 7th–31st May
Distance between rows: 2 ft
Distance between plants: 6 ins
Season of use: July–September
Seed quantity: 1 pt per 60 yd row

Bean (RUNNER)
Propagation: Seed
Sowing time: 7th–31st May
Distance between rows: 6 ft sticks
Distance between plants: 8 ins
Season of use: July–October
Seed quantity: 1 qt per 60 yd row

Beetroot
Propagation: Seed
Sowing time: 15th–30th April
Distance between rows: 15 ins
Distance between plants: 6–8 ins
Season of use: September–April
Seed quantity: 1 oz per 50 ft row

Broccoli
Propagation: Seed
Sowing time: 1st–15th April
Transplanting time: June–July
Distance between rows: 30–36 ins
Distance between plants: 30–36 ins
Season of use: November–May
Seed quantity: 1 oz per 8 sq yds

Brussels Sprouts
Propagation: Seed
Sowing time: 1st–15th April
Transplanting time: June–July

Distance between rows: 30 ins
Distance between plants: 24–30 ins
Season of use: November–April
Seed quantity: 1 oz per 8 sq yds

Cabbage (RED)
Propagation: Seed
Sowing time: 1st–10th August
Transplanting time: March–April
Distance between rows: 30 ins
Distance between plants: 30 ins
Season of use: November–March
Seed quantity: 1 oz per 8 sq yds

Cabbage (WHITE)
Propagation: Seed
Sowing time: April–July
Distance between rows: 24 ins
Distance between plants: 18–24 ins
Season of use: April–October
Seed quantity: 1 oz per 8 sq yds

Carrot
Propagation: Seed
Sowing time: April
Distance between rows: 12 ins
Distance between plants: 4–8 ins
Season of use: August–March
Seed quantity: 1 oz per 50 yd row

Cauliflower
Propagation: Seed
Sowing time: 1st–15th April
Transplanting time: May–June
Distance between rows: 30 ins
Distance between plants: 24–34 ins
Season of use: July–October
Seed quantity: 1 oz per 50 yd row

Chicory
Propagation: Seed
Sowing time: April
Distance between rows: 14 ins
Distance between plants: 6–9 ins
Season of use: November–March
Seed quantity: 1 oz per 60 yd row

Cucumber
Propagation: Seed and cuttings
Sowing time: February–May
Transplanting time: April–June

Distance between rows: Ridge 4 ft
Distance between plants: 4 ft
Season of use: June–September

Leek
Propagation: Seed
Sowing time: February–March
Transplanting time: May–July
Distance between rows: Early – 3 ft, late –
12 ins
Distance between plants: 8 ins
Season of use: October–April
Seed quantity: 1 oz per 50 yd row

Lettuce
Propagation: Seed
Sowing time: February–August
Transplanting time: April–September
Distance between rows: 9–12 ins
Distance between plants: 6–9 ins
Season of use: May–October
Seed quantity: 1 oz per 16 sq yds

Kale
Propagation: Seed
Sowing time: 1st–15th April
Transplanting time: June–July
Distance between rows: 26 ins
Distance between plants: 24–30 ins
Season of use: December–April
Seed quantity: 1 oz per 8 sq yds

Onion
Propagation: Seed or sets
Sowing time (seed): January–March
Transplanting time: March
Distance between rows: 12 ins
Distance between plants: 3–8 ins
Season of use: September–March
Seed quantity: 1 oz per 50 yd row

Parsnip
Propagation: Seed
Sowing time: February–March
Distance between rows: 15 ins
Distance between plants: 6–9 ins
Season of use: November–March
Seed quantity: 1 oz per 60 yd row

Pea
Propagation: Seed

Sowing time: January–February (early),
March–April (mid), 15th–30th May (late)
Distance between rows: Dwarf, 2 ft; medium,
4 ft; tall, 12 ft
Distance between plants: 6 ins
Seed quantity: 1 qt per 60 yd row

Potato
Propagation: Tubers
Sowing time: 1st–15th April (early); 15th–30th
April (late)
Distance between rows: 20–24 ins (early);
26–30 ins (late)
Distance between plants: 15–18 ins (early);
20–24 ins (late)
Season of use: June–August (early);
September–May (late)

Radish
Propagation: Seed
Sowing time: February–September
Distance between rows: 6 ins
Season of use: April–October
Seed quantity: 1 oz per 6 sq yds

Spinach
Propagation: Seed
Sowing time: April–September
Distance between rows: 12 ins
Season of use: June–April

Turnip
Propagation: Seed
Sowing time: April–July
Distance between rows: 12 ins
Distance between plants: 4–8 ins
Season of use: June–March
Seed quantity: 1 oz per 40 yd row

Vegetable Marrow
Propagation: Seed
Sowing time: April
Transplanting time: May–June
Distance between rows: 4 ft
Distance between plants: 4 ft
Season of use: August–November

MENU

A
Gourmet Guide
To
WILD EATING

And God said, Behold, I have given you every herb bearing seed, which is upon the face of all the earth, and every tree, in which is the fruit of a tree yielding seed; to you it shall be for meat. And to every beast of the earth, and to every fowl of the air, and to every thing that creepeth upon the earth, wherein there is life, I have given every green herb for meat: and it was so.

GENESIS 1: 29, 30

THESE days more and more of our fruit and vegetables are being cultivated for uniform size and colour, much to the detriment of flavour (a comparison with organically-grown produce will verify this). At the same time there is a growing trend for new and exotic plant foods which would appear to be one reaction against this Brave New World greengrocery. Nowhere is this more apparent than in the large supermarkets where such previously unheard-of delicacies as passion-fruit, mangoes, artichokes, sorrel and chicory have made an appearance.

But why rely on imported rare tastes? The fact is that growing wild in the woods, hedge-rows, meadows, wastegrounds, waterways and the sea – even in your own garden – there are dozens of wild plants and fungi which can be eaten. And they're all free!

Many of these edible plants not only possess startling and exciting tastes and textures, but are rich in vitamins and trace elements not always found in cultivated foodplants. In some cases, as with fathen (a close relative of spinach) the nutritive value is greater than that of its cultivated brother.

Naturally the novice wild food gourmet will feel a certain amount of trepidation. After all, there are a number (though very few) of poisonous plants and fungi to be found in Great Britain. Yet provided the guide set out below (and further on for fungi) is rigorously adhered to, there will be no need for worry.

This chapter not only contains a compre-hensive guide to plants, seaweeds and fungi, but includes many tasty and unusual recipes as well. Where the food can be eaten raw it says so. Where it states 'cook as for spinach' it means the leaves should be thoroughly washed and placed in a saucepan with just the water left on the leaves after washing and cooked in their own juice. The addition of butter and chopped onions, chives or garlic often improves the flavour. Where it states 'cook as for asparagus' it means the stems or shoots should be tied in bundles, boiled upright in salted water and served with butter.

A Guide to Picking and Eating

(1) Before even contemplating walking out for your first wild lunch, *arm yourself with a reputable field guide to both wild flowers and fungi* (see bibliography at end of book). NEVER rely solely on photographs or illus-trations as a method of identification but use the texts and keys as well. Check and double check and if you are in any way uncertain – *forget it.*

(2) Never pick wild plants indiscriminately, in particular the flowers and seed heads. Many are protected species and so picking is illegal.

(3) NEVER uproot a protected species and be discriminating even with those that are excessively common: many rare plants were once common and have been picked almost to extinction.

(4) NEVER hack a single plant to bits but rather pick small pieces from a number of plants. Try to leave every plant in a good shape.

(5) NEVER pick anything that is growing by the side of busy roads or where chemicals such as pesticides have been used.

(6) Always thoroughly wash whatever you pick.

(7) Always sample a small portion of a wild food *a good time in advance* of making a meal of it. This way you can see if there is any trace of side-effects should the plant be unsafe to eat through wrong identification.

PLANTS: Trees, Shrubs, Herbs

All plants listed below prefixed by an asterisk are uncommon or rare species and *should not be picked*. Although they have been included for interest's sake there is a possibility that you may find one or two of them growing in a garden, on private land or building land in which case there are no strong moral reasons for not sampling them. In some cases, the seeds and cuttings of these rarer plants can be purchased for culti-vation (see end of book).

*ALEXANDERS (*Smyrnium olustratum*)
A stout bushy hairless biennial widespread in hedgebanks and waste places. Use the young leaves and flower buds raw in salads. Boil the upper part of the root and the stems as a vegetable.

ANGELICA (*Angelica sylvestris*)
A tall stout perennial found widespread in wet woods, fens, damp grassy places and on cliffs. Add the leaves, diced, to stews and soups during the last minutes of cooking. Blanch the stems and cook as for asparagus.

Candied Angelica
Cut the young shoots and stems into four-inch lengths, cover with water and boil for 15–20 minutes. Peel and boil again until green. Dry the roots and stems. To every ounce add an ounce of sugar and leave this mixture for two days. Boil ingredients until the syrup begins to crystallize. Remove angelica and cover liberally with sugar and allow to dry.

APPLEMINT (*Mentha rotundifolia*)
Generally rare in ditches and roadside verges.

Use one or two leaves as a flavouring in custards and milk puddings or as a garnish for savoury dishes.

*ARROWHEAD (*Sagittaria sagittifolia*)
A hairless aquatic perennial found widespread and locally common in fresh water. Use the roots, ground and dried as a substitute for arrowroot.

ASH (*Fraxinus excelsior*)
Deciduous tree found common and widespread in hedgerows and woods. The young and tender fruit, 'ashen keys', can be preserved as a pickle. Boil the young keys in water, strain, and boil again. Strain the keys and then immediately preserve in boiling, well-spiced vinegar.

*ASPARAGUS (*Asparagus officinalis*)
A domestic vegetable delicacy now naturalized in some places. Poach the tender young shoots in water or eat raw in salads.

BALM (*Melissa officinalis*)
A garden species now naturalized in places in the south. Use the leaves in stuffings or as a garnish to salads.

BARBERRY (*Berberis vulgaris*)
A deciduous shrub found widespread but rare in hedgerows and bushy places. The berries should not be eaten raw, but use the fruit for tart jellies and preserves, tart sauce and pies. Crush and infuse with lemon and mint for a cooling summer drink.

Pickled Barberries
Dissolve half a pound of sugar in one quart of cider vinegar. Add one pint fruit and sufficient pickling spice or seasoning and boil until a good colour appears. Cover and allow to cool. Strain and bottle.

BARGEMAN'S CABBAGE (*Brassica campestris*)
An annual form of the common turnip, found widespread on bare ground, usually near rivers. Boil the leaves as for ordinary cabbage.

BEECH (*Fagus sylvatica*)
A deciduous tree found widespread in hedgerows and woods. Both nuts and leaves are edible. Collect the nuts in late autumn and eat the kernels raw or roasted with salt. 'Beechmeal' – the dried and powdered nuts – makes a wholesome flour for bread. Crush the nuts in a mill to extract beechnut oil, rich in fats and proteins. Use the young spring leaves raw in a salad.

BILBERRY (*Vaccinium myrtillus*)
An erect hairless deciduous undershrub found widespread and locally abundant on heaths, moors and acid soils. The fruit is deliciously tart eaten raw but can be used extensively in preserves, jellies, pies and tarts.

BIRCH (*Betula alba*) Silver Birch
A deciduous tree found common and widespread on heaths, hills and in woods. Use the young spring leaves raw in salads or cook as for spinach. Use the young catkins raw in salads. The sap can be made into a delicious syrup by boiling, or made into wine.

BIRD CHERRY (*Prunus padus*)
A deciduous shrub or small tree found frequently in woods and hedgerows, especially in the north of England and Wales. The fruit is tart but makes an agreeable preserve or jelly.

BISTORT (*Polygonum bistorta*)
A hairless unbranched perennial found widespread and frequent in wet pastures and in the hills. Rare in the south. Use the leaves as a vegetable cooked as spinach, or in soups and stews.

Easter Ledger Pudding
Take a pound of young bistort leaves, a handful of young nettle leaves, and a handful of blanched dandelion leaves. Wash and blanch in boiling water. Strain and chop the leaves. Add one minced hard-boiled egg, one beaten raw egg, one diced onion, butter, salt and seasoning to taste. Mix ingredients and cook in a pudding bowl till set.

*BITTER VETCH (*Lathyrus montanus*)
A frail hairless perennial found widespread and often common on heaths, moors, in woods and on acid soil. Use the chestnut-tasting tuberous roots boiled as a vegetable.

BLACKBERRY (*Rubus fruticosus*) Bramble
Widespread and very common in hedges, woods, heaths and waste places. As everyone must surely know, blackberries are delicious eaten raw, or cooked in pies, puddings, tarts, conserves and jellies. Use the dried fruit as a substitute for currants in buns. Makes a delicious wine. Use the tender leaf tips, dried, as a substitute for tea.

BLACK BINDWEED (*Polygonum convolvulus*)
A hairless, prostrate or climbing perennial

found widespread and common on waste and cultivated ground. The black seeds can be ground into a flour as an addition to bread mixtures. Use the crushed seed in muesli or cooked with oats in porridge.

BLACKTHORN (*Prunus spinosa*) Sloe
A very thorny, deciduous shrub found widespread and common in woods, shrub, hedgerows, and on sea cliffs. The fruit is too tart for eating raw, or even for cooking, unless it has been 'bletted' by the frost. Makes a tangy but agreeable jelly if mixed with crab apples.

Sloe Gin
Collect the fruit after a good frost and pack into a large Kilner jar. Pour over as much gin as will fill the jar and then seal for three months. Sugar can be mixed with the sloes, measure for measure, if a sweet/sour liqueur is required.

*BLADDER CAMPION (*Silene vulgaris*)
A shiny greyish-green hairless perennial found widespread and common by roadsides and on thinly grassed ground. Use the leaves with other greens as a vegetable. Use the tender young shoots cooked as for spinach.

BORAGE (*Borago officinalis*)
A stout hairy perennial found only rarely in the wild. Use the young leaves as a refreshing addition to summer claret cups.

BRACKEN (*Pteridium aquilinum*)
A stout, tall, gregarious fern found widespread and locally abundant in woods, on heaths and hills. Break off the tender young spring fronds (shoots) when still tightly curled and cook in salted water as for asparagus, only longer. The dried and ground roots have been mixed with barley flour to make a basic bread.

BROOKLIME (*Veronica beccabunga*)
A creeping, hairless, fleshy perennial found widespread and frequent in wet places. A pungent tasting but otherwise excellent little salad herb. Wash the leaves quickly in cold water before serving.

BROOM (*Sarothamnus scoparius*)
A virtually hairless deciduous shrub found widespread and abundant on heaths and dry acid soils. Use the young flower buds raw in a salad or pickled in vinegar with spices.

BULLACE (*Prunus domestica*) Wild Plum
Once domesticated before plums and gages were cultivated, now found only occasionally in hedgerows. The acid fruit is not suitable for eating raw but once the frost has reduced the acidity, bullaces can be cooked with other fruit, such as apples, in pies, tarts, etc.

BURDOCK (*Arctium minus*)
A stiff, stout downy perennial found widespread and common in woods, on roadsides and waste ground. In May, use the young stems raw in salads or cooked as for asparagus. First the stems must be peeled to the soft core. It is best to steam the stems in as little water as possible and serve seasoned with herb vinegar or lemon.

Burdock Beer
Take equal quantities of burdock and dandelion roots (about a quart of each), scrub them clean, slice lengthwise and cut in half. Boil in a gallon (4·5 litres) of water, strain, and when cool, add half a pint (0·56 litres) molasses or sugar and sufficient yeast to promote fermentation. Ready for drinking after three days.

*BUTCHERS BROOM (*Ruscus aculeatus*)
A stiff evergreen bush found locally in dry woods in the south. Use the young shoots boiled as a vegetable, or in soups and stews.

*CARAWAY (*Carum carvi*)
A hairless biennial umbellifer found locally in meadows in Scotland. Use the seeds to spice savoury dishes. The roots are especially delicious, cooked like carrots after having the outer skin removed. Use the tender young leaves raw in salads or as a garnish for savoury dishes.

CATSEAR (*Hypochoeris radicata*)
An erect tufted perennial found widespread and common in grassy places. Use the young leaves raw in salads, or mixed with other greens cooked as a vegetable.

*CHARLOCK (*Sinapis arvensis*) Wild Mustard
A coarse annual found widespread and abundant on waste and cultivated ground. Use the bitterish leaves cooked as for spinach.

CHERRY-PLUM (*Prunus cerasifera*)
A large shrub or small tree found frequently in hedgerows only in England. Use the tart fruit cooked with plenty of sugar or honey, in pies, tarts, conserves, etc.

CHERVIL (*Anthriscus sylvestris*) Cow Parsley
An erect white umbellifer found widespread and abundant in shady places. A close relative of the cultivated chervil. Pick only the young stems in spring and use chopped in salads, or cooked as a vegetable in soups, stews, etc. Excellent with potato dishes and omelettes. WARNING: Although Cow Parsley is our most common white umbellifer, there are others which resemble it and which are dangerously poisonous, *so double and treble check from your field guide.*

CHICKWEED (*Stellaria media*)
A weak, prostrate, pale green annual found widespread and abundant in disturbed ground. A really under-estimated vegetable, far superior to spinach in my view and having the advantage of being available all through the year. Use the leaves and stems cooked as for spinach. Serve with butter and lemon.

*CHICORY (*Cichorium intybus*)
A stiff perennial found widespread but local in grassy and wet places, especially on chalk or limestone. Use the leaves raw in salads or cooked as for spinach. The early spring roots may be cooked and eaten as a vegetable. Roast and ground, the roots are a good substitute for (or addition to) coffee.

CHIVES (*Allium schoenoprasum*)
A cultivated plant but found wild, widespread but very local on limestone cliffs and by lakes and rivers. Use the stems chopped raw in salads or in any savoury dish.

CLARY (*Salvia horminoides*)
A small, slightly aromatic perennial found widespread and locally frequent in dry grassy places. Use the young tender leaves as a garnish or seasoning in savoury dishes. Makes an excellent wine.

Clary Pancakes
Mix up a traditional pancake batter. Add a few chopped clary leaves and a small tub of cream. Fry in butter and serve with sugar or honey and lemon juice.

CLOUDBERRY (*Rubus chamaemorus*)
A low, downy, creeping perennial found locally on damp mountain heath-moors in the north. Use the fruit for puddings and preserves and as a colouring for marmalade.

COLTSFOOT (*Tussilago farfara*)
A low growing perennial found widespread and frequent on wet ground by roadsides, streams and ditches. In the old days coltsfoot flowers were used for making a distinctive wine. The leaves can be boiled in water for coltsfoot syrup.

Coltsfoot Candy
Chop and crush a bowlful of coltsfoot leaves and stew in a pint of water. Strain the liquid well and while still hot, add to a toffee mixture of 1 lb raw Barbados sugar, 1 lb raw treacle and 1 lb butter. Boil ingredients together until it hardens when dipped in cold water. Remove from heat and thoroughly whisk until mixture is stiff. Allow to set on shallow trays.

Coltsfoot Cream
Chop and sauté a handful or two of small coltsfoot leaves. Add water to cover and cook until soft. Add a tablespoon of toasted sesame seeds to the strained leaves and beat into an ever cream.

COMMON CALAMINT (*Calamintha ascendens*)
A small, mint-scented, tufted, hairy perennial found locally on dry grassy banks on chalk and limestone. Use the minty, marjoram flavoured leaves in savoury dishes or where mint is normally required.

COMMON COMFREY (*Symphytum officinale*)
A bushy, hairy perennial found widespread and frequent on river banks and in ditches. Use the leaves cooked as for spinach, with plenty of seasoning. Dip the whole leaves in batter and fry in deep oil as comfrey fritters.

COMMON MALLOW (*Malva sylvestris*)
A hairy, coarse, sometimes sprawling perennial found widespread and frequent in waste places. Use the leaves cooked as spinach with plenty of seasoning. The nut flavoured seeds – 'cheeses' – can be eaten raw.

Mallow Soup (MELOKHIA)
In Egypt, melokhia is one of their national dishes and includes meat and meat stock. Here is a vegetarian version:

Place in a saucepan one pound of washed and blended (or puréed) mallow leaves, garlic sauce (i.e. two crushed garlic cloves lightly fried in olive oil, with cayenne, ground coriander, salt and pepper), and a pound of minced mixed vegetables (chopped and sautéd) in season. Cover with water, bring to the boil, and simmer for fifteen minutes.

COMMON MELILOT (*Melilotus officinalis*) Sweet Clover
A hairless biennial found widespread and fairly common on waste ground. Use the young shoots cooked as asparagus. Use the small pea-like fruits in stews and soups, or with other peas or beans. Also White Melilot (*Melilotus alba*).

COMMON ORACHE (*Atriplex patula*)
A weedy annual found widespread and abundant on bare ground. Use the leaves cooked as for spinach. Also Hastate Orache (*Atriplex hastata*) and Grass-leaved Orache (*Atriplex littoralis*).

COMMON PENNY CRESS (*Thlaspi arvense*)
A stoutish, hairless annual found widespread and locally common on arable and waste ground. Use the leaves raw in salads.

*COMMON SCURVY GRASS (*Cochlearia officinalis*)
A hairless perennial found widespread and common on sea-cliffs. Use the leaves, not unlike watercress, raw in salads or cooked in pea soup.

*COMMON SOLOMON'S SEAL (*Polygonatum multiflorum*)
A creeping hairless perennial found locally in woods in England and Wales. Use the shoots

boiled as a vegetable. Use the roots dried and ground as a flour for bread mixtures.

COMMON SORREL (*Rumex acetosa*)
An unbranched, tufted perennial found widespread and abundant in grassy places and on mountains. One of our most versatile yet largely ignored wild foods. Use the leaves in early spring chopped raw in salads, or in egg or cream cheese sandwiches. Use the leaves cooked as for spinach. This way the sorrel breaks down readily into a purée which can then be used as a basis for many exciting dishes e.g. in omelettes, souffles and soups. Serve the purée (to which butter, cream, cinnamon and seasoning have been added) as a sauce for egg dishes. Dip the leaves in a very light batter and fry them in oil as sorrel pancakes.

Sorrel Soup
Melt 1½ oz (42 g) butter in a saucepan and cook half a finely grated onion till soft. Add two medium-sized potatoes, peeled and dried, and pour over 1¾ pints (1 litre) of vegetable stock. Season well with seasalt, nutmeg, a pinch of raw sugar, and simmer till the potatoes are soft. Wash two good handfuls of tender young sorrel leaves. Purée together with the soup in a blender and reheat. Add one or two large tubs of cream according to taste and remove from the heat. If you don't have a blender, add the sorrel towards the end of cooking.

Sorrel Green Eggs
Wash and cook 3 oz (85 g) of sorrel leaves in ¾ oz (21 g) butter until tender. Drain and chop or purée finely in a blender. Take shelled hardboiled eggs, cut them in half and remove the yolks. Mix the yolks with the sorrel and cream cheese, seasalt, pepper and nutmeg to taste. Put the mixture back into the egg whites and serve with a green salad.

*COMMON STAR OF BETHLEHEM (*Ornithogalum umbellatum*)
A hairless, unbranched perennial found widespread but locally rare in grassy places in East Anglia. Use the bulbous roots, cooked as a vegetable.

COMMON WINTERCRESS (*Barbarea vulgaris*)
A hairless, mustard-like perennial found widespread and frequent by roads and streams. Use

the leaves and stems raw in salads or gently steamed for two minutes in a little water.

CORIANDER (*Coriandrum sativum*)
A hairless, foetid annual found only rarely in the wild. Use the seeds as a flavouring for breads, cakes, and savoury and pudding dishes.

*CORN MINT (*Mentha arvensis*)
Our commonest land mint found widespread and common in damp places and arable fields. Use the leaves as for garden mint.

CORN POPPY (*Papaver rhoeas*) Field Poppy
Our commonest poppy found widespread and sometimes abundant on roadsides and arable land. Collect the seeds in September when the seed heads have turned grey-brown. Use the seed sprinkled on breads, pastries or as a garnish for fruit and savoury dishes.

CORNSALAD (*Valerianella locusta*)
A low, many-forked, hairless annual found widespread and reasonably common in arable land and on walls. Use the tops and leaves raw in salads or cooked as for spinach.

CORN SOW-THISTLE (*Sonchus arvensis*)
A bright perennial found widespread and common in wet and cultivated ground. Use the leaves, trimmed of their bristles, raw in salads.

CORN SPURREY (*Spergula arvensis*)
A frail, weedy annual found widespread and common on arable land. Use the seeds, ground down to meal in muesli or cooked like porridge.

*CORSICAN MINT (*Mentha requienii*)
A prostrate, carpet-forming perennial occasionally found naturalised in a few damp woodland areas. Use the leaves as for garden mint.

COUCHGRASS (*Agropyron repens*)
A creeping, coarse perennial weed found widespread and common in cultivated and waste ground. Use the roots cooked as a vegetable in soups and stews.

COWBERRY (*Vaccinium vitis-idaea*)
A creeping, evergreen undershrub found locally common on moors in the north and west and Ireland. Use the tart berries in jellies and conserves.

CRAB APPLE (*Malus sylvestris*)
A small deciduous tree found widespread and frequent in hedgerows and woods. Use the acid fruit for jellies, jams, pickles and for an excellent wine. Use the flowers dipped in a light batter and fried in butter as crab apple fritters.

Lambs Wool
Vary ingredients according to taste. Roast a pound or two of crabs. Remove the skins and cores and pulp in a blender. Add a little sugar and spice (nutmeg, allspice, etc.) and mix the lot with as much real ale as is needed.

CRANBERRY (*Vaccinium oxycoccus*)
A prostrate, evergreen undershrub found widespread yet local in bogs. The fruits are inedible raw, but excellent for jams, jellies and sauces.

Cranberry Bread
Sift together 1 lb (453 g) wholemeal flour, 14 oz (400 g) raw sugar, 1 teaspoon baking powder, 2 teaspoons seasalt. Add to the mixture $\frac{3}{4}$ pint (450 ml) of halved cranberries, 4 oz (113 g) chopped walnuts, grated peel from 6 oranges. Make a mixture of 4 fl oz (113 ml) water, 8 fl oz (226 ml) pure orange juice, 2 fl oz (56 ml) corn oil, and 2 beaten eggs. Stir into the flour until moist. Pour into 2 greased bread tins and bake for 50–60 minutes at 350°F (180°C).

Cranberry Relish

Blend together 4 cups cranberries, 1 orange, 1 lemon (seeded), $2\frac{1}{2}$ cups honey. Chill and store in a refrigerator. Keeps indefinitely.

CROWBERRY (*Empetrum nigrum*)
A trailing, prostrate, carpet-forming under-shrub found locally common on moors in the north and west and Ireland. Use the fruits for jellies and conserves.

CURLED DOCK (*Rumex crispus*)
Our commonest dock found widespread and abundant in fields and waste places. Use the young spring leaves cooked as for spinach.

DAISY (*Bellis perennis*)
Our commonest wild flower found widespread and abundant on lawns and short grassy places. Use the flower heads to make a really ancient spirit:

Daisy Whisky

Put one gallon of daisy heads (no stalks) in a fermenting bucket and pour over one gallon (4·5 litres) of boiling water. After 24 hours strain off the flowers and add to the must, $3\frac{1}{2}$ lbs (1·8 kg) white sugar, 1 lb (453 g) chopped raisins, 1 lb (453 g) wheat, the thinly peeled yellow rind (no pith) and juice of two lemons and two oranges. Mix 1 oz (28 g) yeast with a little of the liquid and add to the lukewarm must. Strain and pour into a fermenting jar and allow fermentation to proceed. Rack and bottle in the normal way.

DANDELION (*Taraxacum officinale*)
A common flower found widespread and abundant in grassy and waste places. All parts of the plant are edible. Wash and dry the roots in the sun, then roast and coarsely grind and use as an excellent substitute for coffee. Use the roots cooked as a vegetable: slice into rings, sauté in a little oil then braise until tender. Use the tender young spring leaves raw in salads. Use the leaves cooked as for spinach, seasoned with basil, lemon peel or garlic. Use the flowers to make a delicate country wine.

DEWBERRY (*Rubus caesius*)
Similar to bramble, found widespread and frequent in grassy and bushy places, fens and dune slacks. Use the fruit as for blackberry.

*DITTANDER (*Lepidium latifolium*)
A greyish, hairless perennial found locally in damp places on the coasts of east and south-east England, Wales and Ireland. Use the hot pungent roots as a relish.

DOUGLAS FIR (*Pseudotsuga menziesii*)
A tall, pyramidal pine tree found rare in the wild, mostly naturalized. Use the young and tender fir tips in soups, stews and savoury dishes. Imparts a delicate woody flavour.

*DROPWORT (*Filipendula vulgaris*)
A close relative of meadowsweet, found wide-spread but local in grassy areas growing on chalk and limestone. Use the bitterish roots cooked as a vegetable.

*DWARF CORNEL (*Chamaepericlymenum suecicum*)
A low slender perennial found locally frequent on northern hills. Use the berries eaten raw.

*EARLY PURPLE ORCHIS (*Orchis mascula*)
A common orchid found widespread and locally frequent in woods and certain meadows. Absolutely FORBIDDEN to touch but if you are lucky enough to have any growing in your garden/private land, then try eating the bulbs raw in salads or cooked as a vegetable. The bulbs can be dried and ground into a flour for bread mixtures.

*EAU-DE-COLOGNE MINT (*Mentha citrata*)
Very rare in the wild but naturalized in a few southern places. Use the leaves as for ordinary mint.

ELDER (*Sambucus nigra*)
A large shrub or small tree found widespread and common in woods, hedgerows and waste places, especially on chalk downs. A very versatile wild food, most parts of which are edible i.e. berries, flowers, buds, shoots. Dry the berries before absolutely ripe and use as a substitute for currants in puddings and cakes. Also the following:

Elderberry Rob

Fill a stone jar or suitable vessel with berries and place in a hot oven until the juice runs. To every pint of strained juice add half a pound of sugar and a quarter of a teaspoon ground cinnamon. Mix well and boil slowly until it thickens. Pour into bottles and store. Dilute with water for hot or cold drinks.

Elderberry Sauce

Bake 2 pints berries with $\frac{1}{2}$ pint vinegar in a

closed vessel. Leave for 24 hours then strain in a saucepan and add 1 minced shallot, piece bruised root ginger, 1 teaspoon peppercorns, and 1 teaspoon cloves. Boil well then bottle in hot jars and seal well.

Elderberry Soup

Cook for 40 minutes: $1\frac{1}{2}$ pints elderberries, $2\frac{1}{2}$ pints water (1·14 litres), 4 cloves, 1 teaspoon ground cinnamon, 1 sliced lemon. Sieve well and add to the mixture: 1 pint crab apple juice, 5 oz (142 g) Barbados sugar. Cook for 10 minutes. Add 1 teaspoon arrowroot dissolved in a little cold water and cook further until soup thickens. Serve chilled with a dash of nutmeg.

Elder Bud Pickle

Fill a saucepan with thoroughly washed buds. Add 1 teaspoon mace, 1 teaspoon peppercorns, the diced peel of 1 lemon, 1 teaspoon seasalt. Bring to the boil then take from the heat, strain off the liquid and allow both to cool. Put the buds into jars, pour over the liquid and seal securely.

Elder Flower Fritters

Make a thin batter. Dip the flowerheads in the batter and plunge into deep oil which is very hot. Serve golden brown with mint or sugar.

Elder Flower Lemonade

Cover 2 quarts fresh elder flowers with 2 quarts water. Add 1 sliced lemon, 1 tablespoon malt or cider vinegar, 10 oz (283 g) sugar. Stir well and leave for 24 hours. Strain and simmer mixture for 15 minutes. Leave chilled for 1 week before serving.

Elder Flower Pickle

Put 2 cups elder flowers in a pickle jar and pour over 1 cup boiling cider vinegar. After 1 hour, strain the flowers and serve in a tossed salad.

Elder Shoot Asparagus

Cut off the young spring shoots when 5–7 inches high and tie in small bundles. Quickly cook in hot water as for asparagus.

*ELECAMPANE (*Inula helenium*)
A tall, stout, hairy perennial found widespread but rare on roadsides and in copses. Use the stems candied (see instructions for angelica).

*FALSE BULRUSH (*Typha latifolia*) Reedmace
A tall aquatic perennial found widespread and common in small ponds and swamps and by fresh water. Use the root stalks collected in the autumn, dried and ground into a flour for thickening soups and stews. Use the inner portion of the root boiled as a vegetable or raw (only in the spring) in salads. Use the tender young spring shoots cooked as for asparagus. Use the pollen from the flowerheads mixed with wholemeal flour for a superlative bread.

FATHEN (*Chenopodium album*)
Our commonest goosefoot found widespread and abundant in cultivated and waste ground. Use the leaves cooked as spinach. Use the seeds, dried and ground in flour for breads and pastry.

FENNEL (*Foeniculum vulgare*)
A tall, aniseed aromatic, bluey-green perennial found widespread and locally common on waste ground and by the sea. Use the finely chopped leaves raw in salads or cooked in savoury dishes and apple pies. Use the thinner young stalks cooked as a vegetable. Use the seed as a flavouring for savoury dishes.

*FENUGREEK (*Trigonella ornithopodioides*)
A small hairless prostrate annual found widespread but uncommon near the sea in dry, sandy places. Use the chopped leaves and seeds as a flavouring for savoury and spicy dishes.

*FLOWERING RUSH (*Butomus umbellatus*)
An umbellifer aquatic perennial found widespread but local in and by fresh water. Use the peeled roots cooked as a vegetable.

FRENCH HALES (*Sorbus latifolia*)
A tree – a cross between the wild service tree and whitebeam – found locally in woods in the south-west and in south-east Ireland. Use the orange-brown berries for jellies and preserves.

*GALINGALE (*Cyperus longus*)
A hairless perennial found rare in moist places in the south. Use the roots dried and ground as an aromatic spice in savoury dishes. Cultivated species – *Cyperus esculentus*.

GARLIC MUSTARD (*Alliaria petiolata*)
A common biennial found widespread and common in light shade in woods or hedgebanks. Use the leaves chopped raw in salads or as a garnish in vinegar for savoury dishes.

*GIANT BELLFLOWER (*Campanula latifolia*)
A beautiful soft-haired perennial found widespread and locally frequent in woods and hedgebanks. Use the young shoots cooked as spinach.

GOATSBEARD (*Tragopogon pratensis*)
A small greyish perennial found widespread and common in grassy areas. Use the leaves and roots raw in salads.

*GOLDEN SAXIFRAGE (*Chrysosplenium oppositifolium*)
A low, creeping perennial found widespread and locally common in wet shady places. Use the leaves raw in salads.

GOOD KING HENRY (*Chenopodium bonus-henricus*)
A perennial goosefoot found widespread but local near roadsides, farmyards and houses. Use the leaves cooked as for spinach.

GOOSEBERRY (*Ribes uva-crispa*)
A garden fruit found naturalized and widespread in woods and hedgerows. Use the tender young leaves raw in a salad or cole-slaw. Use the fruit in jellies, preserves and pies etc.

GOOSE GRASS (*Galium aparine*)
A straggling, weedy annual found widespread and abundant in fens, hedgebanks and on coastal shingle and disturbed waste ground. Use the flowering burrs, dried and roasted as the finest coffee substitute.

GORSE (*Ulex europaeus*)
A dense, evergreen shrub covered with sharp thorns found widespread and common on heaths and common land. Use the flowers picked in May for a delightful country wine.

GREATER PRICKLY LETTUCE (*Lactuca virosa*)
A stoutish biennial found near the sea on chalky soils. Use the tender young leaves raw in salads.

*GREEN-WINGED ORCHID (*Orchis morio*)
Similar to the early purple orchid and equally sacrosanct unless you have access privately. The tubers, dried and ground have been used in the past to make a beverage called 'salop'.

GROUND ELDER (*Aegopodium podagraria*)
A hairless, creeping perennial found widespread and common in shady places, often in gardens. Use the leaves cooked as for spinach.

GROUND IVY (*Glechoma hederacea*)
A low growing aromatic perennial found widespread and common in woods and hedge banks. Use the leaves for flavouring and clarifying beer.

GUELDER ROSE (*Viburnum opulus*)
A large deciduous shrub or small tree found widespread in bushy places on chalk and limestone. Use the sickly fruits cooked only, in jellies and sauces.

HAIRY BITTERCRESS (*Cardamine hirsuta*)
A low, hairy annual found widespread on walls, dunes, rocks and bare places. Use the leaves raw in salads.

HARDHEAD (*Centaurea nigra*) Lesser Knapweed
A downy perennial found widespread and common in grassy areas. Use the purple petals raw in salads.

HAWTHORN (*Crataegus monogyna*)
A thorny deciduous shrub or small tree found widespread and common in open woods, thickets and hedges. Use the young buds and leaves raw in salads. Use the flower petals to make wine. Eat the fruit raw or use for jellies and preserves.

HAZEL (*Corylus avellana*)
A tall deciduous shrub found widespread and common in hedgerows, woods and bushy places. Use the nuts raw for eating, or grind to a rough meal and use in nut roast and other vegetarian savoury dishes.

HEATHER (*Calluna vulgaris*) Ling
An evergreen undershrub found widespread and abundant on moors, heaths, bogs and open woods. Use the dried flowers as a substitute for tea.

HENBIT (*Lamium amplexicaule*)
Similar to red deadnettle and found widespread but locally on cultivated ground. Use the leaves cooked as for spinach.

*HERB BENNET (*Geum urbanum*)
A hairy perennial found widespread and common by woods and on hedgebanks. Use the roots sparingly, cooked in soups and stews, or as a substitute for cloves in sweet dishes.

HOGWEED (*Heracleum sphondylium*)
Another very common white umbellifer, *not to be confused with other poisonous species*. Use the young shoots cooked as for spinach.

HOP (*Humulus lupulus*)
A hairy perennial climber found widespread and common locally in damp thickets and hedges. Use the young shoots cooked as for asparagus. Use the green flowers for brewing real beer.

HORSE CHESTNUT (*Aesculus hippocastanum*)
A familiar deciduous woodland tree found widespread and common. The young aromatic buds have been used as a substitute for hops in the manufacture of beer. The fruit – conkers – *is poisonous raw*, but the poisonous element can be removed by 'leaching' and the resulting product is said to be rich in nourishment value. In America, they still roast chestnuts as a coffee substitute.

*HORSE-MINT (*Mentha longifolia*)
Similar but larger than spearmint and found widespread but locally by streams. Use the leaves as for garden mint.

HOTTENTOT FIG (*Carpobrotus edulis*) Kaffir Fig, Mesembryanthemum
A fleshy, prostrate perennial found frequent on waste ground. Use the tangy fruits which can be eaten raw.

JAPANESE KNOTWEED (*Polygonum cuspidatum*)
A stout hairless perennial found frequent on waste ground. Cook as for asparagus.

*JEWEL-WEED (*Impatiens capensis*)
A bushy balsam found frequent by the sides of streams and rivers. Use the very young shoots cooked as a vegetable in soups and stews. Eat sparingly.

JUNEBERRY (*Amelanchier intermedia*)
A deciduous shrub or small tree found naturalized in scrub and woodland in the south. Use the fruit cooked in jellies, preserves, pies, etc.

JUNIPER (*Juniperus communis*)
A grey-green evergreen shrub found widespread but infrequent on chalk and limestone hills, heaths, moors and in pine and birch woods. Use the berries to flavour savoury dishes and gin liqueurs.

Juniper Berry Sauce
In four tablespoons of melted butter, cook 3 tablespoons finely chopped onion and 1 teaspoon finely chopped garlic until tender. Remove from heat and add 4 lightly crushed juniper berries, 1 tablespoon chopped parsley, 3 teaspoons lemon juice, salt and pepper to taste. Blend thoroughly. Delicious on potato and asparagus dishes.

KNOTGRASS (*Polygonum aviculare*)
A small, generally prostrate annual found widespread and abundant on waste and cultivated ground. Use the ripe seed, ground into a wholesome flour for bread mixtures.

LADY'S BEDSTRAW (*Galium verum*)
A yellow sprawling perennial found widespread and common in dry grassy places. Use a decoction of the herb as a substitute for rennet in the preparation of junkets and cheeses.

LADY'S MANTLE (*Alchemilla vulgaris*)
A low, pale green perennial found widespread and frequent in grassy areas. Use the leaves cooked as for spinach.

*LADY'S SMOCK (*Cardamine pratensis*)
A graceful perennial found widespread and common in woods, mountain ledges and damp meadows. Use the leaves cooked as for spinach.

*LARGE EVENING PRIMROSE (*Oenothera erythrosepala*)
A striking downy annual or perennial found widespread but local on dunes and in waste places. The roots have been cooked as a vegetable and the leaves cooked as for spinach.

*LESSER EVENING PRIMROSE (*Oenothera biennis*)
A rather beautiful annual or biennial found rarely in waste places and on dunes. Use the roots with their carrot-like flavour, cooked as a vegetable.

LIME (*Tilia europaea*)
A deciduous tree abundantly common in gardens, parks and occasionally naturalized in hedges and copses. Use the young spring leaves, minus their stalks, as a delicious sandwich filling. Use the blossom in summer as a refreshing and fragrant tea. The sap of *Tilia americana* is used to make a delicious syrup and an agreeable wine.

*LORDS AND LADIES (*Arum maculatum*) Cuckoo Pint
A low, hairless perennial found widespread and common in hedgerows and copses. It causes bad upsets if eaten raw, but use the roots baked as a vegetable or boiled, dried and ground, as a substitute for sago – known traditionally as 'Portland starch'. WARNING – *keep well clear of the berries*.

LOVAGE (*Ligusticum scoticum*)
A stocky, hairless perennial found locally on rocky sea cliffs in Scotland, Northumberland and Northern Ireland. Use the young celery-tasting stems in soups and stews. Use the stems candied (see the recipe for angelica).

LUCERNE (*Medicago sativa*) Alfalfa
A hairless perennial found widespread and

frequent in waste and grassy places. A highly nourishing wild food. Use the tender young leaves raw in salads.

*LUNGWORT (*Pulmonaria officinalis*)
A more or less downy perennial found naturalized in hedgebanks and woods. Use the leaves boiled as a vegetable.

MAIDENHAIR FERN (*Adiantum capillus-veneris*)
Found locally in moist crevices in rocks and cliffs by the sea. Use the leaves as a garnish for sweet dishes and for flavouring.

MARJORAM (*Origanum vulgare*) Oregano
A downy aromatic perennial found widespread and locally common in grassy places. A widely-known but little-used herb whose leaves fresh or dried give a distinctive and appetising flavour to soups, stews, savoury dishes and milk puddings.

*MARSH MALLOW (*Althaea officinalis*)
A grey, velvety perennial found widespread and local by salt marshes and dykes near the sea. The roots were once used to make the real marshmallow sweets.

MARSH MARIGOLD (*Caltha palustris*) Kingcup
A hairless buttercup-type perennial found widespread and common in marshy areas. NOT TO BE EATEN RAW. The leaves, however, are rendered harmless by cooking and are excellent prepared as for spinach. Use the flower buds pickled in vinegar as a substitute for capers.

MARSH SAMPHIRE (*Salicornia europaea*) Glasswort
An erect, yellow-green perennial found widespread and abundant in salt marshes. Difficult to harvest but a none-the-less excellent vegetable. Use the young spring shoots raw in salads or boiled as a vegetable or cooked as asparagus. Use the chopped shoots preserved in vinegar as a delectable pickle.

*MARSH THISTLE (*Cirsium eriophorum*)
An impressive biennial thistle found locally in scrub, grassland and on chalk or limestone cliffs. Use the young shoots, stripped to the core, cooked as asparagus, or raw in salads.

*MEADOWSWEET (*Filipendula ulmaria*)
A much-loved wild flower with sensuous blooms found widespread and common in fens, damp woods and by fresh water. Use the tubers dried and ground as a flour for bread mixtures.

MEDLAR (*Mespilus germanica*)
A small thornless tree occasionally found naturalized in hedgerows. Use the fruits baked with cloves like apples, or eaten raw once they have been 'bletted' by the winter frosts. (This can be achieved artificially by keeping the fruit in moist bran for a fortnight.)

MILK THISTLE (*Silybum marianum*)
A stout annual or biennial thistle found widespread and locally common in waste places, scrub, and on limestone near the sea. Use the leaves boiled (trimmed of their prickles), as a vegetable. Use the stems stewed like rhubarb after soaking for some time in water. Use the spring flowerhead bracts cooked and eaten like globe artichokes.

*MONK'S RHUBARB (*Rumex alpinus*)
A stout perennial found locally by streams and roadsides, generally near buildings. Use the leaves as a pot herb.

MORELLO CHERRY (*Prunus cerasus*)
A deciduous shrub found naturalized and rare in hedges and woods. Use the fruits for making wine and liqueurs.

NIPPLEWORT (*Lapsana communis*)
A stiff, leafy annual found widespread and common in gardens and shady places. Use the leaves raw in salads.

OAK (*Quercus robur*)
A large and familiar deciduous tree found widespread and abundant in woods and hedgerows. The acorns of oak trees are a highly nutritious though unexciting food source. They can be ground into a flour, which can then be mixed with cereal flour for breads, or roasted and used as a substitute for coffee.

Acorn Coffee
Crush the acorns to a rough meal and then boil for half an hour in water, strain, dry and then roast until brown. Grind to a granular consistency in a coffee grinder.

Acorn Flour
Soak the acorns in a pot of boiling lye of wood ash and water. This removes the bitterness caused by the tannin content. Dry and then grind down to a fine meal.

OREGON GRAPE (*Mahonia aquifolium*)
An evergreen shrub found widespread and frequently naturalized in shrubberies and gaming land. Use the berries raw, or made into jellies and preserves.

*OX-EYE DAISY (*Chrysanthemum leucanthemum*)
A familiar perennial daisy found widespread and abundant in grassy areas. Use the roots cooked as a vegetable.

*OYSTER PLANT (*Mertensia maritima*)
A prostrate, carpet-forming, fleshy grey perennial found rare on shingle coasts in Scotland. Use the leaves raw in salads or cooked as a vegetable.

PARSLEY (*Petroselinum crispum*)
A hairless, bright green perennial found mostly naturalized on rocks near the sea. A familiar and Vitamin C-rich pot herb.

PARSLEY PIERT (*Aphanes arvensis*)
A small, generally prostrate, downy grey annual found widespread and common on dry and arable ground. Use the young shoots preserved in vinegar as a pickle.

PEAR (*Pyrus communis*)
A deciduous tree found widespread but infrequent in woods and hedgerows. Use the fruit for pies, tarts, jellies and preserves.

*PEPPERMINT (*Mentha piperita*)
Larger than spearmint and found infrequent and naturalized in the south and west. Use the leaves as for ordinary mint.

*PIGNUT (*Conopodium majus*)
A slender, hairless perennial umbellifer found widespread and common in meadows and woods. Use the tubers raw in salads.

PIGWEED (*Amaranthus retroflexus*)
A downy, grey-green annual found occasionally in waste places and arable fields. Use the young leaves raw in salads or cooked as for spinach. Use the seeds, dried and ground into flour for bread mixtures.

*RAMPION (*Campanula rapunculus*)
A lovely hairless perennial found widespread but very rare on banks and shady places near houses. Use the roots boiled as a vegetable and the leaves chopped raw in salads.

*RAMSONS (*Allium ursinum*)
A broad-leafed garlic found widespread and locally frequent in damp woods. Use the leaves as a garlic flavoured relish in savoury dishes.

RAPE (*Brassica napus*)
A swede-like annual found locally common on sea cliffs, stream banks, disturbed ground and waste places. Use the oil from the crushed seed for cooking and dressings.

RASPBERRY (*Rubus idaeus*)
A familiar suckering perennial found widespread and frequent in woods and on heaths. The fruit is at its best eaten raw but is excellent for all pudding dishes, jellies, preserves and conserves.

RATSTAIL PLANTAIN (*Plantago major*)
Our commonest plantain found widespread and common in lawns and wayside places. Use the young leaves cooked as for spinach.

RED CLOVER (*Trifolium pratense*)
Our commonest red clover found widespread and abundant in grassy areas. Use the tender leaves raw in salads or sandwiches, or cooked as for spinach. Use the flower heads to make a traditional wine or as a flavouring and garnish for sweet dishes.

RED CURRANT (*Ribes rubrum*)
A deciduous bush found widespread but infrequent in hedgerows and woods. Use the berries to make a superlative jelly and a reasonable jam.

RED DEADNETTLE (*Lamium purpureum*)
A sprawling, downy perennial found widespread and abundant on cultivated ground. Use the young leaves cooked as for spinach. Also White Deadnettle (*Lamium album*).

REDLEG (*Polygonum persicaria*)
A generally sprawling, hairless perennial found widespread and abundant on bare ground and in damp ditches. Use the leaves cooked as for spinach.

RED VALERIAN (*Centranthus ruber*)
A greyish, hairless perennial found widespread and locally frequent on chalky banks, cliffs and quarries. Use the leaves raw in salads or cooked as for spinach.

REED (*Phragmites communis*)
A tall, stout, hairless perennial found widespread and locally abundant in swamps, brackish water, and on cliffs. The green stalks can be dried and ground into a flour which needs to be sifted. The flour, toasted was eaten in the past like marshmallow.

*REST-HARROW (*Ononis repens*)
A downy, woody perennial found widespread and common on dunes and dry grassland. The roots can be chewed like liquorice.

ROCK SAMPHIRE (*Crithmum maritimum*)
A yellowish maritime umbellifer frequently found on rocky coasts. Use the young stems cooked as a vegetable, or pickled in vinegar.

ROSE-BAY (*Epilobium angustifolium*)
A striking perennial found widespread and abundant on railway banks, heaths and waste ground. Use the young leaves cooked as for spinach.

ROUGH HAWKBIT (*Leontodon hispidus*) Greater Hawkbit
A dandelion-like hairy perennial found widespread and common in grassy places. Use the young leaves raw in salads.

ROWAN (*Sorbus aucuparia*) Mountain Ash
A small deciduous tree found widespread and common in northern dry woods and rocky places and locally in the south. Use the bright red berries for making jelly.

*RUSSIAN THISTLE (*Salsola pestifera*)
An erect, bushy annual found casually but rare. Use the stems, trimmed of their thorns, cooked as a vegetable.

SALAD BURNET (*Poterium sanguisorba*)
A cucumber-smelling perennial found widespread and locally abundant in grassy areas. Use the leaves raw in salads or as a garnish for cold summer drinks.

*SALSIFY (*Tragopogon porrifolius*)
An ancient root vegetable now found only occasionally in waste places, or by the sea. Can sometimes be obtained from the greengrocers. Use the peeled roots boiled or steamed as a vegetable. Even better boiled and then fried in egg and breadcrumbs as a fillet.

Salsify Pie
Boil the salsify and then scrape or peel off the outer skin. Pack into a pie dish and then pour over a white sauce, made with butter, flour, salt and pepper. Top with chopped parsley and finally cover with a good potato crust. Bake until golden brown, or as for fish-pie.

*SAND LEEK (*Allium scorodoprasum*)
A relative of garlic and found very locally in hedgebanks and rough pasture. Use the stems and bulbs as for garlic.

SCOTS PINE (*Pinus sylvestris*)
A tall, evergreen tree found widespread and frequent in woods and on heaths. Use the pink, aromatic tips of the fir to flavour custards, milk puddings and sweets. Best used in a *bouquet garni* bag, removed after cooking. Use the pine seeds (from the cones) as a garnish for puddings.

SEA BEET (*Beta vulgaris*) Wild Spinach
A sprawling perennial found widespread and common by the sea. Use the very young leaves raw in salads, or cook as for spinach.

Sea Beet Fritters
Use the tough outer leaves and cook in a little water until tender – about 1 lb leaves in all. Allow the moisture to boil away, then chop the leaves finely and mix together with $\frac{1}{2}$ cup flour, $\frac{3}{4}$ cup milk, 1 egg, $\frac{1}{4}$ teaspoon salt, $\frac{1}{4}$ teaspoon rosemary, $\frac{1}{4}$ teaspoon Barbados sugar, pepper to taste. Spoon into a pan of hot fat and fry like pancakes. Another way is to dip the uncooked leaves in batter and deep fry in oil.

*SEA HOLLY (*Eryngium maritimum*)
An unmistakable bluey-green, stiff, hairless perennial found widespread but locally on sand and elsewhere by the sea. Use the roots candied (see the recipe for angelica), or in a jelly or conserve.

Eyringo Toffee
Boil the roots, remove the outer skin and slice into small pieces (toffee size). Use a little of the

boiled water to make up a toffee mixture – 1 lb (454 g) Barbados sugar, 3 oz (84 g) butter – and drop the pieces of root into it. Allow to cool on a flat tray.

*SEA KALE (*Crambe maritima*)
A thickish, cabbage-leafed perennial found widespread and locally by the sea on sand and shingle. One of our most ancient vegetables, now sadly disappearing. Use the young white stems cooked as asparagus in salt water.

SEA PURSLANE (*Halimione portulacoides*)
A straggly, greyish undershrub found frequently in saltmarshes. Use the fleshy leaves raw in salads.

SHEPHERDS PURSE (*Capsella bursa-pastoris*)
A dull-green, downy annual found widespread and abundant in waste and cultivated areas. Use the cabbage-tasting leaves cooked as spinach.

SILVERWEED (*Potentilla anserina*)
A silky, prostrate perennial found widespread and common in damp grassy and waste areas. Use the parsnip-flavoured roots boiled or roasted as a vegetable, or dried and ground as a flour for bread mixtures.

*SPEARMINT (*Mentha spicata*)
Our common garden mint, sometimes found as an escape. The usual mint for mint sauce, etc.

*SPIGNEL-MEU (*Meum athamanticum*)
A hairless, aromatic perennial found locally in north Wales and the Central Highlands hill pastures. Use the roots boiled or roasted.

*SPIKED STAR OF BETHLEHEM (*Ornithogalum pyrenaicum*) Bath Asparagus
An unbranched, hairless perennial found widespread but rare in grassy places, usually as an escape. Use the stems cooked as for asparagus.

SPOTTED CATSEAR (*Hypochoeris radicata*)
A tufted, erect perennial found widespread and common in grassy areas. Use the leaves raw in salads or cooked as for spinach.

SPRING BEAUTY (*Claytonia perfoliata*)
A pale green, hairless annual found widespread and locally in sandy soils and some cultivated ground. Use the chestnut-flavoured tubers roasted as a vegetable.

STINGING NETTLE (*Urtica dioica*)
A gregarious weed with stinging hairs found widespread and abundant almost everywhere. Perhaps the most unusual yet at the same time most useful and nourishing wild food. Use the young spring leaves (not later than June) stripped from the stems and cooked as for spinach, with plenty of seasoning. Use the leaves as a substitute for hops in the brewing of beer, or for an unusual yet excellent wine.

Nettle Porridge
Mix 1 teacup boiled pearl barley with 6 handfuls nettle leaves, 1 handful watercress, 1 handful dandelion leaves, 1 handful sorrel leaves, a sprig of mint, a sprig of thyme, 8 blackcurrant leaves and 1 onion. Dice everything together, add salt and pepper to taste, a big knob of butter and 1 well-beaten egg. Pour into a pudding basin and steam for 1½ hours. Serve with a white or cheese sauce, or rich gravy.

Nettle Soup
Cook the nettles as for spinach and then reduce to a purée. Make 1 pint (0·57 litres) white sauce using 1 pint milk, 1 oz (28·3 g) flour, 1 oz butter, salt and pepper, and let it simmer for a few minutes. Pour onto the purée, mix thoroughly (preferably whip), and serve with grated cheese.

STRAWBERRY TREE (*Arbutus unedo*)
A small evergreen tree or large shrub found rare in rocky woods in Ireland, otherwise naturalized elsewhere. Use the fruit to flavour sweets and liqueurs.

SWEET CHESTNUT (*Castanea sativa*)
A large deciduous tree found widespread in woods and parks. A most versatile nut. Eat them raw, minus the peel, or ground into a meal and used in stuffings and nut roasts. Use the nuts boiled as a vegetable, or chopped in soups and savoury dishes. And of course, chestnuts are heavenly roasted!

Chestnut Pudding
Make a slit in the skins of approximately 1 lb (454 g) nuts and boil until tender. Remove the skins and dry in a warm place. Grind the nuts down to a meal and mix ½ lb (227 g) of this with 6 oz (170 g) whipped butter, 2 tablespoons Barbados sugar, 1 cup milk, 6 well-beaten eggs, salt and pepper to taste. Mix thoroughly and turn into a buttered pudding dish. Cover with baking paper and bake slowly for 1½ hours.

SWEET CICELY (*Myrrhis odorata*)
An aromatic white umbellifer found in grassy

areas, mainly in the north. Use the roots boiled as a vegetable. Use the aniseed-smelling leaves raw in salads.

SWEET GALE (*Myrica gale*) Bog Myrtle
A deciduous, highly aromatic shrub found widespread and locally common in fens, marshes and bogs.

Gale Beer
Fill a large wooden tub or open-topped fermenting jar with gale leaves. Carefully measure in enough water to cover the leaves and then strain off. Take half the amount of water it needed and boil with honey at the rate of ½ pint (0·23 litre) per gallon (4·5 litres). Pour this onto the leaves; pressing them down well afterwards. Add the other half of water, boiling, so that the tub is full, and then allow to cool until lukewarm. Add sufficient yeast, remove the gale and allow to ferment 1 week. Remove the froth and strain off the beer into uncorked jars. A week later, cork up the jars and leave for 1 month before drinking, or better still, until the first frosts.

*SWEET VIOLET (*Viola odorata*)
Widespread and common in hedgebanks or shady areas. Use the flowers to impart a delicate flavour to milk dishes, sweets and icecreams. Use the leaves raw in salads or as a pot herb.

SYCAMORE (*Acer pseudoplatanus*)
A familiar deciduous tree found widespread and common in woods, hedgerows and parks. The sap of the sycamore can be boiled to make an agreeable syrup, or fermented to make wine.

*TANSY (*Chrysanthemum vulgare*)
A thick, aromatic, dark green perennial found widespread and frequent near gardens and on walls. Use the leaves dried or fresh as a pot herb, or as a substitute for nutmeg or cinnamon. Excellent in omelettes and other egg dishes, as well as breads and pastries.

WALL LETTUCE (*Mycelis muralis*)
A slender, purplish perennial found widespread but local on walls, rocks and shady banks. Use the leaves raw in salads.

WALL-PEPPER (*Sedum acre*)
The common yellow stonecrop found widespread and common on walls, roofs, sand-dunes and shingle. Use the leaves raw in salads.

WALNUT (*Juglans regia*)
A large deciduous tree naturalized in gardens and parks. Use the young fruits in July for walnut pickle, or ripe in November as nuts eaten raw.

WATERCRESS (*Rorippa nasturtium-aquaticum*)
A hairless, creeping, aquatic perennial found widespread and common in shallow fresh water and mud. A most nutritious food, bursting with Vitamin C and iron. Use only the older leaves raw in salads. Never pick watercress from streams running through sheep grazing land as infection from liverfluke may occur.

*WATER LILY (*Nymphaea alba*)
Our most common floating flower found widespread and locally frequent in fresh sheltered water. Use the roots cooked as a vegetable.

*WATERMINT (*Mentha aquatica*)
Our commonest aquatic mint found widespread and common in wet places. Use the leaves as for garden mint.

WHITEBEAM (*Sorbus aria*)
An impressive deciduous tree or shrub found widespread and locally frequent on the edge of woods, on crags, or in scrub. Use the bletted fruit raw or in cooked fruit dishes.

WHITE MUSTARD (*Sinapis alba*)
The mustard of 'mustard and cress' found widespread and common on arable land. Use the young leaves raw in salads.

WHORLED MINT (*Mentha verticillata*)
A hybrid of cornmint and water mint. Use the leaves as for garden mint.

WILD BASIL (*Clinopodium vulgare*)
A mild aromatic perennial found widespread and frequent in dry bushy areas. Use the leaves as a pot herb.

*WILD CARROT (*Daucus carota*)
A common white umbellifer found widespread and common in grassy areas. Use the roots lightly steamed as a vegetable and the seeds as a substitute savoury flavouring for anise or caraway.

WILD CELERY (*Apium graveolens*)
A celery-smelling, yellow-green, hairless perennial found widespread but local in wet places near the sea. Use the tangy stems raw in salads or as a pot herb.

*WILD PARSNIP (*Pastinaca sativa*)
A more or less hairy biennial found widespread and locally common in waste areas and dry places. Use the roots boiled or roasted as for cultivated parsnip.

WILD STRAWBERRY (*Fragaria vesca*)
A low, hairy perennial found widespread and common in woods and grassy areas. The exquisite flavoured fruit is best eaten raw, but wild strawberries make a heavenly jam if you can pick enough.

WILD THYME (*Thymus drucei*)
A prostrate, carpet-forming, mildly aromatic perennial found widespread and locally common in grassy areas. Milder than the garden thyme but just as useful as a pot herb or in stuffings and savoury dishes.

*WINTER GREEN (*Pyrola minor*)
A hairless perennial found widespread but local on moors, mountain ledges and in coniferous woods. Use the leaves raw in salads.

WOODRUFF (*Galium odoratum*)
An erect, carpet-forming perennial found widespread and locally frequent in woods. Use sprigs of the leaves to flavour summer drinks, especially those made from apples.

WOOD SORREL (*Oxalis acetosella*)
A delicate, creeping pale-green perennial found widespread and common in shady places or on

mountains. Use small quantities of the leaves raw in salads.

YARROW (*Achillea millefolium*)
A small, aromatic, dark-green perennial found widespread and common on lawns and grassy places. Use the leaves sparingly in salads, or boiled (minus the stems) as a vegetable. The flavour is improved by a final sauté in butter. Use as a substitute for chives.

YELLOW ARCHANGEL (*Galeobdolon luteum*)
Similar to a dead-nettle and found widespread and locally common in woods. Use the leaves cooked as for spinach.

POISONOUS PLANTS

The plants in the following list are all poisonous in one way or another and *should not be picked*.
ALDER BUCKTHORN (*Frangula alnus*)
BANEBERRY (*Actaea spicata*)
BITTERSWEET (*Solanum dulcamara*)
BLACK BRYONY (*Tamus communis*)
BLACK NIGHTSHADE (*Solanum nigrum*)
BUTTERCUPS (*Ranunculus*) all species

CHERRY LAUREL (*Prunus laurocerasus*)
COLUMBINE (*Aquilegia vulgaris*)
COMMON BUCKTHORN (*Rhamnus cathartica*)
COWBANE (*Cicuta virosa*)
DARNEL RYE-GRASS (*Lolium temulentum*)
DEADLY NIGHTSHADE (*Atropa bella-donna*)
DOG'S MERCURY (*Mercurialis perennis*)
FINE-LEAVED WATER DROPWORT (*Oenanthe aquatica*)
FOOLS PARSLEY (*Aethusa cynapium*)
FOXGLOVE (*Digitalis purpurea*)
FRITILLARY (*Fritillaria meleagris*)
GREEN HELLEBORE (*Helleborus viridis*)
HEMLOCK (*Conium maculatum*)
HEMLOCK WATER DROPWORT (*Oenanthe crocata*)
HENBANE (*Hyoscyamus niger*)
HOLLY (*Ilex aquifolium*)
IVY (*Hedera helix*)
LABURNUM (*Laburnum anagyroides*)
LILY OF THE VALLEY (*Convallaria majalis*)
LUPIN (*Lupinus*) all species

MEADOW SAFFRON (*Colchicum autumnale*)
MEZEREON (*Daphne mezereum*)
MISTLETOE (*Viscum album*)
MONKSHOOD (*Aconitum anglicum*)
PRIVET (*Ligustrum vulgare*)
SPINDLE-TREE (*Euonymus europaeus*)
SPURGE (*Euphorbia*) all species
SPURGE-LAUREL (*Daphne laureola*)
STINKING HELLEBORE (*Helleborus foetidus*)
THORN-APPLE (*Datura stramonium*)
TUBULAR WATER DROPWORT (*Oenanthe fistulosa*)
WHITE BRYONY (*Bryonia dioica*)
YEW (*Taxus baccata*)

FUNGI

There are well over 3,000 species of large-bodied fungi to be found in the British Isles. Out of this vast number just over twenty are seriously poisonous, which makes the case for not eating fungi at all a shallow one. Of course, there are many which are indigestible for one reason or another, yet there still remains a hard core of delicious species which are a joy to eat.

As with the wild plants, get yourself a reputable field guide. Learn by heart the names and characteristics of all the deadly species. If you are unsure about any particular fungus *leave it well alone*. Only pick fresh specimens and on dry days. Never cut a fungus from the earth – *gently twist* and pull up the whole stem and 'root'. Transport the fungi back home in a well-ventilated container – never in a plastic bag. Finally, test anything picked with a small piece before tucking in good and proper. *Allow at least two hours between tasting and eating.*

Agaricus (MUSHROOMS)

AGARICUS ARVENSIS (*Horse Mushroom*)
Found in fields and pastures between July and November. Excellent baked with tomatoes. Simply pack the whole skinned and salted

66

tomatoes into the insides of the mushrooms and bake until a rich sauce is formed. Equally good baked in a white sauce with bilberries or redcurrants, and a little nutmeg.

AGARICUS AUGUSTUS
Found under coniferous and frondose trees between August and November.

AGARICUS BISPORUS
The wild form of our cultivated mushroom found by roadsides and on manure heaps.

AGARICUS BITORQUIS
Found in gardens and on roadsides between May and October.

AGARICUS CAMPESTRIS (*Field Mushroom*)
Our most familiar mushroom found locally common in meadows and pastures between August and November. In my opinion field mushrooms are best eaten raw but of course they are excellent cooked in a variety of ways. Cooking in milk brings out the strongest flavour.

AGARICUS LANGEI
Found under deciduous trees between September and November.

AGARICUS SILVATICUS
Found under conifer trees between September and November.

AGARICUS SILVICOLA (*Wood Mushroom*)
Found in woods between August and November.

AGARICUS SUBPERONATUS
Found in straw stacks and on roadsides between September and October.

Amanita

AMANITA FULVA (*Tawny Grisette*)
Found in woods under deciduous trees especially birch on peaty soils between May and November.

AMANITA RUBESCENS (*The Blusher*)
Found in deciduous and coniferous woods between July and November. Only eat cooked.

AMANITA VAGINATA (*Grisette*)
Found in woods under deciduous trees especially beech, also on heaths, between July and October.

Armillaria (GILL FUNGI)

ARMILLARIA MELLEA (*Honey Fungus*)
Found on deciduous and coniferous trees between July and November.

Boletus

BOLETUS BADIUS
Found under coniferous trees between August and November.

BOLETUS (GYROPORUS) CYANESCENS
Found in woods on poor soils, especially under birch, between July and November.

BOLETUS EDULIS (*Cep*)
Found mostly in deciduous woods, especially under beech, between August and November. A nutty tasting and excellent fungus which can be cooked in a variety of ways as for cultivated mushrooms.

BOLETUS ELEGANS
Found between March and November.

BOLETUS ERYTHROPUS
Found in woods on poor soils between August and November.

BOLETUS LUTEUS
Found mostly in grass between August and November.

BOLETUS PULVERULENTUS
Found in damp deciduous woods between August and November.

BOLETUS TESTACEOSCABER
Found in birch and coniferous woods between July and November.

Cantharellaceae (FUNNEL FUNGI)

CANTHARELLUS CIBARIUS (*Chanterelle*)
Found in deciduous woods between July and December. Best stewed in milk or served in or with egg dishes.

CANTHARELLUS INFUNDIBULIFORMIS
Usually found in clusters in deciduous and coniferous woods on acid soils between July and January.

CRATERELLUS CORNUCOPIOIDES (*Horn of Plenty*)
Found amongst dead leaves in deciduous woods, especially beech, between August and November.

Clavaria (FAIRY CLUBS)

CLAVARIA (CLAVARIADELPHUS) FISTULOSA
Found on deciduous trees' leaves and branches, mainly beech, between September and February.

CLAVARIA (CLAVARIADELPHUS) PISTILLARIS
Found in deciduous woods between September and December.

Clitocybe (GILL FUNGI)

CLITOCYBE (CANTHARELLULA) CYATHIFORMIS
Found along paths and on rich soils in woods between September and January.

CLITOCYBE FLACCIDA
Found in rings or clusters in mainly coniferous woods between September and December.

CLITOCYBE GEOTROPA
Found in wood clearings on rich damp soils between September and December.

CLITOCYBE (LEUCOPAXILLUS) GIGANTEA
Found in pastures, roadsides, hedgerows and grassy places between August and November.

CLITOCYBE NEBULARIS
Found mainly in coniferous woods between August and December.

CLITOCYBE ODORA (*Anise Cap*)
Found mainly in deciduous woods between August and November.

Coprinus (INK CAPS)

COPRINUS ATRAMENTARIUS
Found usually in clusters at the base of deciduous trees, in gardens and fields between

August and December. (This can be upsetting if eaten with alcohol.)

COPRINUS COMATUS (*Shaggy Cap, Lawyer's Wig*)
Found in clusters on roadsides, in fields and rubbish tips, between May and November. Extremely delicious.

Hydnaceae (TOOTH FUNGI)

HERICIUM CORRALLOIDES
Found on the dead trunks of fir and deciduous trees, especially beech, between October and November.

HYDNUM REPANDUM (*Wood Hedgehog*)
Found in groups or rings in deciduous woods between August and November. More palatable after boiling, first in water, then in milk.

HYDNUM RUFESCENS
Found in coniferous woods between August and November.

SARCODON IMBRICATUM
Found in sandy coniferous woods between September and November.

Hygrophorus (GILL FUNGI)

HYGROPHORUS CAMAROPHYLLUS
Found in coniferous woods.

HYGROPHORUS NIVEUS
Found in meadows and pastures between September and December.

HYGROPHORUS PRATENSIS
Found in meadows and pastures between August and December.

HYGROPHORUS PUNICEUS
Found in grassy areas between August and December.

Laccaria (GILL FUNGI)

LACCARIA AMETHYSTINA
Found in deciduous woods between August and December.

Lactarius (GILL FUNGI)

LACTARIUS DELICIOSUS
Found between August and November. *Wash thoroughly before eating.*

LACTARIUS PIPERATUS (*Pepper Milk*)
Found in deciduous woods between August and November. Hotter than the hottest chillies! Excellent in pickles and curries. *Use with discretion.*

LACTARIUS VOLEMUS
Found in mixed woods between August and November.

Lepiota (GILL FUNGI)

LEPIOTA EXCORIATA
Found in pastures on light soil between August and November.

LEPIOTA LEUCOTHITES
Found in pastures and gardens between August and October.

LEPIOTA PROCERA (*Parasol Mushroom*)
Found in clearings, on the edge of woods and in grassy areas between July and November. An excellent fungus for eating. Pick off the stems and steam the caps in butter, or quickly fry in oil. Do not overcook.

LEPIOTA RHACODES (*Shaggy Parasol*)
Found in gardens, woods, parks, etc., between July and November.

Lycoperdon (PUFF-BALLS)

LYCOPERDON (CALVATIA) CAELATUM
Found on sandy pastures between July and November.

LYCOPERDON (CALVATIA) EXCIPULIFORME
Found in pastures, woods, and on heaths, between August and November.

LYCOPERDON (CALVATIA) GIGANTEUM (*Giant Puff-ball*)
Found in gardens, woods and fields between August and November. A superb edible fungus. Only pick those whose flesh is pure white. Can be sliced into 'steaks' and fried, or dipped in egg and bread crumbs and deep fried. Small puff-balls can be boiled whole in milk spiced with bay leaves and served with a white sauce.

LYCOPERDON PERLATUM (*Common Puff-ball*)
Found in coniferous and deciduous woods between July and December.

Marasmus

MARASMUS OREADES (*Fairy Ring Champignon*)
Found in grass, especially lawns, as the well-known fairy rings. An excellent fungus for eating.

Morchella (MORELS)

MORCHELLA CONICA
Found in copses on rich soil and conifer plantations.

MORCHELLA ESCULENTA (*Common Morel*)
Found under deciduous trees on rich soil and in hedgerows and grass banks. A delicacy but very rare these days. Use for flavouring soups and stews.

MORCHELLA (MITROPHORA) SEMI-LIBERA
Found in damp woods on rich soil.

MORCHELLA VULGARIS
Found in woods on rich soil and in gardens.

Pleurotus (GILL FUNGI)

PLEUROTUS OSTREATUS (*Oyster Mushroom*)
Found on deciduous trees, especially beech, between January and December. Excellent when picked young. Fry sliced like steaks.

Pluteus

PLUTEUS CERVINUS
Found on the stumps and trunks of deciduous trees between January and December.

Russulineae

RUSSULA AERUGINEA
Found between August and November.

RUSSULA AURATA
Found in beech woods between August and November.

RUSSULA CLAROFLAVA
Found between September and November.

RUSSULA CYANOXANTHA
Found in deciduous woods, especially oak, between July and November.

RUSSULA OLIVACEA
Found between August and November.

RUSSULA PALUDOSA
Found in sphagnum moss between August and November.

RUSSULA VESCA
Found in deciduous woods, especially oak, between August and November.

RUSSULA VIOLEIPES
Found in mixed woods between September and November.

RUSSULA VIRESCENS
Found in deciduous woods, especially beech, between August and November.

RUSSULA XERAMPELINA
Found in mixed woods between August and November.

Tremallales

AURICULARIA AURICULA (*Jew's Ear*)
Found on deciduous trees between October and

November. Use only the soft young fungi and stew in milk for about an hour.

Tricholoma

TRICHOLOMA ARGYRACEUM
Found mostly under deciduous trees, especially beech, between August and November.

TRICHOLOMA CINGULATUM
Found on damp ground under willows between August and November.

TRICHOLOMA COLUMETTA
Found in deciduous woods on acid soil, especially beech, between August and September.

TRICHOLOMA FLAVOVIRENS
Found in sandy pine woods between August and November.

TRICHOLOMA GAMBOSUM (*St. George's Mushroom*)
Found in pastures and grassy places between April and June.

TRICHOLOMA (LEPISTA) NUDUM (*Wood Blewits*)
Found in coniferous and deciduous woods, and in gardens, between September and December.

TRICHOLOMA PORTENTOSUM
Found under old pine trees between September and November.

TRICHOLOMA (LEPISTA) SAEVUM (*Blewits*)
Found, often in rings, in grass and pastures, or in deciduous woods or hedgebanks. A delicacy possessing the texture and aroma of tripe. They are best cooked in milk, the caps stuffed with chopped onions and sage.

Tuberales (TRUFFLES)

HYDNOTRIA TULASNEI
Found in light soil or under leaves in deciduous woods in late summer.

TUBER AESTIVUM
Found in calcareous soil, especially under beech, between August and October. Not the truffle of commerce but nearly as good. Truffles are very hard to locate but if you have any luck you should eat them raw on bread and butter, or preserved in vinegar. They are mostly used, however, to impart a delicate flavour to dishes.

Volvariella

VOLVARIELLA SPECIOSA
Found on compost and manure heaps or rich soils between July and October.

SEAWEEDS

Seaweeds are still a mystery food to many people, mainly, I suppose, because of their relationship with the sea. In fact they are packed with goodness, especially trace minerals, and once the unusual tastes have become familiar, they can become a major part of the daily diet.

With any seaweed it is important to thoroughly wash it in fresh water. Don't pull seaweeds off their rock or sandy strongholds; always cut with a knife as this will allow new growth to form.

ALARIA ESCULENTA
Found mostly on exposed shorelines. Use the leaves mixed with dulse to make a composite jelly.

BLADDER WRACK (*Fucus vesiculosus*)
Found mostly on the middle of the shore. Cook as for spinach.

DULSE (*Rhodymenia palmata*)
A purplish-red alga found widespread and abundant on stones on the lower and middle shores. Eat it raw in salads or chewed, dipped in vinegar. Can be fried or boiled (for at least five hours because of its toughness).

Dulse Crisps

Drop some dulse leaves into a frying pan of hot oil and remove almost immediately. Drain on a paper towel before serving.

ENTEROMORPHA INTESTINALIS
Found widespread and abundant in dikes, rockpools and salt marshes. Harvest in early spring. Cook as for spinach.

GIGARTINA STELLATA
Found widespread and sometimes abundant on the lower and middle shores, more on the west coast. Cook as for spinach.

ICELAND MOSS (*Cetraria islandica*)
A reddish-brown lichen commonly found amongst heather in the moorlands of the north east and Scotland. Though not a seaweed this food plant is definitely worth investigating.

Iceland Moss Jelly

Wash a handful of moss in cold water and then simmer in a quart of boiling water until it dissolves completely. Add the juice of two

lemons and a dash of cinnamon. Strain and bottle.

IRISH MOSS (*Chondrus crispus*)
Found widespread on rocks and stones, especially on western shores. Use to thicken soups and stews.

Irish Moss Blancmange

Wash the moss in cold water. Simmer 1 cup of moss (with sugar and flavouring to taste) in three cups of milk until the moss has completely dissolved. Strain into a mould and turn out when set.

Irish Moss Custard

Dissolve by simmering – 1 cup of washed moss in 2 cups of milk. While hot beat in 1 egg yolk already beaten into $\frac{1}{2}$ cup cold milk. Heat again then remove from heat and fold in the white of 1 egg. Sweeten to taste.

KELP (*Laminaria digitata*)
Found widespread on rocky shores at the low-water level. Use the leaves raw in salads.

LAMINARIA SACCHARINA

Usually found on mud and sand flats adhering to small stones. Use the leaves cooked as for spinach, or combined with dulse to form a composite jelly.

LAVER (*Porphyra umbilicalis*)

Widespread and common all round the coast-line, growing on rocks and stones. Cook with lemon juice as for spinach.

Laverbread

Cook as for spinach which reduces the laver to a purée. Mix this with oatflakes, measure for measure, until the consistency of a bread dough is achieved. Shape into little rissoles and fry in a little oil.

Laver Sauce

Blend together 2 cups of laver purée, the juice of 1 Seville orange and 1 oz butter.

MONOSTROMA GREVILLEI

Found attached to stones on various shorelines, especially where water runs into the sea. Cook as for spinach.

PEPPER DULSE (*Laurencia pinnatifida*)

Uncommon and found in rock crevices on the middle shore. Use the cooked weed as a condiment because of its very strong taste.

ROCK TRIPE (*Umblicaria pustulata*)

A lichen found in the west where it grows on rocks and walls. Cook as for spinach.

SEA LETTUCE (*Ulva lactuca*)

Found widespread and common attached to rocks and stones on various sea shores. Cook as for spinach.

SLOKE (*Porphyra palmata*) Sea Spinach

Similar to laver and found mostly on western shores. Cook as for spinach.

Sloke Cakes

Cook into a purée and add butter, cream, pepper and salt to taste. Add oatflakes, measure for measure, and fry in a little oil.

SUMMER SECTION

CYCLORAM

The open road, the dusty highway, the rolling downs! Villages, towns, cities! Here today, up and off somewhere else tomorrow!
Travel, change, interest, excitement! The whole world before you, and a horizon that's always changing.

FROM 'WIND IN THE WILLOWS' BY KENNETH GRAHAME

THE humble bike must surely rate as one of man's greatest inventions. There is so much to say in its favour that not having one seems almost silly. Just look at the facts.

Cost

From the user's point of view, the bicycle is the most economical form of transport available. It is cheap to buy, requires a minimum of maintenance and has no running costs, increasingly important where motoring costs are escalating year after year. Just eliminating commuting by car within a ten-mile radius of work will save over £150 per year – enough to buy two beautiful new bikes!

From a planner's point of view the bicycle has many advantages. Fewer new roads – more cycleways (which, incidentally, cost about one quarter as much). Traffic flow improves and accidents decrease.

Time

It is a proven fact that the bike is the most efficient form of urban travel. The average speed of motor traffic in towns is 10 m.p.h. – less in the rush hour, and it can stop altogether. A bicycle can weave in and out of traffic and get to the front line time after time. No buses to catch, no cars to start, no traffic jams to get stuck in; the cyclist just goes – always taking the same time. On short commuting journeys (the national average is only $4\frac{1}{2}$ miles) the time getting the car onto the road and hunting for a parking space before walking to work can take as long as the journey itself. The cyclist is already there!

Convenience

The bicycle is the most personal form of transport that exists – with the exception of feet, of course! It literally means door-to-door travel. For the shopper the bike means door-to-door transport. No carrying heavy shopping back to the car park – just on to the bike and away. The bike not only carries the shopping but the shopper as well!

Health

Sitting in a car on commuting journeys which are loaded with stress does absolutely nothing for anyone except advance the deterioration of their heart. On the other hand, cycling is an excellent form of exercise, both stimulating and beneficial. And you can expect to live up to five years longer!

Parking

In a country the size of the United Kingdom supporting nearly sixty million people, we do not have space to spare. The cost of land escalates each year and yet great areas in the heart of our towns, where land is at a premium, are given over to car parks. Visit one at 11 a.m.

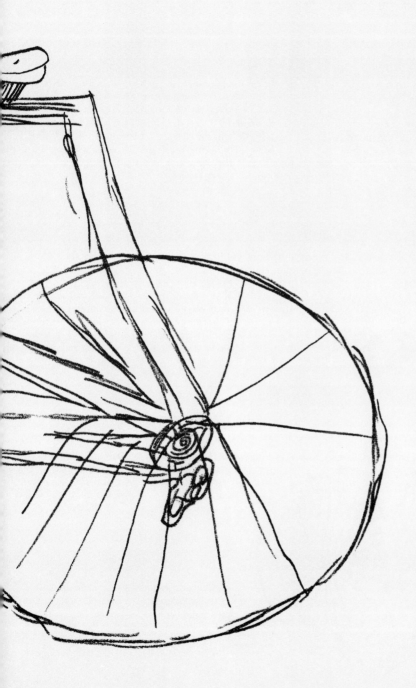

and you're lucky to get in. Visit one at 11 p.m. and you see a bare tarmac desert. One factory manager estimated that every car space in his car park would earn him £500 per annum if used for production.

Sixteen bicycles can be parked in one car space. That is a saving of ninety per cent. Also one car parked in a normal two-direction road effectively halves the width of the road along its whole length. But take it away and you can more than double the road's carrying capacity.

Environmental
The aspects of the environment which concern us in the context of transport are atmospheric pollution, noise, and the depletion of resources. These are caused by the need for mobility.

Investigations into the effect of carbon monoxide and lead concentrations in busy city streets have already shown that they can reach dangerous levels in certain atmospheric conditions. The answer is not just to legislate to reduce exhaust pollution but to encourage an alternative method of transport so that not only is pollution being reduced on one front but it is also being eliminated on another.

The noise in our towns and cities has already grown to scarcely-tolerable levels and is not likely to decrease markedly so long as internal combustion vehicles are with us.

The mineral resources of the world are finite. They will be consumed eventually, so means of conserving them must be found now. The energy and materials used in the manufacture of a bicycle are a small proportion of the amount needed for the manufacture of a car. Furthermore, the bicycle does not consume oil products.

Efficiency
One cyclist can do 1,000 miles on the food energy equivalent of a gallon of petrol which will move a car only some 25 or 35 miles! There surely cannot be a more convincing statistic than that!

Choosing a Bike
The choice will naturally be between a new and a secondhand machine, or, if you live in a city or large town, hiring a bike. Ideally it is better to buy a new bicycle. Not only are there many

79

superb models on the market but unlike cars which fall to bits within a few years, bikes will last a couple of decades or more given proper maintenance.

When buying a new bicycle always go to a reputable dealer or a proper cycle shop. They will stock the best models and give expert advice. Avoid discount and departmental stores wherever possible.

Secondhand Bicycles

These days there are many sources of secondhand bikes. Because of demand, some of them may be offered at grossly inflated prices and you should be on guard for this. Here are a few suggestions.

NEIGHBOURS' SHEDS

Before sorting out the other possibilities, make a preliminary enquiry round friends and neighbours. More often than not they'll have an old bike cooped up in a garage or shed. It may need some attention but this should be no problem.

NOTICE BOARDS AND LOCAL PAPERS

A fine source of secondhand machines which will usually be in good working order. If anything, those advertised in the local rag are just that bit more expensive. Alternatively, place an ad. yourself for a bike. You could be inundated with offers!

MARKETS

In London, Petticoat Lane, East Street and Portobello Road markets always have a few bikes for sale in varying states of repair. Check out your local market if it sells junk, or ask the traders to look out for you.

AUCTIONS

Local auctions according to some friends of mine at Brighton, are *the* place. Really beautiful veteran machines sometimes go for a song, though they might be just one item in a lot which means you may end up with a three-piece suite and a washing machine as well!

G.P.O.

The various Head Post Offices sometimes sell their old red bikes. They don't come sturdier.

BRITISH RAILWAYS LOST PROPERTY OFFICES

It's surprising just how many bicycles get lost each year. Contact the various offices to find out details of their forthcoming auctions.

THE EXCHANGE & MART MAGAZINE

Look under the section for bicycles for hundreds of them. They also carry ads. for secondhand bicycle shops.

BUTCHERS AND GROCERY SHOPS

Some shops still use the old trade or 'heavy roadster' bikes with the big front basket carrier for deliveries. Ask around – they may have an old crate in the back, or they're closing down, or even 'modernizing' to van delivery.

SWOP SHOPS AND JUNK SHOPS

With the demand for secondhand bikes being what it is, the number of shops now dealing in bikes has escalated. Swop shops, junk shops and the various secondhand specialists are worth checking out.

HOLIDAY CAMPS

If you live near one then it may be worth asking. If the camp is worth its salt it will have a bicycle hire service for campers. The way the bikes get handled probably means so many new machines a year. Ask what they do with their oldies.

Hiring Bicycles

If you don't want to be bothered with a bike of your own then hiring one could be the answer. The rates are normally quite reasonable but usually the service is limited to big towns and cities. (See end of book for names and addresses.)

TYPES OF BICYCLES

Excluding children's bikes, there are six categories of bicycles, though they all overlap to a certain extent. The type of machine chosen should be governed not only by the price tag but also the intended use for the bike and the particular physical and environmental circumstances of the area. The six categories are as follows:

Racers

At the top of the league come racing bikes. Their characteristics are: ultra-light frames, dropped handlebars, 10 or 15 speed close-ratio derailleur gears, tubular tyres, and cable brakes. Weight 20–30 lbs (9–13·5 kg). Suitable for racing and long-distance touring. Recommended for anyone living in hilly districts or for those

requiring a lightweight machine because of stairs, etc.

Semi-Racers
Otherwise called Club Sports. Their characteristics are: lightweight frames, dropped handlebars, 5 to 15 speed derailleur gears, 27 × 1¼ inch (685 × 30 mm) high pressure tyres, cable brakes. Weight – 25–35 lbs (10·8–15·4 kg). Suitable for all-purpose touring and general use.

Sports Roadsters
Otherwise called English Racers or Tourist Models. Their characteristics are: medium to lightweight frames, flat handlebars, 1, 3, or 5 speed hub gearing, 26 × 1⅜ inch (660 × 33 mm) tyres, cable calliper brakes. Weight – 30–35 lbs (13·6–15·9 kg). Suitable for general use. Ideal for shopping, errands and other short runs. Sturdy and endurable with a minimum of maintenance.

Heavy Roadsters
The cart-horse of the bicycle world! Their characteristics are: heavy steel frames, flat handlebars, 1 or 3 speed hub gears, 26 × 1½ inch (660 × 38 mm) tyres, toll lever brakes, encased chain set. Weight – 50 lbs (22 kg) approx. Suitable for carting heavy loads and for rough and difficult terrain.

Mini-Bicycles
Otherwise known as small-wheeled bicycles. These machines are enormously popular and constitute the trendy end of the bike market. Their characteristics are: heavy, short frames, flat or shaped adjustable handlebars, 1 or 3 speed hub gears, 16 or 20 inch (406 or 508 mm) wheels, cable calliper brakes. Folding bikes also fall into this category. Suitable for short runs and for carrying (on some models) extra loads. Excellent manoeuvrability but poor braking and speed control. Totally unsuitable for touring – I know, I've tried!

Eccentric Bicycles
In this category come tandems, tricycles, unicycles and social cycles.

Tandems are rarely come-by secondhand and cost a lot of money new. The best types are the lightweight models (40–50 lbs (18–22 kg)), with 10-speed derailleur gears.

Adult tricycles are ideal for elderly people whose balance may not be what it was, or whose bones are in no condition to take the breaks from a fall. Tricycles require cautious handling at bends, especially those with 26 or 27 inch (660 or 685 mm) wheels.

Social cycles are those ridiculous (I love them) four-wheeled jobs that holiday campers fly around on. They seat four people and are basically two bicycles geared together with bench seats slung across both. A rarity to buy but a form of bike transport that could be exploited more, especially in the city.

Unicycles are something else. Like learning to walk all over again! A novel but impractical form of travel.

Choosing the Right Size Bike
The determining factor is the frame size. Ideally you must be able to straddle the frame easily with both feet firmly on the ground. Here are two methods of calculating the correct frame size:
(1) Divide your height by 3 (e.g. someone 5 feet 9 inches tall will require a 23-inch framed bike).
(2) Measure your inside leg from the crotch to the ground, minus 9 inches (e.g. someone with a 30-inch inside leg will require a 21-inch framed bike).

Cycling For Pleasure
Apart from the normal day-to-day errands, commuting and other short runs, the bicycle is a marvellous means of exploring the country. Cycle touring is becoming increasingly popular and it is not difficult to see why. Cheapness, though not the most engaging factor, is none-the-less attractive in these days of astronomical road and rail fares. There is the intimacy with one's surroundings and the total independence of the rider. And though speed and distance are not always the objective of touring, the cyclist can achieve a hundred miles a day or more.

CYCLE CAMPING

Cycle touring can be done in one of three ways.

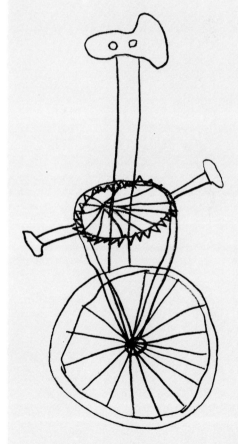

You can travel light and shack up over night in a pub, hotel, youth hostel, etc. You can journey out daily from a base (e.g. a camp site or hostel). Or you can carry full camping equipment and travel around wherever you wish. Most people prefer the latter which certainly has the bigger appeal in terms of adventure and flexibility.

Equipment

Any good touring bike will carry up to 30 lbs (22 kg) extra weight with no trouble, but it is advisable to travel as light as possible. Where camping is concerned this means carrying the lightest tent, sleeping bag, cooking utensils and spare clothing. You can improvise a tent from just a ground sheet and a guyrope slung between two trees, or from a poncho, etc. but the serious camper should get a real tent. Nowadays there is a fantastic range of ultra-lightweight camping equipment, and camping centres – and in particular the Youth Hostel Association camping centre (see end of book) – are the places to go. Whatever you do, buy the best you can afford, especially the sleeping bag. Freezing to death at night after a hard day's touring is not much fun.

A good tool kit is a must. It should contain the following:

PUMP
SCREWDRIVER SET
TYRE REPAIR KIT
TYRE LEVERS
SPOKE WRENCH
ADJUSTABLE WRENCH
SPARE BRAKE CABLES
SPARE BRAKE PADS
SPARE GEAR CABLES
SPARE CHAIN LINKS
OIL AND RAG

Maps are essential too (see below). Clothing is more difficult, but should be basically lightweight and should provide adequate protection against the rain and wind. Acrylic jerseys, shorts or lightweight trousers, a waterproof rain top jacket and leggings for nasty weather, fingerless mittens, a woollen bobble-hat and a pair of bike shoes are the necessary items for most touring trips. Avoid cycle capes as they are not only inadequate protection but can be dangerous as well.

Loading

A surprising amount of gear in terms of bulk can be carried on a bike. At the back of the bike, side and back panniers will carry the bulk of the camping gear. Panniers can be bought separately or, as with my own bicycle, in one unit. A light handlebar pannier can be used to carry items such as rain protective clothing, maps, took kit, etc. Avoid front-wheel panniers as these will make steering dangerously awkward. Aim to spread the load evenly over the bike.

Travelling

Unless the plan is to tour in the local or surrounding counties, it is sometimes a good idea to put the bike on the train to a central jumping off point and start the tour from there; especially as bicycles can now be carried free of charge on British Rail. Cycling from the West Country to Scotland, for instance, could severely fatigue the inexperienced cyclist, and there is the obvious time factor as well. Whichever way is chosen, the aim should not be speed and mile burning. This is especially important at the start of the tour. Going flat out at this stage will take its toll in aching and stiff muscles. Take it easy; enjoy the countryside, and enjoy yourself.

Cycle Touring Routes

The cycle routes suggested below are just some which the cyclist can try, but check all routes in each case. They have one thing in common which will appeal to cyclists everywhere – a lack of cars!

DISUSED RAILWAY LINES
There are hundreds of miles of abandoned railway lines all over the country. Some of them, such as those in Scotland, run through breathtaking scenery. At present only a handful are open to cyclists but there are positive moves being taken by some councils to remedy this.

BRIDLEWAYS
Any cyclist is legally entitled to use the network of bridleways that traverse the countryside – thousands of them! For this sort of cycling, your bike should be equipped with cross-country tyres. Beware of, and give way to, horses and ramblers; and keep on the path.

TOWPATHS
The use of towpaths and other waterside tracks is restricted for cyclists but this seems to be changing. Once again, pedestrians have the right of way.

FORESTRY COMMISSION LAND
The Commission discourages riding on its land but there are sections open to cyclists. Contact the Commission for details, and at the same time complain about the relatively few facilities for cyclists.

B-ROADS
Many of Britain's country B-roads are seventh heaven where cycling is concerned. By arming yourself with an Ordnance Survey map or the Bartholomew Half-inch Series maps and planning your route you can often travel all day without hitting the main roads at all. Please beware of motorists on these roads. Bends in the road and humpbacked bridges are especially precarious as some motorists drive like lunatics along the lanes.

COUNTRY TRAILS
Certain country trails, such as the Ridge Way which runs across the top of the Berkshire Downs, and the South Downs Way, are open to cyclists. They offer sweeping views of the countryside and the sea – often spectacular, always interesting. Details available from the British Cycling Bureau or Ramblers Association (see under Societies at end of book).

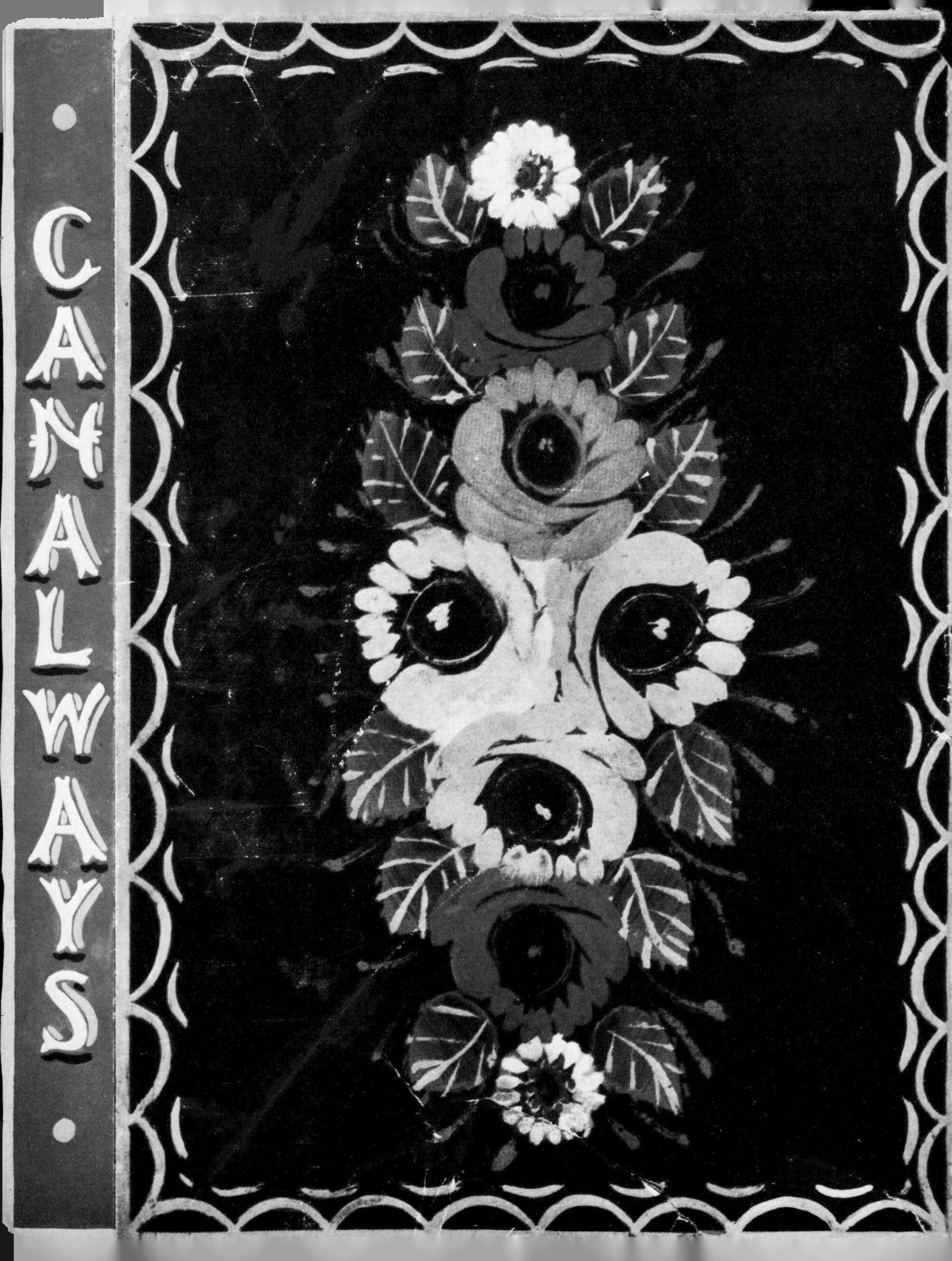
CANALWAYS

My room's a square and candle-lighted boat
In the surrounding depths of night afloat
My windows are the portholes, and the seas
The sound of the rain in the dark apple trees.
ANON

THE British Isles possess one of the finest canal systems in the world, and yet much of the original network lies redundant, or unnavigable, or even filled in and lost for good. Happily, restoration work – much of it voluntary – is reversing the trend and, apart from the expanding canal pleasure cruising industry, there is renewed interest being shown in the commercial viability of canal transport for industry.

Our canal heritage has provided us with not only waterways through some of our loveliest countryside, but a feast of engineering works, architecture, traditional folk art and customs that can still be seen today. What follows will provide a condensed yet comprehensive guide to this marvellous heritage.

CANALS IN USE TODAY

Ashby Canal
A contour canal extending from the Coventry Canal at Marston Junction, Nuneaton, to Snarestone. Known locally as the 'Moira Cut' it was once the origination of the Measham Canal teapots which are now collectors' items. *Navigable length:* 22 miles. *Original length:* 30 miles. *Maximum boat sizes:* Length 72 ft; Draught 3 ft; Beam 7 ft; Headroom 6 ft 6 ins. *Authority:* British Waterways Board (B.W.B.).

Ashton and Lower Peak Forest Canals
Two canals which form the north segment of the 'Cheshire Ring', a circumnavigable waterway network consisting of the Trent and Mersey, Macclesfield, Peak Forest, Ashton, and Bridgewater canals. Both have recently been made navigable, thus making it possible to navigate from the Derbyshire Hills all the way down into Manchester. The Ashton Canal extends from Ashton-Under-Lyme to Manchester, with 18 deep locks. The Peak Forest Canal descends from Whaley Bridge to Marple, and on to Hyde and Ashton through a series of 16 locks and over a masonry bridge crossing the River Goyte. *Authority:* B.W.B.

Basingstoke Canal
Extends from Greywell tunnel, Basingstoke, to the River Wey at West Byfleet. At present only light boats are allowed and all power craft are prohibited. Work is in progress to restore all the locks.

Birmingham and Fazeley Canal
Extends 20 miles from Farmers Bridge, Birmingham, through a series of 27 locks to Fazeley Junction where it joins the Coventry Canal. Most of the canal passes through industrial or suburban landscape, and a tunnel (57 yards) at Cudworth. *Authority:* B.W.B.

Birmingham Canal Navigation
A network of canals lying between Walsall, Stourbridge, Wolverhampton and Birmingham, and a major commercial system serving industry in bygone days. The network comprises – Soho Loop, Icknield Port Road Loop, Oozells Street Loop, Hockley Basin, Dudley Canal, Haughton Arm, Haines Branch, Wednesbury Oak Loop Line, Bentley Canal, Anson Branch, Toll End Branch, Dudley Canal No. 2 Line (with Gosly Hill tunnel), and Ridgeacre Branch. There are also three aqueducts – Telford Aqueduct, Steward Aqueduct, and Tividale Aqueduct. For detailed guide see *Nicholson's Guide to the Waterways No. 5 – Midlands.*

Brecon and Abergavenny Canal
An isolated canal of great beauty which passes through the Brecon Beacons National Park. Extends for 33 miles through 6 locks, from Brecon to Pontypool where it joins the now abandoned Monmouthshire Canal. There is one tunnel (375 yards) – the Ashford Tunnel. *Maximum boat sizes:* Length 34 ft; Draught 2 ft 6 ins; Beam 9 ft 2 ins; Headroom 5 ft 10 ins. *Authority:* B.W.B.

Bridgewater Canal
Part of the Cheshire Ring that links the Liverpool and Leeds Canal at Preston Brook, and passes through industrial areas in the north stretch, and rural countryside in the south. The canal has no locks but passes over the Manchester Ship Canal via the Barton Swing Aqueduct. *Maximum boat sizes:* Length 70 ft; Draught 4 ft; Beam 14 ft 9 ins; Headroom 8 ft 6 ins. (At Preston Brook – maximum beam is 7 ft and draught 3 ft 6 ins.) *Authority:* Bridgewater Canal c/o Manchester Ship Canal.

Bridgwater and Taunton Canal

A 14-mile waterway linking Bridgwater and Taunton in Devon, but now cut off from the sea since the closure of the dock at Bridgwater. There are 6 locks, none in working order. *Authority:* B.W.B.

Caldon Canal

Extending from the Trent and Mersey Canal at Etruria, Stoke-on-Trent, this beautiful canal is at present navigable for 17½ miles to Froghall and is still used commercially on its lower section. There is a disused branch line from Froghall, 13¼ miles to Uttoxeter.

Caledonian Canal

This waterway which extends through Scotland's Great Glen is noted for its fabulous scenery. Only 22 miles of its total length of 60 miles is actual canal, the rest being the waters of Loch Dochfour, Loch Ness, Loch Oich, and Loch Lochy. The canal, which passes as a navigational short cut from Corpach, Fort William, to the far eastern Clachnaharry, Inverness, has a sea loch at each end and 29 locks all told along its waters, including the superb Banavie flight of 8 locks covering a change in level of 64 feet. There are also swing bridges of note including 2 railway swing bridges. *Maximum boat sizes:* Length 150 ft; Draught 13 ft 6 ins; Beam 35 ft. *Authority:* B.W.B.

Chesterfield Canal

This once-derelict canal has recently been restored for 26 miles of its length and is approachable from the Trent Waterway near Trent Falls at Stockwith, passing through cheerful scenery to Worksop and Retford. The canal contains 16 locks. The Norwood Tunnel, which collapsed at the beginning of the century, prevents access to the full length of the canal. *Authority:* B.W.B.

Coventry Canal

Extending from the Trent and Mersey Canal at Fradley Junction, to the Coventry Basin, this waterway passes through the lovely Tame Valley, as well as the urban and industrial areas in the north, and makes a useful link between canal systems in the north and south. *Maximum boat sizes:* Length 72 ft; Draught 3 ft; Beam 7 ft; Headroom 6 ft 6 ins. *Authority:* B.W.B.

Crinan Canal

Built by the famous Thomas Telford between 1793 and 1801, this small canal with its 15 locks enables fishing vessels, yachts, etc. to avoid the time-consuming journey around the Mull of Kintyre en route to the Western Isles. *Maximum boat sizes:* Length 88 ft; Draught 9 ft 6 ins; Beam 20 ft. *Authority:* B.W.B.

Erewash Canal

Due to much needed voluntary restoration the Erewash Canal is now navigable for 11¾ miles from the Trent Waterway, up to Langley Mill. With its 15 wide-beam locks, it was once part of the Grand Union Canal system and today is used mainly by pleasure-craft. *Authority:* B.W.B.

Exeter Ship Canal

This 5-mile long canal links the Exe estuary at Turf with the City of Exeter and is Britain's oldest ship canal. A maritime museum at the canal's terminal basin displays historical craft from all over the world. There are 2 locks. *Authority:* City of Exeter.

Fossdyke Canal

Together with the Witham Navigation, these two waterways which meet at Lincoln, form a passage between the Wash at Boston and the Trent Waterway at Torksey. There are no locks along the Roman-built Fossdyke except for the Torksey Lock on the River Trent which is the gateway to the canal. *Authority:* B.W.B.

Gloucester and Sharpness Ship Canal

Part of the Severn Waterway which is a 58-mile waterway extending from the main canal system at Stourport and Worcester to the Bristol Channel. The Gloucester and Sharpness section is between Gloucester Dock and Saul Junction and has no locks, though a number of swing bridges are in operation. Prospective canal cruisers should contact the B.W.B. for details concerning lock opening times before attempting to explore this canal. *Authority:* B.W.B.

Grand Union Canal

This famous canal system, now designated a Cruising Waterway, comprises four sections, beginning at Brentford, London, and reaching up to Birmingham and Leicester.

(1) LONDON TO BERKHAMSTED SECTION
The canal can be entered either at Brentford Creek from the tidal Thames, or from the Regent's Canal via Paddington Arm. In its climb to the Chiltern hills, this 35-mile long section passes through 55 locks and traverses both London suburbs and rural countryside.

(2) BERKHAMSTED TO BRAUNSTON SECTION
Fifty-four miles long and the most picturesque section of the Grand Union. There are 39 locks, an iron aqueduct over the River Ouse, and two lengthy tunnels – Braunston Tunnel (2,042 yards), and Blisworth Tunnel (3,056 yards). Three canal tributaries, or arms, branch off along the way – the Welford Arm from Marsworth, the Aylesbury Arm from Marsworth (with 16 locks to Aylesbury), and the Northampton Arm from Gayton Junction (with 17 locks to Northampton).

(3) BRAUNSTON TO BIRMINGHAM SECTION
On this section there are 57 locks between Braunston Top Lock and Camphill, including a remarkable flight of locks at Hatton. There is a tunnel at Shrewley (433 yards). The Oxford Canal joins this section and is incorporated in part of the main waterway of the Grand Union, between Braunston and Napton Junctions. The Stratford-upon-Avon Canal joins the Grand Union at the Kingswood Junction.

(4) LEICESTER JUNCTION
From Norton Junction to the River Soar at Leicester, there are 44 locks along this 43-mile long section, passing through picturesque countryside. There are 3 tunnels – Chirk Tunnel (1,528 yards), Husbands Bosworth (1,166 yards), and Saddington (880 yards). There are two arms – the Market Harborough Arm from Foxton, and the Welford Arm from North Kilworth. *Maximum boat sizes:* From Norton Junction to Foxton Junction – Length 72 ft; Draught 2 ft 6 ins; Beam 7 ft; Headroom 7 ft 6 ins. From Market Harborough to Leicester – Length 72 ft; Draught 2 ft 6 ins; Beam 10 ft; Headroom 7 ft. *Authority:* B.W.B.

Grand Western Canal

Once linking up with the Bridgwater and Taunton Canal, this 10¾-mile long waterway connects Loudwelis with Tiverton and since its takeover by Devon County Council, has become part of a Country Park. Restoration is being carried out and at present, no motorised craft are allowed on the canal.

Huddersfield Broad Canal

Part of the Aire and Calder Navigation. Access is from the Wakefield Branch, and the 3-mile Broad Canal runs from Cooper Bridge through 9 broad locks to Huddersfield. *Maximum boat sizes:* Length 120 ft; Draught 7 ft; Beam 17 ft; Headroom 11 ft. *Authority:* B.W.B.

The Kennet and Avon Canal

Extends from Newbury, where it takes over from the River Kennet Navigation (Reading to Newbury), to Bristol, where it joins the River Avon Navigation (Bristol to Bath). The total waterway system forms a link between London and the Thames, and the Bristol Channel, but only sections are navigable at present: 10 miles of the Kennet Navigation from Reading to Towney Lock (8 locks), and 12 miles of the Kennet and Avon canal from Bulls Lock to beyond Hungerford (10 locks). Restoration is being carried out by the Kennet and Avon Canal Trust. *Maximum boat sizes:* River Kennet and Newbury sections – Length 72 ft; Draught 3 ft 6 ins; Beam 13 ft 10 ins; Headroom 8 ft 6 ins. River Avon section – length 75 ft; Draught 3 ft 6 ins; Beam 16 ft; Headroom 9 ft. *Authority:* B.W.B.

Lancaster Canal

Once extending 57 miles from Preston to Kendal in the Lake District, this canal is now only navigable for the 4 miles from Preston to Tewitfield Locks. It still remains one of England's most beautiful (and lock-less) canals, passing over a remarkable John Rennie masonry aqueduct which crosses the River Lune, giving panoramic views of Morecambe Bay. A branch, extending to Glaston Dock from Lodge Hill Junction, has 6 locks. *Maximum boat sizes:* Length 72 ft; Draught 3 ft; Beam 14 ft 6 ins; Headroom 8 ft. *Authority:* B.W.B.

Leeds and Liverpool Canal

The 127-mile long Leeds and Liverpool Canal is the sole surviving trans-Pennine water link, connecting Liverpool and the Mersey Estuary (and thus the Irish Sea), with Leeds and the Aire and Calder Navigation (and thus the North Sea). There are 91 locks all told, including 5 sets of stairway locks and a number of swing bridges. There are 2 tunnels – Gannow Tunnel (559 yards), and Foulridge (1,640 yards). The canal winds its way through remote moorlands and Dale country and gives spectacular views of the Pennines, and also passes over the famous Burnley Embankment which cuts through Burnley, way above the roof tops. *Maximum boat sizes:* Length 72 ft (Liverpool to Wigan), and 62 ft (Wigan to Leeds); Draught 3 ft 9 ins; Beam 14 ft; Headroom 8 ft.

Llangollen Canal

This waterway is the Welsh arm of the Shropshire Union Canal consisting of the Pontcysyllte Branch, from Llantysilio near Llangollen, to Frankton Junction, and the old Ellesmere Canal from Frankton Junction to Hurleston. There are 21 locks serving the canals' 46 miles, including a staircase flight at Grindley. There are two aqueducts, both by Telford – the Chirk Aqueduct over the River Ceiriog, and the famous Pontcysyllte Aqueduct over the Dee. The latter consists of nineteen elegant stone pillars and is considered Telford's finest work. There are three tunnels – Chirk Tunnel (459 yards), Whitehouse Tunnel (191 yards), and Ellesmere Tunnel (87 yards) – as well as numerous drawbridges. Arguably Britain's most beautiful canal. *Maximum boat sizes:* Length 70 ft; Draught 2 ft 6 ins; Beam 6 ft 10 ins; Headroom 9 ft. *Authority:* B.W.B.

Macclesfield Canal

Part of the Cheshire Ring linking the Peak Forest Canal at Marple with the Trent and Mersey Canal at Kidsgrove. The canal is 27 miles long, with 12 grouped locks at Bosley, and passes over a number of embankments and aqueducts. *Maximum boat sizes:* Length 70 ft; Draught 2 ft 9 ins; Beam 7 ft; Headroom 6 ft. *Authority:* B.W.B.

Manchester Ship Canal

This is the largest inland waterway in Great Britain and extends from Manchester to Eastham Locks on the south bank of the Mersey. It also connects with the Weaver Navigation (at Weston Marsh Lock), the Shropshire Union Canal (at Ellesmere Port), and the Bridgewater Canal (at Manchester). Permission is needed from the Harbour Master at Dock Office, Trafford Road, Manchester, before entering the waterway. *Authority:* The Manchester Ship Canal Company.

Montgomery Canal

Closed in 1944, but currently being restored by the Shropshire Union Canal Society in conjunction with the Inland Waterways Association. Already the lock at Welshpool has been officially opened and 6 miles of the canal is due for service in the near future. At present there is a passenger service on the section through Welshpool.

New Junction Canal

Britain's newest waterway, connecting Yorkshire's Aire and Calder Navigation with the Sheffield and South Yorkshire Navigation at Bramwith Junction.

Oxford Canal

From the Coventry Canal at Hawkesbury Junction to the Thames at Oxford, the canal extends for 77½ miles and passes through some very pleasing countryside. There are 43 narrow-beamed locks and one tunnel at Newbold (250 yards). Of particular interest are the wooden drawbridges on the canal's southern section. For 5 miles, between Braunston and Napton Junction, the canal forms part of the Grand Union Canal. The canal is entered at the Oxford end from the River Thames above Osney Lock, or via Dukes Cut branch above Kings Lock. *Maximum boat sizes:* Length 70 ft; Draught 3 ft 6 ins; Beam 7 ft; Headroom 7 ft. *Authority:* B.W.B.

Pocklington Canal

A short Yorkshire canal 9½ miles long extending from the River Derwent at East Cottingwith, to the foot of the Yorkshire Wolds near Pocklington. Much of the canal is unnavigable but restoration work is gradually opening up the waterway again. There are 9 locks, 4 road bridges, and 8 swing bridges.

Regent's Canal and Hertford Union Canal

Together with the River Lee, Paddington Arm, and lower section of the Grand Union Canal, the Regent and Hertford Union canals form part of an extensive network of waterways north of the Thames. Of them all, the Regent's Canal is the most interesting, containing 13 locks between the Grand Union and Regent's Canal Dock, Limehouse. The canal passes by London Zoo after leaving Little Venice, and then cuts a path through a netherworld of old buildings, derelict land and industrial landscape before reaching the Thames. There is a tunnel at Maida Vale and another at Islington. *Maximum boat sizes:* Length 72 ft; Draught 3 ft 6 ins; Beam 14 ft 6 ins; Headroom 9 ft. *Authority:* B.W.B.

Ripon Canal

The River Ouse in Yorkshire extends up from York at Swale Nab, near Boroughbridge where it changes its name to the River Ure. At the top of the Ure on the left bank, the entrance cut to the Ripon Canal leads to Oxclose Lock and the start of the canal proper. The canal originally extended all the way to Ripon town but is no longer navigable beyond the 1¼ miles of waterway from Oxclose Lock. *Maximum boat sizes:* River Ure Navigation (Swale Nab to Oxclose Lock) – Length 57 ft; Draught 4 ft; Beam 14 ft 6 ins; Headroom 8 ft 6 ins; Ripon Canal – Length 57 ft; Draught 4 ft; Beam 14 ft 6 ins; Headroom 11 ft. *Authority:* B.W.B.

Rochdale Canal

The Rochdale once ran from Manchester and over the Pennines to the Calder and Hebble Navigation at Sowerby Bridge. Today, only that part of the canal on the Cheshire Ring between the Bridgewater and Ashton Canals remains navigable. There are nine wide-beam locks on this section. *Authority:* Rochdale Canal Company, 75 Dale Street, Manchester M1 2HG.

Selby Canal

A short stretch of waterway connecting the Ouse Navigation at Selby with the Aire and

Calder Navigation at Knottingley, enabling canal craft to reach York without embarking on the tidal reaches of the River Ouse. *Authority:* B.W.B.

Shropshire Union Canal

This waterway was constructed in four sections and incorporates the old style contour canal with Thomas Telford's direct route style including aqueducts, cuttings and embankments. It extends from the Staffordshire and Worcestershire Canal at Autherley Junction, near Wolverhampton, for 66 miles to Ellesmere Port on the River Mersey. There are junctions at Aldersley (for Birmingham Mainline Canal), Chester (for River Dee), Barbridge (for the Wardle Branch to the Trent and Mersey Canal), and Hurleston (for the Llangollen Canal). There are 46 locks, with a 15-lock flight at Audlem. There is a tunnel at Cowley (81 yards). *Maximum boat sizes:* Length 70 ft; Draught 3 ft; Beam 7 ft; Headroom 8 ft. *Authority:* B.W.B.

Staffordshire and Worcestershire Canal

One of our oldest canals and passing through some exceptionally fine countryside. From the River Severn at Stourport, the canal winds its way northwards via Kidderminster to Penkridge and the Trent and Mersey Canal. There are 43 locks including 'The Bratch', a noted steep-rising flight. There are junctions at Stourton (for the Stourbridge Canal), Aldersley (for the Birmingham Canal), and at Autherley (for the Shropshire Union Canal). There is a tunnel at Cookely (65 yards). *Maximum boat sizes:* Length 70 ft; Draught 2 ft 6 ins; Beam 7 ft; Headroom 7 ft 6 ins. *Authority:* B.W.B.

Stourbridge Canal

A short waterway connecting the Staffordshire and Worcestershire Canal at Stourton Junction with the Birmingham Canal Network and Stourbridge. The canal passes through the Netherton Tunnel, the longest and last built tunnel in Britain. *Authority:* B.W.B.

Stratford-upon-Avon Canal

The southern section of this canal, which extends from Stratford-upon-Avon to Kingswood Junction at Lapworth, is administered by the National Trust, having been restored in the sixties by volunteers. This section is 13½ miles long with 36 locks, and passes through much beautiful scenery. The northern section is 12 miles long, with 20 locks, and is administered by the B.W.B. There is an exceptionally fine aqueduct – Bearley Aqueduct – and another at Wootton Warren on the southern section. The Stratford-upon-Avon Canal links the upper and lower Avon Navigations with the Grand Union Canal at Kings Norton Junction. *Maximum boat sizes:* Length 71 ft; Draught 2 ft 6 ins; Beam 7 ft; Headroom 6 ft. *Authority* (Southern Section): National Trust, Canal Office, Lapworth, Warwickshire.

Trent and Mersey Canal

A 93-mile long waterway connecting the Bridgewater and Manchester Ship canals at Preston Brook with the Trent Navigation at the old canal port of Shardlow. The canal passes through the heart of the Potteries and much attractive countryside. There are 75 locks on the main line, including one remarkable flight – the Cheshire Locks. There are junctions at Fradley (for the Coventry Canal), Great Haywood (for the Staffordshire and Worcestershire Canal), Etruria (for the Caldon Canal), Hall Green (for the Macclesfield Canal), Middlewich (for the Shropshire Union Canal), and via the Anderton Boat Lift for the River Weaver. There are tunnels at Preston Brook (1,239 yards), Saltersford (424 yards), Barnton (572 yards), Harecastle (2,919 yards). *Maximum boat sizes:* Preston Brook to Middlewich section – Length 72 ft; Draught 2 ft 9 ins; Beam 7 ft; Headroom 6 ft; Middlewich to Burton – Length 72 ft; Draught 2 ft 9 ins; Beam 7 ft; Height 5 ft 9 ins; Burton to Trent Lock – Length 72 ft; Draught 3 ft; Beam 13 ft 6 ins; Headroom 7 ft.

Worcester and Birmingham Canal

At Farmers Bridge the Birmingham and Fazeley Canal flows into the Worcester and Birmingham which descends 30 miles from the Midlands plateau to the River Severn at Digilis Basin, Worcester. The canal is very heavily locked – 58 in all – and includes the famous flight of 30 locks at Tardebigge, the longest in the country. There are junctions at Hanbury (for the abandoned Droitwich Junction Canal), Kings Norton (for the Stratford-upon-Avon Canal), at Fazeley Junction (for the Coventry Canal), and at Worcester Bar (for the Birmingham Mainline Canal). There are 6 tunnels. *Maximum boat sizes:* Length 71 ft; Draught 3 ft; Beam 7 ft; Headroom 7 ft. *Authority:* B.W.B.

Wyrley and Essington Canal

Along with the Tame Valley and Rushall canals, the Wyrley and Essington completes an outer waterway ring on the Birmingham Canal Navigations network, extending northwards until rejoining the Birmingham Canal Mainline Canal close to Wolverhampton. *Authority:* B.W.B.

CANALOLOGY

Aqueducts

These architectural devices for transporting canals in the air across rivers, roads, railways and other canals are often of great beauty. The Romans originated the art of building aqueducts but it was during the Canal Age that the most impressive examples were built. Whether constructed from iron, brick or stone, there are many fine examples throughout the canal network, the most famous being Thomas Telford's masterpiece, the Pontcysyllte Aqueduct on the Llangollen Canal.

Architecture

Canal buildings consist mainly of lock-keeper's cottages, toll-houses, 'Barge' or 'Navigation' inns, warehouses and stables. Many of the buildings, and in particular the cottages, were built to the individual designs and requirements of the many canal companies; using local materials and reflecting a functional beauty and utility of design. There are a number of distinctive shapes, such as the roundhouses built of castellated brick peculiar to the Birmingham and Fazeley Canal. Many of the toll-houses were octagonal in plan and this enabled the toll keepers to view the oncoming traffic from two windows. A good example of this type of toll-house can be seen at Bratch Locks, Trysull, on the Staffordshire and Worcestershire Canal.

One characteristic of canal architecture is the use of cheaper materials in place of the traditional, for example, slate for roofing instead of tiles. Other characteristics include overhanging eaves, decorative brickwork with contrasting types of brick, false windows, barge-boarding around the gables, and observation windows.

Bridges

There are many types of bridges of varying shapes and sizes crossing the waterways. Some of them are of great beauty, not because of their size or structure, but because of their simplicity and the loving care with which they were made. Generally speaking, they can be classed into the following groups.

Bascule Bridges: Constructed principally of wood with winch mechanisms for lifting them up and down like a drawbridge.

Cast Iron Bridges: Iron bridges were often highly decorative and are the glory of certain canals. There are many examples of the style but one exceptionally fine bridge can be found over the Wendover Arm of the Grand Union Canal near Tring.

Below: Decorated cabin slides

Lift Bridges: These were constructed with counterbalances and were operated manually by means of a rope. Examples can be found on the Brecon, Llangollen, Shropshire Union and northern section of the Stratford-upon-Avon Canals.

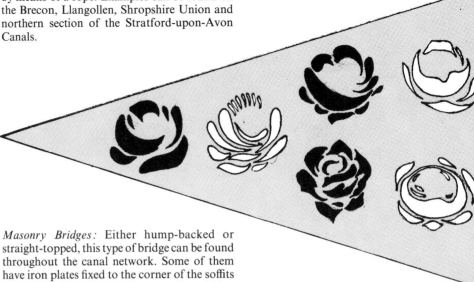

Below: Traditional rose patterns

Masonry Bridges: Either hump-backed or straight-topped, this type of bridge can be found throughout the canal network. Some of them have iron plates fixed to the corner of the soffits to prevent the coarse towing ropes from biting into the masonry.

Split Bridges: Built in two halves with a two-inch gap running across the centre of the bridge for the tow-rope to pass, thus enabling the horses (in the days of horse-drawn boats) to travel from one bank to another without being unhitched. Examples can be seen on the southern section of the Stratford-upon-Avon Canal.

Swing Bridges: There are two kinds. One is operated from the middle of the canal such as the Barton Swing Aqueduct on the Manchester Ship Canal, and the other is operated from one bank of the canal such as those found along the Macclesfield Canal.

Ironwork

The canal system was created in the age of industrial expansion where iron was being newly exploited. Apart from the cast iron bridges already mentioned, all manner of ironwork was used, especially at the locks for bollards, mile posts, engine houses, and even on the canal boats themselves. Many of these industrial relics bear the name of the maker or family.

Lifts

In order to try and reduce the time and effort of taking a boat through a series of locks as a means of going up or downhill, engineers built lifts. The most famous example is the Anderton Lift built in 1875 which links the River Weaver with the Trent and Mersey Canal, where there is a difference of 50 feet in their respective levels of water.

Locks

The locks found on the British canal network are all of one type. Commonly called 'pound' locks (with upper and lower gates), they replaced the ancient 'flash' locks which had single gates. On some canals the locks have one gate each end, while on other waterways, the locks have pairs of mitre-gates. Some locks are in pairs, side by side, which enables craft to travel up and down at the same time – a sort of dual carriageway. Where the water has to travel up a lengthy and steep inclination, the locks are often arranged in flights known as a 'staircase'. At Tardebigge on the Worcester and Birmingham Canal, the flight has 30 locks, raising boats up 217 feet in 2½ miles. Because a flight of locks can consume a vast amount of water, some of them have side ponds or 'pounds' to prevent the locks from running dry.

Reservoirs
These were built to provide the canals with an adequate water supply for, unlike rivers and streams, the waterways have no natural water source. Many of the reservoirs were supplied with pumping houses or engine houses, and dwellings for the keepers. Examples of these are still in existence, complete with their original machinery. The engine houses are of considerable architectural and industrial interest as the pumping engines were of the beam engine type. Nowadays the beam engines have been superseded by electric pumps.

Tunnels
Most of the tunnels in existence were built at a time when power machinery was non-existent and the business of burrowing into the hillsides was done by arduous labour and at the cost of many lives. And once they were built there were

no motorized boats to pass through them. Instead the boatmen had to unhitch their horses and 'leg' it through; a painfully slow manoeuvre on the longer tunnels. This involved laying planks across the fore-end of the boat on which the boatmen lay and propelled the boat along using their feet on the tunnel roof. At certain tunnels, professional 'leggers' were employed for this unenviable task.

The longest tunnel is 3 miles 135 yards long, on the closed Huddersfield Narrow Canal. The longest operational tunnel is the Dudley Tunnel (3,172 yards) on the Birmingham Canal Navigation.

Canal Craft
The history of canal boats is a fascinating and extensive study; from the early horse-drawn barges to the modern motor-powered narrow boats in use today.

The first boats were all horse-drawn; and because the horse was the most important factor in the boatman's life, great care was taken to ensure it was well-fed and kept healthy. Then gradually the steam engine replaced the horse, followed by the internal combustion engine, and the narrow boat powered by a 'National', 'Bolinder', or 'Lister' engine became a familiar sight on the canals.

The boatman and all his family lived on board as it required many hands to work the

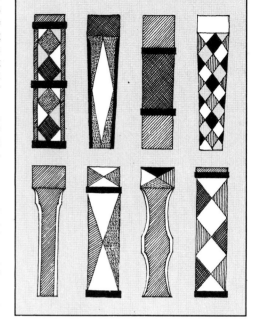

Above: Decorated stands

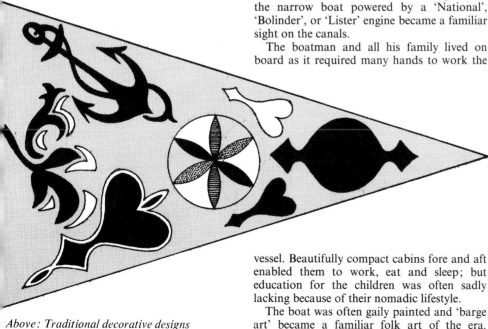

Above: Traditional decorative designs

vessel. Beautifully compact cabins fore and aft enabled them to work, eat and sleep; but education for the children was often sadly lacking because of their nomadic lifestyle.

The boat was often gaily painted and 'barge art' became a familiar folk art of the era.

Detailed and elaborate carvings on the hawse timbers and stern rails of many wooden vessels were a common sight, though only on certain canals did the boatmen paint intricate designs on their boats. Many of the painted designs were traditional, such as the brightly coloured 'roses and castles' decoration that embellished the boats inside and out. Legend has it that it was gypsies who taught the boatmen their art, but it is more likely that they picked it up from the Potteries through which the Trent and Mersey Canal passed. Other traditional decorations include moons, stars, playing card symbols and geometric designs, and these were often painted on the boatmen's domestic equipment too, such as stools, cans, pots and dippers. Graining on the wood was equally popular.

Modern narrowboats are built of steel, or steel and wood. Early steel boats were of a riveted construction but these have been superseded by welding. There is very little commercial

93

trade on the canals now although there appears to be renewed interest of late. What trade there is belongs to small companies or individual boatmen. Most of the old narrow boats still in existence have been acquired and subsequently restored by enthusiasts for pleasure cruising which is now the canals' biggest money spinner.

MODERN BOATS FOR SALE OR HIRE

We are experiencing the dawn of a new Canal Age for never before has there been so much interest shown in our waterways as a source of pleasure and recreation. Today there are many types of craft available to buy and hire. The following comes from the Inland Waterways Authority's annual magazine.

Motor Cruisers

Motor cruisers are the most popular type of craft for inland waterway holidays. Modern craft with from two to ten berths are available for hire, with either petrol or diesel engines. Some of the smaller craft are powered by

outboard motors. On rivers and the Broads, motor cruisers are fitted with wheel steering, whilst on the canals many boats are tiller steered. All craft are equipped with cooking facilities, utensils and a toilet. Some of the more luxurious craft are fitted with showers, bath and heating installation. Canal craft are usually shallower draught and narrower beam than river boats. No driving licence is required to operate a motor cruiser, but instruction is normally given by the proprietor at the outset of the holiday.

Sailing Yachts

Sailing craft for hire on inland waterways are available mainly on the Norfolk and Suffolk Broads. They have from two to six berths and most of them have an auxiliary engine. The degree of skill required to handle the yacht is usually given in the operator's brochure. As with motor cruisers, yachts are fitted with galley, cooking utensils and toilet. On the Broads a small dinghy may also be hired as a tender.

Camping Boats

A number of operators offer an economical holiday in camping boats. These are available mainly on the canals and the boats are either converted working narrowboats, with diesel engines and accommodation for up to twelve persons, or purpose-built camping pontoons powered by an outboard motor and with accommodation for four persons. For youth groups and camping enthusiasts these boats are ideal, but we do not recommend the use of former working narrowboats by novices with no experience. Some companies operate camping boats in pairs with crews provided.

Skiffs and Canoes

Traditional camping skiffs and canoes may still be hired on the River Thames and they remain popular despite the tremendous increase in the use of powered craft. They usually accommodate two or three persons and offer an adventurous outdoor holiday for those who prefer the leisurely progress and exercise of a sculling holiday. The boats are fitted with canvas awnings which spread over metal frames to form a cosy tent at night. Cooking utensils and other camping equipment may also be hired. Most canoeists own their own boats, but there are a few firms who hire out canoes by the week.

Hotel Boats

Several hotel boats operate on the canal system. They are usually former carrying craft which have been well converted to offer accommodation for up to twelve passengers. The boats normally operate in pairs, one towing the other, and work to a schedule from the Spring through to the Autumn. A regular crew is carried to operate the boat and catering staff to prepare the food.

Charges

Charges for the hire of pleasure craft operate on a sliding scale – the more accommodation the boat has, the higher the charge, and charges are higher in July and August than in the Spring and Autumn months.

NAVIGATION NOTES

To ensure the smooth running of the waterways there are rules and regulations (most of them are common sense) which should be followed. Remember that the waterways serve other important uses, notably commercial traffic and water supply. It is essential therefore that pleasure craft should always be navigated with care and attention and in accordance with the Navigation Authority's Bye-laws.

1. Speed

There is usually a speed limit of four miles per hour on canals and six miles per hour on rivers. This limit must be strictly adhered to. Never cause excessive wash or a breaking wave on the bank. Excessive speed causes damage to banks, moored craft and causes a general nuisance. Slow down when approaching or passing moored craft; other craft under way; locks; bridgeholes and tunnels; engineering works and on bends. When the view ahead is obstructed slow down and sound your horn and listen. Give way to larger craft – they cannot stop as quickly as you. Go slow when passing an angling match or regatta.

2. Rule of the Road

(a) Craft meeting should sound one short blast on horn, steer to starboard and pass each other port to port (left to left).

(b) A deep loaded commercial boat will sometimes indicate by two short blasts on its horn that it is steering to port and will want to pass starboard to starboard (right to right). This usually happens only on bends in rivers where the deep water channel is on the outside of the bend.

(c) When a vessel is being towed from the bank pass outside the vessel and thus avoid the towline. Never pass between the towed vessel and the bank.

3. Locks

Except on rivers such as the Thames, Severn and Trent, and heavily used commercial waterways the navigator works the locks for himself. Hirer of craft should be instructed on the operation of locks before they set off from the hire base.

The golden rule is never waste water. A leaflet on lock drill may be obtained from the British Waterways Board, and should be studied before starting. The lock drill should be followed systematically.

The following points should be observed:

(a) To conserve water, all gates should be left shut and paddles wound down when leaving lock.

(b) Where side ponds are provided, use them. Follow the directions which are usually displayed on the notice board beside them.

(c) Never slam gates shut or drop paddles out of control. This causes damage. Close gates by hand and wind down paddles.

(d) If two pleasure craft approach a lock together they should work through the lock together if they will both fit in.

(e) Craft should be securely moored when locking through.

(f) Draw gate paddles open slowly on river locks where no ground paddle is provided. This prevents turbulence in the lock and damage to your boat.

(g) Do not open lock gates with the bows of your boat.

(h) Keep your boat clear of the cill when locking downhill.

4. Commercial Craft

Working narrowboats will be met on a number of canals. On large rivers and other commercial waterways larger barges and sometimes small coasters will be met. Commercial craft should always be given priority. They are working for a living and time is important for them. Give plenty of room to commercial craft – they need the deep water in the centre of the channel and on the outside of bends. On large rivers keep well clear of large barges which are often difficult to steer in a confined waterway and especially so when empty. Look and listen for signals from commercial craft. On narrow canals always allow working boats to pass you, especially when working up a flight of locks.

5. Tunnels

Canal craft should be equipped with a suitable headlamp for navigating tunnels. Torches should also be carried. Go dead slow when approaching other craft in tunnels. Do not stop in tunnels except in an emergency. Give one long blast when entering and approaching the end of a tunnel. Canoes are generally prohibited from passing through long tunnels.

6. Mooring

Do not moor in bridgeholes or where your craft will cause an obstruction. Do not moor on bends or in winding holes. Whenever possible, do not moor on the towpath side of canals where horsedrawn craft are in use. Do not stretch ropes across towpaths where they will obstruct and endanger towpath users. Do not drive metal spikes deep into the towpath – this can cause damage to the clay puddle which lines the canal bed. Do not moor in the short pounds of a flight of locks. Craft moored or anchored in the fairway of large rivers should display a white light at night.

7. Lifting Bridges

At lifting and swing bridges not attended by a member of the Navigation Authority's staff, operate the safety gates across the road before opening the bridge for the passage of your boat. Where no gate is provided a member of your crew should warn road traffic.

8. General

Respect the life of the countryside. Do not leave litter or pollute the waterway. Protect the wild life of the waterway. Always respect the pleasure of other waterway users.

Moorings

With the large increase in private boat ownership over the last decade good moorings in coastal waters are becoming scarce; on inland waterways the problem is not yet so great and there are a number of alternatives.

Owners of small trailable craft often keep their boats at home throughout the year, taking the boat onto the waterways at weekends or for holidays, behind the family car. However, this is not possible with larger craft and owners must find a suitable mooring; near to their homes or perhaps on more distant waterways on which they prefer to go cruising.

On rivers and canals pleasure craft can be moored against the bank of the waterway in specified lengths allocated for this purpose. The British Waterways Board publishes a list of mooring places where craft can be kept for non-residential purposes on the waterways under their administration. A copy of this list, which gives details of charges, may be obtained from the Board's pleasure craft office at Willow Grange, Church Road, Watford, Herts. These sites are graded according to the facilities available and the degree of security offered.

The best place to moor a boat is at a boatyard or a marina where craft are kept off the main navigation channel. The cost is usually greater than for a bankside mooring but the facilities available and the security offered usually make this worthwhile. The best marinas have refuse and chemical closet disposal facilities, water, fuel and gas, slipway, telephone, chandlery and sometimes provisions. Perhaps most important of all, they offer greater security and an owner may leave his boat in the knowledge that it will be safe from floods and vandals.

DERELICT CANALS

There are over 100 lost canals in Britain. Some of them have been sufficiently obliterated by roads, railways and general filling in to be beyond repair. Others, however, are within the range of restoration and a number of volunteer organizations are showing interest. Many of these canals pass through glorious countryside and, in the same way as abandoned railways, they have become artefacts of romantic beauty.

Listed below are some of the canals which can be discovered by anyone with the aid of an Ordnance Survey map and an explorative nature. More detailed information can be found in the various books available mentioned in the bibliography, and in public libraries and the various County Record offices.

ANDOVER CANAL
Andover to Redbridge (22 miles).

BARNSLEY CANAL
Barnsley Basin to Heath Junction on the Aire and Calder Canal (15 miles).

BUDE CANAL
Bude to Thornbury, with branches to Tamar Lake and Druxton, near Launceston ($35\frac{1}{2}$ miles).

CARLISLE CANAL
Carlisle to Port Carlisle ($11\frac{1}{4}$ miles).

CHARD CANAL
Chard to Creech St. Michael Junction on the Bridgwater and Taunton Canal ($13\frac{1}{2}$ miles).

CONG CANAL
Lough Mask to Lough Corrib, County Mayo, Ireland (3 miles).

DONNINGTON WOOD CANAL
Hughsbridge to the Shrewsbury Canal (Wellington) ($7\frac{1}{2}$ miles).

DORSET AND SOMERSET CANAL
Frome to Edford (8 miles).

DRIFFIELD CANAL
Last 5 miles of the Driffield Navigation.

GLAMORGANSHIRE CANAL
Cardiff to Merthyr Tydfil ($25\frac{1}{2}$ miles).

GLASTONBURY CANAL
Glastonbury to Highbridge ($14\frac{1}{4}$ miles).

GRAND UNION CANAL (Buckingham Branch)
Old Stratford to Buckingham ($10\frac{1}{2}$ miles).

GRAND WESTERN CANAL
Taunton to Tiverton ($24\frac{1}{2}$ miles).

GRANTHAM CANAL
Grantham to the River Trent, West Bridgford, near Nottingham (33 miles).

HEREFORDSHIRE AND GLOUCESTERSHIRE CANAL
Hereford to Gloucester (34 miles).

HORNCASTLE CANAL
Horncastle to the River Witham (11 miles).

HUDDERSFIELD NARROW CANAL
Huddersfield to Duckinfield Junction, Ashton Canal (19¾ miles).

KINGSTON, LEOMINSTER AND STOURPORT CANAL
Leominster to Marlbrook, near Mamble (18½ miles).

LEVEN CANAL
Leven to River Hill (3¼ miles).

LISKEARD AND LOOE UNION CANAL
Moorswater, near Liskeard, to Terras Pill, near Looe (6 miles).

LOUTH CANAL
Louth to Tetney Haven (12 miles).

MANCHESTER, BOLTON AND BURY CANAL
Manchester (River Irwell) to Bolton. Branch line to Bury (15¾ miles).

MARKET WEIGHTON CANAL
Weighton to Weighton Lock on the River Humber (9 miles).

MONMOUTHSHIRE CANAL
Newport to Pontymoile Junction on the Brecon and Abergavenny Canal (11 miles). Branchline from Crumlin to Malpas (11 miles).

NEATH CANAL
Glyn-Neath to Giants' Grave, near Neath (13 miles).

NORTH WALSHAM AND DILHAM CANAL
Wayford Bridge to Antingham Ponds (8½ miles).

NORTH WILTSHIRE CANAL
Swindon (Wiltshire and Berkshire Canal) to Latton (9 miles).

NOTTINGHAM CANAL
Nottingham to Langley Mill (14¾ miles).

OAKHAM CANAL
Oakham to Melton Mowbray (15¼ miles).

ROYAL MILITARY CANAL
Winchelsea to Shorncliffe (30 miles).

ST. COLUMB CANAL
St. Columb Porth to Trenance Point, Cornwall (6 miles).

ST. HELENS CANAL (SANKEY BROOK NAVIGATION)
Blackbrook to Sankey Bridges, near Warrington (8 miles).

SALISBURY AND SOUTHAMPTON CANAL
Southampton to Redbridge, and Kimbridge to Alderbury Common (13 miles).

SHREWSBURY CANAL
Shrewsbury to Hadley (17 miles).

SHROPSHIRE CANAL
Coalport to Oakengates. Branch line to Coalbrookdale (10½ miles).

SOMERSETSHIRE COAL CANAL
Limpley Stoke Junction on the Kennet and Avon Canal, to Radstock and Paulton (17¾ miles).

STOVER CANAL
River Teign, Newton Abbot, to Teigngrace (2 miles).

SWANSEA CANAL
Swansea to Abercrave (15½ miles).

TAVISTOCK CANAL
Tavistock to Morwellham. Branchline to Millhill (6 miles).

TENNANT CANAL
Port Tennant to Aberdulais Junction on the Neath Canal (5 miles).

THAMES AND MEDWAY CANAL
Gravesend to Frindsbury (7 miles).

THAMES AND SEVERN CANAL
Stroud to the River Thames at Inglesham (28¾ miles). Branchline from Siddington to Cirencester (1½ miles).

ULVERSTON CANAL
Ulverston to the River Leven estuary (1½ miles).

UNION CANAL (FORMERLY EDINBURGH AND GLASGOW CANAL)
Falkirk to Edinburgh (31 miles).

WEY AND ARUN JUNCTION CANAL
River Wey, Shalford, to the River Arun, New Bridge (18½ miles).

WILTSHIRE AND BERKSHIRE CANAL
Semington Bridge Junction on the Kennet and Avon Canal, to Abingdon (51 miles).

WOMBRIDGE CANAL
Donnington Wood to the Shrewsbury Canal (1¾ miles).

Pulborough, Midhurst, Chichester
– So ran the ancient track,
But where the steel and sleepers were,
The stealthy plants come back.

Mark you that hole within the hill
Above the gravel bed?
A tunnel, yes, where coaches still
Glide softly with their dead.

PHILIP BURCHETT

FOR anyone old enough to remember travelling on a steam train, the memories will probably invoke a deep affection for what was one of the world's superlative and romantic forms of transport. Steam locomotives represented a pinnacle of traction engineering design that many consider has not been surpassed; a point of view that's hard to refute when comparisons are made with some of today's dreary diesels. Fortunately for us, the numerous railway preservation societies throughout the country have managed to keep the memories of steam alive by not only renovating hundreds of abandoned locomotives and coaches to their former glory but also in the re-opening of many disused branch lines for the public benefit and pleasure.

Most people will have heard of the Bluebell Line, and the Ffestiniog railway in Wales, but these are only two amongst an ever-expanding network of steam lines that can be visited. The following guide, divided into counties, gives details of these lines, with references to location and timetables. There is also a complete list of societies and museums to be found at the end of the book.

Avon

BLAISE CASTLE MINIATURE RAILWAY
A $10\frac{1}{4}$-inch gauge passenger line operating within the grounds of Blaise Castle, Bristol.

BRISTOL SUBURBAN RAILWAY
A standard-gauge passenger line under construction along part of the former track of the Midland Railway line from Bristol to Bath.

DODINGTON PARK LIGHT RAILWAY
A 2-foot gauge passenger line running within the grounds of Dodington Park Carriage Museum, near Chipping Sodbury.

Bedfordshire

LEIGHTON BUZZARD NARROW GAUGE RAILWAY
2-foot gauge passenger-carrying railway running 3 miles over the tracks of the Leighton Buzzard Light Railway, from Stonehenge to Pages Park Station, Billington Road, Leighton Buzzard.

WHIPSNADE UMFOLOZI RAILWAY
2-foot 6-inch gauge passenger line running internally through the animal paddocks at Whipsnade Zoo Park near Dunstable.

WOBURN ABBEY RAILWAY
2-foot gauge passenger line running through the grounds of Woburn Abbey.

Buckinghamshire

FAWLEY HILL RAILWAY
Private standard-gauge railway belonging to Mr W. H. McAlpine, Dobson's Farm, Fawley.

QUAINTON RAILWAY SOCIETY
Operates open days when steam-hauled passenger trains run between Aylesbury and Quainton Road stations. Many locomotives in varying states of restoration on view.

Cambridgeshire

PETERBOROUGH RAILWAY SOCIETY
Various locomotives and coaches in varying states of restoration at Wansford Station, Old North Road, Stibbington, Wansford, near Peterborough. Steam days held during the year.

Cleveland

SALTBURN MINIATURE RAILWAY
A 15-inch gauge passenger railway running $\frac{3}{4}$ mile between Valley Gardens and Catnab Stations, Saltburn-by-Sea.

Clwyd

LLANGOLLEN RAILWAY
A proposed standard-gauge passenger line to run 10 miles between Llangollen and Corwen through the lovely Dee Valley.

Cornwall

CORNWALL LIGHT RAILWAYS LTD.
A society recently established and now working to establish a $5\frac{1}{2}$-mile-long 2-foot gauge line between Wadebridge and Padstow along the former L.S.W.R. line.

FOREST RAILWAY, DOBWALLS
A $7\frac{1}{4}$-inch gauge passenger line running for 1 mile at Dobwalls, Liskeard, with access at Liskeard B.R. Station. Open to the public from Easter to October; every day from Whitsun, and selected days before.

INNY VALLEY RAILWAY
A 1-foot $10\frac{3}{4}$-inch gauge private railway owned by Mr J. J. A. Evans, Trecarrell Mill, Trebullett, Launceston.

LAPPA VALLEY RAILWAY
A 15-inch gauge passenger line running from Benny Mill, near Newlyn East, south to East

Wheal Rose Mine, along the former G.W.R. Newquay to Chacewater line.

LISKEARD AND LOOE RAILWAY

A standard-gauge passenger line running $8\frac{3}{4}$ miles from Liskeard to Looe.

NEWLYN RAILWAY

A 2-foot gauge line under construction at Penlee.

TOWANS RAILWAY

A $10\frac{1}{4}$-inch gauge passenger line running at Hayle.

Cumbria

LAKESIDE AND HAVERTHWAITE RAILWAY

A standard-gauge passenger line running from Haverthwaite station $3\frac{1}{2}$ miles to Lakeside station and operated by the Lakeside and Haverthwaite Railway Co. Ltd.

RAVENGLASS AND ESKDALE RAILWAY

A 15-inch gauge passenger line operated by the Ravenglass and Eskdale Railway Preservation Society, running 7 miles from Ravenglass B.R. station through the beautiful Mitedale and Eskdale valleys in the Lake District.

Derbyshire

HALL LEYS MINIATURE RAILWAY

A $9\frac{1}{2}$-inch gauge passenger line running through Hall Leys Pleasure Gardens, Matlock.

LONG EATON LIGHT RAILWAY

A 2-foot gauge passenger line currently being converted to $10\frac{1}{4}$-inch gauge and running 250 yards through West Park, Long Eaton.

MANOR MINIATURE RAILWAY

A $7\frac{1}{4}$-inch gauge passenger line running through Manor Park, Glossop.

Devon

BEER HEIGHTS LIGHT RAILWAY

A $7\frac{1}{4}$-inch gauge passenger line running through parkland at Beer from Mondays to Fridays from 10.00 to 17.00, Saturdays 10.00 to 12.30.

BICTON WOODLAND RAILWAY

A 1-foot 6-inch gauge passenger line running for 1 mile through Bicton Gardens, Budleigh Salterton.

CULM VALLEY LIGHT RAILWAY

A standard-gauge goods line running $7\frac{1}{2}$ miles from Tiverton Junction through picturesque

countryside to Hemyock.

DART VALLEY RAILWAY

Britain's only privately-owned commercially-operated standard-gauge steam line. The line runs for 7 miles from Buckfastleigh Station (between Plymouth and Exeter off the A.38 trunk road) along the glorious River Dart to Totnes.

KINGSBRIDGE MINIATURE RAILWAY

A $7\frac{1}{4}$-inch gauge passenger line running $\frac{1}{4}$ mile round part of the quay car park at Kingsbridge. Open at weekends till June and then daily to September.

NORTH DEVON AND CORNWALL JUNCTION LIGHT RAILWAY

A standard-gauge goods line running $10\frac{1}{2}$ miles from Meeth to Torrington.

PLYMOUTH, DEVONPORT AND SOUTH WESTERN JUNCTION RAILWAY

A standard-gauge passenger line running $4\frac{1}{2}$ miles from Beer Alston in Devon to Gunnislake in Cornwall.

SEATON AND DISTRICT ELECTRIC TRAMWAY

A 2-foot 9-inch gauge passenger tramway

running 1½ miles from Seaton, along the former L.S.W.R. Seaton branch line, to Colyford. The line is due for extension a further 1 mile to Colyton.

TORBAY STEAM RAILWAY

A standard-gauge passenger line running 7 miles from Paignton B.R. Station to Kingswear along the former G.W.R. line. Operated by the Dart Valley Light Railway Ltd. This line passes through some very picturesque countryside and passes over a viaduct of some distinction.

Dorset

AXE AND LYM VALLEYS LIGHT RAILWAY

A 15-inch gauge passenger line running 1¼ miles from Comboyne Station, along the former Axminster and Lyme Regis Light Railway, to Hartgrove.

BOWLEAZE COVE RAILWAY

A 7¼-inch gauge passenger line running in a continuous circuit 150 yards long at Bowleaze Cove, Weymouth.

CHRISTCHURCH MINIATURE RAILWAY

A 10¼-inch gauge passenger line running for 440 yards around a circular route at the Quay, Christchurch. Open to the public every weekend from Easter to Spring Bank holiday and then daily to October.

CROCKWAY LIGHT RAILWAY

A 2-foot gauge private line running through the grounds of Crockway Farm, Maiden Newton, near Dorchester.

SWANAGE RAILWAY

A passenger-carrying service is currently being negotiated to operate along the former Wareham to Swanage branch line on the Isle of Purbeck.

Co. Durham

NORTH EASTERN RAILWAY

A 15-inch gauge passenger line running for ½ mile through the grounds of Haswell Lodge, Haswell. Open to the public every Saturday and Sunday from Easter to September and on Sundays only to October.

WHORLTON LIDO RAILWAY

A 15-inch gauge passenger line running for ½ mile through picturesque countryside at Whorlton Lido, near Greta Bridge, Barnard Castle. Open to the public every weekend from Easter to September.

Dyfed

BURRY PORT AND GWYNDRAETH VALLEY RAILWAY

A standard-gauge light railway goods line running 21 miles from Burry Port to Cym Mawr, Gwyndraeth Valley.

DYFED RAILWAY

A proposed 3-foot 6-inch gauge passenger line to run along part of the B.R. Newcastle Emlyn branch line.

GWILI RAILWAY

A proposed standard-gauge passenger line to run eventually from Abergwili Junction, Carmarthen, to Llanpumsaint, a distance of 6 miles along the former 24-mile-long Carmarthen to Newcastle Emlyn branch line.

VALE OF RHEIDOL RAILWAY

A 1-foot 11½-inch gauge passenger line running 11¾ miles from Aberystwyth B.R. Station to Rheidol Mine, Devil's Bridge. The line, operated by British Rail, passes through exceptionally fine countryside and 7 stations on the way.

Essex

AUDLEY END MINIATURE RAILWAY

A 10¼-inch gauge passenger line running for 1 mile through the grounds of Audley End House, Saffron Walden. Open to the public at the weekend from May to September and on Sundays only during October.

BUTLINS MINIATURE RAILWAY

A 2-foot gauge passenger line running through the grounds of Butlins Holiday Camp, Clacton.

COLNE VALLEY RAILWAY

A proposed standard-gauge passenger line to operate on the former Colne Valley and Halstead Railway.

STOUR VALLEY RAILWAY

A proposed passenger line to run 11½ miles from Marks Tey to Sudbury along the former Marks Tey to Sudbury line. Another line is also proposed (as an alternative to the above)

between Sudbury and Long Melford.

WALTON-ON-THE-NAZE PIER RAILWAY

A 2-foot gauge passenger line running ½ mile along the pier at Walton-on-the-Naze.

Fife

LOCHTY PRIVATE RAILWAY

A standard-gauge passenger line running 1½ miles between Lochty and Knightsward along part of the former East Fife Central Railway. Open to the public every Sunday from June to September.

Mid Glamorgan

CONEY BEACH RAILWAY

A 15-inch gauge passenger line running ¼ mile along Coney Beach, Porthcawl.

Gloucestershire

COTSWOLD LIGHT RAILWAY

A metre-gauge passenger line running for 1 mile inside the Cotswold Marina, South Cerney, near Cirencester.

DEAN FOREST RAILWAY

A proposed passenger line to run 3½ miles from Parkend to Lydney Town in the Forest of Dean, a section of the former Severn and Wye Railway.

Grampian

FRASERBURGH MINI-RAILWAY

2-foot gauge passenger line owned by Fraserburgh County Council.

operated by Fairbourne Railway Ltd., Beach Road, Fairbourne.

FFESTINIOG RAILWAY

A 2-foot gauge passenger line running between Porthmadog and Gelliwrog, Minffordd, along the former Blaenau Ffestiniog to Porthmadog line.

GREAT ORME RAILWAY

A 3-foot 6-inch gauge passenger line running from Victoria Station, Llandudno to the summit of the Great Orme headland, 679 feet above sea level.

LLANBERIS LAKE RAILWAY

A 1-foot 11½-inch gauge passenger line running 2 miles from Llanberis to Penllyn along the former Padarn Railway.

MEIRION MILL RAILWAY

A 2-foot gauge passenger line running for 600

Gwynedd

BALA LAKE RAILWAY

A 1-foot 11½-inch gauge passenger line running 3 miles between Llanuwchllyn and Llangywair along the former Mawddach to Ruabon line.

BUTLINS RAILWAY

A 2-foot gauge passenger line running in the grounds of the Butlins Holiday Camp, Pwllheli.

CEADWLL LLECHWEDD RAILWAY

A 2-foot gauge passenger line running for ¼ mile into the Llechwedd Slate Mines at Blaenau Ffestiniog. Open to the public daily from March to November.

FAIRBOURNE RAILWAY

A 15-inch gauge passenger line running for 2 miles from Fairbourne to Penrhyn Point and

106

yards along the former Mawddwy Railway, Dinas Mawddwy.

SNOWDON MOUNTAIN RAILWAY

A 2-foot 7½-inch gauge passenger rack railway line running for 4¾ miles through majestic countryside, from Llanberis to the Summit Hotel, Snowdon.

TALYLLYN RAILWAY

A 2-foot 3-inch gauge passenger line running 7¼ miles from B.R. Tywyn Station to Abergynolwyn Station, and from Abergynolwyn to Nant Gwernol.

Hampshire

HAMPSHIRE NARROW GAUGE RAILWAY

A 2-foot gauge passenger line in private ownership at 'Four Winds', Durley.

HOLLYCOMBE WOODLAND RAILWAY

A 2-foot gauge passenger line running ½ mile through the grounds of Hollycombe House, Hollycombe Woodland Garden, near Liphook. Open to the public every weekend from Easter to October.

HYTHE PIER ELECTRIC RAILWAY

A 2-foot gauge passenger electric railway running for 700 yards along Hythe Pier.

MID-HANTS RAILWAY

A proposed passenger line to operate from Alton to Alresford along the former Alton to Winchester Junction Mid-Hants Line.

Hereford and Worcester

BROMYARD AND LINTON LIGHT RAILWAY

A 2-foot gauge passenger line running for 1 mile along the former Worcester to Bromyard branch line.

HEREFORD WATERWORKS MUSEUM TRUST

A 2-foot gauge passenger line running 300 yards at the Broomy Hill Waterworks Museum, Hereford.

Hertfordshire

KNEBWORTH WEST PARK AND WINTER GREEN RAILWAY

A 1-foot 11½-inch gauge passenger line running for 1¼ miles through the grounds of Knebworth House, Stevenage. Open to the public daily from Easter to September.

WATFORD MINIATURE RAILWAY

A 10¼-inch gauge passenger line running ⅓ mile through Cassiobury Park, Watford.

Highland

STRATHSPEY RAILWAY

A standard-gauge passenger line running 5½ miles from Aviemore to Boat of Garten and passing through beautiful moorland terrain along the former Inverness and Perth Junction Railway.

Ireland (including Northern Ireland)

GALWAY MINIATURE RAILWAY

A 10¼-inch gauge passenger line running through Galway.

IRISH STEAM PRESERVATION SOCIETY

A 3-foot gauge passenger line running ¾ mile at Stradbally.

NORTH-WEST OF IRELAND RAILWAY

A proposed 2-foot gauge passenger line to run for 1 mile between Riverside Park and Londonderry along part of the former County Donegal Railway.

ROSMINIAN FATHERS RAILWAY

A 2-foot gauge passenger line at Upton, Innishannon, County Cork.

SHANE'S CASTLE LIGHT RAILWAY

A 3-foot gauge passenger line running for 1½ miles through the grounds of Shane's Castle, Antrim, Northern Ireland. Open to the public on Wednesdays, Saturdays and Sundays from Easter to September.

TRANMORE MINIATURE RAILWAY

A 15-inch gauge passenger line situated at Tranmore, County Waterford.

Isle of Man

DOUGLAS HORSE TRAMWAY

A 3-foot gauge passenger horse tramway running for 1½ miles from Victoria Pier to just north of the Manx Electric Railway Station.

ISLE OF MAN RAILWAY

A passenger line running 5½ miles along one section of the former South Line from Port Erin to Castletown.

MANX ELECTRIC RAILWAY

A 3-foot gauge passenger electric light railway running 18 miles through beautiful countryside from Derby Castle, Douglas, to Ramsey.

QUEENS PIER TRAMWAY

A 3-foot gauge passenger tramway running for ½ mile along Queens Pier, Ramsey.

SNAEFELL MOUNTAIN RAILWAY

A 3-foot 6-inch gauge passenger electric mountain railway running 4¾ miles from Laxey to the summit of Snaefell.

Isle of Wight

ISLE OF WIGHT STEAM RAILWAY

A 1¾-mile long passenger line running between Haven Street and Wootton Stations.

Kent

BIRCHLEY RAILWAY

A 10½-inch passenger line running ¾ mile through the grounds of Birchley House, Biddenden, Ashford.

DREAMLAND MINIATURE RAILWAY

A 15-inch gauge passenger line running for ¾ mile within Dreamland Park, Margate.

EAST KENT RAILWAY

A standard-gauge light railway goods line running for 2 miles between Shepherdswell and Tilmanstone Colliery along the former East Kent Railway.

KENT AND EAST SUSSEX RAILWAY

A standard-gauge passenger line running 10 miles between Tenterden and Robertsbridge.

KENT COUNTY NURSERIES

A 10¼-inch gauge line running through the grounds of Kent County Nurseries Ltd, Challock, near Ashford.

ROMNEY HYTHE AND DYMCHURCH RAILWAY

A 1-foot 3-inch gauge passenger line running 13¾ miles from Hythe via Dymchurch to Dungeness.

SHEPPEY LIGHT RAILWAY

A 2-foot gauge passenger line running for ½ mile along part of the former Sheppey Light Railway.

SITTINGBOURNE AND KEMSLEY LIGHT RAILWAY

A 2-foot 6-inch gauge passenger line operating between Sittingbourne and Kemsley.

Lancashire

BLACKPOOL COASTAL TRAMWAY

A standard-gauge passenger electric tramway running for 11 miles between South Shore, Blackpool and Fleetwood Ferry.

BLACKPOOL PLEASURE BEACH RAILWAY

A 21-inch gauge passenger line extending ⅔ mile along South Shore, Blackpool.

BLACKPOOL ZOO MINIATURE RAILWAY

A 15-inch gauge passenger line running within the 'World of Animals' Zoological Gardens.

LYTHAM GREEK RAILWAY
A 1-foot 10¾-inch gauge passenger line extending ⅓ mile within the Motive Power Museum, Lytham.

MORECAMBE PLEASURE PARK RAILWAY
A 20-inch gauge passenger line extending ⅓ mile within the Pleasure Park, West End Promenade, Morecambe.

Leicestershire
MAIN LINE STEAM RAILWAY
A proposed standard-gauge passenger line to run between Leicester and Loughborough, along the former Great Central main line.

NEWBOLD VERDON RAILWAY
A 1-foot 10¾-inch gauge private passenger line running within the grounds of Church Farm, Newbold Verdon.

SHACKERSTONE RAILWAY
A proposed standard-gauge passenger line to extend 2¾ miles between Shackerstone and Market Bosworth, possibly further on to Shenton.

STAPLEFORD MINIATURE RAILWAY
A 10¼-inch gauge passenger line extending 1 mile within Stapleford Park, Melton Mowbray. Open to the public Sunday, Wednesday and Thursday from May to September.

Lincolnshire
CLEETHORPES MINIATURE RAILWAY
A 10¼-inch gauge passenger line nearly ½ mile long and situated alongside the boating lake on the Marine Embankment, Cleethorpes.

LINCOLNSHIRE COAST LIGHT RAILWAY
A 2-foot gauge passenger line extending for 1 mile from North Sea Lane and South Sea Lane, Humberston, Grimsby.

London, Greater
RUISLIP LIDO RAILWAY
A 12-inch gauge passenger line extending ⅔ mile within The Lido, Reservoir Road, Ruislip.

TONECOT HILL MINIATURE RAILWAY
A 10¼-inch gauge passenger line operating within the grounds of Queen Mary's Hospital for Children, Carshalton.

Manchester
BELLE VUE STEAM RAILWAY
A 15-inch gauge passenger line running for 600 yards within the Zoological Gardens, Belle Vue, Manchester.

Merseyside
LAKESIDE MINIATURE RAILWAY
A 15-inch gauge passenger line extending ¾ mile at Southport. Open to the public every weekend from Easter to Spring Bank holiday, then daily till October.

SOUTHPORT PIER RAILWAY
A 2-foot gauge passenger line extending 900 yards along the length of Southport Pier.

WEST LANCASHIRE LIGHT RAILWAY
A 2-foot gauge passenger line extending 350 yards at Hesketh Bank, near Preston.

Norfolk
BARTON HOUSE RAILWAY
A 3½-inch gauge passenger line extending 80 yards in the grounds of Barton House, Wroxham.

CAISTER CASTLE RAILWAY
A standard-gauge private passenger railway at Wymondham.

MIDLAND AND GREAT NORTHERN JOINT RAILWAY
A standard-gauge passenger line extending three miles from Sheringham to Weybourne along the former Midland and Great Northern Line.

YAXHAM PARK LIGHT RAILWAY
A 2-foot gauge private passenger line in the grounds of 'The Beeches', Station Road, Yaxham, Dereham.

Northamptonshire
BILLING MINIATURE RAILWAY
A 2-foot gauge passenger line extending for ¾

mile in the grounds of Billing Aquadome, Billing.

OVERSTONE SOLARIUM LIGHT RAILWAY
A 2-foot gauge passenger line extending for 1,300 yards inside Overstone Park, Sywell.

WICKSTEED PARK LAKESIDE RAILWAY
A 2-foot gauge passenger line extending for 1½ miles inside Wicksteed Park, Kettering.

Northumberland

SOUTH TYNEDALE RAILWAY
A proposed standard-gauge passenger line to operate between Haltwhistle and Alston in Cumbria.

Nottinghamshire

OLLERTON MINIATURE RAILWAY
A 7¼-inch gauge passenger line extending 350 yards inside Sherwood Forest, near Ollerton Roundabout, Newark.

THORESBY HALL MINIATURE RAILWAY
A 10¼-inch gauge passenger line extending 750 yards in the grounds of Thoresby Park, Ollerton, Newark.

TOLLERTON RAILWAY
A standard-gauge line within the grounds of Hill Farm, Tollerton.

Oxfordshire

BUSCOT LIGHT RAILWAY
A 11½-inch gauge private goods line in the grounds of National Trust property at Buscot.

PENDON MUSEUM TRUST
A miniature 1930 railway landscape laid out at the Pendon Museum of Miniature Landscape and Transport, Long Whittenham, Abingdon.

Powys

BRECON AND MERTHYR RAILWAY
A 2-foot gauge passenger line being constructed to extend for 8 miles along the former Brecon and Merthyr Railway between Torpantau and Pontsarn.

SOCIETY OF ENVIRONMENTAL TECHNOLOGY RAILWAY
A 2-foot gauge passenger line within the Society's grounds at Machynlleth.

WOODROFFE RAILWAY
A 15-inch gauge private passenger line extending 1,500 yards at Welshpool.

Salop

HILTON VALLEY RAILWAY
A 7¼-inch gauge passenger line extending for 1 mile through woodland countryside at Hilton near Bridgnorth.

SEVERN VALLEY RAILWAY
A standard-gauge passenger line extending 13 miles between Bridgnorth and Bewdley and passing through beautiful countryside alongside the Severn River.

Somerset

BUTLINS RAILWAY
A 1-foot 9-inch gauge passenger line running within the grounds of Butlins Holiday Camp, Minehead.

Staffordshire

ALTON TOWERS RAILWAY
A 2-foot gauge passenger line extending 750 yards within the grounds of Alton Towers, Leek.

CHASEWATER LIGHT RAILWAY
A standard-gauge passenger line extending 2 miles within Chasewater Pleasure Park, Brownhills, along part of the former Cannock Chase and Wolverhampton Railway.

DRAYTON PARK MINIATURE RAILWAY
A 10¼-inch gauge passenger line extending for 1 mile within Drayton Manor Park, Fazeley, near Tamworth.

FOXFIELD LIGHT RAILWAY
A standard-gauge passenger line 4 miles long from Foxfield Colliery, Dilhorne, to Blythe Bridge, Stoke-on-Trent.

TRENTHAM GARDENS MINIATURE RAILWAY
A 2-foot gauge passenger line extending for 1 mile within Trentham Gardens, Stoke-on-Trent.

Strathclyde

BUTLINS LTD
2-foot passenger line running internally at the Heads of Ayr Holiday Camp.

HARDRIDGE GROUSE RAILWAY
A 2-foot gauge passenger line in operation at Hardridge, Kilmacolm.

Suffolk

EAST SUFFOLK LIGHT RAILWAY
A 2-foot gauge passenger line extending 200 yards alongside the East Anglia Transport Museum, Chapel Road, Carlton Colville, Lowestoft.

FELIXSTOWE MINIATURE RAILWAY
A 7¼-inch gauge passenger line running in a circular track along the Promenade at Felixstowe. Open to the public at weekends to Spring Bank Holiday and then daily until September.

Surrey

CHESSINGTON-ZOO MINIATURE RAILWAY
A 12-inch gauge passenger line extending 925 yards within Chessington Zoo. THE ROCKET RAILWAY. A 2-foot gauge passenger line extending 600 yards within the Zoo which features an exact replica of Stephenson's Rocket locomotive.

GREAT COCKROW RAILWAY
A 7¼-inch gauge private passenger line extending for 1 mile at the property of Ian Allan, Hardwick Lane, Lyne, near Chertsey.

WEY VALLEY LIGHT RAILWAY
A 2-foot gauge passenger line extending for ¼ mile within the grounds of Moor Park Venture Scout Unit, Old Pumping Station, Guildford Road, Farnham.

Sussex, East

BLUEBELL RAILWAY
A standard-gauge passenger line running for 5 miles through the heart of the Sussex Weald, from Sheffield Park station to Horsted Keynes station.

DRUSILLA'S RAILWAY
A 2-foot gauge passenger line running through cattle and poultry paddocks at the back of Drusilla's Country Tea and Luncheon Room, Berwick, near Alfriston.

GREAT BUSH RAILWAY
A 2-foot gauge passenger line operating within the grounds of Tinkers Park, Hadlow Down, near Uckfield.

HASTINGS MINIATURE RAILWAY
A 10¼-inch gauge passenger line extending for ½ mile along Marine Parade to Rock-a-Nore, Hastings.

VOLKS ELECTRIC RAILWAY
A 2-foot 8½-inch gauge passenger line running 1¼ miles from the Aquarium, Brighton, to Black Rock.

Sussex, West

LITTLEHAMPTON LIGHT RAILWAY

A $12\frac{1}{4}$-inch gauge passenger line extending for $\frac{1}{2}$ mile from Mewsbrook Park to Littlehampton Common.

Tayside

DALMUNZIE HOTEL LIGHT RAILWAY

A 2-foot 6-inch gauge passenger line extending 2 miles from the Dalmunzie Hotel, Spittal O' Glenshee, Blairgowrie.

KERRS MINIATURE RAILWAY, ARBROATH

$10\frac{1}{4}$-inch gauge line running from West Links station 400 yards to Burnside through West Links Park.

Tyne and Wear

TANFIELD RAILWAY

A passenger line under construction along the former 1725 Tanfield Waggonway between East Tanfield and Sunniside.

Warwickshire

OLDBERROW LIGHT RAILWAY

A 2-foot gauge passenger line operating within the grounds of Oldberrow House, Henley-in-Arden.

WYCHWOOD RAILWAY

A 2-foot gauge private passenger line operating within the grounds of 'Wychwood', Cubbington Wood, Weston-under-Wetherly, Leamington Spa.

West Midlands

DUDLEY ZOO MINIATURE RAILWAY

A 15-inch gauge passenger line extending for $\frac{1}{2}$ mile within the grounds of Dudley Zoo, Dudley.

Wiltshire

LONGLEAT LIGHT RAILWAY

A 15-inch gauge passenger line extending for 1 mile within the grounds of Longleat Park, Warminster.

Yorkshire, North

DERWENT VALLEY RAILWAY

A 4-mile goods line running between Dunnington and Layerthorpe.

NEWBY HALL MINIATURE RAILWAY
A $10\frac{1}{4}$-inch gauge passenger line extending for $\frac{1}{2}$ mile alongside a section of the River Ure in the grounds of Newby Hall, Skelton-on-Ure, Ripon. Open to the public on Wednesdays, Thursdays, Saturdays and Sundays from Easter to October.

NORTH BAY RAILWAY
A 20-inch gauge passenger line extending for nearly a mile within Northstead Manor Gardens, Scarborough.

NORTH YORK MOORS RAILWAY
A standard-gauge passenger line between Pickering and Goathland.

YORKSHIRE DALES RAILWAY
A standard-gauge passenger line undergoing construction from Embsay station to Bolton Abbey along the former Midland Railway line.

Yorkshire, West

HOWDENCLOUGH LIGHT RAILWAY
A 1-foot $11\frac{1}{2}$-inch gauge private passenger line extending 230 yards within the grounds of Mr J. Buckler, 123 Howdenclough Road, Bruntcliffe, Leeds.

KEIGHLEY AND WORTH VALLEY RAILWAY
A standard-gauge passenger branch line from Keighley B.R. station, extending 5 miles to Oxenhope.

MIDDLETON RAILWAY
A standard-gauge passenger line operating on 1 mile of track from Tunstall Road Halt to Middleton Park Gates, Leeds.

OLICANA RAILWAY
A $10\frac{1}{4}$-inch gauge passenger line operating at Ilkley.

SHIPLEY GLEN CABLE TRAMWAY
A 1-foot 8-inch gauge cable-operated passenger tramway operating at Shipley Glen, Middle Airedale.

Fly, fly ever so high!
How I should like to go up to the sky
But I'd rather fly like a bird on the wing
Than fly like a kite that is tied to a string.

ANON

114

THOSE who were lucky enough to catch that fabulous exhibition at London's I.C.A. gallery – 'The Dream of Flight' – back in 1976, will know that the art of kite making and flying knows no bounds. Tom Van Sant's magnificent and often spectacular 'aerial sculptures' and Jacqueline Monnier's riotous 'sky works' set the gallery ablaze with decorative colour and form and the exhibition marked what is now considered a renaissance of the kite.

Kite construction and flight is for some a highly skilled and professional craft and there are respected organizations now in existence catering for their needs. However, for the average bloke and girl, this ancient pastime will probably always be primarily a recreational activity. Indeed, the beauty of kite flying is its wide appeal to people of all ages and professions because it is both stimulating and therapeutically relaxing, as well as being a thoroughly enjoyable form of exercise.

Types of Kite

There are essentially two groups of kite – *decorative* or tailed kites, and the *highflyers*. Decorative kites include the most ancient forms, which were mainly figures or beasts fashioned from lightweight materials, usually paper, and adorned with tails. They were, and still are, used in many parts of the world in ceremonial, religious or celebratory occasions. Highflyers can be categorized into:

PLANE-SURFACE OR FLAT KITES

Most decorative kites are of the plane-surface type but this flat-sail principle can be used for highflyers as well. Some notable examples are the *English Arch Top Kite*, the *Star Kite*, the *Barn-door Kite*, and the *Diamond Kite*. Most plane-surface kites need tails to provide stabilizing drag.

BOWED KITES

These are single-sail kites which have one or more spars sprung in a bow which keeps the sail surface correctly shaped to fly in the wind. The Malay Kite is the most famous example but there are dozens of variations, many of which originate from Malaysia and Indonesia and other eastern countries. Most of them were used as fighting kites, such as the *Indian Fighter*, *Thai Pakpao*, *Korean Fighter* and *Nagasaki Hata*.

BOX KITES

Most of the classic kites have been of eastern origin, but the Box Kite is a western invention and is widely acknowledged as one of the finest of all highflyers. It was invented by an Australian in 1893 for the purposes of lifting men, but over the years it has been extensively used in scientific research in the upper atmosphere. In its simplest form, a Box Kite is a single *cell* box or rectangle, but variations include the *Hexagonal* and *Barrel Kites*.

115

COMPOUND KITES

By constructing a kite from a number of cells, a *compound* kite is formed which often has wings for extra stability. Early compound kites were really the very first aircraft. Examples include the *Coyne Kite, Bell's Multi-celled Tetrahedral Kite*, the *Cody Compound Kite*, the *Washington Weather Bureau Box Kite*, and the *Double Rhomboidal Compound Kite*.

CANOPY KITES

These contemporary kites which consist of *Parachutes* and *Sleds* are perhaps the easiest of all kites to construct. William Allison, an American, was the originator of the *Allison Sled Kite* but a modified version by Frank Scott proved to be a more efficient flyer.

DELTA KITES

These *soaring* kites are the modern equivalent of the spineless *Rogallo Flexible Kite*. They include the *Soaring Delta Kite*, the *Semi-Flexible Soaring Kite*, and the *Modified Delta Kite*, all of which are semi-rigid with their wings adjusting to the wind in flight.

PARAFOIL KITES

The Parafoil is the most recent innovation and was the brain-child of an American, D. C. Jalbert. Unlike other kite forms, the Parafoil contains no rigid spars, spines or other structures; instead, the sail is divided up into a number of wind 'pockets' which set up an internal pressure that keeps the whole thing airborne. This new breed of kite, which now incorporates many features from other kite forms, is regarded as the most efficient controlled wing device ever invented.

FLYING YOUR KITE

Successful kite flying depends on a number of important factors. With a little thought and consideration for wind conditions, location and technique, handling a kite will be a simple and enjoyable activity.

Where to Fly

The ideal location is a large area of flat landscape such as an open field, beach, moorland, or pasture. Obstacles in the landscape, such as hills, trees and buildings, will cause ground turbulence that will grossly affect the kite's performance and make handling difficult. It may even damage the kite. Where the location is marred by obstacles, fly the kite upwind of them, as far away as possible. Where the location is a hill itself, fly the kite half-way up the windward side – not on the top.

Precautions and Regulations

Whatever happens, be extremely careful about overhead obstructions such as power lines. Don't fly near an airport – within three miles at least, as there is a law against it. Don't fly near a main road, otherwise the kite may distract motorists and cause accidents. In London there is a legal limit of 200 feet for kite flying but this does not apply throughout the country.

Wind

In the past, March was always considered the kite flying season because the winds at this time of the year are ideal. In general, winds blowing parallel to the surface of the ground are the most suitable for sustained highflying. However, individual types of kite require different wind conditions (see below). The addition of a bridle will significantly increase adaptability of a kite in winds. Avoid freak wind conditions and heavy or gale-force winds. The ideal winds are those with a velocity between 8 and 16 miles per hour.

Thermal currents (i.e. rapidly-rising columns of air) will enable kite flying to take place on hot days with little wind. Thermals happen when the cool temperature of the morning air is replaced by the heat of the day, a phenomenon more common over extensive dry areas. Certain kites, such as the Soaring Deltas, are more suited for riding thermals.

Launching

This often proves difficult, hence the all-too-familiar sight of the kite handler running like crazy with his or her kite trailing behind like a dead duck. It so happens that this method has little in its favour. In ideal conditions (i.e. with the right kite for the prevailing wind conditions), launching should be no problem. The kite should lift up from the pull of the wind the moment it is thrust in the air.

Single-Person Launch: Stand with your back to

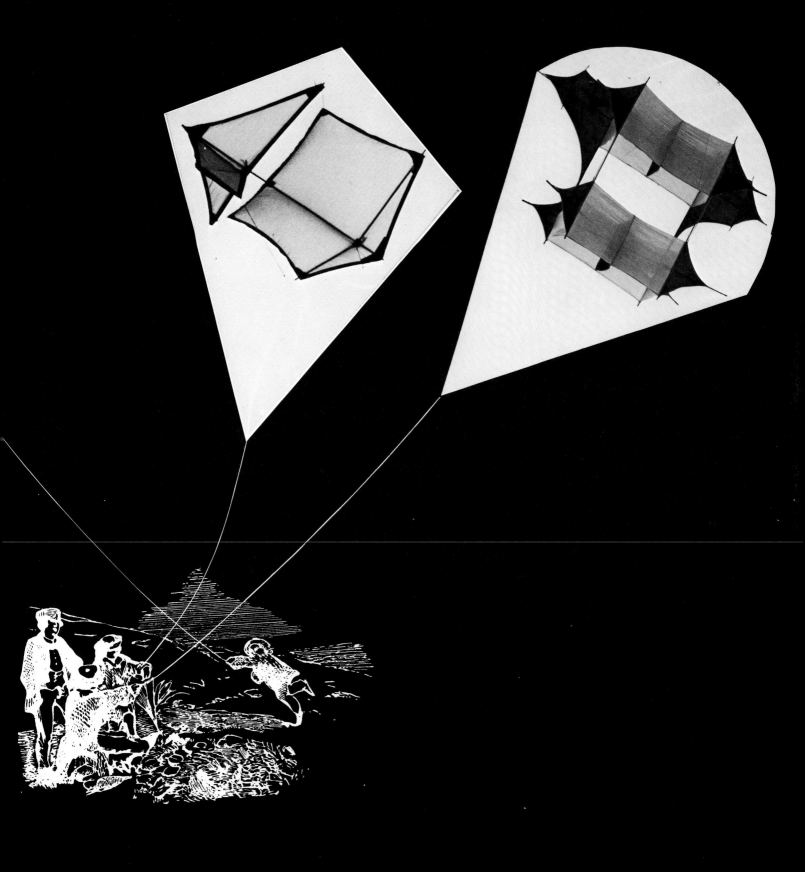

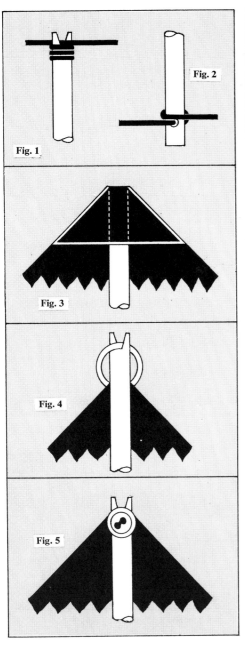

Fig. 1

Fig. 2

Fig. 3

Fig. 4

Fig. 5

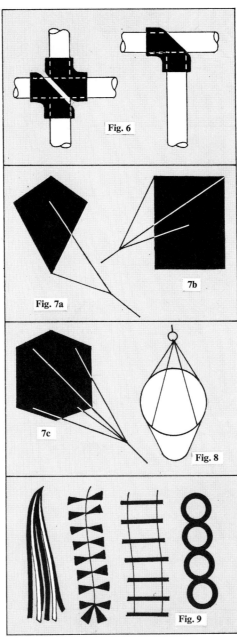

Fig. 6

Fig. 7a

7b

7c

Fig. 8

Fig. 9

the wind with the kite held in both hands and the line let out a few yards. When the wind pulls on the kite, thrust it into the air and let out a little more of the line. If the kite begins to sink, run a few yards and stop letting out the line, until the kite regains its height.

Two-Person Launch: Let out fifty yards of line, with the kite into the wind. With one person handling the line and the other the kite, the idea is that at a given signal, the kite is thrust into the air. At the same time, the person handling the line hauls in some of it as fast as possible – which should launch the kite straight into the sky. Once up, more line can be let out as required.

Performance and Control

Performance depends on the type of kite; its size, structure, weight, bow, tension and whether or not it has a bridle. To some extent this will affect the handler's control of the kite. If the kite tends to dart over to one side, then the bridle should be adjusted accordingly. If darting persists, it may be there is an insufficient length of tail, if the kite is a tailed type, or an insufficient bow, if it is a bowed kite.

All kites have a ceiling height beyond which excessive drag or *catenary* appears in the line. When this happens, the kite is unable to support the weight of its line and sagging appears. Sometimes a kite may reach a stratum of calm air which will prevent further height being reached. In this case, let out more line and give a number of short, sharp pulls.

Winding In

What might seem an easy operation can often be a chore and even a disaster. High-altitude flying where a lot of line is released will really necessitate the use of a reel, otherwise winding-in time can take ages. The golden rule is not to wind in too fast. A kite that is being hauled in quickly can suddenly dart or even plunge, and if this happens, it can end up a broken heap on the ground!

MAKING YOUR OWN KITES

The range of kites on sale today is enormous, from little decorative paper jobs to huge models costing a lot of money. Half the joy of kites however, is making them yourself and really, with one or two tools and a little care and patience, there is no reason why anyone cannot construct beautiful kites at home. Much cheaper too!

Kite Size and Design

The one important factor in any kite design is its proportion. Size does come into it, of course, but if the proportions are ill-designed the kite will simply not fly efficiently, or maybe not at all. Most of the classic kites throughout history were all to the same proportions and it is wise to keep to these. There are a number of excellent books on the market which give specific working plans and it is advisable to keep to these initially. The kite designs featured at the end of this chapter are all tried and tested.

Too much bow in a bowed kite will reduce its lifting power. Too much tail will make a kite's performance difficult and unresponsive. If the cells of a compound kite are constructed too close together, the flight will be erratic.

Tools and Materials

A basic tool kit should contain a sharp cutting knife (a Stanley knife), a mortise saw, a hammer, a ruler, a pencil, and a darning needle. For paper kites, a strong paper glue and scissors will be needed.

Crêpe and tissue paper are ideal for paper kites, otherwise wrapping or kraft paper. For fabric-covered kites, silk is the finest material, but also the most expensive. In ordinary circumstances, use cotton cambric, spinnaker nylon, Terylene, Dacron, Tyvek, Polythene – or any lightweight closely-woven material.

The materials used in the frame or structure of a kite will be governed by its size. For average-sized kites, $\frac{1}{4}$-inch white-wood dowelling is ideal, increasing to $\frac{5}{16}$-inch or $\frac{1}{2}$-inch dowelling for kites with larger spans. Aluminium rod or tubing is a relatively new innovation in kite construction that has obvious advantages. Bamboo and rattan cane is a traditional material suitable for paper kites. Balsa wood can also be used.

There are many types of line available. For paper and other lightweight kites, use nylon fishing line. Heavier kites are best flown on string, cord, twine, braided nylon, or shark-line.

Ensure the breaking strength of the line is at least two-thirds as strong as the maximum pull exerted by the kite. This can easily be calculated by multiplying the surface area of the kite by three (e.g. a kite of 4 square yards will need a 12 lb line). Always use the smallest-gauge line possible for this will help keep drag to a minimum when the kite is flying. Never use second-rate line.

Construction Details

(a) Accuracy is essential, during the whole construction process.
(b) The frame structure of any kite must be symmetrically balanced for even flight. Spars and spines that intersect centrally can have their exact centre of gravity calculated by balancing each separately on a knife edge. When the sticks balance perfectly, that will be the true centre.
(c) Bowed kites will need their spars bent evenly. Soak the rods or sticks in water overnight and then hold over a steaming kettle or some other steam source. The wood should yield to gentle bending and the bow can be held in position by tying the ends together with string like a crossbow once the required shape has been achieved. Remove the string when dry.
(d) A framing line is essential for paper-covered kites. This is a taut line of string running round the perimeter of the frame structure to support the paper. The ends of the spars and spine are notched with a V and, starting from the tail end of the spine, a length of line knotted at the end is passed through the notch and subsequently through all the notches around the kite *(fig 1)*, looping once at each notch. Alternatively, drill a small hole at the ends of the spars and spine and pass the line through *(fig 2)*.
(e) All intersections of a paper kite structure should be securely lashed and doped with glue. Never cut joints at intersections, as this will seriously weaken the structure.
(f) Cloth sails must be secured at the edges and reinforced with fabric tape.
(g) Cloth-covered kites require fastenings to secure the sail to the spars. There are a number of methods of doing this, the usual way being a pocket fastening *(fig 3)*. Alternative methods include ring fastenings *(fig 4)* and button fastenings *(fig 5)*. All fastenings should be reinforced by a double thickness of cloth or

fabric tape sewn into the sail.
(h) Fabric kites, especially compound and other intricate models, require effective, positive joints within the frame structure. At the moment, everyone is using flexible polythene tubing, which is ideal. It can be cut and manipulated by gentle heat to form countless rigid tubular joining sections *(fig 6)*.

Bridles

Kites can be flown without a bridle but they respond much better in flight if one is attached. A bridle is a length of line running from the fore and aft *(two-legged bridle)*, or left, right and centre *(three-legged bridle)*, or four opposite corners *(four-legged bridle)* of a kite *(fig 7a, b and c)*. The towing line is attached to the bridle by means of a metal ring, and this is called the *towing point*.

The towing point is critical for efficient flight and should be positioned one-third of the distance down the length of the spine and outwards half the length of the spine. In exceptionally high winds the kite should fly from the towing point at a low angle and at a high angle in low winds.

Most stunt kites are flown from double towing lines attached to two-legged bridles, thus enabling the handler to effect spectacular loops and dives. There are even four-line stunt kites now which enable the handler to be in perfect control of the kite's performance.

Tails and Drogues

Tails can transform simple kites into something spectacular, as Jacqueline Monnier amply proved. On the face of it, fitting a tail might seem counter-productive to a kite's performance because of the additional drag. However, this can be a positive force on the kite's overall stability, especially during high wind velocities.

The general rule is to make the tail *seven times* the length of the spine but it's worth experimenting with varying lengths of tail for individual kites. Remember, too, that the higher the wind speeds the longer the tail should be. There are plenty of possibilities as well as a number of traditional designs for tails *(fig 9)*. String and paper ribboning are the ideal materials, or offcuts from any lightweight fabrics.

The drogue is a device invented by Sir George Nares for automatically adjusting the amount of drag exerted on a kite during different wind speeds. It is simply an open-ended conical cup suspended from the kite *(fig 8)*. The size of the drogue remains the same whatever the weight of the kite. Instead, the towing line attaching the drogue alters, i.e. heavy kites will need a greater length of line than lighter kites.

Reels

There is a wide range of reels on the market which will greatly increase the efficiency of winding in line and therefore increase the enjoyment of the kite flyer. They range from simple wood-framed hand winders to expensive power-operated winches. For the average kite enthusiast, however, a fishing-rod reel is perfectly adequate.

SIX KITES TO MAKE

(1) Diamond or Two Stick Kite
Dimensions:
Spine: 26 inches (660 mm)
Spar: 22 inches (559 mm)
Intersection: 7 inches (178 mm) from top of spine
Sail: Paper
Bridle: Two-legged
Wind: Light.

(2) English Kite
Dimensions:
Spine: 26 inches (660 mm)
Spar: 20 inches (508 mm)
Intersection: 8 inches (203 mm) from top of spine
Sail: Paper
Bridle: Two-legged
Wind: Light.

(3) Hexagonal Kite
Dimensions:
Spars: 26 inches (660 mm)
Sail: Paper or cloth
Bridle: Three-legged
Wind: Light.

120

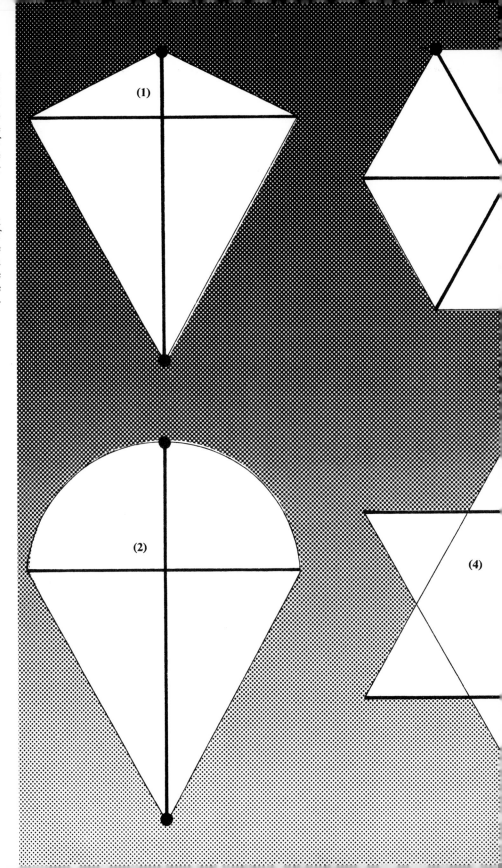

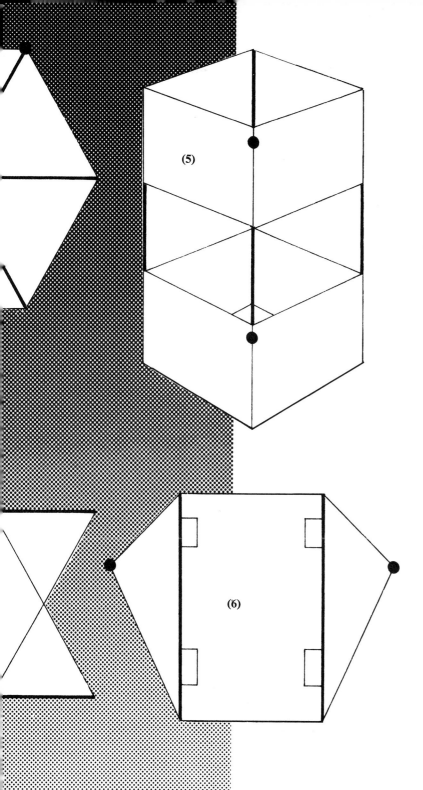

(4) Six-Pointed Star Kite
Dimensions:
Spine: 26 inches (660 mm)
Spars: 22¾ inches (577 mm)
Intersections: 7 inches (178 mm) from top and bottom of spine
Sail: Paper
Bridle: Two-legged
Wind: Light.

(5) Square Box Kite
Dimensions:
Spars: Four at 26 inches (660 mm); four at 17 inches (432 mm)
Width: 12 inches (305 mm)
Sails: 8 × 49 inches (203 × 1,245 mm)
Sails: Paper, plastic, nylon, etc.
Bridle: Two-legged
Wind: Moderate–strong.

(6) Sled Kite
Dimensions:
Spines: Three at 36 inches (914 mm)
Distance between spars: 11 inches (280 mm)
Width of sail: 44 inches (1,118 mm)
Sail: Nylon, plastic, polythene, etc.
Bridle: Two-legged
Wind: Light.

T·H·E
S·T·R·A·N·G·E
W·O·R·L·D
O·F
T·O·P·I·A·R·Y

The climbing street, the Mill, the leafy lane,
The Peacock Yew tree, and the lonely hill.
                                          TENNYSON

ALTHOUGH that strange, almost surreal art of the clipped hedge had its popular origin in the Mediterranean gardens of ancient Rome, it was in this country that the craft of cutting trees and shrubs into quaint devices really blossomed. And like so many other forms of English folk art, topiary revealed that wonderful trait of whimsical eccentricity so peculiarly British.

Sadly the practice of fashioning living sculpture from shrubs and trees has severely declined, but there are still plenty of examples around; from the classical and architectural forms adorning the gardens of our great country houses, to the cats, gnomes, peacocks, teapots and other kitsch cut from the hedges of suburbia. So with luck, this chapter may inspire would-be topiarists to unleash themselves on their hedges, or encourage the planting of new shrubs for a shapely posterity. Who knows, there may even be a revival!

The History of Topiary
From its classical beginnings in ancient Greece, the art of topiary spread to Rome, and then flourished throughout Europe wherever the fingers of the mighty Roman Empire had stretched. This included Britain and many of the villa gardens that grew in the south of England were landscaped with clipped boxwood.

After the empire of Rome had fallen, the onset of the Dark Ages meant the end of many romantic pursuits and topiary completely died out. Then in the eighth century the art flourished again in France and was re-introduced into this country through the Norman invasion. By the twelfth century, the practice was developing into a more and more sophisticated form with mazes and clipped hedge walks and

eventually evolved into the Tudor formal garden where topiary was the essential characteristic.

The next innovation was the knot-gardens of the sixteenth century. These were formal beds of coloured pebbles or earth laid out in heraldic shapes and surrounded by dwarf box hedges. At the same time, trees were becoming fashionable for topiary and cypresses, yews and junipers were clipped into pyramids and other architectural shapes at strategic points in arbours and around the house.

The knot-garden gave way to the parterre of the seventeenth century, replacing the former heraldic forms with embroidery-like patterns of clipped hedges surrounding black-earthed beds filled with colourful flowers. They were designed to be seen from a bedroom window where their elaborate designs could be fully appreciated.

During the seventeenth century influences from the Dutch and French garden styles were assimilated into English formal landscaping and topiary flourished as never before. Great houses such as Kew had their gardens laid out with avenues of clipped yews in the French style, and alleys, vistas, parterres and terraces incorporated topiary in some form or other.

The Golden Age of topiary however came at the end of the seventeenth century when figurative clipping developed into wild and extravagant forms. It was a style largely derived from the Dutch, and all manner of animals, figures, gods and objects were formed through the clipping of hedges, trees and shrubs. Nature, as one writer commented at the time, '. . . was deformed by making her statuesque through the medium of the shears'.

The inevitable backlash against topiary came in the early eighteenth century when writers and philosophers such as Alexander Pope and Joseph Addison led a crusade against the formal concept of garden landscape. No sooner had these influential men aired their views than the whole practice of sculpturing trees and shrubs went into a sharp decline as the new and fashionable interest in 'natural' gardening came to the fore.

It wasn't until the Italianate Revival of 1830 that topiary enjoyed a renewed interest, though it never regained its former popularity or distinction and today is confined to the great historical gardens and the odd few eccentric gardens throughout the country.

TOPIARY FOR THE BEGINNER

It might appear otherwise, but training and shaping a shrub or tree is not a lifetime-before-it's-ready craft. Most trees and shrubs can be brought into roughly their intended form within ten years, and if they are already established in the garden, even sooner. The prime concern is the choice of tree or shrub because it will have to sustain constant clippings over a long period. Not only that, but the foliage should be of a dense nature and with small leaves which do not reveal the damage of clipping.

All the topiarist requires is a sharp pair of shears and secateurs and a little imagination. The following list of species are all suitable for topiary.

Bay (SWEET BAY)
The tree of bay-leaf culinary fame, *Laurus nobilis*, and once greatly revered by the ancient Greeks for their laurel crosses and wreaths. It tolerates most loamy soils but does require full sunlight for healthy growth. Because of the largish nature of the leaves, bay trees are more suited to simple geometric shapes, especially the sphere and pyramid. They are ideal for tubs which can be positioned outside entrances of buildings. Bay survives well near the coast. Use secateurs for clipping as shears will damage the leaves. Can be grown from seed but better bought as a shrub. Plant 2 feet 6 inches (762 mm) apart for hedges.

Beech
The various kinds of beech are very attractive as a shaped hedge as they retain their rich golden or purplish leaves throughout winter. Suited to good loam or clay soils, is tolerant of lime, but will fare poorly on badly drained land. Can be grown from seed or bought as hedging or young trees. Plant 1 foot 6 inches (460 mm) apart for hedges.

Box
There are many varieties of this widely-used shrub. They are extensively used in topiary and although rather slow in growth will tolerate most soils and some degree of shade. The two principal varieties are the dwarf box (*Buxus suffruticosa*) which is ideal for edgings, and the common box (*Buxus sempervirens*) which can reach up to 20 feet (6 m) in height. Both will tolerate quite severe clipping. Box can be propagated from cuttings, struck at the end of summer. Plant the cuttings deeply to encourage healthy root growth. *Buxus suffruticosa* can be bought by the yard from many reliable garden centres, and the other species as individual shrubs. Plant 1 foot (305 mm) apart for hedges.

Cypress
Many forms of cypress have been used throughout the history of topiary and in particular the upright Italian cypress (*Cupressus sempervirens*). They tolerate moderate clipping but this can render them more susceptible to frost if planted in an unsheltered area. For this reason coastal-situated cypresses do far better than those inland. Plant 1 foot 6 inches (460 mm) apart for hedges.

Hawthorn
Though not as suitable for fancy shaping as the evergreen species, hawthorn makes a beautiful clipped hedge. Tolerant of most soils and fast-growing, too. Can be grown from seed, cuttings, or can sometimes be obtained in bulk from certain garden centres. Hawthorn will tolerate severe pruning. Plant 1 foot (305 mm) apart for hedges.

Holly
Holly is one of our most lovely evergreens and though it tends to shed leaves untidily in the summer, is well suited for hedges and topiary work. Apart from the common holly (*Ilex aquifolium*), there are countless variegated forms of great beauty (Hillier & Sons of Winchester stock 148 different varieties!) with romantic names such as 'Golden Gem', 'Silver Milkbay' and 'Silver Sentinel'. Holly grows well in most soils and is very hardy, being tolerant of polluted city air and strong winds. Can be grown from seed but as it grows slowly at first, it is advisable to take 4-inch (102-mm) cuttings in August. Ensure the cuttings include a reasonable heel from the parent wood and remove all lower leaves before striking into sandy soil, preferably in a greenhouse or cold-frame. Transplant the cuttings in late spring or autumn and avoid disturbing the roots. All clipping should be relegated to the spring or autumn months and secateurs used instead of shears. Plant 2 feet (610 mm) apart for hedges.

Honeysuckle
The sun-loving shrubby honeysuckle (*Lonicera nitida*) can be pruned into shape for topiary purposes. *Lonicera nitida* 'Bagesen's Gold' has handsome foliage which turns golden bronze in winter. Other forms include *Lonicera* 'Ernest Wilson'; *Lonicera* 'Fertilis' and *Lonicera* 'Yunnan'. Tolerant of most soils but prefers a good loam on the moist side.

Hornbeam
Similar to beech but more hardy. The common hornbeam (*Carpinus betulus*) makes a beautiful hedge. By clipping in mid-summer the consequent new growth will be retained throughout the winter. Can be grown from seed or bought in shrub or tree form. Plant 1 foot (305 mm) apart for hedges.

Juniper
The slender grey Irish form (*Juniperus communis hibernica*), which can attain the height of 60 feet (18 m), grows in the wild in this country but can be cultivated for hedges and simple topiary. Cuttings taken from the new year's growth are the most successful method of propagation, although it can be grown from seed, or bought as a shrub.

Laurustinus (VIBURNUM)

Laurustinus (*Viburnum tinus*) is a favourite winter-flowering evergreen that takes well to topiary. It tolerates most conditions and will form into an excellent hedge. Cuttings can be taken in late summer in the usual way.

Lavender

Not so widely used these days but nevertheless an evergreen shrub which produces a beautiful clipped hedge and ideal for simple topiary. Taking 3-inch (76-mm) heeled cuttings in August is the easiest form of propagation, or the young plants can be obtained from most garden centres. Lavender prefers well-drained soil on the chalky or sandy side. Clipping should be carried out primarily in the spring. Plant 1 foot (305 mm) apart for hedges.

Myrtle

The fragrant myrtles are sturdy evergreens bearing white rose-like flowers in summer. They require shelter from the south and need full sun to do well in this country. *Myrtus communis* is the classic ancient myrtle which is the most suitable variety for clipping, surviving in most good soils. Can be struck successfully from cuttings. Prune with secateurs to protect the foliage.

Phillyrea

This is a broad, dense, slow-growing evergreen, sometimes referred to as the 'mock privet'. It is tolerant of moist soils and sea winds, which makes it an ideal shrub for coastal areas. It will also tolerate shade. Excellent for topiary as the sheer hardiness of this shrub means it can endure severe clipping. Cuttings can be taken in late summer in the normal way.

Privet

The favourite hedge of suburbia. The somewhat unexciting dark green privet is the more commonly planted variety but the Golden Privet (*Ligustrum ovalifolium aureum*) and the Silver Privet (*Ligustrum argenteum*) are rather fine

shrubs. Privet will tolerate almost every soil and condition which is the reason why it is so widely grown. It grows fast from cuttings (which are easy to strike) or from young bushes. Severe clipping two or three times during the growing season is necessary to prevent the hedge or topiary from growing out of shape. Plant 1 foot 6 inches (460 mm) apart for hedges.

Pyracantha

The Firethorn. This genus of shrub is second to none for adaptability and it is beautiful too. Will grow in most soils, in the ground or in tubs; against a wall or as a cut shrub or hedge. The clusters of brilliant red berries which grow in profusion are replaced by lovely white blossom in the spring. Can be cultivated quite happily on a north wall. Propagate from seed or from late summer cuttings. Prune with secateurs to avoid leaf damage. Plant 1 foot 6 inches (460 mm) apart for hedges.

Rosemary

Of Rosemary, cut out with curious order,
In satyrs, centaurs, whales and half-men-horses
And thousand other counterfeited courses.

This ancient and well-beloved gem of a shrub from the Mediterranean makes a lovely hedge, and is suited to topiary as well. Rosemary prefers a light, well-drained soil and needs good protection from the winter winds as it is apt to suffer from the cold and bleak conditions. *Rosmarinus officinalis* is the common form but the White Rosemary (*Rosmarinus albus*) and *Rosmarinus fastigiatus* are beautiful variations. Can be grown quite easily from seed, or propagated from shoots layered in the summer. Plant 1 foot (305 mm) apart for hedges.

Sage

Still used in some herb gardens as a formal edging hedge. With over 500 varieties to choose from, the sage is useful for unusual low hedges and simple shaping. Grow from seed or cuttings. Plant 1 foot (305 mm) apart for hedges.

Yew

Last but not least, the yew is the topiarist's first choice and the finest of all shrubs for either detailed, creative clipping or monumental hedges. It can be trained into almost any shape and can be twisted or bent. Although it is renowned for its longevity – some yews grow for 500 years or more – it grows surprisingly fast in its early years. Yews prefer well-drained lime soils, though any good deep loam will be suitable. They are not suited for town planting as they will not grow well in polluted air. Can be grown from seed but it is usual to buy 2-foot (610-mm) high shrubs which take readily for hedge work. *Taxus baccata* is the common form but there are nearly 50 varieties to choose from. Plant 2 feet (610 mm) apart for hedges.

Where to Plant

The two most important considerations in choosing a site for topiary are sunlight and shelter. Although certain species of shrubs tolerate varying degrees of shade, the best results will always occur when they are grown in full sunlight. Shade from trees or from the shifting shadows caused by other obstructions may result in uneven growth. Shelter is equally important because severe winds can totally ruin a beautifully clipped hedge.

The ideal situation is an area in the garden which is slightly below the level of everything else, surrounded by a high hedge 10–12 feet (3–3·5 m) high. Obviously this is impractical for most suburban gardens but commonsense must be the deciding factor, bearing in mind what has been said. In the past, topiary trees and shrubs were planted in beds of herbs and flowers and edged with box, but nowadays it is customary to plant in grass. From a purely practical point of view, planting in grass makes clipping and the subsequent clearing of leaves an easier operation. Topiary shaped out of a hedge will require the same conditions as free-form topiary.

Planting

Nursery-bought trees and shrubs should come from the nearest reliable garden centre to ensure climatic suitability. The planting season for all species is from October to May, unless

129

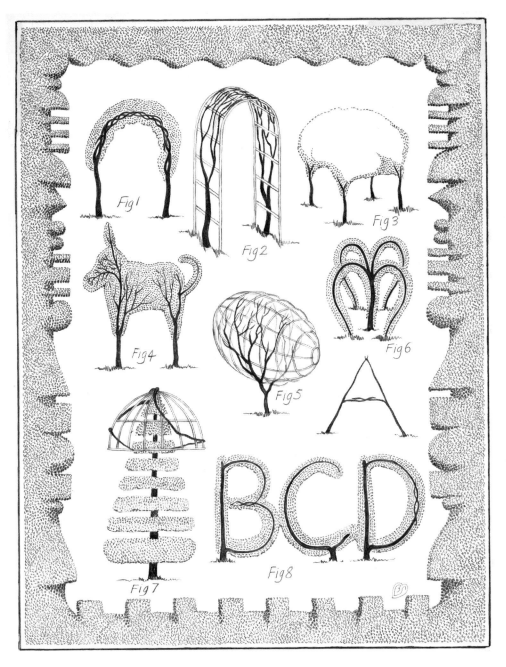

Fig 1

Fig 2

Fig 3

Fig 4

Fig 5

Fig 6

Fig 7

Fig 8

container-grown plants are used which can be planted any time during the year.

The soil is the most important consideration in the planting procedure. It should be sufficiently enriched with manure or compost to ensure healthy growth over the many years. (Bonemeal is particularly beneficial for long-term feeding.) This may mean digging out a good-sized hole or trench and replacing with richer soil. When plants arrive from the nursery or garden centre, soak the roots in water for a day before planting, unless they are already in soil. Dig the hole or trench of sufficient size to allow the roots to spread out fully and tread down the soil carefully once in position. Firmness is very important. Tread around the plants once a week for several weeks after planting. Trees should be staked and tied securely. Water in well and mulch with a good layer of compost or well-rotted stable manure.

In the summer, especially in exceptionally dry conditions, the shrubs and trees must be given a regular soaking at the roots, preferably once a day. This is even more important once clipping has started because clipped trees keep the rain from their roots.

SHAPING

Allow all trees and shrubs to grow naturally for the first year as this will strengthen and consolidate the roots. Aim to clip lightly the following spring (about May) and again in July. Evergreens should not be clipped later than September.

The general aim should be to get the shrub, hedge or tree into roughly the required shape within three years. As for the choice of shape, this is a personal affair but often the plant itself will suggest a shape. It is easier to adjust to what the plant wants to do than vice versa. Some of the more traditional folk-art forms in topiary are: peacocks, teapots, rabbits, chickens, bottles, horses, cats and doves. However, to begin with, aim for simple shapes, as these will not only be easier to achieve but will quite often be very effective.

More intricate shaping such as those suggested above involves the training and bending of leading shoots. For really bulky forms, two

130

or three shrubs should be planted together and clipped into one shape. To assist in this shaping thin wires and bamboo can be used to support the plants, insulated at strategic points with rubber or cork to protect the branches.

Individual shapes will now be discussed in more detail.

Arches

Used in the right place an arch can beautifully enhance a garden. To achieve this there are two methods to choose from depending on the size and shape of the intended arch. Trees should be selected for the vigour of their leading shoots as these will be required for forming the curve of the arch. The simplest way is to bend the leading shoots on the two trees planted on either side of the path, gate etc. and plait them together as they grow *(fig 1)*. For larger arches, a framework of wire or wood will be useful in support of the shoots until mature *(fig 2)*.

Animals

Plant four trees or shrubs where the feet are to rest. These should be clipped hard at first so as to form their shape. Once this has been achieved, allow them to grow uninhibited for the bulk shape of the head and body *(fig 3)*. Ears, tails and snouts can be formed by extending shoots at the required places *(fig 4)*.

Birds

Birds have always featured strongly throughout the history of topiary. Box and yew are perhaps the best trees to use. Begin by training the tree into a form from two leading shoots, which will be the feet (for large birds plant two trees and proceed as for animals). Another way is to train the leading shoots around an oval wire frame fixed to the main stem *(fig 5)*. This will form the body. The head can be formed later by training shoots around another smaller oval frame. Alternatively, tie shoots into bunches as they extend from the body. This can form the basis of a head or tail.

Cones, Cubes, Spheres, etc.

Simple geometric forms are the easiest shapes to achieve and can usually be trained within a couple of years. Straight sides present little trouble if some kind of straight edge such as a plumb line is used. All these shapes form the basis of more complicated forms. The cone can be readily adapted to form a jug or coffee pot by training away shoots to form the spout and handle. Chessmen and other bulky figures can also be clipped from cones and cubes.

Crowns

In this case, four or more leading shoots are bent down *(fig 6)* into the four corners of the crown and tied to the main stem. Tying down, as opposed to tying up, is essential as this ensures good full shapes.

Finials

These are classic topiary ring shapes which are often used to top off cones and spirals. The main shape must be fully formed before any attempt is made to train the finial. This is achieved by drawing down shoots out of the cone or spiral. The shoots are trained round a circle of wire held to the main plant; one in a clockwise direction and one the other way *(fig 7)*.

Letters

Any letter from the alphabet can be formed by bending leading shoots. Two trees will be needed (or two leading shoots, depending on size) for the letters A, H, M, N, O, Q, W. All other letters can be formed from just one shoot or plant. To create an H, for instance, a leading shoot is drawn out of each plant half way up the stem and twisted together for the cross-bar *(fig 8)*.

Spirals

Another traditional shape and not half as difficult as might be expected, provided a young pliable tree such as yew is used. The simplest spiral can be formed by driving a thick stake into the ground as close to the main stem as possible (ideally this should be put in when the tree is planted). The main stem, with every other shoot removed, is then twisted around the stake and secured with wire or string. For wide spirals, or for tapered spirals, a number of stakes are used to form a bigger bulk or pyramid and the tree trained around in the same way.

AUTUMN S

THE TREASURE FOUND

134

TREASURE ISLAND

Peggy could not speak. Not a single word would come to her lips. She just pointed.

"What is it?" said Susan. "Is it —? Is it —?" She could get no farther.

"What?" said the others, and then, following Peggy's outstretched arm and pointing finger, they all saw the thing at once. Brown and sandy, in the brown and sandy earth, they saw the corner and a bit of the side of a box.

FROM 'PETER DUCK' BY ARTHUR RANSOME

THERE must be precious few of us who have never dreamt of discovering treasure at sometime in our lives; digging up a crock of gold pieces from underneath an old tree, or a chest of doubloons, pearls and jewels from the beach or from a sunken wreck from the Spanish Main. Children's literature is full of such tales and yet hunting for treasure is one of those childhood fantasies that lingers on long into adult life. These days, however, what constitutes treasure is no longer confined to buried casks of gold coins and chests of pearls and jewels. Neither is treasure hunting limited to sandy beaches or sunken wrecks. Antique relics of all kinds – bottles, badges, buttons, coins, pipes – are being dug out of the ground, or discovered in old houses, and many people are making a good profit from selling these finds on market stalls up and down the country. In fact, a whole new 'industry' has developed from the antics of the amateur treasure hunter, with reputable organizations, magazines and an international network of clubs and communication. Even Long John Silver himself would have approved!

RULES, REGULATIONS AND THE LAW

The first task of the prospective treasure hunter is to acquaint himself with the various laws and the unwritten code of conduct concerning treasure finds. This is very important as breaking the law not only may be costly but may also harm the good name of treasure hunting. And contrary to what might appear, the laws are *beneficial* to treasure buffs.

Treasure Trove
Any hoard or find of gold or silver coins *must be reported immediately to the local coroner* via the police or local museum. A receipt will be given and a coroner's inquest held at a later date to decide whether the find is Treasure Trove. This will depend on where the treasure was found and the assumed intention of the person who buried it. If the treasure is deemed Treasure Trove then the finder will receive a reward equal to the full current market value of the find.

Permission to Search
Always be sure to get permission from the owner of land or property intended for search as he will have the rights to anything discovered and without permission you would be trespassing. This includes rubbish tips, old mines and derelict houses. If possible get written permission.

Archaeological Digs
Anything dug up from an archaeological site, or any ancient coins and antiquities made from base metals do not have to be reported to the coroner as they are not considered Treasure Trove. They should, however, *be reported to the local museum and, in all fairness, donated to the museum, being of historical interest to the public.* Having said that, it would be very much better if treasure hunting completely excluded archaeological sites.

Treasure from Wrecks
All finds washed ashore *must be handed in to the local coastguard* who will return them if the finds are unclaimed, subject to a fee for storage.

Prospecting for Gold
Unfortunately panning for gold is not a free right. A Crown Estate Permit must first be

obtained (£2 approximately) and permission obtained from the landowner in whose stream the panning is to be carried out.

Modern Treasure

All modern finds such as purses, wallets, jewellery and other valuables must be handed in to the police. They will be handed back if the owner fails to claim within a certain period of time. Individual coins need not be handed in.

The Treasure Hunter's Code of Conduct

This is an unwritten code prepared by the various treasure-hunting organizations, professional treasure seekers and the Department of the Environment which all treasure buffs should follow. It is in everybody's interest that the code is carried out.

(1) *Don't interfere with archaeological sites or ancient monuments.* Join your local archaeological society if you are interested in local history.

(2) *Don't leave a mess.* It is perfectly simple to extract a coin or other small object buried a few inches under the ground without digging a great hole. Use a sharpened trowel or knife to cut a neat circle; extract the object; replace the soil and grass carefully and even you will have difficulty finding the spot again.

(3) *Help Keep Britain Tidy – help yourself.* Bottle tops, silver paper and tin cans are the last things you should throw away. You could well be digging them up again next year. So do yourself and the community a favour by taking all rusty junk you find to the nearest litter bin.

(4) *Don't trespass.* Ask permission before venturing on to any private land.

(5) *Report all unusual historical finds to your local museum and get help if you accidentally discover a site of archaeological interest.*

(6) *Learn the Treasure Trove laws and report all finds of gold and silver objects to the police.* You will be well rewarded if the objects you find are declared Treasure Trove.

(7) *Respect the Country Code.* Don't leave gates open when crossing fields and don't damage crops or frighten animals.

(8) *Never miss an opportunity to show and explain your detector to anyone who asks about it.* Be friendly. You could pick up some clues to a good site.

(9) *If you meet another detector user while out on a hunt, introduce yourself.* You could probably teach each other a lot.

(10) Finally, remember that when you are out with your detector you are an ambassador for the whole amateur treasure hunting fraternity. *Don't give us a bad name.*

COINSHOOTING

The most popular branch of treasure hunting is the search for coins and is affectionately known as 'coinshooting'. When one considers that over 100 million coins disappear from circulation each year it is not difficult to see why it is so widely pursued. To practise coinshooting in a serious and productive way, a metal detector is required. This is an electric device that locates, more or less accurately, any metal object lying in the ground by a sound signal. *A licence to use one should be obtained from the Home Office (£1.40 for five years).*

Using a Metal Detector

The sales of metal detectors have mushroomed in recent years and considerable hoards have been discovered by amateur treasure seekers using the simplest of equipment. As with every other piece of equipment, it is *how* it is used that matters because for all its electrical wizardry, a detector in the wrong hands will not come up with the goods.

There is a wide range of detectors on the market, ranging from the cheapest types around £15–£20 to really sophisticated equipment costing hundreds of pounds. The choice will inevitably be a personal one, related to the price that can be afforded.

Types of Detectors

There are four main groups of detector:

1. *Transmitter/Receiver (TR) Detectors.* Every detector transmits and receives electronic signals but this particular type is more sophisticated than the BFO detectors (see below). They are easy to operate and have a good penetration of depth down to large objects. They also give out a clear signal. Ideal for locating large objects.

2. *Beat Frequency (BFO) Detectors.* These were the earliest detectors on the market and they are cheap and easy to operate. They are extremely accurate in locating small objects but do not have a far-reaching depth of penetration. Ideal for beginners.

3. *Induction Balance (IB) Detectors.* These detectors require considerable skill in handling and are not really suitable for beginners. They are used by many professional treasure hunters because, once the technique of handling the IB has been mastered, they can locate objects at a greater depth than either the BFO or TR types.

4. *Pulse Induction Detectors.* These are the new generation detectors which can locate coins at over a foot in depth with ease. The one disadvantage, however, is their sensitivity to iron which can waste an awful lot of time for the inexperienced treasure seeker. Also they do not have the same pin-pointing accuracy as the other types of detectors.

Apart from the actual detector unit there are accessories on the market which can aid the search for buried treasure.

Headphones are the most useful extra as they enable the user to hear any signals given out by the detector more clearly. There are also visual meters, search coils and tuner refiners, but these are all luxuries which the beginner can pass by.

For searching in streams and rivers a *water-immersible detector* is essential (a detector labelled 'waterproof' is not necessarily water-immersible).

It will be quite helpful for the beginner to join one of the reputable treasure-hunting organizations who will be able to give expert advice on the purchase and handling of detectors. There will be opportunities to try out the various types of equipment and even possibly to hire them for a trial run. Also, certain manufacturers operate a hire service and a seven-day trial scheme which can be useful when trying to decide which type of detector to buy.

Using the Detector

Apart from the detector itself it will be useful to take on treasure-seeking forays: a large plastic bag (to keep the detector dry if it rains); smaller plastic bags (for the treasure); an Ordnance Survey map of the area; a pencil; a long screwdriver; spare batteries for the detector; a sharp knife or trowel.

The three golden rules of operation are:

(1) *Keep the head of the machine as close and as parallel to the ground as possible.*
(2) *Search diligently and thoroughly over the ground.*
(3) *Search slowly.*

To search an area of ground thoroughly it is necessary to be systematic in the way the detector is used. Instead of a haphazard random swing of the detector head here there and everywhere, aim to go from side to side snake-fashion moving ahead about 3 inches (76 mm) at a time. Searching, say, a path, this way is easy because the sides of the path will be the boundary of each swing of the detector. When searching larger areas such as a field, it will be helpful to mark out a strip 3 yards (3 m) wide with string lines.

Once a strong signal is picked up, locate the area exactly. This will be where the detector gives out the strongest signal. Then dig neatly into the ground with the sharp knife or trowel and remove the object. If the area is covered in grass, use the sharp knife to cut the turf which can then be replaced once the hole is refilled.

It will be beneficial to jot down in a notebook exactly where each find is made or better still, to mark the spot on a sketch map of the area. This may be useful when searching sites with a similar environmental history, and it is important when reporting a find to the local museum.

Areas to Search

Certain areas in parks, woodlands, and open spaces are more likely to harbour treasure than others. Knowing what to look for and concentrating on these areas first will save untold wasted labour.

1. *Beneath old trees:* People sit beneath trees and the older the tree the more likely the chance of finding antique coins and objects. Search in close concentric circles from the trunk outwards.
2. *Beauty spots and prominent places:* A rewarding source of treasure.
3. *Grassy slopes:* At the foot of grassy slopes there may be any number of coins and jewellery which have tumbled down over the years.
4. *Secluded areas:* Try searching areas frequented by courting couples, and other secret beauty areas.

Beachcombing and Buried Treasure

The seashore has long been a great source of treasure of all kinds; from that washed ashore from shipwrecks, to the thousands of valuables lost each year by holidaymakers. In fact, the beaches in and around our coastline provide the biggest bonanza of finds for the seasoned treasure seeker.

Although a detector will not be necessary for simple beachcombing, it will be extremely useful for searching eddy pools and other areas of the beach which, though not showing any visible signs of treasure, may well have valuables buried in the sand or shingle.

A spade, a trowel, and a sand sifter (see under sand sifting) are all useful tools for beach hunting. And obviously, the major coast resorts will provide the most generous amounts of finds.

As with inland searches, knowing where to look can save valuable time. In this case, a knowledge of the tidal movements and the make-up of the shoreline will be most beneficial.

The Tides

Every beach is more or less subjected to tidal movement, not only in-shore, but in one particular direction up or down the beach. This latter movement is known as 'tidal' or 'long-shore drift'. The direction of tidal drift on individual beaches will vary considerably but the general directions for the country as a whole are as follows:

South Coast: From West to East
West Coast: From South to North
East Coast: From North to South

A knowledge of tidal drift is important because the tide is continually lifting up and depositing sand, pebbles and anything else on the sea bed, along the high-tide line and in the direction of its drift. Any obstructions such as breakers and groynes will have a build-up of material on the tidal side and this will be an invaluable source of treasure.

While on the subject, it must be said that the most rewarding time to visit the shoreline is during the winter months; the reason being that the weather during this time is fiercer than during the rest of the year and the waves and breakers bigger and more powerful as a direct result. Powerful breakers churn up the sand and shingle and may release buried objects that the milder tides and waves haven't disturbed during

the summer. Violent storms will be especially good; so check with the local coastguard station for weather forecasts and try to explore as soon after the gales have subsided as possible.

Currents and the Beach

Apart from the action of the waves and breakers and the tidal drift, there is one other important factor determining the most likely areas for finding treasure. This is the various eddy currents working in the water which cause objects to be lifted up from the sea bed and deposited in certain areas unaffected by tidal drift. A close scrutiny of the shoreline between high and low watermarks will provide useful clues. Look out for isolated patches of shingle on otherwise sandy beaches as these are likely to be areas where the currents have weakened and deposited any material carried in the water. Look out, too, for shallow pools of water left exposed by the retreating tide and search thoroughly with the detector.

Sand Sifting

On dry sandy beaches where hundreds of holiday revellers have spent the day frolicking around, there will be untold valuables lying in the top 3 inches (76 mm) of sand. By skimming the surface with a sand sifter, these valuables can be easily retrieved. A sand sifter is very easy to make. It consists of nothing else but a broom stick on which one end is fixed a rectangular wooden frame three feet wide by one foot deep over which wire netting (e.g. chicken-wire) has been stretched. Use the sifter systematically in the same way as a detector when searching the beach.

Shipwrecks

Literally thousands of ships have been wrecked in the treacherous waters around our coasts. Many of these ships carried only coal, wood, food and other basic provisions, but there were more than a few which carried great cargoes of treasure which has never been recovered. In recent times, well-known wrecks have been searched by professional divers but there are countless unmarked wrecks that can still provide rich rewards for the sharp-eyed and diligent treasure seekers. The sea will continue to pound the seabed littered with wrecks, and so any

Lynne opened the cash-box to disclose the hoard of glittering gold coins. "So the legend was true!" Bert Blane exclaimed.

I'M SICK OF THIS! I WISH I WERE ON A DESERT ISLAND!

unexpected finds of really old coins or valuables on the beach may well provide a clue to greater finds in the vicinity. But the same constraints on underwater finds of historic interest apply as for dry-land archaeology.

Treasure from River, Stream and Canal Banks

Next to the beach, the banks of rivers, streams and canals are the finest source of treasure. Right from earliest times, valuable cargoes have been transported on the waterways, some of which found their way into the water through accident or design. Not only that, but the waterways have been used as a dumping ground for 'rubbish' – rubbish such as pottery, buttons, bottles, pipes and other relics which are now regarded as antiques.

Precautions

Searching the riverbanks and water's edge is not dangerous provided common sense prevails and the following rules are adhered to:

1) Don't venture into deep water. Most finds occur on the riverbanks and in shallow water.

2) Don't venture into the river until the riverbed has been tested with a rake or stick.

3) Don't walk into the water at one point and come out at another – always enter and leave the water at the same spot.

4) Don't walk along in the water parallel with the river bank.

Equipment

Apart from a water-submersible detector, other essential equipment will be a stout rake for the river bed and mud banks, a spade, a trowel, and a pair of waders. Plastic bags will also be required for the finds.

Where to Search

Certain points along the riversides are more likely to produce finds than others. These will depend on areas of human proximity and eddy currents in the water. Bridges, fords, landing places, piers, staithes, steps and other points along a river which people frequent will provide a rich source of finds. Coins are always being thrown into the water from bridges – apart from the valuables lost by accident. A thorough search of the riverbanks in the vicinity of such areas will prove fruitful, but there are other factors at work which need to be understood. These are the eddy currents which are caused by obstructions and imperfections on the riverbed. Eddy currents can affect the final resting place of coins and other valuables that are lost or thrown into the water. Watch out for points along the river where pebbles and debris have been deposited. It is a fair bet that amongst them will be objects of value.

Another likely place is on the inner bend of a fast flowing river or stream immediately below a bridge or other human meeting place. On such a bend, the flow of water will strike the outer bank and leave the inner bank exposed. Here on the exposed shingle or mud objects of value will often be deposited.

Treasure from Houses

There are three principal sources of treasure to be found in old houses and other dwellings from which some people have discovered small fortunes: lost valuables, hoards, and antiques.

LOST VALUABLES

Consider how much money passes through your own house over a period of, say, ten years and you can see how easy it can be for some of it to 'disappear'. Jewellery and other valuables can be apparently lost and never found again by the owners, yet the knowledgeable treasure seeker can discover them many years later by knowing exactly where to look.

The first area to search, whether in your own house or in an old property, is down the backs of armchairs and settees. It has been estimated that the average three-piece suite will contain ten coins. If the furniture is old there is a good chance of finding antique coins or rings. A careful search of the backs of chairs will probably prove the point. Whatever happens, don't turn the furniture upside down as the valuables may become trapped in the springs and become impossible to retrieve without damage to the upholstery.

Another likely place is the gap between the skirting boards and floorboards, especially near the entrances to the house where money has been used to pay the milkman etc., and where coats have been hung. For this purpose, a piece of wire bent into an L shape is the best tool for searches. Any coins lying in the gaps can be carefully hooked out, avoiding knocking the coins further back and off the ends of the floorboards.

One seemingly unlikely source of coins is the locks on doors of Victorian houses. Children have a habit of poking objects in secret places and coins poked into the keyholes are no exception. By removing the backing plate, any coins lying inside can easily be removed.

Finally, check any waste sump beneath the sinks. It is surprising how easy it is for rings to fall down the plug hole and get trapped there.

TREASURE HOARDS

Before the use of banks became widely available to the population as a whole, ordinary people kept their money and all their worldly possessions tucked away in their own homes or buried in their gardens. This way their valuables were kept relatively safe from looters and thieves. As often happened, however, people died and left no indication as to where they 'hoarded' their wealth. And so it remains there to this day; hidden away out of sight and out of mind.

Some quite spectacular hoards have been discovered by treasure hunters in recent years who have coupled their knowledge of where to look in a house with the skilful use of a detector. And some of these hoards were found in the treasure hunters' own homes! So to begin with, if your house has had more than one owner, start with a search of your own home.

Here is a list of likely places where hoards may be hidden.

(1) Inside any old crockery left behind from the previous owner.

(2) Inside mattresses or seats. Look out for any new or different stitching, e.g. the use of different colour threads.

(3) In the loft. Thoroughly search beams and rafters for money boxes tied or screwed down. Look inside the water tank for submerged boxes. Look underneath felting, between joists and in all the nooks and crannies.

(4) Up the chimney breast. Use a chimney broom or stick to probe around.

(5) Under the stairs.

(6) Behind cupboards. Check for false backs and bottoms.

(7) In cellars outside dwellings.

(8) Beneath floorboards, in pipework, and behind faulty brickwork. Use a detector for this purpose, which will otherwise mean tearing the house to pieces.

(9) Beneath steps, especially those leading from back doors.

(10) In the garden. Use the detector to systematically search the whole garden area.

It can often prove useful to find out about the previous owners of the house from neighbours and other people in the neighbourhood old enough to know the history of the house. The knowledge of a sudden death, of previous eccentric householders, or of suspect criminal tenants, may indicate the possibility of a hoard.

ANTIQUES

Those wonderful tales of people who discover Rembrandts in their attics are certainly not fairy stories. I know personally of someone whose granny had a Ming vase on her Welsh dresser for most of her life without ever knowing what it was! So a thorough check of every relic and 'antique' object, including old pictures and crockery that is around the house or stashed away in the loft or attic, is more than worthwhile. You just never know! If in doubt as to the value of an article, a local antique dealer can help. Beware, however, of sharks in the business. Go to a reputable dealer who is guaranteed to tell you precisely the value of the object in question. *You may have to pay for this service.*

DUMP DIGGING

Without a doubt, this has become the most popular and widespread branch of the treasure hunt boom in recent years. So popular, in fact, there is now a British Bottle Collectors Club to serve the interest of the 'bottle buffs' who dig the many Victorian rubbish dumps and sites for beautiful pot lids, bottles, jars and pipes, often to be found in their hundreds. Market stalls and antique shops are doing a roaring trade in all this dump-ware and what was once thrown away as rubbish is now adorning mantelpieces and windowsills as *objets d'art* in homes all over the country.

Where to Look

Remembering that bottles, pot lids and pipes were yesterday's throwaways, it is to the ancient rubbish sites, tips, and dumping grounds that the collector must go. These are the likely places to search but please remember – *ask permission beforehand.*

RUBBISH TIPS

Old municipal refuse tips are probably the prime source of all relics found each year. Vast amounts lie buried just beneath the surface of the soil in most instances and only require digging out. Where to track down these sites is discussed later.

QUARRIES

Chalk pits, mining excavations and quarries of the Victorian era that have been filled in are most likely to contain tons of rubbish. The smaller quarries are the ones to search because they will not be still in use and therefore covered by a layer of modern rubbish.

LAND RECLAMATIONS

Marshland and other low-lying waterlogged sites were reclaimed by disposing domestic rubbish on them to form a solid foundation for factories and other industrial works, parks, civic projects, etc.

CLIFFS

Where the coastline suffered from erosion, the authorities dumped rubbish over the cliff tops to help stem the decline.

DEMOLITION SITES

Any nineteenth-century and Victorian building(s) being demolished may yield some fine bottles. Likely places will be under the floor boards on the ground floor, cellars, and out buildings.

BREWERIES AND GLASSWORKS

Check out the grounds of any Victorian breweries or glassworks. Even if the buildings are no longer standing there may well be many bottles buried on the site.

WASTE INDUSTRIAL LAND

Old factory sites and other industrial land are well worth investigating, as buildings were often constructed on 'rubbish' foundations.

ALLOTMENTS

It was a common practice to convert rubbish tips into allotments. This is why old bottles and other relics can often be discovered around the perimeter of allotments, discarded by the gardeners who have dug them up.

TOWN GARDENS

Town gardens were often dumping grounds for rubbish in the Victorian era. It is more than

likely that your own garden may be harbouring some fine specimens of Victorian bric-à-brac.

RIVERS
As with coinshooting, the river can be a treasure house for the bottle buff. Investigate the riverbanks in exactly the same way.

CANALS
A good source, especially by locks, canal pubs and landing places.

VILLAGE PONDS
It is a fact that hundreds of village ponds have 'disappeared' in recent years. They have dried up or become neglected or filled in. Most of them will contain all sorts of treasures. A friend of mine has recently recovered not only some fine bottles and pot lids, but also a beautiful array of ornate brass knobs, knockers and locks! Fish ponds and farm ponds are worth investigating too.

TIDAL SITES
The estuaries of tidal rivers can provide exciting treasure hunting. It is advisable to check the times of the tides beforehand, either from local people or the local port or river authority.

Researching Sites
Knowing that bottles can be found in rubbish tips is one thing, but where do you find the tips? This is not so difficult and it is surprising just how many there are, even close to home. Here are a few suggestions:

TOWN HALLS
A visit to the local Town Planning Department will provide many clues. Look in the Planning Register which will provide a record of all construction and demolition work carried out in the district. It will provide details of the nature of work being executed, what is being built and who are the contractors.

LIBRARIES
The local library should contain records of local history. Here may be found details of local industries and maps of the areas earmarked as refuse sites. Look out for clues leading to the whereabouts of bottleworks etc.

NEWSPAPERS
There is a good chance that the local newspaper may date back to the Victorian era. Even if it doesn't there may well have been another in print at the time, the records of which will be in the local library. By studying these old newspapers, all manner of local information can be gleaned, such as proposals for opening or closing rubbish dumps, proposals for recreation grounds, and opening or closing industries. Look out for articles concerning any unauthorized dumping. Compare topographical photographs with the present-day landscape and make a note of any change in the landscape, such as the disappearance of depressions, slopes or even valleys.

OLD PEOPLE
A kindly word to one or two of the elderly people in the area may provide valuable information. They may know of rubbish dumps that were in existence and may even be able to help with identification of finds.

BOTTLES AND RELICS PUBLICATIONS
The various issues of *Bottles and Relics Quarterly* are a mine of information. Issue No. 1 (series 4) for instance contains a complete list of Victorian potteries and glassworks and their addresses! See bibliography at end of book.

Tools
The essential tool for dump-digging is a narrow-pronged garden fork; no bottle buff can seriously search without one. Also required is something suitable for transporting the finds back home. Sacks are ideal providing each bottle or relic is individually wrapped in newspaper to prevent breakage.

A useful tool is a probe-rod. This can be made from a length of half-inch (13-mm) diameter steel rod. Cut one piece about 4 feet (1219 mm) long and another 1 foot (305 mm) long and weld or tap and screw one end of the long piece to the middle of the shorter piece; the shorter being used as a handle. Sharpen the other end of the long piece. A probe-rod is useful for driving into the ground to locate bottles, lids etc.; the sharp point of the steel making a distinctive noise on contact with china or glass.

Two other useful tools are a pick and shovel for difficult sites where there is a lot of brick and rubble.

Cleaning and Restoration
Many specimens may be found that will only require a thorough wash and scrub in soapy water to restore them to their original condition. There will, however, be just as many that will be heavily coated with iron stain and these will need special attention.

EQUIPMENT AND MATERIALS
You will need:
   A bath, sink or some other large receptacle.
   Two plastic buckets
   Builder's sand
   Washing soda
   Rubber gloves

METHOD
Allow at least 24 hours from when the bottles were dug up to cleaning. This will give the bottles time to acclimatize to their new atmospheric conditions.

Add 1 lb (454 g) soda to the bath half-filled with cold water. Add 1 lb (454 g) soda to a bucketful of cold water. Fill the other bucket with clean cold water. Take each bottle and fill up with the soda solution from the bucket and then place in the bath. Allow to soak for 2–3 days and then thoroughly rinse in cold water. Severely stained bottles may need further treatment. This should consist of grinding the bottles by the neck in a bucketful of sand. Rotate continuously until the abrasive action of the sand has worn away the stains.

To remove internal stains, half fill the bottles with gravel and a little water and with a thumb over the top, shake thoroughly for a few minutes. Severe internal iron stains can be removed with rust remover sold in hardware shops.

To remove chemical stains from medical bottles, soak for a week or more in soda. If this fails, soak in a weak acid solution. Vinegar can be helpful but a really excellent treatment is soaking them in the juice strained from freshly boiled rhubarb. Household bleach is also effective. If certain stains remain after the various treatments, *do not use an abrasive*. It is

better to leave them on the glass than to spoil the bottles. This is especially so with 'iridescence', a rainbow-coloured stain which is very difficult to remove.

Bottle brushes are a must for any bottle-cleaning work. They come in various shapes and sizes and the serious collector can make his own. Old toothbrushes are ideal for this job.

Once the bottles are clean they will look ten times better if given a polish. This is done with a piece of felt dampened with water, and cerium oxide powder (available from chemists or lapidary shops). Place a little of the powder on a damp cloth and apply to the bottles using small circular movements. Rinse under a cold tap.

Identification

Unfortunately, space doesn't allow an identification section because the range of bottles, pot lids, pipes and other relics is vast. The reader is advised to refer to the bibliography at the end of the book, where there are books listed which specialize in this subject.

Selling

The market stall has proved to be a favourite selling point for dump-ware. The cost of renting stalls is still very reasonable and hiring one for an evening or one day a week can be a good beginning for those interested in starting up a business.

The type of market is important. Avoid the expensive antique-type affairs and instead try to set up a stall in a junk market which offers a wider range of goods. Avoid selling uncleaned, cracked and damaged specimens.

Pricing is always a thorny problem as the market is subject to constant change. The British Bottle Collectors Club will give up-to-the-minute information of the types of bottle most in demand. Otherwise refer to the columns of *Exchange & Mart* or enquire at other stalls for current prices.

*Crystal is ice through countless ages grown
(so teach the wise) to hard transparent stone:
And still the gem retains its native force,
And holds the cold and colour of its source.
Yet some deny, and tell of crystal found
Where never icy winter froze the ground.*

MARBODUS

A 'ROCKHOUND' is not a marble statue of a dog as the term might suggest but the definitive title given to someone who collects semi-precious gemstones, crystals and ornamental pebbles as a hobby. 'Rockhounding' and in particular pebble hunting, has become enormously popular in recent years and it is not hard to see why. It involves an open-air activity by the sea, stream, river, or on hills and mountains, which is a pleasure in itself, and the materials are there free for the taking. Added to this there is the lapidary aspect whereby polishing and maybe cutting the pebbles at home will transform them into gems; as articles of beauty in themselves, or used for pendants and jewellery.

Types of Rock

In order to recognize the many different types of pebbles and gemstones to be found in and around the British Isles it will be helpful to have a basic knowledge of the various rock formations from which all ornamental, precious and semi-precious stones have been formed.

IGNEOUS ROCKS

This class of rock provides the widest variety of gems. They were formed millions of years ago through intense heat, solidifying from the molten substances in the earth's core. Igneous rocks consist of two distinct forms:

a) *Volcanic* – i.e. extrusive rocks – formed when molten lava erupted through volcanic action and was quickly cooled. Most of these rocks consist of fine-grained *basalt* (black, dark green, dark brown, dark grey).

b) *Plutonic* – i.e. intrusive rocks – formed when molten material was thrust up from the earth's core but found its way into other rocks near the surface, cooling slowly beneath the ground. Most of these coarse-grained rocks consist of granite, which is itself made up of *quartz* (pure silica), *felspar*

(white) and *mica* (black).

Other forms of plutonic rocks are *Dolerite* (felspar and augite) – formed in dykes and sills between other rocks; *Diorite* – resembling granite (dark grey with a white and green mottled effect); *Gabbro* (felspar, augite and olivine) – dark-coloured, containing green, grey and black crystals; *Syenite* – resembling granite (grey or reddish in colour); *Andesite* – fine-grained and lighter in colour than basalt.

SEDIMENTARY ROCKS

These consist of particles of rocks and organic material that were washed down from the land surface and deposited into lakes or the sea. Over a long period of time the particles compressed into a solid mass and so formed new rock formations. Sedimentary rocks consist of three distinct groups:

(a) *Sandstones and Grits* – consisting wholly of sand grains, of which there are a number of different types varying in composition and hardness. The sand grains are mostly quartz particles. Grits refer to the more coarsely grained sandstones such as *Millstone Grit*, the most familiar, which is widely used for millstones and sandstones. One category of sandstone rocks is the *Conglomerates* or pudding-stone. These are multi-coloured or opaque and comprise fragments of rocks cemented together by other materials.

(b) *Limestones* – formed from the skeletons of sea creatures which sank to the bottom of the sea and became compressed by their own weight.

(c) *Slates and Shales* – formed from clay. Shale is compressed clay, a laminated rock made up of thin layers which were laid down where rivers meet the sea. Slate is extensively compressed shale found in mountainous districts and contains minute flakes of mica and other materials.

METAMORPHIC ROCKS

These rocks were all originally very ancient sedimentary or igneous forms which became transformed into new structures through the action of intense heat or pressure. The three most familiar groups are:

(a) *Schist* – usually made up of quartz and

mica and consisting of a great many planes which are formed in flakes. The arrangement of the quartz and mica crystals in schist is in streaks or bands and this is called foliation.

(b) *Gneiss* – a highly foliated coarse-grained crystalline rock comprising quartz, felspar and mica.

(c) *Marble* – a metamorphosed limestone.

Recognition of Decorative Pebbles

The following list, though by no means complete, will be a comprehensive guide to the many beautiful and exciting gems and stones that can be found by the enterprising rockhound.

AGATES

Mostly almond-shaped, these come from rocks formed from silica solutions that cooled in steam and gas cavities. They have defined banding when cut. *Colour* – white, yellow, brown, black and blue. There are five principal groups of agates: *Banded agate* – having parallel bands of colour across the surface; *Eyed agate* – having bands in concentric rings; *Fortification agate* – having angular bands; *Onyx* – having straight and alternating bands of colour; *Sardonyx* – having brown, red, or white bands. *Location* – beaches between Porthleven and Newlyn, Cornwall; beaches between Clevedon and Portishead, Avon; the beach at Fleswick Bay, Isle of Man and near Whitehaven, Cumbria.

AMBER

Theoretically not a stone but fossilized resin. Originally, liquid amber exuded from pine trees and became solidified with insects and other organic life over a great period of time. *Colour* – pale yellow to deep orange. *Location* – beaches between Yorkshire and Essex, especially Aldeburgh, Cromer, Felixstowe, Southwold and Yarmouth.

AMETHYST

Transparent rock-crystal quartz (i.e. crystallized silica), formed in granite, where large crystals formed in vein cavities or 'druses'. *Colour* – usually purple, violet or green. *Location* – beaches on Scotland's east coast; the north-east coast of England; Cornwall; Old Mines at Mwyndy and Garth Ward, Dyfed.

ANDALUSITE

Cube-shaped crystals formed in metamorphic

aureoles (i.e. the perimeter of igneous rocks). *Colour* – pink, red, yellow, brown or dark green. *Location* – Cumbria and Durham.

APATITE
Formed in gabbro or near ore-bearing lodes (i.e. deposits of valuable minerals that have solidified in extrusive rocks). *Colour* – mainly green, sometimes blue, yellow or earthy red. *Location* – tips and spoil heaps in and around abandoned Cornish tin mines; and Knoweston, Powys.

AZURITE
Consisting of a blue carbonate of copper normally found in grape-like formations, encrusted on rocks or bordering ore-bearing lodes. *Colour* – azure blue. *Location* – Dolgellau, Gwynedd; Snowdonia; spoil heaps of disused copper mines in Cumbria; Cornwall; Cheshire; and Lancashire.

BERYL
Long hexagonal crystals found in granite druses in vein formation. *Colour* – blue, yellow or green. *Location* – Devon, Cornwall, Arran, Cairngorm Mountains; Mourne Mountains.

BLOODSTONE
Sometimes called Heliotrope, a variety of jasper. *Colour* – rich green with mottled ice spots. *Location* – rare but widespread.

CAIRNGORM
Rock-crystal quartz sometimes known as Smoky Quartz formed in the Cairngorm Mountains in Scotland. *Colour* – yellow, deep orange to smoky brown. *Location* – Cairngorm Mountains; Scottish and eastern England beaches.

CALCITE
Crystals formed in gangues (i.e. minerals immediately surrounding ore-bearing lodes). *Colour* – colourless or white. *Location* – North Yorkshire; Cornwall; and Gwynedd.

CARNELIAN
Formerly known as Cornelian, and a variety of quartz. *Colour* – translucent, mostly flesh pink, but also yellow, brown, or red. *Location* – beaches at Felixstowe; Cromer; Essex; beaches at Deal, Kent; beaches on the Isle of Wight; Yorkshire; Suffolk; Cumbria; and Arran.

CASSITERITE
Tin oxide found in gangues surrounding ore-bearing lodes in granite. *Colour* – red-brown to black. *Location* – tips and spoil heaps of disused Cornish tin mines.

CHALCEDONY
A non-crystalline translucent quartz cemented together by opal (hydrated silica) and found in grape-like clusters (botryoidal) that originally formed in cavities of igneous rocks. *Colour* – pale brown or blue-grey. *Location* – beaches between Porthleven and Newlyn, Cornwall; beaches in Cumbria; Arran; the Scottish coast and on the eastern and southern coasts of England.

CHERT
Non-crystalline silica, similar to flint, and occurring in limestone. *Colour* – grey, brown or black. *Location* – southern and western beaches of England.

CITRINE
Yellow quartz sometimes known as Scotch Topaz, and similar to amethyst in form. *Colour* – lemon to golden yellow. *Location* – beaches between Porthleven and Newlyn, Cornwall.

CLEAR QUARTZ
Clear six-sided rock quartz, pyramid-shaped at each end. *Colour* – colourless. *Location* – rare on southern and Cornish coasts.

CONGLOMERATES
Usually rounded fragments of rock cemented together and the surviving sections of ancient beaches. *Colour* – multicoloured and/or opaque. *Location* – widespread on ancient beaches.

EPIDOTE
Elongated pencil-like crystals formed in igneous rock formations. *Colour* – yellow, brown, bluey-green, dark green. *Location* – Gwynedd; and Cornwall.

FELSPAR
Occurs in plutonic rocks, especially in granite. *Colour* – dull white. *Location* – Builth Wells and Llandrindod Wells, Powys; Criccieth Castle, near Portmadoc, Gwynedd.

FLUORITE
Cuboid crystals found in gangues surrounding ore-bearing lodes and in metamorphic aureoles. *Colour* – yellow, green, blue, violet. *Location* – Derbyshire; Durham; Cumbria; Minera, Halkyn Mountain, Pen-y-Bryn and Coed Cymric, Wales.

GARNET
Multi-faceted crystals found in metamorphic aureoles or granite formations. *Colour* – mainly red, otherwise yellow, green, brown. *Location* –

northern Scotland; Fifeshire; Cumbria; and Devon.

GRANITE
Formed from quartz, felspar and mica. *Colour* – various shades of grey. *Location* – Dartmoor; the Cornish Peninsula; Mourne Mountains; Cumbria; Scottish Highlands; and Wales.

HAEMATITE
Otherwise known as Kidney-ore, referring to its distinctive kidney-shape formations. Found throughout igneous rocks, usually in gangues surrounding ore-bearing lodes. *Colour* – red to brown. *Location* – Cumbria.

JASPER
An opaque type of quartz formed from an admixture of clay materials in silica. *Colour* – dull red, brown, or yellowish green. *Location* – beaches around Felixstowe, Suffolk; beaches on the east coast of the Isle of Wight; beaches between Porthleven and Newlyn, Cornwall; beaches at Llanddwyn Island and Newborough Warren, Anglesey; most beaches in Scotland; and Northern Ireland.

JET
An organic ornamental stone, closely related to coal, being wood that has fossilized in rock into which the mud on the sea bed has slowly transformed. *Colour* – glossy black or brownish black. *Location* – only from cliffs and nearby dales at Whitby, on the Yorkshire coast.

LABRADORITE
Usually found in basalt and similar in its reflection of colours to opal. *Colour* – yellow, green, pale blue. *Location* – Derbyshire; Co. Antrim.

MALACHITE
Similar to azurite but instead a green carbonate of copper. *Colour* – various shades of green. *Location* – tips and spoil heaps of disused copper mines. Mainly in Cumbria, Cheshire, Cornwall, Derbyshire, Durham, Lancashire and North Wales.

NATROLITE
Elongated cuboid crystals, pyramid-topped, usually found in basalts. *Colour* – yellow, pink or white. *Location* – Staffordshire; Strathclyde; and Northern Ireland.

OBSIDIAN
The most familiar form of natural glass, formed by the rapid cooling of silica-rich lava. *Colour* – mostly black, otherwise dark grey, red or yellow

OLIVINE

Found in basalts and other plutonic rock formations. *Colour* – olive green to bright green, otherwise brown. *Location* – Co. Antrim; Derbyshire; and Lothian.

ONYX

Similar to banded agate but much rarer and once highly favoured for cameo work, *Colour* – black and white stripes, otherwise white and various graduations of grey.

OPAL

Formed from a very fine mixture of tiny crystals of silica and minute droplets of water; usually found in basalts and lava formations. *Colour* – a distinctive 'pearl' sheen reflecting a multitude of colours. *Location* – Devon; Co. Antrim; Co. Tyrone; and Highland.

PORPHYRITIC PEBBLES

Formed from a variety of rock formations including perfect crystals of felspar and quartz. *Colour* – grey to pink.

PREHNITE

Usually found in botryoidal formations, formed in cavities in extrusive lava flows. *Colour* – white, yellow, green. *Location* – Strathclyde; Isle of Skye; and Northern Ireland.

QUARTZ

Formed from solid silica and one of the commonest minerals on earth. There are a number of quartz types: *Milky quartz* – translucent white or creamy yellow; *Banded crystalline quartz* – multicoloured bands or patterns of white to light brown; *Rose-quartz* – an opaque quartz coloured pink; *White quartz* – found in Slapton Ley lagoon, Devon; *Smoky quartz* (see Cairngorm); *Agate, Carnelian, Onyx* and *Sard* – a translucent brown quartz similar to chalcedony. *Location* – beaches around Felixstowe, Suffolk; beaches at Sandwich and Deal, Kent; beaches around Beachy Head, East Sussex; beaches on the east coast of the Isle of Wight; beaches in south and north Devon and Cornwall; beaches in Gwynedd; beaches at Colwyn Bay.

QUARTZ BRECCIA

Consists of angular pieces of rock cemented together with silica. *Colour* – multicoloured and opaque. *Location* – similar areas to quartz.

QUARTZITE

A hard sandstone composed of quartz grains cemented together with silica. *Colour* – white,

yellow, brown sometimes patterned blue or purple. *Location* – Llandudno; and beaches around Milford Haven.

RHODONITE

A manganese silicate found mostly in gangues surrounding ore-bearing lodes in granite. *Colour* – waxy or pearly lustres of pink and red, sometimes with shading. *Location* – Devon; Cornwall; and Strathclyde.

SARD

A variety of carnelian but harder and richer in colour and form. *Colour* – brown, red, and dark pink. *Location* – beaches at Sandwich and Deal, Kent.

SARDONYX

A combination of sard and onyx and very rare. *Colour* – parallel bands of white with red or brown.

SPHENE

Tubular or wedge-shaped crystals found in diorite and granite. *Colour* – a lustrous brown, green, yellow or black. *Location* – Grampian; Dyfed; and Builth Wells and Llandrindod Wells, Powys.

SPINEL

Occurs in metamorphic aureoles and other intrusive igneous formations. *Colour* – red, brown and blue. *Location* – the Hebrides; the Cairngorm Mountains; Cornwall.

SYENITE

A coarse-grained rock similar to granite. *Colour* – darker than granite, with a red or grey hue. *Location* – Gwynedd; and Ireland.

TOPAZ

Multifaceted crystals with flattened pyramid tops found in gangues surrounding ore-bearing lodes in granite. *Colour* – yellow. *Location* – Arran; Highland; Grampian; Lewis; Cairngorm Mountains; and Cornwall.

TOURMALINE

Long prismatic crystals found in metamorphic aureoles in granite. *Colour* – red, dark green, dark blue, brown, black. *Location* – Highland; Tayside; Devon; and Cornwall.

ZIRCON

Occurs in granite rocks. *Colour* – lustrous red, pale green, pale yellow or colourless. *Location* – Highland and Fifeshire.

Where to Search

Pebble beaches are widely distributed around

the coasts of Britain so there will be little trouble for most people in getting to a pebble-hunting area. There are, however, certain stretches of coastline which are more favourable than others.

Generally speaking the best areas are:

(a) Beaches along the northern coast of Scotland.

(b) Beaches along the Fifeshire coast.

(c) Beaches along the old Ayrshire coast.

(d) Beaches around Anglesey, north Wales.

(e) Beaches along the west coast of Cornwall.

(f) Beaches along the North Yorkshire coast.

(g) Beaches along the Suffolk coast.

(h) Beaches along the Norfolk coast.

Which Part of the Beach?

In the chapter on treasure hunting, the phenomenon of tidal or longshore drift was discussed. It was on the areas of the beach where the drift deposited debris that treasure was most likely to be found. The same goes for the best pebbles.

Equipment

Rockhounding at the simplest level, i.e. pebble hunting, requires a minimum of equipment. This should consist of:

(a) A penknife with one good strong blade. This is for scraping the surface of pebbles to determine their hardness, and to remove their 'skin'.

(b) A small hammer with a heavy head. Special geological hammers can be bought from rock shops and some good hardware stores. This is needed for fracturing pebbles to determine their structure. NEVER crash stones one against another – fragments may fly off and blind you or anyone else nearby.

(c) A good pocket lens for close observation of crystalline and grain structure.

(d) A piece of sharp-edged flint. This is for testing extra hard rocks that the penknife will not scratch.

(e) A bag or rucksack to carry the equipment and pebbles.

Useful but not essential is a geological map of the area in question. This will reveal at a glance the nature of the rocks and soil.

Safety

Three points to watch out for on the beach.

Beware of being cut off by the tide should the search take you out to headlands or promontories. Beware of falling rocks from cliffs – check up beforehand about any dangerous stretches of coastline. Beware of quicksands. Inland, the dangers are more abundant. Rock climbing of any sort requires a respectful attitude for the terrain and sheer common sense. Confine rockhounding activities to the summer months if possible. Be extra careful when searching disued mine spoil heaps.

Rules and Regulations

Remember to obtain permission from any landowner whose land is intended for searching. Special permission may be required for searching old mine spoil heaps and quarries.

PEBBLE POLISHING

Any pebble, no matter how ordinary, can look beautiful when polished. This is how it's done.

Selecting the Right Pebbles

A single beach may comprise millions of pebbles from which the rockhound must select but a few to take home. Knowing exactly what to look for comes with practice, and of course personal taste is important, but there are certain rules which apply where selection is concerned, especially where the pebbles are intended for polishing in a tumble machine.

(a) *Size:* Most tumble polishers accept only a small size-range of pebbles. Aim, therefore, to collect pebbles from about the size of a fingernail to the length of the little finger.

(b) *Shape:* For jewellery-making, look for those pebbles which have a pleasing shape. Those which will be most useful are the spherical, ovoid and flat disc pebbles. Avoid really odd shapes for the tumble polisher.

(c) *Quantity:* Unknown to many, there are restrictions on lots of beaches on removing large quantities of pebbles. Shingle is a natural barrier against erosion by the sea and removing sackloads of pebbles can get you into trouble. Try not to be seduced by the sheer volume of beautiful pebbles, and just take a few at a time.

(d) *Quality:* For tumbling purposes there are certain types of pebble that will not polish successfully. These will be mostly pebbles which are too soft to withstand the abrasive action in the tumble machine and can be identified into one of the following groups:

(1) *Flaky pebbles* – made up of parallel layers of material which can easily be pulled apart (e.g. slates, schists, and mudstone).

(2) *Porous pebbles* – usually sandstone. They remain wet longer than other pebbles and have a coarser texture.

(3) *Veined pebbles* – often very beautiful. They will be mostly sandstone and can be identified from the fact that the veins, usually of a harder material, stand out as ridges on the surface.

(4) *Granular pebbles* – usually sandstone.

(5) *Damaged and pitted pebbles* – of *any* type. Pebbles with a pitted surface will take ages to wear down in the tumble polisher. Cracked or damaged pebbles may disintegrate in the tumbler. Only collect perfect specimens.

(6) *Man-made material* – such as brick, earthenware, concrete, glass or china. The passing of time can render these materials into attractive pebbles but they are useless for polishing.

Grading the Pebbles

Pebbles of varying degrees of hardness cannot be polished together, for the obvious reason that they will require different lengths of time in the tumble polisher. Soft pebbles which must be polished separately are limestone, serpentine and marble. A good test for hardness is to scrape the surface of the pebbles with a knife. If they have a coating or 'skin' then scrape this away down to the true surface. If the knife can make an impression on the true surface, then these can be classed as soft pebbles. If the knife makes no impression then they can be classed as a hard type.

Tumble Polishing Machines

This is the most expensive angle of rockhounding. Pebbles can be polished by hand but

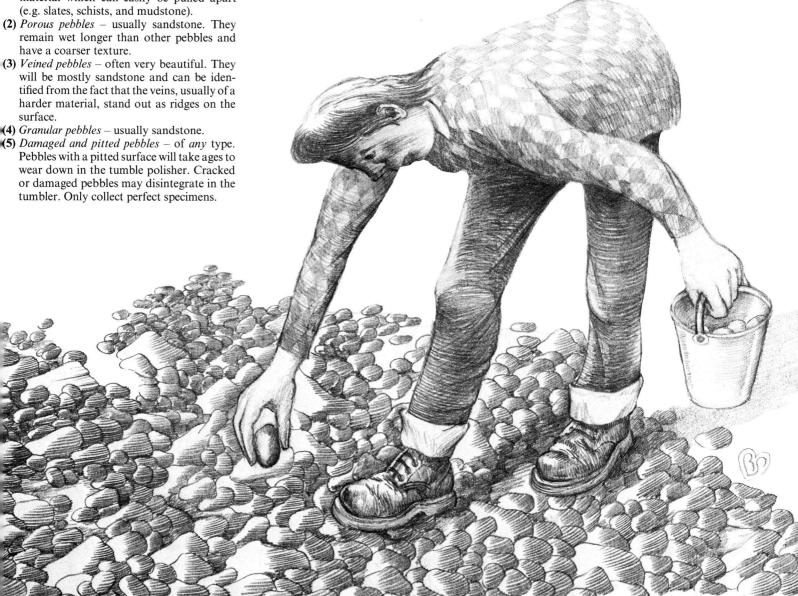

it is a very long-winded and arduous process. For those interested in serious polishing of large quantities of pebbles, a tumble polishing machine is a must. Unfortunately they will cost a few pounds – £15 will buy the very cheapest of any decent quality, and they can cost an awful lot more. However, after the initial outlay, a good machine should last almost indefinitely with care and maintenance; so it is still really a cheap hobby.

Types of Machine and How They Work

There are various types of machine on the market, all of which have special advantages and disadvantages. All of them work on the same principle, though, which is to copy nature, only on a speeded-up time scale. Rocks in the sea are pounded and pummelled by the waves on the sand until they are smoothed into pebbles. This is what happens on a miniature scale inside the tumble polisher. Pebbles, silicon carbide grits, and water are loaded into the barrel of the machine and in a matter of a week or two, the surface of the pebbles is reduced to a high-gloss finish.

There are five principal groups of polishers:

SMALL ROUND BARREL TYPE

These are the most popular machines. They consist of a round removable barrel set on its side, activated by an electric motor. The barrel must be removed from the motor rollers in order to load and empty the pebbles and abrasive materials. This type of machine comes in various sizes, usually with a barrel capacity of $1\frac{1}{2}$ lb (680 g); 3 lb (1,360 g); 6 lb (2,721 g); or 12 lb (5,443 g). The $1\frac{1}{2}$ lb machine will suit most people's needs.

HEXAGONAL BARREL TYPE

By using a hexagonal instead of a round barrel, a positive movement of pebbles is ensured which avoids the possibility of slippage and subsequent damage.

MULTI- OR TWIN-TUMBLERS

These machines have two or more barrels running simultaneously off the one motor. The obvious advantage here is the facility for tumbling hard and soft materials at the same time, each in separate barrels. Alternatively, pebbles at various stages in the polishing procedure can be tumbled at the same time, which helps save time.

CEMENT-MIXER TYPE

The one disadvantage with the previous models is that once the machines are in motion it is impossible to see what is going on without stopping the motor. The cement-mixer tumbler has the barrel mounted like a cement-mixer machine and so inspection can be carried out with the motor still in motion. This also prevents gas building up inside the barrel.

VIBRASONIC TYPE

This machine works on an entirely different principle to the other models. Instead of the barrel revolved by rollers driven from the motor, here it is vibrated at the rate of 2 to 3 dozen times per second. It has many advantages over the revolving tumblers. It eliminates fracturing and chipping which sometimes occurs with conventional tumblers. It grinds much more easily. It is ideal for 'preforms', i.e. stones of odd or irregular shape. The high-speed action reduces the polishing time from weeks to days. The one big disadvantage is cost – they are pretty expensive.

Whatever type of machine is acquired, it must fulfil certain requirements. The barrel must be tough, waterproof and easy to clean. The motor must be strong, efficient, and reliable. The pulley and drive belt or other driving mechanisms must be strong and soundly made. The rollers and bearings must be strong enough to withstand the friction of the continuously revolving barrel, and lastly, the machine must be easy to lubricate. Most of the machines available from lapidary firms will fulfil these requirements though like any other business, watch out for inferior products.

Before actually starting tumble polishing, it is essential to determine a good place in the house to position the machine. Consider the fact that it will make a certain amount of noise as it tumbles the pebbles one against another, and from the electric motor. This noise will be in evidence for days on end, so an out-of-the-way corner but near to an electric point is desirable.

Polish and Grits
Silicon carbide grit is the abrasive which is used initially in the tumble machine. It comes in various grades from coarse to fine and most tumble-polishing machine manufacturers will give instructions as to which grades should be used with their particular product. Generally, three grades of grit will be needed for each batch of pebbles. Once the pebbles have been ground down by the abrasive, a polish such as tin oxide or cerium oxide will give them a beautiful mirror-like finish.

Loading
Generally speaking, pebbles of varying shapes and sizes tumble more efficiently than those of uniform character. Each barrel load should be no more and no less then three-quarters full. Overloading will inhibit the tumbling action and underfilling will damage or ineffectively grind the pebbles.

The loading order is as follows: pebbles first, then the grit, then the water. Pebbles must be placed in the barrel gently. The amount of grit needed for each load will depend on the size of the barrel. A $1\frac{1}{2}$ lb barrel will need 1 heaped tablespoon of grit. A 3 lb barrel will need 2 heaped tablespoons, and so on. Finally, water should be added until it barely covers the top of the pebbles. Remember to ensure the barrel lid is replaced tightly.

First Grinding
Each grinding process should take approximately 4 or 5 days depending on the nature and quality of the pebbles. At the end of the first day the pebbles should be inspected to see how the process is progressing. Inspection is necessary at the end of each day following and those pebbles which have had all surface pits and blemishes worn down should be removed (leaving every pebble inside until the worst specimen is smooth may drastically reduce the size of smaller, softer specimens).

When all the pebbles are blemish-free they must be washed and the barrel thoroughly cleaned. Any traces of coarse grit left in the barrel during the following finer grinding may ruin the surface of the pebbles. (Remember to dispose of the slurry in the barrel out in the garden or dustbin and *not down the sink*.)

Second Grinding
At this stage all the pebbles must be scrutinized for any damage or surface irregularities. Those which are imperfect should be rejected. The barrel should be loaded in exactly the same way as before. Inspect the pebbles at the end of each day. At the end of the second grinding, the imperfections and scratches left behind from the coarse grit of the previous grinding should all but disappear. Again, reject any pebbles that may have become damaged as these may damage perfect specimens in the barrel.

Third Grinding
The final grinding process should render the surface of the pebbles absolutely smooth. Tiny scratches or blemishes will show up horribly after the polishing stage so any which possess imperfections should be put to one side for more grinding in a future batch. To test for surface imperfections, take a little of the polish and vigorously rub a specimen pebble on a piece of soft cloth. If the result is a gleaming mirror-like finish then the batch is ready for the final process.

Polishing
First the pebbles must be thoroughly washed. At this stage they must be handled very gently so as not to damage their surface. Likewise, the barrel of the tumbler should be scrupulously cleaned (with multi-barrelled machines, it is worth keeping one barrel exclusively for polishing). After the barrel has been loaded in the normal way – this time with the polish instead of grit – the pebbles should be inspected daily during a period of about one week. At the end of this time, each pebble will be a beautiful gem.

Washing
Because the polish deposits a film over the pebbles during the tumbling, they must be given a wash in detergent. Load the barrel and cover with water and add a half-teaspoon of detergent. After 8 hours, remove the pebbles and wash in clean running water.

Cutting and Polishing
On a final note it is worth mentioning the more advanced and sophisticated areas of lapidary, namely cutting and shaping pebbles. As this is a skilled craft in its own right, only the briefest outline is given here and the reader is advised to refer to the many suitable books on the subject in the bibliography at the end of the book and/or attend classes.

For jewellery purposes, ornamental stones often need to be cut in half, especially for earrings, cufflinks, etc. involving identical pairs. Alternatively, beautiful stones of, say, agate can be cut into thin slices called *cabochons* which reveal the patterns inside. For these purposes a rotary saw powered by an electric motor, called a *trim saw*, is used. These have diamond-tipped blades and come mounted on a cutting table to enable the operator to work with both hands free.

For polishing cabochons and other flat surfaces, an electric *lapping* unit is necessary. These machines consist of a turntable or *lap* mounted horizontally inside a bowl and capable of revolving at between 300 and 500 revolutions per minute. The cabochon is held against the lap, on which silicon carbide abrasive has been sprinkled, until a smooth surface has been achieved.

WHITE MAN TALK
WITH FORKED STICK:

THE
ART OF
DOWSING

The ends of the stick were lifting her thumbs. She fought against them, trying as hard as she could to hold them still. But the fork of the stick was dipping, dipping. Nothing could stop it. Her hands turned in spite of her. 'Titty! Titty!' They were all talking to her at once. The next moment the stick had twisted clean out of her hands. It lay on the ground, just a forked hazel twig with the green showing through the bark where Nancy's knife had trimmed it. Titty, the dowser, startled more than she could bear, and shaking with sobs, had bolted up into the woods.

FROM 'PIGEON POST' BY ARTHUR RANSOME

FOR a very long time dowsing has been looked upon by many people with much scepticism and suspicion, or simply designated under the label of the supernatural which defies logical explanation. Both these viewpoints do little justice to what is now becoming appreciated as a skill, albeit a paranormal skill, but one which is not beyond the scope of the man in the street. Indeed, the art of dowsing has undergone a considerable revival of interest of late, what with programmes on the radio, new instruction books being published, and even evening classes being held by the I.L.E.A.

Can anyone really dowse? Tom Graves, teacher, in his excellent little book *Dowsing* says that no one can teach you to dowse – 'the most anyone can do is help you to learn'. It would appear that an awareness and feel for the medium is very important, but as with any other skill, practice is the governing factor.

This chapter, then, far from being a do-it-yourself dowsing manual, is primarily an introduction; a taste of what dowsing has to offer but, it is to be hoped, enough to arouse interest and perhaps spur more people to pursue what must be one of the most intriguing and fascinating activities around.

What is Dowsing?
Most of us will probably associate dowsing with the image of a man holding a forked hazel twig in his hands, striding across some field or other in search of subterranean water which will manifest its presence by forcing the end of the stick downwards to the ground. While this image is by no means inaccurate, it is none-the-less a popular myth which has obliterated the true nature of dowsing with its far wider implications. In simplistic terms, dowsing is a method of using an implement to find the whereabouts of hidden material by a non-physical means. The dowser concentrates his mind on the subject of his search while the implement in his hands focuses the unconscious awareness of the dowser's perception of that subject.

Dowsing's most popular application is in the search for underground water supplies (i.e. artesian wells, pools, streams, etc.), but it is widely used for discovering mineral deposits such as coal, iron and precious metals. Medical dowsing, whereby the nature of an illness and the whereabouts of that illness within a patient's body is determined, is another branch of the practice. It is also used to find lost objects, to find dead bodies in police investigations, to determine the position of archaeological remains, and to find missing relatives. In fact there is no end to the practical uses to which dowsing can be applied.

The forked hazel stick is another popular myth because not only will any forked stick serve as the dowsing implement but also bent metal rods or wires, or even one long rod with a right-angle bend for holding. Alternatively, the implement can be a pendulum, which is used extensively in *map-dowsing* and other indoor techniques. One well-known British dowser uses nothing more than a pencil and a map for dowsing, preferring to visit the sites later to confirm and accurately establish his findings.

How Does it Work?
There are a number of plausible explanations of the dowsing phenomenon and many dowsers have their own ideas as to what causes their particular reaction and response to the presence of the material being searched for through the medium of the dowsing implement. Some say that it is unconscious neuro-muscular contractions which affect the stick, rod or pendulum because of the dowser's finely-tuned ability or awareness of the medium, and this subliminal ability or awareness can only make itself apparent through the dowsing implement.

Another explanation claims the dowser actually 'tunes in' to the material through his paranormal awareness of its presence. The dowser sends out a mental ray or probe which bounces back from the material and registers through the dowsing implement in a similar fashion to a radar screen and scanner. Some dowsers claim they are even able to see the material of their search.

The area of ESP (*Extra-Sensory Perception*) which is often referred to where dowsing is concerned is *directional instinct* such as that which animals and birds use to find their way back home over long distances. This instinct also includes the ability that some animals, such as those who live in the desert, have to sense the presence of water beneath the ground in seemingly unlikely places. It may be that the dowser, as with the birds and animals, unconsciously knows where water, or whatever, is located – by instinct.

The most recent explanation, however, concerns what is broadly described as *radiesthesia*. This is a dowsing term used to explain the *radiations* which, it is claimed, are given off by the materials themselves. Basically what is implied is that every substance and object gives off its own particular radiations. So the dowser, using his paranormal perception, picks up the radiations of the material he is seeking which then manifests itself through the medium of the stick, rod or pendulum.

As yet there is no really concrete or scientific explanation as to how dowsing really works. We know that it is broadly an ESP phenomenon but beyond that it is merely speculation. No doubt in time, scientists may be able to rationalize what actually happens and enlighten us all.

Dowsing Instruments

There are three main groups of dowsing instruments, classified according to the principle each uses. These are:

(1) *The Spring Rod.* This is the most traditional group and includes the forked hazel spring rod. Other instruments in this group are the bowsaw and the bucket handle.

The forked or Y-shaped spring rod can either be cut from a twig taken from a tree or hedge, or made from two pieces of springy material tied, glued, or pinned together. Although hazel is the wood most generally associated with this instrument, there are in fact many other springy and resilient woods just as suitable, such as cherry, dogwood, hawthorn, rowan and ash. Other materials sometimes used are whalebone, metal, and plastic. In fact any springy or resilient material will suffice.

The arms of the forked rod are generally about eighteen inches (457 mm) long where wooden twigs are used and between eight and eighteen inches (203–457 mm) for other types. They are all held in the hands in what is known as an *unstable tension* position due to the rod's natural springiness (i.e. with the pointed end of the fork facing outwards and the two arms of the instrument held in upturned hands). Held in this way the rod is in the neutral position and will react by the pointed end forcing itself

154

upwards, or downwards to the ground.

(2) *Angle Rods*. This group consists of metal rods bent at right angles (i.e. into an L-shape) with one long arm and a shorter arm which is used for holding (wire coat-hangers are excellent for this purpose). The dowser can work with two such rods, one held in each hand, or just the single rod. Either way, the angle rods use what is known as a *static neutral balance*. In the neutral position, the rod (or rods) point directly forwards from the dowser and react by swivelling round into a cross-over position when a pair are in operation, or to left or right with a single rod.

(3) *The Pendulum*. Perhaps the most interesting instrument, yet the least-known to the non-initiated. The pendulum consists of a weight or *bob* suspended on a piece of string or cord. There is no special significance in the nature or type of bob required apart from being more or less symmetrical in shape and weighing approximately between $\frac{1}{2}$ oz and 5 oz (14–142 g) – determined by the pendulum technique involved. Such an instrument uses what is referred to as *dynamic neutral balance*. The pendulum is held by the string between the forefinger and thumb so that between 3 and 5 inches (76–127 mm) of string and the bob are left hanging below.

The pendulum reacts by oscillating to and fro, or gyrating in either a clockwise or an anti-clockwise direction. Some dowsers keep the pendulum at rest in the neutral position while others prefer to oscillate the instrument backwards and forwards, the reaction being a change in the directional swing, or a change to gyration.

Applications

It has already been explained that the application of dowsing is not restricted to water divining. Here is a more detailed description of just some of the many purposes for which dowsing is still used.

MAP DOWSING

Many dowsers are now using this technique, which can be carried out in the comfort of their own home by moving their rods or pendulum above Ordnance Survey maps of the area being searched. The dowser concentrates on moving

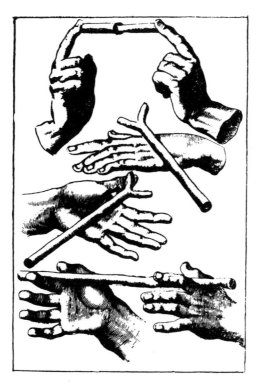

around the area as he holds the pendulum above the map, systematically 'walking' it in a defined fashion, square by square or by triangulation. All reactions over the map are checked on the actual site at some future date, which means valuable time is saved by knowing exactly where to search.

TIME DOWSING

Here dowsing is used to determine the age of a given object or even the date it was manufactured or first used. The pendulum is the usual instrument for this purpose, worked backwards and forwards along a *time-line* (i.e. a rule graduated in years) of the historical past. A variation of this technique is *psychometry*. Here an antique object or even a picture is held in the hands, or against the forehead or crown, and the time and situation is 'felt' from images stored inside it. It is a controversial and seemingly difficult form of dowsing.

MEDICAL DOWSING

The uses of dowsing here are mainly analytical; to determine the presence of damage or disease within the body and providing information which helps towards diagnosis. In this way the cause of the disorder is discovered. Even more remarkable is another branch of medical dowsing which locates body disorders *before* they actually reveal themselves through physical symptoms. This is a pure form of preventive medicine and probably the most useful application of the dowser's skill. Often the pendulum is used in conjunction with a rule or protractor-like disc which has been graduated especially for the individual purpose. Such graduations can refer to, say, lists of organs or nerve cells.

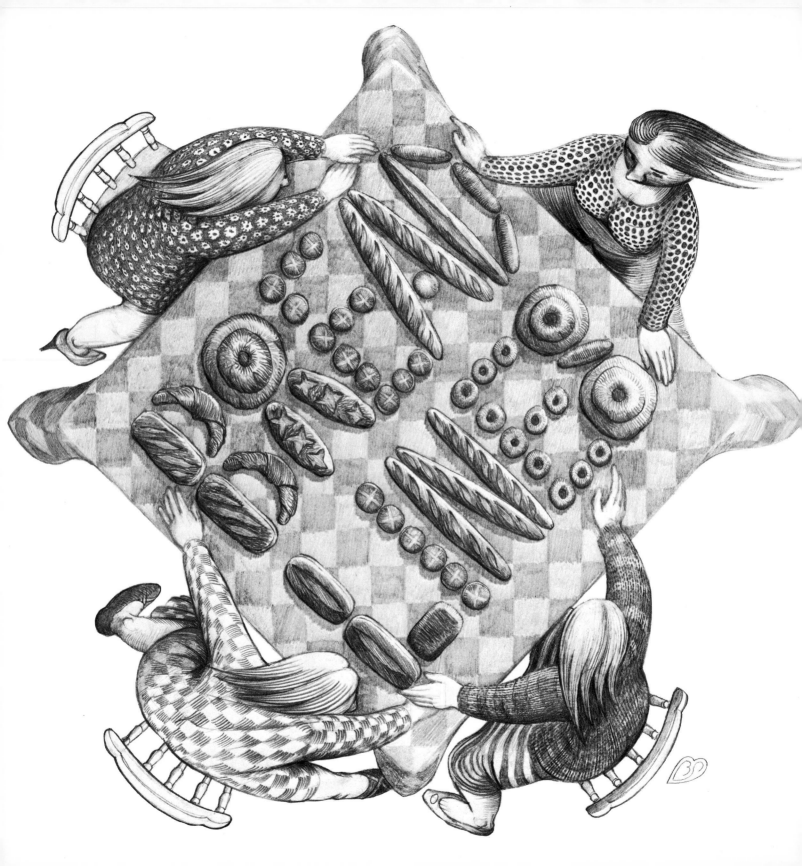

'Twas beautiful dough, like a milking breast it was.'

A COUNTRYWOMAN

IN our house we have reverted back to the bread-eating habits of the nineteenth century where white bread was considered a speciality and eaten mainly as a treat. It's a bizarre treat, of course, because your good old hundred per cent stone-ground wholemeal loaf wins hands down in terms of goodness and taste. But as home-made white bread is far superior to the reconstituted cotton-wool being sold these days in the bakers it certainly makes a change. Dietetics apart, however, this chapter is about the basics of home baking because, contrary to popular belief, making a loaf is nowhere near as difficult and time-consuming as people make out. And anyone who has ever smelt that gorgeous aroma of baking bread knows there is nothing more pleasurable and satisfying.

Equipment
Apart from the obvious oven, all the home baker will need is a large mixing bowl, a wooden spoon, a measuring jug, a sharp knife, and an assortment of vessels to bake the bread in. Special baking tins are obtainable from most hardware shops but try experimenting with earthenware flowerpots and other heat-resistant containers. A useful but not essential tool will be a pastry brush for giving special glazes to loaves.

Flours
There are many types of flour suitable for bread and each one has its own distinctive taste. However, wheatflour, because of its high gluten content, makes the finest bread and it is advisable to include some in recipes using other flours. Make your choice from the following:

BARLEY
Barley on its own makes a sweet but very heavy bread because of its lack of gluten and consequent inability to hold the yeast fermentation gases. Mix with wheatflour in the ratio of 2 or 3 of wheat to 1 of barley. Try toasting the barley flour for an unusual alternative.

CORNMEAL
On its own, cornmeal will make a dense, crumbly bread. A more stable loaf should consist of cornmeal and wheatflour, measure for measure.

MAIZE
Produces a distinctive, yellowish, gritty texture, but tasty nonetheless.

MILLET
Sometimes called sorghum, this flour makes a rather dry bread and should be mixed measure for measure with wheatflour.

OATS
Oatflour, oatmeal and rolled oats can all be used to make a sweet, heavy bread, or mixed measure for measure with wheatflour.

RICE
Ground rice on its own is not very good but O.K. if mixed measure for measure with wheatflour.

RYE
Makes a wholesome bread with a distinctive sour taste. Superb if mixed 2:1 with wheatflour.

SOYA
Makes a protein-rich loaf but needs the addition of some wheatflour.

WHEAT
From the most bland, bleached white, supa-sifted stuff to the nutty, chewy wholesomeness of wholewheat, there is a range of wheatflours to suit everyone's taste. Canadian wheat is considered to be the best.

WILD FOOD FLOURS
The roots, tubers and fruit of certain wild plants can be dried and ground into flour (*see Chapter 4*). All of them should be mixed with wheatflour.

MISCELLANEOUS
Try cooking whole cereal grains and using measure for measure with wheatflour. Try using ground nuts, broken seeds (poppy, sesame, sunflower, etc.) and dried fruit, or even muesli. The recipes that follow later on will give some idea of the versatility of breadmaking.

Leavened and Unleavened Bread
Long ago, before some bright spark discovered yeast, bread was very different to that which we eat today. Now known as unleavened bread, it was baked very thin and ended up as a hard crisp bread. No one knows who invented yeast bread but it was probably one of those happy accidents of which history is made. If un-leavened bread dough was left for a day or so, it started to ferment through wild yeasts reacting with the sugar content of the flour. If this was then baked, a crude leavened bread would have been the result.

The next innovation was probably the *sour-*

159

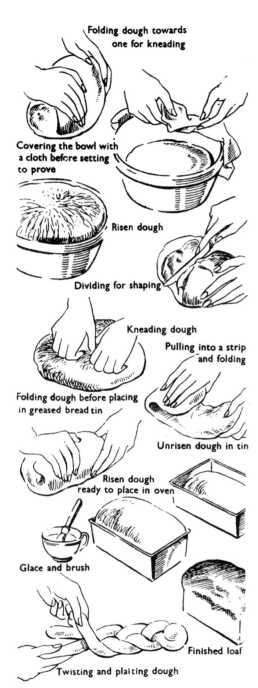

Folding dough towards one for kneading

Covering the bowl with a cloth before setting to prove

Risen dough

Dividing for shaping

Kneading dough

Pulling into a strip and folding

Folding dough before placing in greased bread tin

Unrisen dough in tin

Risen dough ready to place in oven

Glace and brush

Finished loaf

Twisting and plaiting dough

dough breads which were very popular in America during pioneering days. During the bread-making process, a little of the dough – the *starter* – containing the wild yeasts was kept back to mix with the next batch of dough.

Nowadays with the wide availability of modern yeasts, most breads are leavened throughout the world.

Yeasts and Other Rising Agents

Yeasts are microscopic uni-cellular plants which reproduce dramatically when fed on sugar in warm conditions. Too much heat or sugar will kill the yeasts, whereas cold conditions will slow down their reproduction. There are a number of different ways of obtaining these yeasts as now follows; alternatively, other rising agents can be used.

BAKER'S YEAST
Fresh baker's yeast should be used wherever possible. It can be obtained from the local baker if he is a kind sort of chap, otherwise at an inflated cost from a Health Food shop. Fresh yeast in mint condition should have the consistency of soft putty and be easy to break apart. Avoid any which crumbles on touch or that is discoloured in any way. Store in an airtight container in the refrigerator until use.

BAKING POWDER
If you run out of baking yeast then this is an acceptable stand-by.

BREWER'S YEAST
Once widely used in bread-making before baker's yeast was specially cultivated. Try using the yeast in the froth of home-made or 'real' beer, or simply the fresh or dried brewer's yeast from a wine- and beer-making shop.

DRIED YEAST
Available in any decent grocer's shop – the most convenient form of baker's yeast. To use dried yeast it must be sprinkled in warm water containing a little sugar until it froths up to a good head. As a general guide, use half as much dried yeast in any given recipe using fresh yeast, as it is twice as potent.

SOURDOUGH
Apart from saving back a piece of dough the size of a tennis ball each time bread is made, try this other method. Boil 1 lb flour, ¼ lb Barbados sugar, and a pinch of salt in two gallons of water for an hour. Bottle and cork when lukewarm.

Ready for use in 24 hours. 1 pint of this mixture is sufficient for 18 lbs of bread.

SPLIT PEAS
Pour boiling water on to a cup of split or bruised peas and place in a container near a fire or some other warm place for 24 hours. It should ferment nicely and the froth can be used as yeast.

MAKING A BASIC LOAF

I don't know anyone who makes bread the same way as anyone else and I certainly know that my own recipes and methods are unique to myself. However, there are certain fundamental rules in all successful bread-making whatever the methods may be. The following recipe is for a good-sized (approx. 1½ lb) wholemeal loaf, and the other for four medium-sized loaves.

1 lb wholemeal flour	3 lbs flour
½ oz or 1 heaped teaspoon dried yeast (1 oz fresh yeast)	1 oz dried yeast (2½ oz fresh yeast)
1 teaspoon sea salt.	1 dessertspoon sea salt
1 teaspoon sugar or honey	1 dessertspoon sugar or honey
1 dessertspoon oil, or 1 oz butter or margarine (optional)	2 dessertspoons oil, or 2 oz butter or margarine (optional)
¾ pint water.	1½ pints water.

Metric conversions

1 oz	= 28·35 g
2 oz	= 56·7 g
4 oz (¼ lb)	= 113 g
8 oz (½ lb)	= 226·5 g
1 lb (16 oz)	= 454 g
2 lb	= 907 g
1 fl oz	= 28·35 ml
¼ pt (5 fl oz)	= 142 ml
½ pt (10 fl oz)	= 284 ml
1 pt (20 fl oz)	= 568 ml
1¾ pt (35 fl oz)	= 1 litre
2 pt (40 fl oz)	= 1·136 l

¼ in	= 6·35 mm		
½ in	= 12·7 mm		
1 in	= 25·4 mm	5 in	= 127 mm
1½ in	= 38·1 mm	1 ft	= 304·8 mm

160

All utensils and ingredients must be kept warm throughout the various procedures. Pour the flour and salt into the mixing bowl and gently warm in the oven or by a fire. Dissolve the yeast and sugar/honey in 1 cup of the water (*which should also be warm*), or cream the fresh yeast in the same. Allow the mixture to stand for about 15 minutes, or until there is a good head of froth. Make a well in the bowl of flour. Add the oil or margarine and pour in the yeast. Add the rest of the water and mix well with the wooden spoon.

From here onwards there are three separate methods to follow, depending on the type of loaf, and the amount of time at hand. In the first, or 'traditional' method the mixture is poured on to a floured surface and *kneaded* into a dough. It is then put back into the bowl, covered with a damp cloth and allowed to *rise* in a warm place until the dough has doubled in size. The dough is then poured back onto the floured surface and kneaded again or *knocked back* to its original size. Finally the dough is placed in a greased baking vessel and allowed to double back in size or *prove* in a warm place. The bread is then baked.

The second method (the one I use) leaves out the first kneading. The mixture is allowed to rise in the mixing bowl. It is then kneaded, allowed to prove and then baked.

The third or quick method leaves out both kneading and rising, but the texture suffers because of it. The mixture is poured into a greased baking vessel and allowed to rise a little and then baked.

Kneading

The kneading process is really the most important in bread-making because it brings out the gluten content in the flour which in turn gives the dough its elastic quality. Kneading also ensures the even and thorough mixing of dough which is essential for trouble-free rising and proving. The mixture should be poured out on to a flat lightly floured surface. With lightly floured hands it should then be pummelled, punched, slapped and twisted. Lift one end and bring it across and pummel, punch, slap and twist it again. Pull it, twist it, turn it; thoroughly knead it until the dough becomes soft, smooth and elastic. If the dough becomes sticky in the process then flour the hands, not the dough (be careful not to over-flour the dough). Knead for about 10 minutes.

Rising

Once the dough has been kneaded it should then be put back into the bowl and covered with a damp cloth. Ideally the dough should be left in a warm place to rise overnight but it will be ready for the next procedure once it has doubled in size.

Knocking Back

Here the risen dough is poured back on to the floured surface and kneaded for the second time, for about 2–5 minutes. This removes any excess air bubbles in the dough.

Proving

At this stage the dough is placed in a baking tin for proving (i.e. *the second rise*). Nowadays it is customary to grease the tin or whatever, but old-fashioned bakers preferred to preheat their containers in a hot oven and lightly dust with flour, which works just as well. Any surface decoration, incidentally, must be carried out immediately before proving (see below).

Baking

Because domestic ovens differ enormously in performance and design, only a fundamental guide to baking will be given. *The oven should be pre-heated – as hot as it will go – for about 10 to 15 minutes.* The bread tins can then be put in the oven but it is crucial not to knock them at this stage as it may affect the consistency of the finished bread (i.e. make it hard). Place the tins at the top of the oven and bake for about 20 minutes at gas mark 7 (220°C, 425°F). Turn the tins around and bake for a further 15 minutes. After baking, immediately remove the bread and allow to cool on a wire rack. (Some people prefer to let their bread cool outside in the air.) A standard test to determine whether bread is sufficiently cooked is to tap the bottom of the loaves. If they sound hollow then they are ready.

Points to Remember

1. Always use fresh yeast, as stale yeast will give the bread a sour taste or may simply not work at all.

LOAVES

Brick

Coburg

Cottage

Sandwich

Farmhouse

Bloomar

Brown

Vienna roll

Tin

Twist or Callas

Household

Bermaline

Wholemeal

2. All ingredients and utensils must be kept warm and free from draughts, otherwise the bread may not rise and prove.
3. Too much water will produce an open, spongy bread.
4. Always cover the dough with a damp cloth when allowing to rise and prove.
5. If the water for dissolving the yeast is too hot it will kill the yeast.
6. Placing the loaves for baking in too cool an oven will produce bread full of holes and an uneven texture due to the continuing action of the yeast.
7. Baking in an overheated oven will produce bread with rock-hard crusts and uncooked middles.
8. Baking in too cool an oven will produce bread that will be dry and light in colour.
9. Any fruit and other flavourings should be added to the dough when knocking back.
10. Proving for too long will produce a heavy bread.
11. The greater the amount of flour in a recipe, the less yeast is needed in proportion, e.g. $\frac{1}{2}$ oz yeast for 1 lb flour, 1 oz yeast for 3 lb flour.

Once the hang of making a basic loaf has been mastered, there is the fun of experimenting with the numerous traditional bread shapes, as well as the fancy 'engraving' and relief decoration for the crust including surface glazing and trimmings. This is known as *gilding*.

Bread Shapes

Half the joy of a loaf of bread is its shape and appearance. During our own history of bread-making there have arisen numerous traditional bread shapes, many of which are still in use today. Here is a look at most of these shapes. (*Remember that shaping is done after knocking back and before proving.*)

BAKESTONE
Probably the earliest shape of all, and the simplest. The dough is formed into a round ball and baked on a flat stone, emerging as an elliptically shaped loaf.

BAP
A large elliptical breakfast roll baked like a bakestone.

BATCH
A general term for loaves baked together in a large tin or tray which are separated afterwards in much the same way as scones and buns are sometimes made.

BATON
French in origin. The dough is rolled into a flat square and then into quarters diagonally. Each triangle is then rolled and baked.

BLOOMER
A long loaf with horizontal cuts along the top.

BRICK
These are moulded in two parts like cottage loaves (see below) only instead of being round, the pieces are in two rolls, the top one being much smaller than the bottom. 'Sister Bricks' are those which are set in the oven in pairs so that one side of each loaf is crusty and the other side soft.

BUN TWIST
The dough is rolled into a long sausage and the ends tied together like a knot.

CHURCH AND CHAPEL
Shaped like the end view of a church. By putting more dough into the baking tin than normal, it will prove over the top of the tin which will form the church shape.

CLOVER LEAF
Three balls of dough placed together and baked so they are joined as a clover leaf shape.

COB, COBURG
Round loaves with two deep cuts on the crust in the form of a cross which open out with baking to form the four points of a crown shaped top. Otherwise known as 'cakes' in the west country and 'skulls' in Ireland.

COLLAR
An elliptically-shaped plain flat loaf, pointed at the ends, and with a narrow plait stretched lengthways along the top.

COTTAGE
Perhaps our most traditional loaf but varying to some extent in various parts of the country. The dough is cut into two with one piece being approximately $\frac{1}{3}$ the size of the other. Both pieces are rolled into balls and the smaller placed on top of the other. A floury finger is then pushed down the centre of both, which binds them together. The top can be scored (as they do in Oxfordshire) or left plain.

CRESCENT

Simply a baton bent into a crescent.

CRUMPETS, MUFFINS AND PIKELETS

Cooked on a hot plate or griddle and not in the oven. Crumpets should be cooked in crumpet rings which prevent the batter from running all over the place. Pikelets are similar to pancakes which are buttered both sides. The traditional muffin is small, flat and round like a bap.

FARL

One portion of a scone round.

FARMHOUSE

Same as a bakestone but with the addition of a cross cut on the top.

HOUSEHOLD

Moulded in two parts like cottages except that both parts are the same size, or the top part slightly larger than the bottom. The loaves are packed close together in the oven so that the crust forms on the top and bottom only, the sides being square and 'crumby' (i.e. soft). Now only baked in Ireland.

KNOBBLY-TOP

Here the bread tin is filled with balls of dough piled on top of each other, with one in the middle on top.

PLAIT

A beautiful loaf when made correctly. The dough is cut in 3, 5 or 7 pieces, according to the plait, which are then rolled into long sausages. One end of all the pieces are pressed together and the free ends plaited loosely like girls' hair.

POT

Much of the bread in the past was baked in earthenware pots and these were called pot loaves. Nowadays flowerpots can be used in the same way to make a good pot loaf.

PUNCH

A roughly shaped, mis-shapen lump of dough baked as it is.

SALLY LUNN

A little round cakebread with a big cob, which is baked in a cake tin or some other round vessel. The top is deep cut diagonally to form a batch as in a scone round. Traditionally this bread is torn open when cool, buttered, placed together, and popped back in the oven again for a few minutes more.

SANDWICH OR TIN

A commercially-produced bread that is tailor-made for sandwiches. The dough is baked in enclosed square or round tins. A boring shape, often with the taste to match, but the nation's favourite nonetheless.

SCONE OR BUN ROUND

Scones and bunloaf are traditionally made in the shape of a bakestone and cut into sections diagonally in the tin or on the tray before proving. The sections are not separated and baking binds them together though each section can be pulled apart like a batch.

SCOTCH

Oblong tin loaves packed tight in the oven to produce a crust only on the top and bottom. The smooth and glossy appearance of the crumby part of the bread is due to the greasing of the sides and ends of each loaf before it is set in the oven.

SMALL TOP

Same as a cottage loaf except that here the top is very small compared to the bottom and the 'closings' of the bottom part are turned upwards so that they open out and show small cracks while baking in the oven. As a rule the loaves are moulded in flour to make them white.

VIENNA

A long elliptical loaf with slanting cuts set at equal distances along the top.

WHEATSHEAF OR HARVEST FESTIVAL

The most impressive and decorative, as well as one of our best traditional breads. A certain amount of skill is needed for this loaf, details of which are given below.

Ordinary yeasted dough is unsatisfactory for this decorative loaf because of the length of time involved for fashioning the shape. A less leavened mixture will be needed, one that will not rise and alter shape too much during the proving.

Make up a dough from:
  3 lbs flour
  4 tablespoons oil
  2 teaspoons sea salt
  1 level teaspoon dried yeast
  1½ pints water, approximately.

The dough must be as thick as possible, so add water or flour until really thick. Pour on to a floured board and knead for 10 minutes and then cut into two pieces, one a bit larger than the other. Shape the largest piece into a ball and then flatten with a rolling pin until 1 inch thick. Lay out the dough on a greased tray and cut out

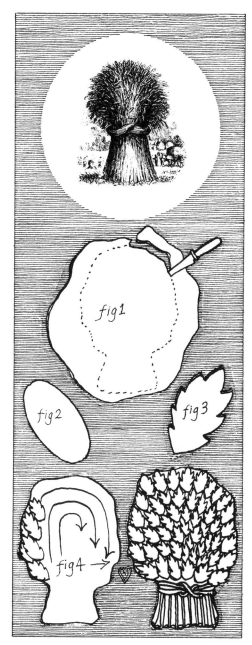

the basic shape *(fig 1)*. Brush with an egg glaze (2 egg yolks in $\frac{1}{2}$ pint milk). Divide the other piece of dough into approximately 50 equal pieces, each the size of a small plum, and flatten into an elliptical shape *(fig 2)*. Cut out of each piece the simple shape of an ear of wheat and arrange them on the base like a wheat sheaf *(fig 3)* – beginning with the outside row and working towards the middle. With the dough left over, roll into thin strands and press them lengthwise beneath the wheat ears to form the stalks, with a few wider strands laid across and knotted for the sheaf band *(fig 4)*. Brush all over with egg glaze and bake in a moderate oven (340°F – 175°C) for about 1 hour. *Do not lift from the tray until perfectly cool.*

Engraving

By 'engraving' is meant cutting or scoring a pattern into the surface of the dough just before proving as a form of decoration. There are a number of traditional patterns (see illustration p. 162), but there is no reason why you shouldn't make up your own. Use only a sharp knife and cut into the surface of the dough no more than $\frac{1}{2}$ inch. A floured finger can be used for indenting the surface where holes are required.

Relief Decoration

The opposite process to engraving, whereby small pieces of dough are pressed on to the top of the main dough before proving (e.g. as for the wheatsheaf loaf). All sorts of patterns and even simple pictures can be used in this form of decoration.

Glazes

Glazes – i.e. brushing the loaves with a solution to enhance its appearance – can give a really professional touch to bread making. The following is a complete list of them:

PRE-BAKE GLAZES

Brush rolls and small loaves before baking. Large loaves brush 20 minutes before the end of baking.

Egg Yolk: Produces a dark, almost black crust.

Egg Yolk and Milk: Produces a deep brown, semi-matt crust.

Beaten Egg: Produces a gleaming crust, ideal for milk breads.

Cream; Rich Milk; Evaporated Milk: Produce a shiny, yellow crust, ideal for twists and rolls.

Salt Water: Produces a crisp crust.

POST-BAKE GLAZES

Apply while the bread is still hot from the oven.

Thick Milk and Sugar: Produces a sticky, shiny crust, ideal for malt loaf, bun loaf and tea breads.

POST-BAKE GLAZES (RETURNED TO OVEN)

These should be applied when the bread is cooked and the loaves returned to the oven for a few minutes.

Cold Water: Produces a hard, crunchy crust.

Melted Butter or Margarine: Produces a crisp, crunchy crust and highlights the natural colours.

Loaves dried quickly in a warm place will produce crisp crusts. Loaves wrapped in a thick cloth and cooled slowly will produce soft crusts.

Toppings

As an added decorative and pleasing effect, glazed loaves can be strewn with poppy seeds, cereal kernels such as wheat and barley, or aromatic seeds such as cardamom, caraway and coriander. Poppy seed is the traditional topping for plaits and twists, while cereal kernels are used for wholemeal breads. Alternatively, the loaves can be dusted with flour when they are removed from the oven.

Colouring and Flavouring

The traditional colouring for bread is saffron. This comes from the stigmas of the bulbous flower *Crocus sativus* which was once extensively used in breads from the West Country, and in particular Cornwall. Saffron will impart a beautiful golden colour to breads and cakes, though the full effect of this is more dramatic with white flours. It is also good for the digestion. Saffron is added to the fermenting yeast at the beginning of bread-making.

There are many flavourings which can be used in bread. Traditionally, caraway seed is used extensively, especially in rye bread. Coriander seed imparts a beautifully delicate flavour and aroma. The seeds of dill, fennel, onion and celery as well as various savoury herbs are worth trying. Garlic bread is unbelievably delicious. Cut a loaf into slices but

not all the way through so that it is still intact at the bottom. Spread both sides of each slice with butter or margarine into which one or two garlic cloves have been mashed. Wrap the loaf in silver foil and bake in a fairly hot oven for $\frac{1}{2}$ hour.

Try coconut flavouring for an unusual bread. Steep the grated flesh of a whole coconut in a pint of hot milk and use this liquid (strained) for fermenting the yeast.

TRADITIONAL BREADS

Behind the nutty loaf is the mill wheel;
Behind the mill wheel is the wheat field;
On the wheatfield rests the sunlight;
Above the sun is God.

JAMES RUSSELL LOWELL

Bara Brith (WELSH)

$\frac{1}{2}$ lb flour
$\frac{1}{2}$ lb oatmeal
$\frac{1}{2}$ lb mixed dried fruit and peel (or $\frac{1}{4}$ lb dried fruit and $\frac{1}{2}$ lb blackberries in season)
4 oz butter
$\frac{1}{2}$ teaspoon mixed sweet spice
$\frac{1}{2}$ teaspoon sea salt
1 egg
$\frac{1}{4}$ pint warm milk
$\frac{1}{4}$ lb Barbados sugar (or 2 tablespoons black treacle)
$\frac{1}{2}$ oz dried yeast
$\frac{1}{4}$ pint water

Soak the mixed dried fruit overnight in the $\frac{1}{4}$ pint of *hot* water. Warm the milk and add to the water strained from the fruit. Mix the yeast with the milk and water and allow to ferment. Thoroughly rub the butter into the flour and then beat in the egg. Add the fermenting yeast, mix, and then knead for 10–15 minutes. Allow to rise and then knock back with the rest of the ingredients. Prove in a greased tin and bake at gas mark 5 (190°C, 375°F) for 1–1½ hours. Glaze after baking with sweetened milk.

Country Herb Bread (ENGLISH)

1 lb flour
$\frac{1}{4}$ lb grated mature Cheddar cheese
2 oz mixed dried herbs (to taste)
3 oz margarine

1 small finely-chopped, lightly cooked onion
   (optional)
½ pint warm water
1 teaspoon sea salt
½ oz dried yeast
1 teaspoon Barbados sugar

Ferment the yeast in the water sweetened by the sugar. Mix the flour, salt, margarine and fermented yeast in a bowl and knead for 10–15 minutes. Allow to rise. Knock back with the rest of the ingredients and allow to prove. Bake for ½ hour at gas mark 7 (218°C, 425°F). Glaze with a beaten egg.

Harvest Festival Sweetbread (ENGLISH)

1 lb flour
¼ lb raisins
1 oz grated lemon and orange peel
1 oz Barbados sugar
2 oz melted butter or oil
1 egg
1 pint warm milk
1 oz dried yeast
½ teaspoon sea salt
Topping – mixed broken nuts, toasted almond
   flakes, chopped glacé cherries.

Mix the yeast in the warm milk into which the sugar and egg have been beaten. Mix the flour, salt, peel and fruit and add the fermenting yeast and melted butter. Thoroughly mix and then knead for 10–15 minutes. Allow to rise and then knock back. Fashion the dough into a plait as described earlier on and allow to prove on a greased tray. Bake for ½ hour at gas mark 6 (204°C, 400°F). Glaze after baking with sweetened milk syrup and immediately top with nuts, almond flakes and cherries.

Maizebread

¾ lb maize flour
¼ lb wheatflour
½ pint buttermilk (optional), or 1 egg
¾ pint boiling water
1 teaspoon baking powder

Mix the flours and baking powder with the boiling water and beat in the egg or buttermilk. Bake for 40 minutes at gas mark 6 (204°C, 400°F).

Maltbread

1 lb flour
½ pint milk or water
2 oz butter or margarine
2 tablespoons malt extract
2 tablespoons black treacle
2 oz dried fruit (optional)
1 egg
½ teaspoon sea salt
1 oz dried yeast

Ferment the yeast in the milk or water sweetened by a little of the treacle. Mix the flour and other ingredients and add the fermenting yeast. Mix well then knead for 10–15 minutes. Allow to rise, knock back, and then prove in a greased tin. Bake for 40–50 minutes at gas mark 5 (190°C, 375°F). Glaze after baking with sweetened milk syrup.

Millet Bread

½ lb millet flour
½ lb wheat flour
1 teaspoon baking powder
1 teaspoon sea salt

Mix the ingredients with as much water as will make a stiff dough and bake for 45 minutes at gas mark 4 (180°C, 350°F).

Monk's Bread or Monastery Oatmeal

(ENGLISH)
12 oz wholemeal flour
½ lb white flour (plain)
½ lb oat flakes
¾ pint warm milk
2 oz oil or melted butter or margarine
½ teaspoon sea salt
1 teaspoon sugar
1 oz dried yeast.

Ferment the yeast in the milk sweetened by the sugar. Mix half of the wholemeal flour and the white flour together with the oil or butter and add the fermenting yeast. Mix well and knead for 10–15 minutes. Allow to rise for 1 hour. Mix remaining wholemeal flour, oats, margarine and salt and knead into a soft dough. Allow to rise for 1 hour. Shape into 2 loaves, allow to prove, then bake for 45 minutes at gas mark 7 (218°C, 425°F). Top with broken wheat kernels.

Newcastle Bread

Proceed as for the basic bread recipe given earlier on and add 2 teaspoons of caraway seeds when mixing the ingredients prior to kneading.

Northumberland Bread Cakes

1 lb barley flour
½ teaspoon bicarbonate of soda
¼ teaspoon cream of tartar
½ pint skimmed milk
1 teaspoon salt

Mix all the ingredients into a good dough and divide into 5 pieces. Roll into balls and press flat until about ¾ inch thick. Bake until nicely brown – ideally on a griddle where each cake can be cooked separately.

Oatbread

1 lb oatflour (or oatmeal, or oat flakes)
¼ lb margarine
3 oz honey
¾ pint boiling water
2 tablespoons warm water
1 oz sea salt
½ oz yeast.

Ferment the yeast in the warm water sweetened by a little of the honey. Mix the oatflour, margarine, salt and honey in the boiling water. When cool add the fermenting yeast and allow to rise for 2–3 hours. Knead for 10–15 minutes, divide and shape into two round bakestones and allow to prove on a greased tray. Bake for 40–50 minutes at gas mark 8 (230°C, 450°F).

Rice Bread

Sift together a cup of rice flour, 1 teaspoon baking powder. Add a pinch of salt and 1 egg beaten into 1 cup milk. Add 1 tablespoon of melted butter and turn the mixture into a shallow tin. Bake in a moderate oven for about 40–45 minutes.

Rye or Black Bread

2½ lb rye flour
1 oz butter
1 teaspoon caraway seeds
1 teaspoon sea salt
1 teaspoon Barbados sugar
¾ pint warm milk and water, mixed half and half
½ oz dried yeast.

Ferment the yeast in the milk/water solution sweetened by the sugar. Mix the flour with the rest of the ingredients and add the fermenting yeast. Knead for 10–15 minutes, allow to rise and then knock back. Divide and shape into two oval loaves and allow to prove on a greased tray.

Bake for 45 minutes at gas mark 7 (218°C, 425°F). Glaze with a beaten egg.

Selkirk Bannock (SCOTTISH)

1 lb flour
2 oz melted butter or margarine
1 teaspoon sugar
½ teaspoon sea salt
3 oz mixed dried fruit
1 oz candied peel (or chopped orange or lemon peel)
½ pint warm water
½ oz yeast

Ferment the yeast in the water sweetened with the sugar. Mix the flour, salt and melted butter or margarine and add the fermenting yeast. Mix and knead for 10–15 minutes. Allow to rise and then knock back with the other ingredients. Allow to prove and then bake for 45 minutes at gas mark 6 (204°C, 400°F). Glaze with sweetened milk syrup.

Soda Bread

1½ lb wholemeal flour
½ lb strong white unbleached flour
2 level teaspoons bicarbonate of soda
4 level teaspoons cream of tartar
1 pint milk or buttermilk
1 oz butter or margarine
1 teaspoon sea salt
1 dessertspoon Barbados sugar

Mix all the dry ingredients. Rub in the butter or margarine and then fold in the milk. Shape into a cob and deep cut into the dough to give four farls. Bake for ½ hour at gas mark 6 (204°C, 400°F).

Sourdough Bread

Keep back a piece of dough the size of a tennis ball from a previous bread-making session. Keep it covered for 4 days in which time it will have soured. The ingredients are:

1½ lb rye flour
½ lb wheat flour
3 oz margarine
½ pint warm milk
2 teaspoons salt
sourdough paste.

Sourdough paste:
dough from previous baking
1 lb rye flour
¾ pint warm water

Mix the sourdough with 1 lb rye flour in ¾ pint warm water until it makes a runny batter. Let it stand overnight in a warm place and cover with

a cloth. Mix the sourdough paste with the rest of the ingredients and knead for 10–15 minutes. Allow to rise, knock back and then divide into two loaves for proving. Bake for $\frac{1}{2}$ hour at gas mark 6 (204°C, 400°F). Remove and glaze with salted water. Bake for a further 1–1$\frac{1}{2}$ hours at gas mark 2 (150°C, 305°F).

Yuletide Bread

1 lb flour
$\frac{1}{4}$ lb margarine
$\frac{1}{4}$ lb raisins
$\frac{1}{4}$ lb sultanas
2 oz currants
2 eggs
$\frac{1}{2}$ teaspoon cinnamon
$\frac{1}{2}$ teaspoon mixed spice
2 oz Barbados sugar
1 dessertspoon black treacle
$\frac{1}{2}$ pint warm milk
2 oz dried yeast
Ferment the yeast in the milk sweetened with the sugar. Mix the flour, salt, spices, eggs and margarine and add the fermenting yeast. Mix thoroughly and allow to rise. Knock back with the rest of the ingredients and allow to prove in a greased tin. Bake for about 1 hour at gas mark 6 (204°C, 400°F). Glaze with sweetened milk.

Miscellaneous:

Rolls

Use the same recipe for the basic bread given earlier on. After knocking back, divide the dough into small pieces, the size of a small apple, and roll into balls. Allow to prove for 1 hour and then bake for 10–15 minutes at gas mark 8 (232°C, 450°F). Decorate with poppy seed or cereal kernels to taste.

Crumpets

1 lb flour
1 pint warm milk
$\frac{1}{2}$ teaspoon salt
$\frac{1}{2}$ oz dried yeast
$\frac{1}{2}$ teaspoon sugar
These vary throughout the country as to size and ingredients but all are toasted before being eaten. It is necessary to cook crumpets on a griddle or metal sheet and to use crumpet rings which prevents the batter from running amok.

Ferment the yeast in the milk sweetened by the sugar. Mix the flour and salt and add the fermenting yeast. Mix and leave to rise in a warm place for 1 hour. Grease the crumpet rings and griddle and pour in the batter to a depth of $\frac{1}{2}$ inch. Cook one side and then the other. Before serving, toast one side well, the other lightly and smother in butter or margarine.

Muffins

1 lb flour
$\frac{3}{4}$ pint warm milk
$\frac{1}{2}$ teaspoon sea salt
$\frac{1}{2}$ oz dried yeast
$\frac{1}{2}$ teaspoon sugar
Proceed as for crumpet recipe, except that instead of a runny batter it should be a soft dough. Allow to rise and then knock back. Divide into small rounds and allow to prove on a floured board or tray. Bake on a hot plate or griddle until lightly brown on each side. Muffins must never be cut open. Open the edges all round with the fingers to allow the heat to penetrate and toast both sides. Pull apart and butter, and put back together for eating.

Bran Muffins

8 oz wholemeal flour
8 oz bran
1 teaspoon bicarbonate of soda
2 tablespoons black treacle
1 oz melted butter
$\frac{1}{4}$ pint milk
pinch of salt
Mix the bran, flour, salt, bicarbonate of soda and add the treacle and butter. Mix to a stiff dough with the milk and bake in small tins in a hot oven for 20–30 minutes.

Pikelets

$\frac{1}{2}$ lb flour
2 eggs
$\frac{1}{2}$ teaspoon sea salt
$\frac{1}{2}$ teaspoon sugar
$\frac{1}{2}$ oz dried yeast
$\frac{1}{2}$ pint warm milk (approximately)
Ferment the yeast in the warm milk sweetened with the sugar. Mix the other ingredients and add the fermented yeast. The mixture should be the consistency of runny batter (add more warm milk if necessary). Allow to rise for 1 hour and

then cook like pancakes in a frying pan or on a griddle. Cook both sides and serve with butter.

Home & Dry

IN these inflationary seventies, more and more people are seeing the sense of growing as much of their own food as possible. The satisfaction gained from cultivating, harvesting and eating home produce now takes on an even rosier glow in view of the economic attractiveness of such a scheme. Unfortunately, when the winter months come round and the vegetable plot is more or less at rest, the old reliance on the greengrocer and supermarkets crops up again. Yet this need not be so. By storing and preserving part of the harvest and at the same time growing some winter crops, a more or less perpetual supply of food can be ensured all the year through.

Storing Vegetables

Many vegetables and fruits can be stored during the autumn for winter use. Methods of storing crops will be dealt with individually, but the one golden rule to observe which concerns each and every crop is to use only *sound and healthy specimens*. Anything bruised or diseased will soon affect the rest of the produce.

ARTICHOKE (CHINESE)

The tubers, which should normally be ready for eating in the autumn, can be left in the ground throughout the winter. Individual tubers can be dug when needed for eating but must not be exposed for any length of time before cooking, as discolouring will occur.

ARTICHOKE (GLOBE)

The heads should be cut off, leaving them with long stalks, which can be stuck into moist sand in a frostproof shed or outhouse. It is wise to cut off a little of the stalks every week and replace the artichokes in the sand.

ARTICHOKE (JERUSALEM)

The tubers can be left in the ground until needed or lifted at the end of November and stored in bone dry soil or sand in a cool building like a shed.

BEETROOT

There are two ways of storing beet. The traditional way is to use a *clamp* (see fig p. 170). Choose a dry corner in the garden, free from frost if possible, and away from overhanging trees. Dig out a circular base 6 inches deep by approximately 1 yard in diameter. Fill the depression halfway with dry straw or ashes. After removing the leaves with a sharp twist (*do not use a knife*) lay out the beet in circles with the crowns facing outwards. Cover with sifted ashes and arrange another batch in similar fashion on top but in a smaller circle than the first layer. Continue until a conical mound of beet has been built and then cover with 4 inches of straw. Top with 4 inches of sifted moist soil, allowing a tuft of straw to penetrate into the open at the top for ventilation.

The other more straightforward method is to store the beet in deep boxes of dry sand, ashes or sifted dry soil, in an upright position, crowns upwards. The boxes should remain in a dry cool place to prevent sprouting and mildew. Best varieties for storing are the long or winter beet varieties such as 'Cheltenham Green Top'.

CABBAGE

Remove all the outside leaves and any that are discoloured or damaged, and store in net bags or hammocks suspended from the roof of a cool dry room. When cutting the cabbage, leave the lower leaves on the plant; this will help the development of an autumn crop of collets which will be tender and won't be caterpillar-ridden.

CARROT

Maincrop carrots sown in May and June are the most suitable for storing. They should be lifted not later than the end of October when the leaves have curled and lost their fresh green colour. Remove the leaves as near to the crown as possible to prevent sprouting and store in a clamp outside or in boxes of peat or sand with 2 inches between layers.

CAULIFLOWER

Can be left in the ground or stored in boxes of straw in a cool dry place.

CELERIAC

Celeriac can be left in the ground and lifted as needed, but can also be stored in a clamp, or in sand inside a cool dry shed. Remove all the leaves except the centre growth which is essential to prevent new leaves appearing.

CELERY

Can be left in the ground until needed for eating. In harsh weather where heavy frosts are likely, heel the plants in with plenty of dry soil to protect them.

CHICORY

Store as for carrots.

CUCUMBER

Cut them before they are fully developed and either bury them in a dry box of sand, or stand

At the top of the house the
Apples are laid in rows
And the skylight lets the moonlight in, and those
Apples are deep-sea apples of green.

                                    JOHN DRINKWATER

them in a bucket, their stem ends resting in an inch of water. They can be kept for some time by either of these methods.

FENNEL

Clumps of fennel can be lifted during October and replanted in good-sized boxes or pots of peat. They require the warmth of a greenhouse or warm part of the house (around 10–15°C).

GARLIC

During July when the leaf tips turn yellow, the garlic bulbs should be pulled from the soil. Allow them to ripen on the ground under the protection of cloches for a week and then store them on some sort of wire rack until all the foliage has withered. Finally, separate each bulb, remove any surface soil and dirt, and then string together in a rope (see under onion) or store in cloth bags until needed.

HORSERADISH

Remove the tops in the usual way and store in sifted ashes or moist sand.

KOHL RABI

Can be left in the ground throughout the winter.

LEEK

Leeks will survive left in the ground over winter but in severe weather it is advisable to lift some for inside storage. Stored in boxes filled with sand, they will keep for a month or more.

MARROW

Use only full-grown fruit and those which have a full rounded butt end. Only cut one marrow from each plant. Store in a kitchen or some other room where the temperature will not fall below 10°C. Lay the marrows on sacking in boxes or on a shelf but *make sure the fruits are not in contact with each other*. Alternatively store separately in string bags suspended from the ceiling.

ONION

Lift the onions and allow to ripen in a sunny place until the foliage has withered. The traditional method of storing onions is to form them into a rope which can then be hung in a dry, cool place. Alternatively they may be stored in shallow boxes or in net bags.

Onion Ropes: Tie a length of stout string into a loop and hang the loop from a hook from a suitable height for working. Proceed as illustrated opposite.

PARSNIP

It is customary to leave parsnips in the ground as frost improves their flavour. After February, however, they must be lifted, otherwise the roots will start sprouting. Remove the leaves close to the crown and store head to tail in dry sand or sifted soil.

POTATO

It is essential to use only healthy unblemished tubers and even these must be periodically checked for signs of disease. The simplest method is to spread out the tubers on straw or sacking in an airy shed or outhouse and cover with the same. Excluding the light will prevent greening. Alternatively the tubers can be put carefully into sacks or boxes and stored in a larder, or outside in a straw or bracken-filled clamp. Where a clamp is used, dig a trench around the base to help drain the clamp and keep it dry. Remove from the clamp in heavy frosts. New potatoes can be kept till Christmas if they are put into a sealed tin immediately they are dug up and buried in the garden.

SALSIFY AND SCORZONERA

In dry districts the roots can be left in the ground. In high-rainfall areas, lift the roots and store in dry sand or sifted soil.

SHALLOTS

Once the foliage has turned yellow in July, lift the bulbs and allow to dry in a sunny place. Store in shallow trays or in bundles where sufficient ventilation will keep them cool and dry.

SWEDES

Twist off the tops, leaving a little of the greenery, and shorten the roots. Swedes can be stored either in a clamp or in peat or sand in much the same way as carrots.

TOMATOES

Green tomatoes can be wrapped in tissue paper, newspaper or flannel and kept in the dark until ripe.

TURNIPS

Store as for swedes.

Storing Fruit

As with vegetables, only sound, unblemished and disease-free fruit must be used. *Never remove the stalks* as this induces decay. Avoid picking fruit for storage in wet conditions.

APPLES

There are a great many varieties of apples but only those classified as Late Autumn Dessert,

Midwinter Dessert, New Year Dessert, Spring Dessert and the various classes of cooking apple can be stored for any length of time. The following varieties are particularly favourable: 'Cockles Pippin', 'Cox's Orange Pippin', "Egremont Russet', 'Golden Delicious', 'Laxton's Reward', 'Red Delicious', and 'Tydeman's Late Orange'.

Pick the apples just before they are perfectly ripe and before the frosts set in. Be careful not to mistake falling apples, which may be infested with maggots, for ripe fruit. Gather the apples in the afternoon and lay them out very carefully in heaps in a cool dry place to 'heat' for two weeks inside. Wrap each apple individually in tissue paper and store in shallow trays, boxes or on shelves – in single layers with none of them touching. A cool, dark but well-ventilated cellar is ideal but a shed or similar place will do. The floor of the store room should have water sprinkled over it now and then to keep the air moist, otherwise the fruit may shrivel. Periodically inspect the fruit and dispose of any diseased or decaying specimens.

PEARS

Only the late-fruiting varieties are suitable for storing. Store in the same way as apples.

Storing Nuts

Kentish cobs, filberts (i.e. hazelnuts) and chestnuts can successfully be kept for quite long periods. Pack them into stone jars, earthenware

flower-pots or boxes, between layers of dry salt. It is essential to prevent the nuts from getting damp; and if no airtight lid or stopper is available then cover with a thick layer of salt. Store in a dry frost-proof place.

·WALNUTS

Place the nuts in single layers in shallow trays to dry out immediately after picking. Later some twenty at a time should be shaken vigorously in a bag to separate the husks from the nuts. Store in any cool, frost-proof place.

Drying

There are two principal methods which can be used successfully to reduce fruit and vegetables to a dehydrated state. Produce stored in this way can be kept for months. In the first method the produce is laid out in the sun to dry out naturally, while in the second, the produce is dried artificially. Because of our unpredictable climate it is generally easier to use the artificial method. A general steam-dry procedure is described here, but other methods for specific produce are listed individually below.

Steam-dry: Use only the very best produce. Wash the fruit or vegetables thoroughly and unless stated otherwise below, slice and peel. Steam in a basket or steam tray to the required steaming time (*see below*) and then either string up the slices or place across trays ready for the oven. Place in a cool oven (*refer to table below for temperatures and times*) until dehydrated and dry. Allow to air for at least 12 hours before storing in dry, airtight conditions in a cool dark place.

The numbers following the temperatures denote the time in hours.

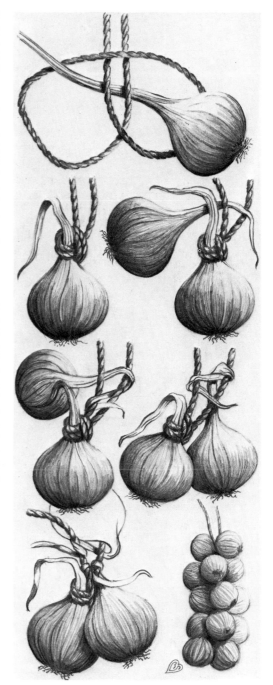

Table of Drying Times and Heats

APPLES	43–120°C/110–250°F (4–5)
APRICOTS (*blanched*)	43–93°C/110–200°F (4–6)
BEANS, BROAD (*shelled and blanched*)	65–120°C/150–250°F (3–4)
BEANS, RUNNER	65–120°C/150–250°F (2–3)
BEETS (*parboiled, skinned and cut*)	65–120°C/150–200°F (3)
BRUSSELS SPROUTS (*blanched for 5 minutes*)	62–78°C/145–175°F (2–3)
CABBAGE	62–93°C/145–200°F (3)
CARROTS	43–62°C/110–145°F (2½–3)
CAULIFLOWERS	62–93°C/145–200°F (2½–3)
CELERIAC	65–93°C/150–200°F (2–3)
CELERY	54–65°C/130–150°F (2–3)
CHERRIES	65°C/150°F (3–4)
CORN ON THE COB	49–65°C/120–150°F (about 3)
KOHLRABI	65–78°C/150–175°F (2–3)
LEEKS	60–93°C/140–200°F (2–3)
MARROW	49–60°C/120–140°F (3–4)
MUSHROOMS	60–65°C/140–150°F (2–3)
ONIONS	60–65°C/140–150°F (2–3)
PARSLEY	230°C/450°F (*must be very hot oven*) (5 mins)
PEACHES	65–93°C/150–200°F (2–3)
PEARS	65–93°C/150–200°F (5–6)
PEAS (*blanched*)	120°C/250°F (2–3)
PLUMS (*blanched*)	65–93°C/150–200°F (4–6)
PUMPKINS	65–78°C/150–175°F (4–6)
QUINCES	65–93°C/150–200°F (5–6)
RHUBARB	54–65°C/130–150°F (6–7)
SALSIFY	43–60°C/110–140°F (3)
SPINACH	49–60°C/120–140°F (3–4)
TURNIPS	43–54°C/110–130°F (3)

172

APPLE

Peel, core and slice into rings about $\frac{1}{8}$ to $\frac{7}{8}$ inch thick. Thread the rings on sticks or lay across a suitable drying rack and place in a cool oven not exceeding 41°C. When ready, the texture should resemble that of chamois leather and if properly dried the rings will separate at once if pressed together and released. Some people prefer to steep the rings in salted water for 10 minutes before placing in the oven.

ASPARAGUS TIPS

Steam for 4–5 minutes and oven dry as described above.

BEANS

Sliced green Dwarf, French or Scarlet runner beans should be steamed for 15–20 minutes and then oven-dried as described above.

To preserve the seed, use one of these two methods:

(1) Allow the pods to ripen on the plants while still growing and then pick and hang up in a cool dry place. Allow to dry out completely. Remove the seed from the pods and store in an airtight container.

(2) Remove the ripe seed and soak for 12 hours in water. Drain and place in a pan with fresh water. Boil until half cooked and then replace in the water to which a little sea salt has been added. Cook till tender, strain and then oven dry as described above.

To preserve the whole bean: Allow 1 lb cooking salt to every 3 lb beans. Wash and dry the beans and slice as you would for cooking. Put a 1-inch layer of salt in an unglazed jar and cover with a layer of beans. Press on top another 1-inch layer of salt and repeat. Cover securely. Wash the beans thoroughly and soak well before eating.

BEETS

Remove the tops but do not peel or slice. Steam for 30–45 minutes. Peel and slice the beets and then oven-dry as described above.

BROCCOLI

Steam for 8–10 minutes and oven-dry as described above.

CABBAGE

Shred the cabbage and steam for 8–10 minutes. Oven-dry as described above.

CARROT

Steam whole for 8–10 minutes. Slice and then oven-dry as described above.

CHERRY (also GRAPE, BLACKCURRANT and PLUM)

Dip the fruit into boiling water for a few minutes and then lay out on a suitable drying rack. Heat in a cool oven at 49°C to begin with, until the skin shows signs of shrivelling. Raise the heat to 57°C until dehydrated. The fruit can be tested by squeezing between thumb and finger. If correctly dry the skin will not burst and there should be no juice. The most suitable plums for drying into prunes are 'Victoria' and 'Pond's Seedling'.

HORSERADISH

Slice and oven-dry as described above. When dry, grate into shreds and store in an airtight container.

MUSHROOMS

The best fungus for drying is *Marasmius oreades* (Fairy ring mushroom), a wild mushroom, but the cultivated kind will dry quite well. Select a quantity of large healthy mushrooms and remove all traces of grit and dirt. Place in a pan with two large peeled onions impregnated with a few cloves, some mace and salt. Place in an oven and heat gently until the mushroom juice has been drawn. Shake the pan over an open flame until the moisture has evaporated (be especially careful not to burn the mushrooms). Dry the mushrooms in a cool oven until crisp, then store in airtight containers.

An alternative method is to thread the mushrooms on a length of string and hang up in a hot airing cupboard till crisp.

ONION

Slice and shred the onions and steam for 4–6 minutes. Oven-dry as described above.

PEACHES

Follow the directions for apple rings, or make a proper 'Peach Leather' as follows:

Stone and slice 1 lb peaches into a saucepan and cover with water. Bring to the boil and simmer until the fruit can be easily mashed with no lumps. Stir in 14 oz sugar and simmer further until almost dry. Spread the mixture thinly on to a lightly-buttered board and either set in the sun to dry or dry in a cool oven. Roll up the leather in cheesecloth when dry and store. Works for other fruit as well, incidentally.

PEARS

Peel, core and cut the fruit into quarters and then place into a sea salt solution for exactly 1 minute (1 oz salt to 1 gallon water). This prevents discoloration. Place the fruit on a drying rack and put in a cool oven at 47°C, raised later to 57°C.

PEAS

Shell the pods and steam for 10 minutes. Oven-dry as described above. Alternatively try one of the following three methods:

(1) Pick the firmest, ripest pods. Shell them and spread the peas out on clean paper in the sun for 5–6 hours. Store in an airtight container.

(2) Shell the peas, put them into dry wide-mouthed bottles and shake them together so that they lie in as little space as possible. Cork or seal the bottles and bury in the driest part of the garden. Use for eating as needed but the peas should keep for 6 months.

(3) Blanch the shelled peas in boiling water for 10 minutes. Drain and then oven-dry as described above, or until the peas are dehydrated and hard.

POTATO

Peel and shred the tubers into 'shoe-string' pieces and steam for 4–6 minutes. Oven-dry as described above.

RED AND GREEN PEPPERS

Steam for 8–10 minutes and then dry as described above.

SWEETCORN

Cook the whole cobs in water until tender. Remove the kernels and allow to dry in a cool oven for a few hours. Store in airtight container.

TOMATO

Dip the fruit into boiling water for a minute or two and then plunge into cold water. Peel and cut into quarters and then oven-dry as described above.

BOTTLING

To my mind the taste of bottled fruit and vegetables leaves a lot to be desired. Not only does steeping in syrup or brine for a long period of time radically alter the quality of the produce but there is the added disadvantage of eating sugar-saturated food. For this reason drying and storing is preferable, but if you enjoy bottled produce or are keen to try it out, here is a basic guide to follow.

Equipment

The common *Kilner* jar is the easiest and most widely-used bottling jar. If old jars are being used they must first be thoroughly checked for any cracks or chips. All perished rubber sealing rings must be replaced – *never use old rings*.

The bottles need to be sterilized before being used. The most straightforward way is to boil them in water. For this purpose a double boiler is needed but you can make do with an ordinary large saucepan with a false bottom inside. This can be a piece of wood, chicken wire, an upturned tray, or even a folded towel. Anything, in fact, that will keep the bottles from touching the bottom of the pan when boiling.

Fruit

All fruit should be ripe and firm and of the highest quality. Grade the fruit in sizes so that each bottle contains fruit of a similar size. Large fruit such as peaches can be skinned and halved but otherwise bottle whole where possible. (The only advantage of halving fruit is that more can be packed into each jar.)

175

Syrups

For flavour, all fruit should be bottled in syrup. A standard syrup mixture, made from $\frac{1}{2}$ lb sugar boiled for 3–5 minutes in 1 pint water, will be suitable for most fruits but adjust to suit the acid content of individual fruits. Most fruits can be bottled in water, though the flavour will not be as good.

Vegetables

All vegetables must be bottled in a pressure cooker. Using the ordinary boiler will not kill all the bacteria which can seriously affect health. Wash all vegetables thoroughly. It is advisable to follow the instructions laid down by the pressure-cooker manufacturers with regard to pre-cooking times and bottling procedure. Vegetables can be bottled in syrup or brine (1 teaspoon salt to 1 pint water).

Bottling Procedure

There are three fruit bottling methods:

COLD WATER METHOD

(1) Wash the bottles with cold water, drain, but leave wet inside.

(2) Pack the jars with graded fruit, taking care to shake down the fruit with the aid of the handle of a wooden spoon. Leave about $\frac{1}{2}$ inch space between the top of the jar and the fruit.

(3) Pour the cold water, brine or syrup on to the jars and then fit the rubber seals (which should have been pre-heated in warm water) and the glass or metal lids.

(4) Screw on the lid bands lightly and then unwind about $\frac{7}{8}$ inch.

(5) Put the bottles in the boiler (with the false bottom) and fill up with cold water up to the level of the shoulders of the jars and cover the boiler with a lid.

(6) Heat for 1 hour so that the temperature of the water slowly reaches 53°C. Keep it at this temperature for a further 1 hour.

(7) Very carefully remove the jars and place on a wooden surface.

(8) Tighten the lids and allow to cool for 48 hours.

(9) Finally, test the vacuum of each jar by removing the metal lid bands and lifting them by their lids. If any of the lids come away with the weight then they must be reheated in the boiler in the same way.

HOT WATER METHOD

(1) Pack the jars as described in the previous method but use *hot* water, brine or syrup instead of cold.

(2) Put on the lids and screw on the bands loosely and place in the boiler containing warm water. Bring to the boil within 30 minutes and simmer for 2 minutes (soft fruit); 10 minutes (stoned fruit); 40 minutes (tomatoes).

(3) Remove the jars and allow to cool as in the previous method.

THE OVEN METHOD

(1) Fill the jars with fruit as described above and water, brine or syrup (cold). Put on the seals and lids but not the bands.

(2) Put the jars in the oven at 104°C, making sure they do not touch the oven bottom and sides, or each other.

(3) Heat for approximately 2 hours (more if there are a lot of jars, less if there are only a few).

(4) Remove the jars to a warm insulated surface and seal with the screw bands.

With the oven method the fruit is liable to shrink and so it is necessary to have a spare jar from which the juice can be used for topping-up purposes.

A helpful tip when bottling is to keep the screw bands greased with cooking oil in between use. This will prevent them going rusty.

Freezing

In a way, freezing makes redundant all the traditional methods of storing and preserving foods, as practically anything will keep in a freezer. However, as with all other aspects of life, variety brings delight, besides which it is not a wise policy to be totally dependent on any form of power device, no matter how convenient. Readers wishing to pursue a freezer-orientated preserving system are advised to refer to the bibliography at the end of the book.

JAMS

That it may please thee to give and preserve to our use the kindly fruits of the earth, so as in due time we may enjoy them.

LITANY

Preserving fruit in a jam is one of the nicest ways of storing and it is still surprisingly economical. There is the added pleasure too, of giving away jars to friends as presents.

Equipment

Kitchen scales – for weighing fruit, sugar, etc.
Jam filler – for scooping up hot jam.
Funnels – for filling jars without getting in a mess.
Measure – for liquids.
Muslin bags – for holding stones, pips, etc. when cooking.
Preserving pan
Sieve
Skimming spoon – slotted or perforated for removing scum, stones, etc.
Spoons – various sizes but must be wooden.
Seals, rubber bands, and labels.
Other items which are helpful but not essential are bottle brushes, bottle tongs (for transporting hot jam-filled jars), corer, lemon squeezer, stoner, stone basket.

Basic Jam Making Procedure

(a) Always use the very finest fruit and vegetables – the better the fruit the better the jam.

(b) Fruit must be picked on a dry, preferably sunny day. Fruit that is wet can result in runny, tasteless jam.

(c) Better to use underripe, than overripe fruit.

(d) Fruits need a certain degree of pectin to make the jam 'set'. Some fruits such as damsons, apples, gooseberries and blackcurrants have a high pectin content and therefore set well. Fruits such as blackberries, strawberries, cherries and apricots have a low pectin content and do not set. To overcome the problem of fruit set, lemon juice should be added at the rate of 1–2 lemons per 4 lbs fruit. Alternatively, fruits with a high pectin content can be added to the main fruit, e.g. blackberry and apple.

(e) Contrary to general belief, it makes no difference which type of sugar is used. The one advantage of preserving sugar is that it dissolves more quickly than lump or granulated. However, by heating ordinary sugar in the oven prior to use, this problem can be eliminated. Sugar is an essential ingredient of jam and unfortunately there are no satisfactory substitutes. Honey can be used to replace up to half the sugar content for any given recipe but it will impart its own distinctive flavour. Treacle can be used likewise.

(f) A special preserving pan should be used exclusively for jam making. This can be any large, thick pan which can take a high boiling temperature over a long period without burning. Avoid iron or zinc pans as these will taint the flavour of the jam.

(g) As jam needs room to rise, never fill the pan more than half full.

(h) Do not allow jam to stand for any period of time in a copper or brass pan.

(i) The most important rule in jam making is cook the fruit (either with or without water) *before* adding the sugar.

(j) Always stir the fruit regularly in the pan to prevent sticking and possible burning.

(k) Always cook the fruit *slowly*.

(l) Boil *quickly* once the sugar is dissolved.

(m) Stir in the sugar until it is *completely dissolved*. This prevents burning.

(n) Test for set after 10 minutes of quick boiling by dropping a little of the mixture on a cold saucer and allowing to cool. Draw a finger across the surface and if the mixture forms heavy wrinkles, the jam is of sufficient set. Some jams may need up to $\frac{1}{2}$ hour quick boiling to set.

(o) Skim off any scum.

(p) Warm the jars prior to filling.

(q) Allow jam to cool for a while before pouring into the jars, otherwise the fruit may rise to the surface.

(r) Fill the jars to the very brim to allow for shrinkage and cover immediately with a waxed disc (wax side down). This helps prevent mould.

(s) When cool, cover the top of the jars with a cellophane wrap, secured by an elastic band. Dampen the top of the cellophane before securing with the elastic band to form an airtight cover.

(t) Label the jars with the name of the jam and the date. You can buy ready-made labels but it is fun to make your own.

(u) Store the jars in a cool, dry, dark place and they should keep a year.

Remember – the hallmark of a fine jam is that it should reveal the true flavour of the fruit; be firm in consistency; have an even distribution of fruit; be brilliant in colour; have a palatable texture of flesh; and store without mould or crystallization.

177

CHERRY
Morello cherries and other cooking varieties are best. Needs added pectin or lemon juice.

DAMSON
Excellent for jam and needs no extra pectin.

FIG
Needs pectin and fruit acid to jam well.

GOOSEBERRY
Excellent for jam. Use when young and still green. Requires no added pectin.

GRAPE
All varieties jam well.

LOGANBERRY
Excellent and needs no added pectin.

MULBERRY

Fruits and Their Jam Qualities

It has already been mentioned that fruits vary in their pectin content. Here is a guide to the fruits and the best sorts to use.

APPLE
Cooking apples and crab apples are best, as dessert varieties do not cook well.

APRICOT
Needs cooking with the kernels. Needs the addition of lemon juice.

BLACKBERRY
Only the early-fruiting wild blackberries are suitable; otherwise mix with apple.

BLACKCURRANT
Excellent for jam and needs no extra pectin.

on occasion.

STRAWBERRY
Excellent – the finest of jams, though needs extra pectin.

WHITECURRANT
A useful fruit for adding acid and pectin to other jams without impairing that fruit's colour.

TRADITIONAL JAM RECIPES

There are so many recipes for jams in existence! The collection here contains some unusual jams as well as the good old favourites. The sugar

Black mulberries jam well, providing they are fresh.

ORANGE
Excellent and needs no added pectin.

PEAR
Makes poor jam on its own, being low in acid and pectin. Best varieties are the cooking pears.

PLUM
Excellent and needs no extra pectin.

RASPBERRY
Jams well.

REDCURRANT
Good and needs no pectin.

RHUBARB
Mature rhubarb sets better, but pectin needed

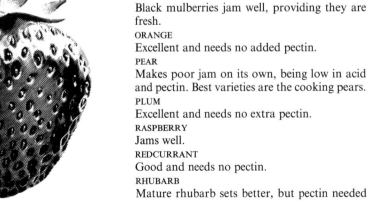

178

content may be reduced a little if a more tart jam is preferred, but be very careful, otherwise the jam may not set. *Add extra pectin whenever the sugar content is reduced.*

Bilberry Jam
Ingredients – 3½ lb bilberries (not too ripe); 2 lb sugar; 1 pint water; ¼ oz tartaric acid. Wash fruit thoroughly and stew with water and tartaric acid until tender. Proceed as for basic jam. This jam is never a firm set.

Blackberry and Apple Jam
Ingredients – 4 lbs blackberries (not over-ripe); 1½ lb cooking apples; sugar; ½ pint water. Pick

over and wash the blackberries and stew with ¼ pint water. Add the peeled, cored and sliced apples and the rest of the water and stew till reduced to a pulp. Add 1 lb sugar to every 1 lb pulp and proceed as for basic jam.

Blackcurrant Jam
Ingredients – 4 lbs blackcurrants; 6 lbs sugar; 3 pints water. Prepare and wash the fruit and stew in the water till soft. Proceed as for basic jam.

Cherry and Gooseberry Jam
Ingredients – 3 lbs cherries; 1½ lbs gooseberries; 4 lbs sugar; ¼ oz tartaric acid. Top and tail the gooseberries and remove stalks from cherries.

Wash the fruit and stew until the juice flows. Add the tartaric acid and simmer for 20 minutes. Proceed as for basic jam.

Damson Jam
Ingredients – 5 lbs damsons; 6 lbs sugar; 1½ pints water. Prepare and wash the fruit and stew with the water for 1½ hours until really soft. Remove stones and continue as for basic jam.

Greengage Jam
Ingredients – 6 lbs greengages; 6 lbs sugar; 1 pint water. Wash and halve the fruit and remove the stones. Crack a few of the stones to remove the kernels. Stew the fruit and water and a few

blanched kernels until soft. Proceed as for basic jam.

High Dumpsie Dearie or Autumn Jam
Ingredients – 3 lbs apples; 3 lbs plums; 3 lbs pears; 6 lbs sugar; ¾ pint water; lemon rind and ginger root to taste. Prepare the fruit and remove the stones. Boil the stones with the water for ½ hour then strain the liquid into the preserving pan. Add the fruit and stew until tender. Add the flavouring and proceed as for basic jam.

Japonica Jam
Ingredients – 4 lbs japonica (quince) fruit; 7

pints water; 1 heaped teaspoon powdered cloves; sugar. Wash the fruit and cut into eighths. Stew with water until tender and then sieve. Weigh the pulp and allow 1 lb sugar for every 1 lb pulp. Add flavourings and proceed as for basic jam.

Kentish Jam
Ingredients – 2 lbs Morello cherries; 1½ lbs raspberries; 1½ lbs mixed red and white currants; 3 lbs sugar. Stone the cherries. Break the stones and place in a muslin bag. Simmer with the water for 20 minutes. Add to the fruit and boil briskly for 20 minutes. Proceed as for basic jam.

179

Latweige (JUNIPER JAM)

Ingredients – 3 lbs juniper berries; ½ pint water; sugar. Wash and then stew the fruit with the water until tender. Pulp the mixture through a sieve and allow 3 lb sugar for every 1 lb pulp. Proceed as for basic jam.

Pear Jam

Ingredients – 3 lb pears; thinly pared rind of 1½ lemons; 3 tablespoons lemon juice; 1 lb 5 oz sugar; 1 pint water. Peel, core and cut the fruit into chunks. Boil the cores and lemon rind in the water for 10 minutes and strain. Stew the pears in the strained liquid with the lemon juice until tender. Add the sugar over a low heat and proceed as for basic jam.

Plum Jam

Ingredients – 6 lbs plums; 6 lbs sugar; 1½ pints water. Follow the recipe for greengage jam and proceed as for basic jam.

Raspberry Jam

Ingredients – 4 lbs raspberries; 4 lbs sugar. Wash the fruit, and then stew very gently until the juice flows. Bring to the boil and simmer gently until tender. Proceed as for basic jam.

Rhubarb and Elderflower Jam

Ingredients – 6 lbs rhubarb; 2 cups elder flowers; 2 lemons; 6 lbs sugar. Cut the rhubarb into small pieces and place in a large bowl. Put the elder flowers in a muslin bag and bury in the rhubarb. Add the sugar, cover with a cloth, and leave for 24 hours, stirring after the first 12 hours. Place the contents in the preserving pan and heat *very gradually* but not to boiling point. Pour back into the bowl and leave for a further 24 hours. Remove the muslin bag of elder flowers and add the juice and grated rind of the lemons. Pour the contents into the preserving pan and bring to the boil. Proceed as for basic jam.

Rhubarb and Ginger Jam

Ingredients – 6 lbs rhubarb; 5 lbs sugar; 2 teaspoons ground ginger; juice of 6 lemons. Gently stew the fruit and lemon juice until pulped. Add the ginger carefully. Proceed as for basic jam.

Strawberry Jam

Ingredients – 4 lbs strawberries; 3 lbs sugar; juice of 4 lemons. Boil the fruit and lemon gently for ½ hour. Proceed as for basic jam.

Wild Strawberry Jam

Ingredients – 1 lb sugar to every 1 lb fruit. Lay out the fruit in a dish and cover with some of the sugar. Leave for 24 hours and then pour the juice into preserving pan. Add the rest of the sugar and bring to the boil. Add the whole fruit and then proceed as for basic jam. *Do not overboil*, as this impairs the jam's delicate flavour.

JELLIES

Here concentrated in this lustrous purple pot,
Are speckled autumn days not easily forgot,
Hedges of graceful fruiting bramble sprays,
Arching the dry and crumbling brown pathways,
Spill out the jelly on to the fresh-made bread
And taste this coloured warmth the sun has shed.

A.G.

A jelly is made along the same lines as jam except that here the juice is extracted from the fruit to form a clear preserve. There are two methods of extracting the juice, the choice depending on the type of fruit and the quantities available. In both methods a jelly bag is needed; these can be purchased, but a perfectly good bag can be made from two thicknesses of muslin or cotton sewn together.

1st Method (SUITABLE FOR SOFT FRUITS)

Put the fruit into a glass jar or some other suitable container and place in a pan containing water. Bring the water to the boil which will cause the fruit to render its juice. Mash the fruit occasionally and then turn into the jelly bag to strain overnight. *Never squeeze the pulp* as this will cloud the jelly.

2nd Method (SUITABLE FOR HARD FRUITS)

Place the fruit in the preserving pan and add water to about ¼ depth of the fruit. Simmer until the fruit becomes pulpy and then turn into the jelly bag to strain overnight.

Making a Basic Jelly

Use 1 lb sugar to every pint of juice except for black-, red- and whitecurrants, which may require more. Bring the juice to boil in the preserving pan and then add the sugar, stirring until dissolved. Remove the scum and test after 10 minutes quick boiling (pure fruit juice should be tested after 3–4 minutes). Bottle as for jam.

Traditional Jelly Recipes:
Blackcurrant Jelly

Ingredients – 6 lbs blackcurrants; 3 pints water; sugar. Wash the fruit and place in the preserving pan with the water. Heat slowly and simmer for 1 hour. Mash the fruit while it cools. Strain in the jelly bag overnight. Return the juice to the preserving pan and bring to the boil. Simmer for 5 minutes and add the sugar. Proceed as for basic jelly.

Crabapple Jelly

Ingredients – 5 lbs crabapples; 6 cloves; small piece root ginger; 1 lemon; 4 pints water; sugar. Thoroughly wash the fruit. Cut into halves and place in the preserving pan with the water, together with the root ginger and cloves tied in a muslin bag. Bring to the boil and simmer for about ¾ hour until soft. Rub the pulp through a sieve and strain overnight in the jelly bag. Put the juice in the preserving pan, bring to the boil and simmer for ½ hour. Add the sugar and proceed as for basic jelly.

Cranberry Jelly

Ingredients – 3 lbs cranberries; 1½ lbs sugar; water. Wash and place the fruit in the preserving pan. Cover with water and cook for 15 minutes until soft. Pour into the jelly bag and strain overnight. Pour the juice into the preserving pan and bring to the boil. Simmer for ½ hour, add the sugar and continue as for basic jelly.

Elderberry Jelly

Ingredients – 3 lbs elderberries; 1½ lbs cooking apples; sugar. Wash and prepare the fruit, cut the apples into slices and put in the preserving pan. Boil the fruit, mashing constantly until soft and pulpy. Strain overnight in the jelly bag and return to the preserving pan. Proceed as for basic jelly.

182

Haw Jelly

Ingredients – 3 lbs hawthorn berries; 3 pints water; sugar. Wash the haws and place in the preserving pan with the water. Bring to the boil and simmer for 1 hour and then strain overnight in the jelly bag. Proceed as for basic jelly.

Mint Jelly

Ingredients – Large bunch of mint; $\frac{3}{4}$ gill vinegar; juice and pared rind of 1 lemon; 2 pints apple jelly (as a base). Remove the mint leaves from stalks. Tie the stalks together and add the apple jelly together with the lemon and vinegar. Boil for about 5 minutes and test for set. Pound the finely-chopped mint leaves and add 3 teaspoons to the boiling jelly. Strain and bottle.

Quince Jelly

Ingredients – 4 lbs quinces; 5 lbs crab or cooking apples; juice and pared rind of 2 lemons; water; sugar. Wash and cut the fruit into quarters and place in the preserving pan. Just cover with water and simmer gently until soft. Strain overnight in the jelly bag. Return juice to preserving pan with the juice of the lemons and the rind tied in a muslin bag. Bring to the boil and proceed as for basic jelly (removing the rind *before* adding the sugar).

Raspberry Jelly

Ingredients – 8 lbs raspberries; sugar. Extract the juice as described in the 1st method earlier on and proceed as for basic jelly.

Red Blackberry

Ingredients – 3 lbs red blackberries; water; sugar. Put the washed fruit in the preserving pan with the water and boil gently to extract the juice. Strain overnight in the jelly bag and return juice to pan. Boil gently for 20 minutes stirring constantly and then add $\frac{3}{4}$ lb sugar to every pint of juice. Proceed as for basic jelly.

Redcurrant Jelly

Ingredients – Redcurrants; sugar. Extract the juice as described in the 1st method earlier on. Allow 1 lb (or $1\frac{1}{4}$ lb to taste) sugar for every pint of juice and proceed as for basic jelly.

Rosehip Jelly

Ingredients – $2\frac{1}{2}$ lbs ripe rosehips; 4 lbs crab or cooking apples; 3 pints water; sugar. Use hips that have had at least one good frost if possible. Wash and cut the apples into quarters. Place in an enamel saucepan (other metals will discolour the hips) with the water and hips and bring to the boil. Simmer gently for 1–1$\frac{1}{2}$ hours until the hips are soft enough to crush (use a wooden spoon to crush them against the side of the pan). Strain overnight in the jelly bag (made of 3 layers of muslin). Proceed as for basic jelly. *Rose hip jelly stores better in small jars.*

Rowan Jelly

Ingredients – Rowan (mountain ash) berries; sugar; water. Wash the fruit and cover with cold water. Simmer for 40 minutes until the water is red and the berries soft. Strain overnight in jelly bag. Return juice to the preserving pan and bring rapidly to the boil. Proceed as for basic jelly.

Sloe and Blackberry Jelly

Ingredients – 2 lbs sloes; 8 lbs blackberries; 3 pints water; sugar. Wash and then boil the fruit in the water until soft and strain overnight in the jelly bag. Use $\frac{3}{4}$ lb sugar for every pint juice and proceed as for basic jelly.

Perfumed Jellies

Using a base of crab-apple jelly, exciting and delicate jellies can be made incorporating fragrant flowers and herbs. Roses, violets, scented geranium leaves, peppermint, verbena and angelica are just some of the possibilities.

Rose Petal Jelly

This procedure can be used for any other fragrant jelly. Pound a good handful of freshly picked rose petals with caster sugar so that the sugar absorbs the juice. Place in a dish, cover with a little water, and stew *very gently* in the oven. Strain in the jelly bag overnight and add the apple jelly. Boil up the mixture and proceed as for basic jelly.

CONSERVES

Generally speaking, a conserve is the whole fruit preserved in a syrup, as opposed to a jam which is the sweetened fruit pulp.

Cherry Conserve

Ingredients – Cherries (preferably Morello or Mayduke); $\frac{3}{8}$ pint redcurrant juice (or apple or gooseberry juice); 1$\frac{1}{2}$ gills water; sugar. Stone the cherries and allow 1 lb sugar for every 1 lb fruit. Dissolve the sugar in the water in a preserving pan over a low heat. Add the cherries and quickly bring to the boil, stirring very gently with a wooden spoon so as not to bruise the fruit. Boil for 10 minutes, remove the scum and then pour into a bowl. Leave for 24 hours and then return to the pan. Add the redcurrant juice and bring back to the boil for 3 minutes. Lift out the cherries into a hot jar and then pour over the hot syrup. This method can be adapted for other fruit such as damsons, plums and apricots.

FRUIT CHEESES

Cheeses are made from fruit pulp and sugar, cooked to a consistency thick enough to cut into slices when cold. Care must be taken to stir constantly when preparing fruit cheeses as they can easily burn.

Apple Cheese

Ingredients – Apples; juice and grated rind of 2 lemons; sugar; cider vinegar. Wash and cut the apples into quarters. Place in the preserving pan and fill to half the level of the apples with vinegar. Cook until soft and pulpy and boil with the lemon juice and rind for 1 hour, stirring constantly over a very low heat.

Bullace Cheese

Ingredients – Bullaces; sugar. Proceed as for apple cheese except to use $\frac{3}{4}$ lb sugar for every 1 lb pulp.

Quince Cheese

Ingredients – 9 lb ripe and unripe quinces; 2 lemons; 2 oranges; water; sugar. Cut up 3 lb quinces and barely cover with water in the preserving pan. Simmer till tender and strain. Peel and core the remaining quinces and slice thinly into the strained juice. Place in the preserving pan and simmer till pulpy (which

may take some time). Rub the mixture through a fine sieve. Allow 1 lb sugar to every 1 lb pulp and return to the pan together with the strained juice of the oranges and lemons. Proceed as for apple cheese.

MARMALADES

There really is nothing quite like home-made marmalade. The following recipes are for traditional marmalades.

Seville Orange Marmalade
Ingredients – Seville oranges; water; sugar. Boil the whole oranges for 1 hour until tender. Cut into quarters and remove the pulp. Extract the pips and thinly slice the peel. Mix the peel and the pulp and add 1 pint of water from the boiled oranges to every 1 lb pulp. To every 1 lb of pulp mixture allow 1½ lb sugar and dissolve in the preserving pan over a slow heat. When the sugar has dissolved boil rapidly for ½ hour or until set. Bottle as for jam.

Grapefruit and Pineapple Marmalade
Ingredients – Grapefruit; pineapple; lemon; water; sugar. Use an equal weight of grapefruit, pineapple and lemon. Slice the lemons and grapefruit finely and pare and shred the pineapple. Mix together in a bowl, with 3 pints water for each 1 lb fruit. Cover and leave for 24 hours and then boil in the preserving pan until tender (approximately 3 hours). Allow 1 lb sugar to every 1 lb of pulp and cook until set.

Bitter Sweet Marmalade
Ingredients – 2 oranges; 2 lemons; 1 grapefruit; 2 apples; water; sugar. Wash the fruit. Halve the citrus fruits and squeeze out the juice, saving the pips from the oranges and lemons. Finely shred or mince the peel. Peel, core and dice the apples. Tie the cores, citrus peel and pips in a muslin bag. Mix together the fruit and juice and add to it twice the quantity of water. Pour the mixture into the preserving pan with the muslin bag and bring to the boil, simmering gently for 1½ hours or until the pulp is thick. Allow 1 lb sugar for every 1 lb pulp and proceed as for Seville orange marmalade.

Lemon Marmalade
Ingredients – 6 large lemons; 6 pints water; sugar. Wash and thoroughly dry the lemons. Thinly pare off the yellow rind and cut into shreds. Cut up the pith into small pieces and tie in a muslin bag with the pips. Place the sliced lemons, the shredded peel and the muslin bag in the preserving pan with the water and boil gently until the contents are reduced and the mixture thickened. Remove the muslin bag and allow 1 lb sugar for every 1 lb of pulp. Proceed as for Seville orange marmalade.

PICKLES

Pickles are simply vegetables or fruits preserved in a spiced vinegar and can be either sweet or sour. For the best result use only the finest ingredients (i.e. not left overs) and a good malt, cider or wine vinegar. Avoid bottled vinegar. Pickling spices can be bought ready-prepared from the grocer or made up from the following ingredients to every 2 pints vinegar:

¼ oz cinnamon
¼ oz mace
¼ oz allspice
¼ oz ginger
¼ oz cloves
6 peppercorns

Avoid using metal utensils as vinegar can react and become poisonous. Pickles must be kept in glass bottles or unglazed earthenware jars and should be closely sealed. Always store in a dry place. Always ensure there is at least 2 inches of vinegar above the level of pickle in each jar.

Ash Key Pickle
Ingredients – Ash keys (i.e. fruit from the ash tree); vinegar; pickling spice; salt. Boil the ash keys in water, strain and repeat twice until tender. Pack the keys in a jar and cover them with spiced, salted vinegar.

Cherry Pickle
Ingredients – Ripe red cherries; caster sugar; spices; vinegar. Put alternate layers of cherries and sugar in a jar and between every two layers of fruit put a small muslin bag of broken

cinnamon, nutmeg and mace. Cover the mixture with vinegar and keep at least 1 month before using.

Marrow Pickle

Ingredients – 1 large marrow; 1 lb small pickling onions; 1 oz ground turmeric; 1 oz ground ginger; 1 oz chilli pods; vinegar; $\frac{1}{2}$ lb sugar; salt. Peel the marrow and remove the seeds and cut the flesh into small chunks. Lay alternate layers of marrow and salt on a dish, and alternate layers of sliced onions and salt on another dish. Leave overnight and then strain well. Put the other ingredients into a pan and simmer for $\frac{1}{2}$ hour. Add the onions and marrow and simmer together till the mixture thickens. Bottle when cool.

Mixed Vegetable Pickle

Ingredients – 1 cauliflower; 4 onions; 6 cucumbers; 2 green peppers; 2 lbs tomatoes; 1 head celery; 1 lb runner beans; 2 oz mustard seed; 1 oz turmeric; 1 oz allspice; 1 oz pepper; 6 peppercorns; 4 pints vinegar; sea salt. Prepare and dice the vegetables. Sprinkle thoroughly with salt and leave overnight. Put the vinegar in a pan with a muslin bag containing the spices. Bring to the boil and add the vegetables. Simmer gently until tender then bottle after removing the muslin bag.

Mushroom Pickle

Ingredients – Mushrooms; spiced vinegar; sea salt. Put the peeled mushroom caps and the trimmed stems into a pan with a little salt and gently simmer until the juice flows. When all the juice has evaporated, add the spiced vinegar and simmer for about 3 minutes. Bottle when completely cold.

Nasturtium Pickle

Ingredients – Nasturtium buds or seeds; spiced vinegar; salt. The buds are more delicate in flavour and should be gathered before the petals protrude beyond the calyx. The seeds, which are more highly flavoured, should be gathered while they are young and as soft as green peas. Put the seeds or buds into glass jars and cover well with spiced vinegar and 2 oz salt to every 2 pints. Keep 12 months before using.

Pickled Onions

Ingredients – 2 quarts pickling onions; 1 quart spiced vinegar; $1\frac{1}{2}$ oz sea salt; 2 oz sugar. Peel the onions and cover with the salt. Leave overnight and then rinse and dry the onions. Boil the vinegar with sugar for 6 minutes and add the onions. Bring to the boil and then remove from the heat. Strain off the onions and pack into jars. Reheat the vinegar and pour over the onions. Seal when perfectly cold.

Radish Pod Pickle

Ingredients – Green radish seed pods (fully formed); spiced vinegar; sea salt. Wash the pods in salted water and pack into glass jars. Pour over the vinegar and cover. As the vinegar becomes absorbed, add more, and seal when the jars are full.

Red- and Blackcurrant Pickle

Ingredients – $2\frac{1}{2}$ lb mixed red- and blackcurrants; 2 lb sugar; $\frac{1}{2}$ pint vinegar; $\frac{1}{4}$ oz cloves; $\frac{1}{2}$ teaspoon ground ginger; 1 oz cinnamon; pinch salt. Boil all the ingredients slowly for 2 hours and bottle in small jars.

Red Cabbage Pickle

Ingredients – Red cabbage; peppercorns; bruised ginger; vinegar; sea salt. Pick a cabbage that has seen the frost and remove the outer leaves. Cut it as finely as possible and sprinkle with salt in a bowl for 24 hours. Add a few peppercorns and a little root ginger (or use spiced vinegar) and pack into jars. Cover well with vinegar. Best eaten within the week – beyond which time the cabbage will soften.

Walnut Pickle

Ingredients – Green walnuts; spiced vinegar; sea salt; water. Use young green walnuts picked around the end of June (*walnuts are suitable for pickling if a needle can be passed through them*). Pierce the walnuts thoroughly with a stout needle and cover with a solution of 6 oz salt to every 2 pints water. Steep for 6 days, strain and repeat with fresh salted water. Strain and place on a tray in a warm, preferably sunny place, turning occasionally. When black and completely dry, pack into jars and cover with spiced vinegar.

CHUTNEYS

Unlike pickles, which preserve large pieces of fruits and vegetables, chutneys are made from vegetable or fruit pulp, cooked together like jam in a preserving pan. Points to remember are (1) *Never use a copper or brass pan*, for this purpose use enamel pans. (2) *Always use a wooden spoon.* (3) Chutneys for the store cupboard should be bottled more runny than those for the table, as they tend to stiffen up over a long period. (4) The ratio of fruit/vegetables to sugar is *2 to 1* (i.e. 2 lb of fruit to 1 lb sugar). (5) Rub the cooked ingredients through a sieve before bottling. (6) *Stir frequently.*

Apple Chutney

Ingredients – 2 lb peeled apples; 1 lb sultanas; ½ onion; 2 lb Demerara sugar; 1 dessertspoon sea salt; 1 teaspoon cayenne; 1½ pints vinegar. Boil the apples and onion till soft and then add the other ingredients, boiling gently for ½ hour. Sieve and bottle.

Blackberry Chutney

Ingredients – 3 lb blackberries; 6 medium-sized onions; 3 oz sea salt; 1 oz ground ginger; 1 oz mustard; ½ teaspoon cayenne; 1 lb Demerara sugar; 1 pint vinegar. Peel the apples and onions and chop into the preserving pan along with the blackberries, spices, salt and vinegar. Cook for 1 hour until tender. Add the sugar and cook gently for 2 hours. Sieve and bottle.

Elderberry Chutney

Ingredients – 2 lbs elderberries; 1 onion; 1 lb raisins; ½ teaspoon cayenne; ½ teaspoon ground ginger; ½ teaspoon mustard; ½ teaspoon cinnamon; ½ teaspoon ground mace; 1 teaspoon sea salt; ½ lb Barbados sugar; 2 fresh chillies; 1 pint vinegar. Prepare the fruit and mash them in the preserving pan with the vinegar. Mince the onion and raisins and add to the pan along with the rest of the ingredients. Simmer gently for 1½ hours. Sieve and bottle.

Gooseberry Chutney

Ingredients – 3 lbs green gooseberries; 1½ lbs dried fruit; ½ oz mustard seed; 2 cloves garlic; ½ oz cayenne; 1 lb sugar; 2 pints vinegar; pinch sea salt. Bruise the mustard seed and garlic.

Cook the gooseberries in the vinegar with the cayenne until tender. Add the sugar. Rub the mixture through a sieve and when cold, mix together with the minced currants and raisins and spices. Bottle and leave for 6 months before use.

Rhubarb Chutney

Ingredients – 2 lbs rhubarb; 1 lb sultanas; 2 lemons; 2 cloves garlic; 1 oz root ginger; 1 oz sea salt; ½ teaspoon cayenne; 2 lbs Demerara sugar; 1 pint vinegar. Cut and shred the rhubarb and mix with the juice of the lemons. Chop the garlic, bruise the ginger and tie in a muslin bag. Put all the ingredients into the preserving pan and gently cook for 2 hours until the mixture thickens. Remove the muslin bag and then sieve and bottle.

Tomato Chutney (GREEN)

Ingredients – 6 lbs green tomatoes; 3 green peppers; 1½ lb apples; 1½ lb onions; 1 lb sultanas; 2 oz root ginger; 1½ oz mustard seed; 1½ oz sea salt; teaspoon cayenne; 1½ lb Barbados sugar; 2 pints vinegar. Finely chop the onions, peppers, tomatoes and the peeled and cored apples. Put the ginger in a muslin bag (after bruising) and put all the ingredients into the preserving pan. Cook gently for 3 hours. Remove the muslin bag and then sieve and bottle.

Tomato Chutney (RED)

Ingredients – 6 lb ripe tomatoes; 1½ lb onions; 1½ lb peeled and cored apples; juice and grated rind of 2 lemons; ½ teaspoon mace; ½ teaspoon ground ginger; ½ teaspoon black pepper; 4 oz sea salt; ½ lb Demerara sugar; 2½ pints vinegar. Peel the tomatoes and remove the seeds and juice. Strain the juice and put into the preserving pan with the chopped tomato flesh. Add the other ingredients and cook gently for 2 hours. Sieve and bottle.

KETCHUPS

Hunger is the best sauce.

CAMDEN'S REMAINES 1614

To end with, there are recipes for three tradi-

tional ketchups which might wean you away from shop-bought ketchups.

Gooseberry Ketchup

Ingredients – 4 pints gooseberries; 1 oz bruised root ginger; ½ oz cloves; ½ oz allspice; ½ oz peppercorns; ½ pint vinegar; 3 lb sugar. Top and tail the gooseberries. Tie all the spices in a muslin bag and place in the preserving pan with the other ingredients. Simmer gently for two hours, remove the muslin bag and then strain through a fine sieve into bottles.

Mushroom Ketchup (FROM A COOKERY BOOK DATED 1896)

'Gather large flap mushrooms in the month of September. If the weather be showery, wait until the mushrooms have had a few hours of sunshine, for no water should enter into the composition of the ketchup. Break into an earthenware pan as many mushrooms as it will hold. Let them be clean, and quite free from grit and dirt, and that portion of the stem removed to which the soil adheres. Sprinkle salt among them and put a layer over the top. Cover them for a few days, occasionally stirring them during the time, then strain through a sieve without giving the mushrooms any pressure. To each quart of the juice so gained, allow three blades of mace, half an ounce of black peppercorns, the same of sliced ginger, with half the quantity of allspice, a few cloves, and more salt if required. Boil the juice for fifteen minutes, uncovered, and before putting in the spices. Add the spice and boil for twenty minutes more. Fill the bottles when quite cold.'

Tomato Ketchup

Ingredients – 8 lb ripe tomatoes; 2 large onions; 3 cloves garlic; ½ oz peppercorns; ½ oz allspice; ½ oz root ginger; ½ oz mace; 1 oz sugar; 2 bay-leaves; ½ pint white vinegar (distilled). Wash and dry the tomatoes and cut into slices. Lay the slices in a dish, sprinkle with salt and leave overnight. Put the contents into the preserving pan, together with the finely-chopped onions and garlic and all the spices tied in a muslin bag. Cook gently until the mixture is reduced to pulp. Remove the muslin bag and sieve the pulp through a fine hair sieve. Return to the pan and simmer gently with the vinegar and sugar until a creamy consistency is reached. Bottle and store.

WINTER

SECTION

Sea-coaling

ALONG the stretch of north-east coast which gently curves from Northumberland to the Tees estuary there was a spot, typical of many on that coast, where 'sea-coal' collected as richly and effortlessly as grime in the crook of a miner's elbow. This coal was a coarse powder, clean and brilliant like particles of crushed jet, and although we guessed it was washed in from the Durham coalfield which mysteriously extended outwards for miles under the North Sea, it seemed to bear little resemblance to the large, filthy lumps which rattled off the shovel into our fireplace. Although it was coal it was perfectly clean and it was silently deposited by the high tide in a glittering carpet a mile long for the coastal community to glean.

The gear used for sea-coaling expeditions was a curious and traditionally proven assortment which to my knowledge never varied from community to community along the entire north-east coast. Sacks were, of course, essential to put the coal in, and string to tie the neck of each sack when it was full. To scrape the coal from the beach a wooden rake was used which was generally made from an old broom handle with a flat piece of wood nailed at a slight reclining angle on the end. Sometimes the edge of the piece of wood was chamfered off to make a more precise tool. The only alternative to the rake was a flat piece of board held in the hand, which children and other ancillary helpers crouched down to use. A flat, broad shovel, to lift the raked coal into the bags, completed the portable hardware.

The crucial item of equipment, however, was a bicycle, a special kind of rusty, stripped-down model which was virtually a symbol of the north-east sea-coaling craft. A lady's bike was no good because it lacked a cross-bar, and that was an essential element in transporting sea-coal. One full sack could be slung through the triangular frame of a man's bike, another over the cross-bar and, sometimes, even a third on top of that. The beauty of this was that it not only enabled one to move the sea-coal from place to place, but the pressure of the metal bars against the full, wet sacks forced excess water out of the coal while it was being wheeled home. On a good day, the path to the beach was generally a double snail-trail of water that had been forced from each end of a caravan of coal-sacks.

Even to veteran sea-coalers, the sight of coal on the beach was always an immense visual shock. It was carelessly and richly flung across it, like Indian ink from a bottle, and it forced onlookers to stare at the drama of it before going down to spoil its stupendous asymmetry. If early sea-coalers had been at work, the black blotch would already be scarred here and there

191

with the regular plough sweeps of a rake. When the sea-coal crunched underfoot, the first job was to examine what depth of coal there was. It was a good day if there was a spread a quarter of an inch thick, with drifts here and there half an inch deep. If the half-inch drifts were extensive it was bonanza day. One peculiarity of the sea-coal deposit was that the deeper the layer, the greater likelihood there was of finding larger pieces of coal in it, washed smooth and round by the sea. These were known locally as 'roundies' or 'nutties' and were often collected separately by old age pensioners and children.

The sources of the two types of coal were also distinctive. Whereas the drifts of finer coal were in fact colliery discard washed in from marine dumps north of Hartlepool, the roundies were fragments quarried out from underwater out-crops of the Durham coalfield by the heavy surge of the North Sea.

There was never any Klondike rush to establish a stake on the beach. Individual sea-coalers and their families simply started work, and automatically new arrivals would give them a wide berth. By midday there would be a wide farm of sea-coalers spread the length of the beach, rhythmically raking and bending like reapers in a sea-scape. Collecting the sea-coal was simple. Sufficient pressure was applied to the rake so that it scraped up the coal without disturbing the bed of sand beneath. In winter it was very odd to separate carefully the layers of this industrial Neapolitan ice: the snow, the coal and the sand beneath. The coal was raked into heaps and left as long as possible to drain while the gatherer moved on elsewhere. The heaps were then shovelled up and put into sacks and the string to tie the sacks was wetted in the sea so that as it dried out, the knot round the neck of the sack would tighten. Greed rarely entered into traditional sea-coaling because no man could take away more than he could carry on his bicycle at any one trip, and, as I have said, this was generally three sacks full.

Wheeling off was the most difficult part of the job, and here the lone sea-coaler could be in trouble. The easiest way was for one person to raise the bicycle from its side one or two feet from the ground. The first sack would then be dropped by his mate through its triangular frame, and when the fulcrum of the sack had been established, the bicycle would be raised to its upright position. As the bike was steadied the second sack would then be heaved over the cross-bar, and sometimes a third on top of that. The difficult and prostrating climb to the dunes would then begin. Once a bike was loaded and underway it was unwise to put it down again as the loading operation would likely have to be repeated, but among some men there was a certain sea-coaler's etiquette which put them under an obligation to help lone women sea-coalers up the steep climb through soft sand to the path.

Even at that time in that part of the country, sea-coaling was looked down on by some members of the community who were not a cut above anyone else in any other respect. To them, gathering 'roundies' was more acceptable because it could be disguised as the by-product of a more sophisticated beach-combing stroll. As sea-coaling was often done on a Sunday some atavistic religious feeling may have entered into it, and certainly some returning sea-coalers tried to avoid wheeling their dripping pack-horses past disgorging churches. But the occasional van on the beach was the real clue to this growing snobbery. Sea-coaling had become a small-time commercial proposition for local youths who could drive off the beach with a comparatively large quantity, bag it and sell it at a competitive price to those women who were too proud to let their husbands wheel it off the beach in the traditional way.

No matter how it was gathered, sea-coal made an incomparable fire and its processing for domestic use was also traditional. Real heating experts put several shovels full into a bucket or basin and after picking out any stray shells, which cracked and spurted from the grate in a terrifying way, would dampen the sea-coal with water. A double sheet of newspaper was then twirled into a cone, twisted at the bottom to make it hold, and the damp sea-coal was packed into it like ice-cream into a cornet. The top end of the cornet was then twisted to secure it and when three or four of these were ready they would be arranged like a row of parcels on top of a small coal fire. Dampening the sea-coal not only washed out any particles of sand but made the coal hold together in entire red-hot bricks, with the surrounding newspaper acting

as a mould until this stage was reached. When the encircling family could no longer read items of news on the scorching coal parcels, the fire was ready to be enjoyed.

That was a child's-eye-view of sea-coaling, pictures in the fire, but now many years later, with the help of that nineteenth-century fuel-history classic, Galloway's *Annals of Mining and the Coal Mining Trade*, I see that my childhood belief in sea-coaling as a strangely innocent activity was not misplaced. Raking coal in the timeless chill of a blank north-eastern beach we were re-enacting man's earliest experience of coal in the North when, at an unverifiable date before 1236 up the coast at Blyth, the monks of Newminster Abbey were allowed by Adam de Camboise to take seaweed from a local beach for tillage and the romantically named *carbo maris* to burn. As in other sea-coaling documents of that period the emphasis was on the word 'take', not 'dig' or 'hew', and in unconsciously following that tradition we too were approaching coal, a mineral so often associated in the North with organised violence and injustice, as gatherers rather than violators, who would themselves be violated.

Alexandra Artley

194

The Miniature Garden

A garden should be rather small
Or you will have no fun at all
It should be sheltered from the cold
As full of flowers as it can hold
FROM 'RECIPE FOR HAPPINESS' BY REGINALD ARKELL

WHEN I was at primary school there used to be a show put on in the assembly hall each year, just before we broke up for the summer holidays. This show mainly comprised paintings, drawings, crafts and three-dimensional work that had been created during the year, but there was also a big nature section with prizes for the best entries. There was a pressed wild flower section, a flower arrangement section, and a vegetable- and flower-growing section. By far the best, though, were the miniature gardens.

Some of these gardens were truly beautiful (at least so it seemed at the time); full of ingenuity and a wildness that only children can create.

They were made in the most weird and wonderful array of biscuit and other tins, pots, trays, and boxes. Plants from gardens, wild flowers, vegetables and weeds were all somehow thrown together with pebbles, paths, pools and all manner of crazy houses, bridges and seats.

Unfortunately, most of these creations were dead within the week, or simply grew out of control because they were planted out with the wrong sort of flowers. Yet this needn't have happened. With a basic knowledge of structure and the right kinds of plants, a real living garden in miniature can be made that will last for years. They look enchanting set in the right position in

any garden but are especially cheering for those without a proper garden, such as flat-dwellers. And anyone with a love of stylized gardening and the miniature will delight in making one.

General Comments
Specific advice is given further on for the various types of miniature garden but here are discussed some of the basic principles.

Containers
For an outside location the ideal receptacle is a shallow stone trough. Unfortunately these are difficult to obtain and are generally very

196

expensive. Old sinks are the next best thing, especially if the stark white porcelain is painted in a subdued neutral or earthen colour. Large earthenware trays are lovely if you can get them, but for an especially effective setting, half logs scalloped out to form a trough are well worth using. Alternatively, troughs can be made from concrete. Moulds should be made from boards and the cement poured in and allowed to set (the inclusion of wire netting will reinforce the concrete). The walls must be at least two inches thick. Before using a newly-made cement trough, it should first be 'cured' by soaking in a strong solution of permanganate of potash for three days.

Only resort to plastic or tin containers for the balcony or inside the house.

Soil and Drainage
Whatever container is used should have adequate drainage holes in the bottom. Cover all drainage holes with old crocks (with sinks cover the drainage hole with a perforated zinc disc to keep out worms). Next, cover the bottom of the container with a layer of small stones and then an inch layer of peat or leaf-mould. Finally, top up with a sandy loam or John Innes compost, pressing down well. As shallow containers are apt to dry out in hot weather, a small piece of tubing can be buried vertically in one corner with the top remaining above the level of the soil (this can be concealed behind a plant or beneath a rock). This way, water can be poured through the tube deep into the container in dry conditions. Evaporation can be reduced if gravel or chippings are spread over areas of exposed soil.

Landscape Materials and Effects
Small attractive stones, rocks, pebbles, flints, marble chippings, gravel and any other similar material can be employed in the miniature garden for the formation of paths, steps, pools, walls and rockeries. Limestone and sandstone rocks are especially beautiful: limestone for alpine plants and sandstone for plants allergic to lime. Even bricks can be made from clay dug from the garden and fired in the oven.

The aim should always be to reproduce nature and the natural garden landscape in direct scale, and therefore care should be given to proportion and design. Little bridges, garden furniture,

sundials, dovecotes, pagodas, arbours, statuettes, terraces, gateways, arches and other decorative features can add charm to the miniature landscape, but beware of figures and buildings, as these will probably be way out of scale.

A miniature pool, or even a fountain or cascade, will add the final touch of magic to a garden. It can be simply a stone, earthenware or plastic tray or dish sunk into the soil and decorated wih pebbles and with plants encouraged to colonize the rim. The bottom should be painted a neutral matt colour. A better pool can be made by actually modelling the pool's basin from cement in much the same way as a full-scale pool. The hollow intended for the pool should be lined with small gravel and the cement spread over, either formally as for a formal garden, or irregularly for a 'natural' pool. Artificial pools can be made using silver sand, with ripples of darker sand for shadows and shading effects. Alternatively cellophane can be used, but avoid using mirror glass or tin as this may cheapen the whole look of the garden.

Cascades, waterfalls and fountains will require an electric pump to obtain a perpetual flow of water. Used inventively, such landscape devices as these can be utterly devastating. Used carelessly, they can look pretty grim. Cascades will require special construction techniques, with the miniature garden built up as a terrace in two or more levels. The top level will have a pool over which the water will cascade into a pool in the level below, and so on.

Location
Miniature gardens must not be subjected to extremes of temperature, wind, heavy rain or exposure to frost, and must be out of reach of drips from trees. Try and select the most sheltered position, preferably facing west.

Setting
Positioning a trough garden outside needs careful consideration. A position too close to flamboyant plants will spoil the miniature effect, and yet in an isolated or exposed position the garden can look absurdly out of place. It is difficult to be specific but some suggestions would be: at the bottom of steps; at the junction

of pathways; against the neutral background of a wall or fence; in a herb garden (because of the subdued colouring and delicate foliage of most herbs).

Suitable Plants
Some plants require strong sunlight, some require shade, while others will need varying degrees of moisture. All this must be taken into consideration, and a garden containing plants with similar needs is what to aim for. For very shallow containers, restrict planting to succulent or xerophytic plants (see separate list).

There are many little plants, dwarf (and *bonsai*) trees suitable for the miniature garden. Here is a good comprehensive list from which to choose. The number following each species denotes height in inches and the colour describes the flower, followed by growing conditions.

Flowers
ACHILLEA LEWISII (6) Yellow/dry, sunny
ALLIUM CYANEUM (2) Blue/sunny
ALSINE PARNASSICA (4) White
ALYSSUM SPINOSUM (6) White/dry, sunny
ANAGALLIS COLLINA (3) Orange/sunny
ANAGALLIS TENELLA (3) Pink/semi-shade
ANAGALLIS WILLMOREANA (3) Blue/moist, shade
ANDROSACE ARACHNOIDA (3) White/sunny
ANDROSACE CARNEA HALLERI (3) Pink/sunny
ANDROSACE SARMENTOSA (4) Pink/sunny
ANDROSACE SEMPERVIVOIDES (2) Pink/sunny
ANDROSACE SUPERBA (3) White/sunny
ANTENNARIA DIOICA ROSEA MINIMA (3) Pink/sunny
ANTENNARIA DIOICA RUBRA (3) Red/sunny
ARENARIA BALEARICA (2) White/moist, semi-shade
ARENARIA TETRAQUETRA (2) White/moist, semi-shade
ARMERIA CAESPITOSA (2) Pink/dry, sunny
ARTEMISIA BRACHYPHYLLA/Sunny
ASPERULA CAPITATA (3) Pink/semi-shade
ASPERULA HIRTA (3) Pink/semi-shade
ASPERULA LILACINA CAESPITOSA (3) Pink/semi-shade
ASPERULA NITIDA (3) Pink/semi-shade
ASPERULA SUBEROSA (3) Pink/semi-shade
ASPLENIUM RUTA-MURARIA (4) Dry, sunny
ASPLENIUM TRICHOMANES (3) Dry, sunny

ASPLENIUM VIRIDE (3) Dry, sunny
CALCEOLARIA TENELLA (2) Yellow/dry, semi-shade
CAMPANULA ARVATICA ALBA (2) White/dry, sunny
CAMPANULA COCHLEARIFOLIA (2) Lilac/sunny
CAMPANULA HALLII (3) White/sunny
CAMPANULA HEDERACEA (3) Blue/dry, semi-shade
CAMPANULA PULLOIDES (4) Violet/sunny
CAMPANULA RAINERI (3) Lilac/dry, sunny
CAMPANULA STANSFIELDII (4) Orange/sunny
CAMPANULA ZOYSII (2) Blue/sunny
CARDUNCULUS RHAPONTICOIDES (4) Purple
CENTAUREA PORTENSE (3) Pink/sunny
CHEIRANTHUS 'MOONLIGHT' (6) Lemon
CHEIRANTHUS 'SUNBRIGHT' (3) Yellow
CYANTHUS LOBATA (3) Light blue/sunny
DIANTHUS ARVERNENSIS (3) Deep pink/sunny
DIANTHUS BOYDII (1) Pink/sunny
DIANTHUS CAESIUS (2) Pink/sunny
DIANTHUS FREYNII (2) Pink/dry, sunny
DIANTHUS MYRTINERVIS (2) Pink/dry, sunny
DOUGLASIA VITALIANA (1) Yellow/semi-shade
DRABA BRUNAEFOLIA (3) Yellow/sunny
DRABA BRYOIDES (2) Yellow/sunny
DRABA MOLLISSIMA (2) Yellow/sunny
DRABA PYRENAICA (2) Lilac/sunny
DRABA RIGIDA (3) Orange/sunny
DRYAS OCTOPETALA MINIMA (3) White/moist, sunny
ERICA CORNEA
ERICA VULGARIS
ERIGERON LEIOMERUS (2) Mauve/sunny
ERINUS ALPINUS (3) Lilac/dry, sunny
ERINUS ALPINUS ALBUS (3) White/dry, sunny
ERODIUM CHAMAEDROIDES ROSEUM (2) Pink
FELICIA BERGERIANA (5) Blue/sunny
FRANKENIA LAEVIS (6) Pink/dry, sunny
GENTIANA VERNA (3) Blue/moist, sunny
GERANIUM ALBUM (4) White/sunny
GERANIUM DALMATICUM (4) Pink/sunny
GLOBULARIA BELLIDIFOLIA (3) Blue
GLOBULARIA NANA (2) Blue
GYPSOPHILA FRATENSIS (2) White/dry, sunny
HELIANTHEMUM ALPESTRE (SERPYLLIFOLIUM) (3) Yellow/sunny
HELIANTHEMUM LUNULATUM (3) Gold/sunny
HELIANTHEMUM OBLONGATUM (3) Yellow/sunny
HELXINE SOLEIROLII (3) Yellow/dry, semi-shade
HERNIARIA GLABRA (3) Green/dry, sunny

HOUSTONIA CAERULEA (3) Lilac and white/moist, sunny
HYPERICUM ANAGALLOIDES (4) Yellow/moist, sunny
HYPERICUM CUNEATUM (5) Yellow/moist, semi-shade
IONOPSIDIUM ACAULE (3) White and lilac/moist, semi-shade
IRIS CRISTATA (4) Lilac/sunny
LAURENTIA TENELLA (2) Lilac/moist, semi-shade
LINARIA AEQUITRILOBA (1) Lilac/dry, sunny
LINARIA ALPINA (5) Lilac/dry, semi-shade
LINARIA ALPINA ROSEA (5) Pink/dry, sunny
LINARIA GLOBOSA ALBA (5) White/dry, semi-shade
LINUM SALSOLOIDES NANUM (3) White/dry, sunny
LOBELIA LINNAEOIDES (2) White/moist, semi-shade

MENTHA REQUIENII (4) Lilac/semi-shade
MORISIA HYPOGEA (4) Orange/sunny
MYOSOTIS AZORICA (6) Blue/moist, sunny
MYOSOTIS COLLINA (3) Blue/moist, semi-shade
MYOSOTIS EXPLANATA (6) White/moist, sunny
MYOSOTIS RUPICOLA (6) Blue/moist, sunny
OXALIS ADENOPHYLLA (2) Lilac/sunny
OXALIS ENNEAPHYLLA (2) White/sunny
OXALIS CHRYSANTHA (3) Yellow/sunny
OXALIS LOBATA (3) Yellow/sunny
OXALIS MAGELLANICA (2) White/semi-shade
POLYGALA CALCAREA (2) Blue/dry, sunny
POTENTILLA NITIDA (3) Yellow/sunny
POTENTILLA VERNA PYGMAEA (2) Semi-shade
PRIMULA CLARKEI (2) Pink/moist, semi-shade
PRIMULA FRONDOSA (3) Lilac/moist, semi-shade
PRIMULA MINIMA (3) Pink/moist, semi-shade
PRIMULA SCOTICA (2) Lilac/moist, semi-shade

SAXIFRAGA (*Aizoon*):
S. AIZOON BALDENSIS (4) White/moist, sunny
S. AIZOON MINUTIFOLIA (6) Pink/moist, sunny
S. AIZOON ROSEA (8) Pink/moist, sunny
S. BURNATII (8) White/moist, sunny.
SAXIFRAGA (*Kabschia*):
S. APICULATA (2) Primrose/moist, sunny
S. ARCO-VALLEYI (2) Pink/moist, sunny
S. BURSERIANA (2) White/moist, sunny
S. CRANBOURNE (2) Rose-pink/moist, sunny
S. CHRISTINE (2) Red/moist, sunny
S. FALDONSIDE (2) Yellow/moist, sunny
S. HAAGII (3) Yellow/moist, sunny
S. JENKINSAE (2) Pink/moist, sunny
SILENE ACAULIS (3) Pink/sunny
SILENE ALPESTRIS (3) White/sunny
SILENE PUSILLA (2) White/sunny
SISYRINCHIUM ANGUSTIFOLIUM (4) Blue/sunny
SOLDANELLA ALPINA (3) Lilac/sunny

SOLDANELLA MINIMA (2) White/sunny
STACHYS CORSICA (4) Pink/sunny
THYMUS SERPYLLUM MINIMA (3) Pink/dry, sunny
VERONICA BOMBYCINA (4) Blue/dry, sunny
VERONICA RUPESTRIS NANA (4) Blue/sunny
VIOLA HEDERACEA (2) White/sunny
VIOLA YAKUSIMANA (1) White and blue/sunny

Miniature Roses
ROSA BO PEEP Red
ROSA ELF Red
ROSA MAID MARION Red
ROSA MIDGET Red
ROSA PEON Red
ROSA PIXIE White
ROSA SWEET FAIRY Pink

Succulent Plants
CRASSULA SARCOCAULIS (6) Pink/sunny
SEDUM ACRE AUREUM (2) Yellow/dry, sunny
SEDUM ACRE MINOR (1) Yellow/dry, sunny
SEDUM ANGLICUM (1) Pink/dry, sunny
SEDUM DASYPHYLLUM (2) Pink/dry, sunny
SEDUM FARINOSUM (1) White/dry, sunny
SEDUM FLORIFERUM 'Weihenstephaner Gold' (4) Gold
SEDUM MIDDENDORFIANUM (6) Yellow/dry, sunny
SEDUM NEVII (1) White/dry, sunny
SEDUM OBTUSATUM (4) Yellow/dry, sunny
SEDUM SPATHULIFOLIUM 'Cappa Blanca' (3) Yellow
SEMPERVIVUM ARACHNOIDEUM (4)
SEMPERVIVUM BROWNII (6)
SEMPERVIVUM 'Commander Hay' (6)
SEMPERVIVUM GIUSEPPII (5)
SEMPERVIVUM GLAUCUM (4)
SEMPERVIVUM KOSANINII (5)
SEMPERVIVUM RUBRIFOLIUM (6)
SEMPERVIVUM TECTORUM TRISTE (6)

Trailing Plants
ALYSSUM MONTANUM (4) Yellow
ARABIS ALBIDA FLORE PLENA (6)
ARENARIA MONTANA (6) White
CAMPANULA GARGANICA (3) Mauve
CAMPANULA PORTENSCHLAGIANA (MURALIS MAJOR) (5) White
CAMPANULA POSCHARSKYANA (10) Lavender-blue
CAMPANULA 'W. H. Paine' (3) Violet and white
HELICHRYSUM BELLIDIOIDES (4) White
PHLOX DOUGLASII (3) Lavender, pink, white
SAPONARIA BRESSINGHAM (3) Rose-pink
SEDUM EWERSII (6) Pink

Dwarf Trees (CONIFERS)
ABIES BALSAMEA NANA
CEDRUS LIBANI 'COMTE DE DIJON' (*Lebanon Cedar*)
CEDRUS LIBANI BREVIFOLIA
CYPRESSES (*Chamaecyparis*):
C. FORSTECKENSIS
C. LAWSONIANA AUREA DENSA
C. LAWSONIANA LUTEA NANA
C. LAWSONIANA MINIMA AUREA
C. LAWSONIANA MINIMA GLAUCA
C. OBTUSA CAESPITOSA

C. OBTUSA ERICOIDES
C. OBTUSA FLABELLIFORMIS
C. OBTUSA INTERMEDIA
C. OBTUSA JUNIPEROIDES
C. OBTUSA NANA
C. OBTUSA PYGMAEA
C. OBTUSA TETRAGONA AUREA
C. PISIFERA FILIFERA
C. PISIFERA NANA
C. PISIFERA SQUARROSA NANA
C. PISIFERA VARIEGATA
C. PLUMOSA COMPRESSA
C. SPHAEROIDES ERICOIDES
CRYPTOMERIA JAPONICA COMPACTA (*Japanese Cedar*)
CRYPTOMERIA JAPONICA SPIRALIS
JUNIPERS (*Juniperus*):
J. CHINENSIS AUREA
J. COMMUNIS COMPRESSA
J. COXII
J. HIBERNICA COMPRESSA
J. SABINA TAMARISCIFOLIA
J. SQUAMATA MEYERI
SPRUCES (*Picea*):
P. ALBERTIANA CONICA
P. EXCELSA CLANBRASSILIANA
P. EXCELSA ECHINAEFORMIS
P. EXCELSA PUMILA GLAUCA
P. ORIENTALIS GRACILIS
PINES (*Pinus*):
P. NIGRA PYGMAEA
P. PUMILA
P. SYLVESTRIS AUREA
P. SYLVESTRIS BEAUVRONENSIS
P. SYLVESTRIS GLOBOSA
TAXUS BACCATA (*Yew*):
TAXUS BACCATA COMPACTA
THUYA COMPACTA
THUYA ELLWANGERIANA AUREA
THUYA ORIENTALIS ROSEDALIS COMPACTA
TSUGA CANADENSIS (*Hemlock Fir*)

Aquatic Plants (CLEAR WATER)
ALISMA NATANS
AZOLLA CAROLINIANA
FONTINALIS
HOTTONIA
HYDROCHARUS MORSUS-RANAE

Aquatic Plants (BOG GARDEN)
ANDROMEDA POLIFOLIA

ARENARIA
ASPLENIUM RUTA-MURARIA
ASPLENIUM TRICHOMANES
COTULA REPTANS
DROSERA ROTUNDIFOLIA
DRYAS OCTOPETALA MINIMA
HYPERICUM ELODES
PRIMULA FARINOSA
PRIMULA ROSEA
SISYRINCHIUM ANGUSTIFOLIUM

Bonsai
Many species of tree can be trained as a *Bonsai* – the Japanese miniature tree. As Bonsai is such an art in itself, the reader is advised to refer to one of the many authoritative books on the subject (see bibliography at end of book).

Some Miniature Garden Arrangements
With such a wide range of plants and ornamental materials available, miniature gardens of great charm and beauty are within the scope of anyone. The keywords are simplicity and ingenuity. Try laying out a garden with unusual plant and rock combinations. Try sunken gardens, rockeries, secret walks, avenues, mazes, arbours, water gardens and cascades. But keep it simple. Overcrowding plants may result in a choking jungle that will obliterate all the landscape features. Better to plant too few than too many. Here are six miniature gardens to make.

THE ROCK GARDEN
One of the most effective miniature rock gardens I have seen was formed of flints and planted out with just sedums and sempervivums. Generally, however, it is the alpine species that are most suited to this setting. The art of a good rock garden is in the arrangement of the rocks. Avoid using too many small rocks; three or four large pieces of rock aesthetically arranged will be far more effective than two dozen pebbles. Rocks of the same kind should be used; try not to mix various types as this will be unnatural. When actually laying out the rockery, the largest rocks should always be placed at the bottom, gradually working up to smaller rocks at the top. Soil must be packed between each rock to enable the plants to grow. Try to emulate nature and reproduce the

natural rock formations that appear in the wild. Alternatively, take a visit to the local park or botanical gardens and see how professional gardeners have designed the rockeries.

THE WATER GARDEN
Combined with a rockery, this is perhaps the most beautiful of all miniature gardens. The water can either be constantly flowing in cascades, fountains, etc., or static in what is called a bog garden. Where a rockery and pool garden without plants growing in it is concerned (with or without flowing water) the depth of the pools need be no more than two inches. Use pebbles or small pieces of rock to naturalize the edges. Certain plants will grow in clear water but the depth of water must be at least four inches and there must be a one-inch layer of soil on the bottom of the pool.

For the bog garden, the depth of water should be a good four inches to enable the various aquatic plants to grow. The water area, whether a part of the total garden or the garden itself, must be filled with a mixture of charcoal, grit and peat. This will make an ideal swamp for the plants. Although the bog garden is a static water area, it will need fresh water quite regularly, otherwise stagnation will set in. The ambitious miniature gardener can overcome this problem by feeding the swamp area from an overflow, say, from surrounding pools, or from a cascade. Alternatively, fresh water can be added daily, and a little of the excess drained off. Incidentally, glass fish tanks are ideal containers for a bog garden.

THE CACTUS GARDEN
This is the simplest form of miniature garden, suited for indoors. Select cacti of varying shapes and sizes – the larger forms taking the part of trees and the smaller species as flowers. The cacti can be planted among coloured pebbles or ornamental stones.

THE JAPANESE GARDEN
This indoor miniature garden is virtually a model of a garden style that is already on a small scale. The Japanese, having very little room at their disposal, developed a form of gardening that incorporated many landscape and ornamental features within a given area to give an

201

impression of distance. These features include mounts crowned with a temple or pagoda from which to view the landscape, various significant rocks, islands, bridges and trees.

For the miniature form, Bonsai trees, cacti and small ferns are the plants most suited and effective in a miniature setting. The temples and bridges can be fashioned from modelling clay or made from wood and painted in bright colours traditional to Japanese culture, i.e. red, blue and gold.

It is especially important to keep this style of garden as simple as possible. One beautiful dwarf tree or Bonsai and one or two 'shrubs' with a temple, bridge and pool will look very effective.

THE HANGING GARDEN

A really effective hanging garden can be made using terracotta strawberry pots, the type that have planting cups up the side. Trailing plants such as those listed earlier on will look lovely pouring down the side of the pot. Try planting with just succulent plants, such as sempervivums, for a more unusual effect.

Hanging baskets provide an orthodox yet attractive way of showing trailing plants to their best advantage. It is advisable, however, to treat them as a purely annual decoration. To prepare the basket for planting, place it the right way up in the top of a flowerpot or some other open container. This will hold it steady for planting. Line the basket with damp sphagnum moss from the bottom upwards, taking care that no gaps remain. Next, fill the basket with potting compost that is sufficiently damp to stay firm when squeezed in the hand. Finally, plant out with species such as ivy, pendulous begonia, ivy-leafed geraniums, campanula isophylla, heliotrope, trailing lobelia, fuchsia, asparagus sprengeri, achimenes and lantana. Water them in well.

Remember that a hanging basket may weigh as much as 25 lb when full and watered. *Make sure that the supporting chains are strong enough and that the hook from which it hangs is firmly secured.*

THE BOTTLE GARDEN

Bottle gardens are virtually replicas of tropical or sub-tropical forests or jungles; because a humid atmosphere is created, the plants will rarely need watering. They are the exotic end of miniature gardening.

The most difficult operation involved in making a bottle garden is getting hold of a suitable bottle! Very large bottles such as those fabulous globular acid bottles are like gold dust and cost just as much. A perfectly reasonable garden, though, can be created inside a four-litre cider bottle, the type that can be purchased in most off-licences.

After thoroughly washing the bottle, let it dry and then pour in a two-inch layer of gravel (this is made easier with the aid of a paper tube inserted like a funnel in the neck of the bottle). On top of this pour in about four inches of good soil compost to which a couple of handfuls of broken or powdered charcoal has been added (to prevent soil acidification). The soil must then be lightly pressed down; achieved quite easily using a cork impaled on the end of stout wire such as that used in a coathanger.

Planting inside the bottle is not half as tricky as it might appear. Holes for the plants' roots can be dug with the coathanger wire – the plants gently inserted in position using the same wire bent at the end to form a semi-circle in a plane at right-angles to the direction of the wire. Once in position, the plants can be bedded into position using the corked wire.

The most suitable plants will be those requiring a constant humidity. Here is a brief list to choose from:

AFRICAN VIOLETS
BROMELIADS
DWARF PALMS
IVIES
LICHENS
LIVERWORTS
MOSSES
PEPEROMIAS
PHILODENDRONS
SMALL FERNS
TROPICAL PLANTS

Although a bottle garden will require minimal maintenance, there will inevitably be the odd plant failure and a certain amount of pruning to deal with. All dead and dying vegetation must be removed, otherwise disease can set in and kill off the rest. Pruning can be achieved using the good old coathanger once more, with a razorblade attached to the end. The position of the bottle, too, is very important. The ideal situation is a north facing window. Direct sunlight may kill off everything inside. Never place outside in the sun, as the heat created inside will reduce the plants to corpses within the hour. Finally, keep the bottle unsealed. Not only will it make visibility inside the jar a lot easier, but also the chances of infection from terminal fungal and bacterial diseases are considerably reduced.

THE
JUVENILE THEATRE

Portrays each sep'rate Part,
And, while we thus our time beguile,
We get the Play by heart.
For there are Combats, great and small,
and Portraits out of number:
Processions, Cars, Stage-Fronts, and all!
To fill one's mind with wonder.

FROM 'THE BRITISH STAGE IN MINIATURE'

DURING my last year at art college I became heavily influenced by 'Art Deco' and the 1930s, which inevitably led to a blinding obsession with Hollywood and the 'Golden Age of Musicals'. One outcome of this infatuation, which embraced the visual splendours of Busby Berkeley and the sheer joy of Astaire and Rogers, was the construction of an art deco toy theatre, with an elaborate static stage set of chorus lines, Fred and Ginger, and opulent scenery, props and lighting. If I say so myself, it was my pièce de résistance and it gave myself and many others immense pleasure.

Now it so happens that most of the know-how for constructing the theatre I picked up from a tutor and good friend, the artist Betty Swanwick, an authority of some note on the juvenile theatre. In fact Betty had been responsible for the near-legendary Goldsmiths' Art College toy theatre productions and had written an article on the subject outlining her experience with the college shows. What follows is that same article, with the addition of my own comments (in italics). Apart from the craft angle involved, there is the opportunity for urbanites to reconstruct landscapes and beautiful rural scenes in terms of stage scenery, bringing an element of those day excursions back to life!

Construction: Proportions and Framework

There is no doubt that Benjamin Pollock, the father of toy theatre, had carefully worked out the right size for the aperture of the Toy Theatre. This is 13 inches (330 mm) high by 18 inches (457 mm) wide. One year in the early days we tried a wider opening for the proscenium arch, but this shape was not satisfactory; we found that it was more difficult to conceal the manipulators' hands and mask the views that the audience had from the sides to behind the scenes.

The basic framework need not be complicated. It must, however, be strong enough to support lights, curtains and any props that may be employed during performances. For this purpose ¾-inch (18 mm) battening for the perimetal framework of the theatre is ideal, with ½-inch (12 mm) battening for side and stage supports. The stage floor can be constructed from either hardboard or plywood. If you're an ambitious

type, try constructing an authentic-looking stage floor from ¼-inch (6 mm) hardwood battening glued together like floor boards. If these are stained and polished you will have a really super stage floor. The front of the stage can be trimmed off with moulding (picture moulding, especially some of the ornate kinds, can look very effective). The front of the theatre – the proscenium – can be a permanent fixture constructed from hardboard or plywood and as simple or ornate as you care to make it. Alternatively, it can be a temporary affair made from card, designed and constructed anew for each theatrical performance. Whichever is chosen, the ornamentation and decoration of the proscenium can be made from papier mâché, paper sculpture, moulding or any other decorative medium and/or painted with matt paints which will not reflect the lights.

Theatre Curtains

The theatre curtain may be made of thick cardboard and painted a plain colour, or designed in traditional theatre curtain draping. We found that a curtain made of nylon is very effective. This has to be slightly ruched, in the way seen in jewellers' windows. Because of the lightness of nylon, little weights have to be sewn to the bottom, so that there will be no gap. The top of either a material or cardboard curtain is tacked to a batten. A piece of cord is placed either end of the curtain; these cords are knotted together about 18 inches (457 mm) up, passed through a centrally-placed screw-eye and taken straight up to a height well above stage. The cord can then be guided through a series of screw-eyes placed horizontally in the partition wall. The end of the cord can be tied in a loop and attached to a hook when the curtain is up, and released when it has to be lowered.

The curtains can also be fixed to wooden dowelling 'rollers' which have wire crank handles for lowering and lifting. Using this method, a whole series of curtains can be employed from the front of the stage to the back. The top of the curtains should be fixed to the dowelling (½-inch (12 mm) diameter) by staples and the rollers fixed to the roof of the theatre by drilling holes in the top side supports and using the crank handles as spindles. Beautiful effects can be made by using netting or see-through fabrics which have scenery

printed or painted on them. Embroidery, tassels, sequins and beads can all be used.

Scene Painting

Perspective. On the whole, it is advisable to ignore rules of perspective in scenery. The stage itself is given depth by the use of side wings, and although some added depth can be suggested in the treatment of the backdrop, it is certainly better not to show objects in perspective on the side wings. The topdrop, however, like the backdrop, can be designed in such a way as to suggest depth. In outdoor scenes, for instance, rows of clouds make a good topdrop, while an interior can be enhanced by a chandelier, suspended from the ceiling. Such things as a row of flags, or a garland of flowers, will also serve to help the illusion of recession.

The side wings and the back drop can also be constructed from papier mâché. This is especially effective for forest scenes where trees and animals can be made in relief. Paper sculpture can be incorporated for special effects. Abstract scenery and props can be made from anything that comes to mind providing it is used with ingenuity – wire, tubing, mirror foil, mirror glass, tin cans, and especially natural materials such as flowers, twigs, leaves, stones and shells which can be collected on trips into the garden or the country-side. Be creative and explore all the possibilities.

Lighting

We fixed our electrical equipment, consisting of a dimming board and switches bought from a firm experienced in making these things for theatres, on a wall to one side of the stage. This board was placed about six feet up the wall, and the electrician sits on a stool set on a stout table. From this slightly higher position he can keep his eye on the rest of the company. The jelly screener is in close contact with the electrician, for he is mobile and has sets of coloured jellies mounted on card frames to insert into slots attached to the stage lights. We had lights and shades made for the stage, but in the old days someone made us a set of lights with shades made from cocoa tins, and with wire frames for putting the coloured jellies into. There are four lights hung on a rod above the stage, one strip for footlight and one strip for top light con-

cealed from view but giving the maximum strength. In addition there is a wanderer which may be used for such effects as a light in a window cut in a backdrop or other similar devices.

Theatrical dimmers can be obtained from any well-known electrical store. Someone who is electrically-minded should contact such a store and seek advice. This is necessary, because if anyone who is not knowledgeable about electricity tampers with it there may be danger of conflagration. During the whole of my experience we have never had a fire, but I always insisted that a qualified electrician looks over our apparatus at regular intervals. In the old Victorian days of Toy Theatre when they often used nightlights, and firepowder for battle scenes, I should imagine that many a Toy Theatre went up in flames.

Lighting effects make a most valuable contribution to Toy Theatre atmosphere. The thunderstorm or firework scene, the dawn growing into daylight, and some examples of new lighting can be used to full advantage. A gauze curtain with the footlights and top lights playing on it will produce a flat surface for perhaps two characters to speak against; then, when the front lights are dimmed out and the back lights put on, a scene set behind the gauze makes a most astonishing transformation. There are endless possibilities for all kinds of effects which the electrician can try out. It is also necessary for the voice, the scene shifter and the music worker to have a masked light apiece to enable them to see what they are about. But these lights need not be under the control of the electrician.

The electrical system is perhaps the trickiest part of the theatre construction. Miniature mains lights are difficult to obtain but still available from certain large electrical retailers. The wiring must be in parallel so that individual lights can be switched on and off. All lights must be encased in tin cowling to prevent the possibility of overheating and fire. These can easily be adapted from empty food tins, or constructed specially from tin sheet and solder. Set the lights out of the public (i.e. the audience's) view. This will mean fixing the footlights below the level of the bottom of the proscenium, or set in a cowling guard fixed to the front edge of the stage. The shades or 'jellies' can

be made from coloured paper, plastic film, or perspex. Alternatively, coloured lights can be used, with extra and more subtle colouring effects achieved when used in conjunction with the jellies. For the electrically ambitious, beautiful lighting effects can be created using Christmas tree fairy lights, wired up in two or more circuits (the effect can be even more stunning if the lights are phased!). I did this with my Busby Berkeley set. I fixed the fairy lights in a star formation to a board covering the whole of the backdrop and each circuit (there were four) operated one specific colour and one section of the star. In front of this I placed a sheet of frosted glass to mask the lights and the end result was pure magic! (See photograph at beginning of chapter.)

Terminate all wiring from the lights to a control box. This can easily be made from plywood, with $\frac{1}{4}$-inch (6 mm) holes drilled in the lid for the switches. On all accounts, though, when wiring up the electrical circuit – BE CAREFUL!

Figures

The figures are divided into the main characters and the lesser characters; these latter we designed on flat card and cut out and fitted them on to wire holders.

For the chief characters we devised a means of scoring down the middle of the cardboard figures and bending them back slightly. The wire holder is put through paper tubes which are sewn on to the figure. This enables it to swivel round.

It is best to paint the figures very simply, with large, clear eyes not heavily made up. As the figures are so small, we made the head rather large in proportion to the body, otherwise the expressions and details of the faces would be quite lost. The body and legs together are approximately equal to three-and-a-half head lengths. The card of which they are made is about $\frac{1}{16}$-inch (1·6 mm) thickness. Public libraries have books with pictures of costumes, military, highland, and oriental. We always paint the backs of the figures.

Another amusing effect may be produced in a witch, a dragon, or a monster by attaching the head to the shoulder by a small wire spring; this makes a shaking movement. For some other evil character the eyes may be cut out and coloured jelly paper stuck behind, so that in certain

lighting their optics appear to glow. We also folded and bent the arms of the main characters. This gives a movement and feeling of life from the shadows cast. The scoring and bending makes the figure look more solid. A very queer effect can be made by having just the large heads of the main characters talking with each other on the stage as in a close-up used by films. It is very interesting to play with the scale and, for instance, to pass through two normal-sized figures, and then to pass them through again in a smaller version farther back. The usual size for figures is $7\frac{1}{2}$ inches (190 mm) for men and 7 inches (176 mm) for women, but there are no rules about this.

Materials of all kinds may be used. Sequins are very exciting when stuck on to eyes. Glitter adds a wonderful sparkle to scenes of climax such as wedding banquets and ballrooms. Seccotine is the best adhesive for glitter, sequins, or jelly paper. For scenery a thick cardboard should be used for strength, and also all figures, objects and gadgets. For lesser things a thinner card or paper may be used. Tissue paper which can be bought in many beautiful shades can make lovely effects when stuck over things. Textured papers such as brick paper, marbled and flocked papers, make good surfaces. Silver paper on the whole is disappointing as it tends to go black in artificial light. A scene of depth and far distance may be attained by using a cut-out trellis in a garden or a cut-out window with a view behind it, and to see figures walking behind these cut-outs is most impressive. There are endless possibilities in effects, which you realize when you begin to experiment with them.

Gadgets and Effects

Over a period of time we invented all kinds of gadgets. Some of these were based on Victorian moving picture post cards and books. Gadgets are simple (some are not so simple, it depends on the mechanical ability of the inventor concerned) devices whereby you produce a movement which animates an object that might become boring if it didn't move. The best gadgets are usually contrived so that the manipulators can work them smoothly. If you have a scene with a conjuror and a table with a top hat on it, behind this table will be in a small container a dozen paper doves strung together

on nylon thread; this thread has been passed to the top manipulator in the shadow of the side wings. At the appropriate moment the conjuror and his table of tricks are pushed on and held firmly down (gadgets are better if fixed on to a batten rather than a wire), and then as the cymbal crashes the top manipulator will pull the nylon thread and out will come the doves. Do this in a mystic type of lighting and the whole thing is amazing. To make a mouse run up a clock one has not only nylon thread to pull it up, but a weight on the back of the mouse for it to go back again. If you do not have weights you always have to have another thread to get it back again. There is enormous scope for gadget-making minds, but it is still advisable not to get them too complicated. For an effect of clouds you can use two gauze nets with clouds painted on, these may just be gently moved from side to side, held by the side manipulators, and with some artful lighting the impression is rapturous. A most interesting technique is to move your inanimate objects to avoid changing scenery. If your princess suddenly finds herself walking from the seashore to arrive in a thicket, you leave the seascape in and the side manipulators can push on a tree or groups of trees fixed on wood battens. There are endless possibilities in this idea. If a policeman should wish to sit down whilst he is waiting for the burglar to appear, you can take off the standing bobby and shove in a separate figure of him seated on a chair. The audience accepts these novelties, they are most logical and convincing, and they afford a welcome movement for the eye of the beholder. A stationary fire engine can be placed on the stage and the landscape moved. The landscape perhaps being four or five feet wide may be passed from one side to the other, also a pillar box, lamp post or passers-by may glide across, and you find that you can keep the fire engine unmoved to the sound of engine throbs and fire bells whilst your narrator is relating how urgent it is for it to get to the fire and how long it seems to take for firemen to arrive to save the hero and heroine. It is extraordinary the way that the fire engine seems to be tearing along without in fact moving.

On the side wall opposite the electrician we arranged a series of large shallow shelves. Each scene used in the play occupied one shelf, the shelf being labelled with the name of the scene

and numbered according to its appearance e.g. Scene I, 'Outside the Palace Gates', on the first shelf, Scene II, 'In the King's Bathroom' on the second. Each scene has to be put back in order immediately it has been played. If the scene has two sets of side wings, each is marked clearly on the back so that it is visible to the players, Left Back, Right Back, Left Front, Right Front. This simple device stops any confusion when the scenes are being changed. The backdrop is similarly marked clearly, Top, so that there is no doubt in a rush, and possible panic is avoided. For nothing can appear so hideous or so spoil the magic for the audience as a piece of scenery put in upside down. These wide wings and drops are clipped by large spring paper clips to wooden struts which form a sort of cage round the stage.

It is most important for each manipulator round the stage to inspect the scenery as it is put in, to see that it is straight and as steady as possible. All built-up gadgets, about which there will be a more detailed explanation later, are usually kept separately in order of appearance on top of the shelves containing the scenery. Of the two scene shifters, the first is in charge of taking out and finally of putting away the scenery. She usually hands out the scene (always being a scene ahead of that being played on the stage) to the second scene shifter, who carries it noiselessly to the manipulators on the far side ready for being put in. Each manipulator has a place for keeping the scenery until ready for changing. The first scene shifter usually feeds the scenery to the two manipulators near her. The process of changing scenery in itself is a most interesting one. We often used a transparent nylon front curtain through which the exciting shadows of the changing scene were visible or, more often, the scene was changed quite openly in front of the audience. The most important thing is never to rush the scenery on or off at a mad speed, for the most unpleasant downfall is likely, but to perform the change in slow measure, as if it were a dance. But, and this is a vital point, you must always keep the previous side wings, backcloth and topdrop on the stage while putting in position new scenery. It is of the greatest importance never to have the stage bare so that the audience can see the backstage works exposed. The following back-

drop is very easily lowered over the old one and the old one removed. By this means you produce a kind of moving picture effect which can be rather a pleasing spectacle, especially with dim and delicate lighting. The scene shifters are also in charge of the stage figures and see that the manipulators are given the ones they need for each scene. We found that by hanging a wire from back to front of the backstage space about 6 feet 6 inches (2 m) from the floor, we could hook a number of figures on to this, and as this is near the manipulators it can eliminate the necessity for the scene shifters to hand them. A golden rule for the organizing of the scenes and figures is always to insist upon each thing being put neatly away as soon as it is finished with. By this method everything is in order for the next performance. Another point: the first scene shifter must have near the shelves some sort of little box or cupboard containing the 'first aid' kit. This comprises sellotape, needles, cotton, wire, paper clips, sharp knife, scissors, pliers, hammer, a little cardboard, paper, drawing pins, and indeed any property that may have to be suddenly used for hasty repairs. I always made a point of impressing upon the scene shifters that they must inspect each scene, figure and gadget before each performance, and if manipulators notice some weakness which may have appeared to report this for repair work. Strange as it may seem, however, the diminutive card and paper world is much stronger than one would suppose.

Manipulators

The manipulators must be a cool and elegant-fingered lot if possible. It must be impressed on them that they must never rush the tiny figures on or off the stage, except for the very occasional reason. Because the stage is so minute, movement must be slowed down, otherwise if the villain enters and whizzes across the 18-inch stage he is gone in a flash and makes no emotional impact on the audience whatsoever, and his voice is left talking his part without him. Accurate timing between voice and manipulator is imperative. On the whole it is better that the characters face the audience when they are talking, and that they move sparingly; most to stress some action, say of anger, horror, or laughter. If they jerk a little at certain key

moments quite a dramatic quality is effected. As on the big stage, over-acting is to be frowned on. It is very trying for the audience to see the beautiful and dreamlike heroine behaving like a dizzy lizzy, jarring their eyes and causing them to feel uncomfortable for her. Although these characters are so small and only made of card, they become very real and living in the minds of the spectators. I have known audiences to laugh and gasp in just the same way as they will at a performance of human actors. There are usually four manipulators, one each side standing on the floor, one seated or kneeling behind the stage on the same level, and it is convenient to have one mobile manipulator who can go from side to side to give a hand when there is heavy traffic and movement of figures. For instance, in a scene depicting lines of soldiers marching or a carnival this floating manipulator is invaluable. Sometimes it is rather interesting to see a human hand removing some property from the stage: this, of course, has to be done with a sense of purpose, a definite air and some style. The casual clumsiness of a bad manipulator can be very irritating.

Voices

Voices are a difficulty unless you have the help of someone who specializes in speech production. I myself favour the natural quality of a pleasing speaking voice for Toy Theatre, especially for narration. If the voice is out of scale and over-trained it would be too grand for the smallness of everything. The narrator was the chief voice in our productions as a rule, and the rest of the company took over different characters' voices according to their abilities. The narrator in his dominant position above the stage has a very exacting job. He has to time his voice with the action going on below him and with the music. To give the time required for the manipulation of the figures or gadgets, he has to count to himself. The whole question of timing is the key to a good production, and requires much patience and self-control on the part of the producer and discipline on the part of the players during rehearsals. When the whole thing is under way it is very like what one imagines an orchestra to be, each player having the cue for his part, and in next to no time it becomes second nature for all to carry this out.

Music

Side by side with the switchboard, on the rest of the wall not used by the electrician, we managed to fit in a small upright pianoforte which can be a great asset to any Toy Theatre even if you have no competent musician. The deep notes may be struck for sudden thunder or the high notes for a bell, and an odd tune fingered out at no more than beginner's standard can make variety to the competence of the record player's polished performance. The music worker is in charge of the all-important interval music and possibly a theme tune, and all other tunes. He has to organize the records carefully for speedy changes, and also to show due respect for their safety. It is best for him to be in sole charge so that he can lay hands on what he wants when he wants it. Records can be obtained of thunder, clapping, birdsong, waves breaking, and many other strange sounds which will help the general atmosphere. Often the whole group can help him with sound effects such as dogs barking, cats miaowing or crowds cheering. This they will find an extremely enjoyable occupation, as it will allow them to let off steam for a few moments. But all this must be kept under strict control and not overdone, for there is no place for an exhibitionist among the crew. The music worker is in close touch with the noise maker, and usually directs him as to shaking out the zinc-sheet thunder, firing the starting pistol, ringing the door bell, dropping a cymbal, banging drums, tinkering on a doll's dulcimer, or blowing the mouth organ or toy trumpet. A very jolly job, this one.

The Auditorium

When we arranged the seating for the audience we built up a miniature auditorium on boxes and tables in a succession of steps. We had a curtained doorway cut in the dividing screen; this was useful during rehearsals for the producer to rush in to those working behind, with directions. Above the stage, well out of the way, we had a small platform upon which the chief voice was seated. Two small ventilators were cut in the dividing screen by this platform to help the voice to penetrate through to the audience. From this dominating position this main voice which is usually concerned mostly with the narration of the play has the advantage of being able to view the whole scene of activity below and time his voice with the cues given him by the manipulators, electrician and the music worker, etc.

The division of the room at your disposal should roughly be one quarter for behind the scenes and three-quarters for the accommodation of the audience. We divided our room with a permanent screen of hardboard from floor to ceiling. The height from the floor for the aperture of the theatre is 3 feet 2 inches (1 m).

Production
The producing of one of these plays is a serious work of art not to be taken lightly, although it is right to keep it a gay and spirited venture. The designing and drawing and making usually took up one evening a week from September until mid-May. Then we had to begin rehearsing for performances proper at the beginning of June. We gave two performances three times a week for three weeks. One accumulates a technique for rehearsing with as little possible time, and if you carry one or two old hands in the cast it is a marvellous help. I should think we rehearsed about two hours for each scene and perhaps about six for a complete run-through, which is not really very much. As for the scene of each member of the cast is tried out, the person responsible can explain to the rest of the cast roughly how it works. After the first two or three performances one has to curb any tendency towards slickness that might creep in, for the players can get almost too quick and clever at changing the scenes and taking the cues. It is rather good for the morale of the cast behind to hear the laughter and clapping of the audience. Sometimes our audiences have been so enthralled they dare not clap at the end of each scene, or guffaw heartily. But our old-established patrons who came year after year got the idea very well, and let the players know when they were appreciated. They also came behind afterwards and told them where they thought they did badly and where they thought they managed well.

HOUNDS OFF OUR WILDLIFE

NOTHING is guaranteed to raise temperatures to boiling point more in many people than the hunting of wild animals. And rightly so. As far as I am concerned I hold in contempt anyone who gets his kicks from chasing innocent creatures to their deaths and so this chapter is devoted to the anti-hunting organizations and in particular the Hunt Saboteurs.

Up till the early sixties the only organized face-to-face opposition to hunts had been the League Against Cruel Sports' banner demos at meets (usually Boxing Days). Some Brixham fishermen had been attempting to disrupt some of the local hunts and a young local journalist, John Prestidge, decided that the time was ripe for the formation of a nationwide direct-action

One morning last winter to Holmbank there came
A brave, noble sportsman, Squire Sandys was his name
Came a-hunting the fox. Bold Reynard must die.
And he flung out his train and began far to cry
"Tally-ho! Tally-ho! Hark, forward away! Tally-ho!"

OLD HUNTING SONG

association to combat bloodsports. Amid a welter of publicity the Hunt Saboteurs Association began life in late 1963.

Groups rapidly sprang up in several parts of the country and in most cases, mainly through lack of experience of management, just as rapidly faded away. Over the next few years, as old members drifted out and no new members took their place, things gradually ground to a halt, apart from an occasional foray by the London group (ex-Surrey group). Then, with a new and enthusiastic small London core and a few advertisements, things started picking up again. An existing Dorset group (CROW) were contacted and the ball has been rolling ever since.

The H.S.A. was formed to fight bloodsports in the very fields where they take place using non-violent direct methods to save the lives of hunted wild animals, to keep the public constantly aware of the unnecessary carnage going on in the name of 'sport' around them, and to keep the hunting fraternity constantly aware that their days are numbered.

H.S.A. members sometimes campaign in a minor way on the parliamentary level but generally leave this aspect to other anti-hunt organizations who are better equipped to deal with it. The H.S.A. currently has more than 2,000 members spread throughout the length and breadth of the British Isles and active, or potentially active groups in most areas. They work on a Group Contact basis whereby H.Q. maintains a regular link with its area reps (Contacts) who, in turn, are expected to maintain a similar link with the active members in their areas. There are no paid officials, the whole thing being run on a voluntary basis. An annually-elected executive committee of ten members endeavours to keep the wheels turning as efficiently as possible. They hold at least one general meeting each year together with occasional tactics meetings as required. Each member receives the official magazine *Howl* at least three times a year.

Here, then, in response to an ever-growing interest in H.S.A. activities, is the first field manual of anti-hunting techniques ever published.

Hunting Seasons

(All hunt at least twice a week, always Saturdays and never Sundays.)
FOX (*206 packs*) November–April 11 a.m. start.
STAG (*5 packs*) August–April 11 a.m. start (only in the West Country and New Forest).
BEAGLE (*79 packs*) October–March Noon–2 p.m. start.

BASIC TACTICS FOR SAVING THE LIVES OF HUNTED FOXES AND HARES

How Do I Find My Hunt?

Baily's Hunting Directory (in your local library) gives full details of hunt area and terrain.

Hunts advertise their meets:
(a) In some local papers. (b) In some pubs. (c) In the magazines *Horse and Hound* and *Shooting Times* under 'Hunting Appointments' (have a browse through in W. H. Smith's). (d) Via fixture cards obtainable from the hunt secretaries.

Try to arrive in time for the meet (usually 11.00 a.m. for foxhunts, 12.00 noon–2.00 p.m. for beagles). N.B. It is often possible to hit a foxhunt first followed by a hare hunt (beagles).

If you are late or if you lose the hunt, have a scout round the area. Country-folk gazing across fields, horses in a field apparently interested in something in the distance, fresh horse droppings on the road, hoof marks and paw prints in muddy gateways, disturbed flocks of birds, running cows or a large number of cars by the side of the road usually mean that the hunt is somewhere nearby. (Supporters' cars are often identified by coloured windscreen stickers, e.g. SDH = Southdown Hunt.)

Basic Operation of Foxhound and Beagle Hunts

Both types of hunt rely on the scenting ability of the hounds and the huntsman's control over them. A still, warm day with damp ground makes ideal scenting conditions.

Both hunts meet at least twice a week, every Saturday but never (except in Eire) on Sunday. They usually meet at a pub or a farm. The hounds are released (unboxed) 10 to 15 minutes before the move off.

Foxhunts take place on horseback, so a large number of horse boxes will be seen near the meet. Beagling takes place on foot, but still at a very fast pace.

Some foxhunts employ 'stoppers' to block earths the night before; this ensures that foxes remain above ground for the hunt.

Farmers very often open all their gates and leave them open for the hunt. This ensures that the hunt has a quick and easy passage across the land.

Beagle packs will spend most of their time in the open, in fields. Foxhunts will put the hounds into woods (*coverts*) to try and draw the fox.

Both hunts will be assisted by their followers – foxhunts more so than beagles. If the followers see the quarry they will 'holloa' the hunt over and point out the direction the quarry took.

When hounds have picked up a scent they will yelp ('give voice') loudly. In both hunts the hounds rely on their greater stamina to overcome the superior speed of the quarry. This means that the chase may last for one or even two hours.

Both hunts pack up when it starts to get dark.

H.S.A. Tactics – Before the Meet

(1) *Lay a false trail.* If you know a friendly fox-owner, drag the bedding of the fox around the area where the hunt are meeting.

(2) *Search for blocked earths.* If these are in soft soil they are often best left blocked – the hunt will dig out foxes from small, easily dug earths. If the soil is hard or full of roots or the earth is a big warren it can safely be unblocked.

(3) *Secure gates in the area.* This will cause the hunt considerable inconvenience and delay.

(4) *Spray roads, gateways and woods (preferably at the dogs' nose height) with harmless but strong-smelling substances such as Antimate. (See 'Materials' below.)*

At the Meet

(1) *If you have contacted the press, hold a banner demo.* Otherwise, it is better to act as followers, mingling with and chatting to the supporters. This way you can find out where the hunt is likely to go.

(2) *Spray hands with Antimate and pat the dogs, rubbing it into their coats.* The hounds are very friendly, never vicious, and love to be made a fuss of.

(3) *If several Sabs are present, split forces and cover all the roads leading from the meet.* As the hounds move off spray the road with Antimate etc. N.B. *Never spray the hounds directly,* always spray well in front of them.

After the Meet

(1) *Keep one step ahead of the hunt.* Spray Antimate etc. in the woods before they get there – keep an eye out for specially-made jumps – the hunt are likely to pass this way.

(2) *Confuse and distract the hounds by using whistles and calling the hounds by name (mimic the huntsman).*

(3) *Pretend you have seen a fox and 'holloa' (a sort of loud, high-pitched 'woooo' yell).* This will often bring the hunt and/or the hounds over. Then either 'disappear', or misdirect the hunt. N.B. *See 'Warnings' no. 1.*

(4) *Use a hunting horn to bring some or all of the hounds over to you and away from the huntsman.*

Used in conjunction with hunting calls (such as 'hark to the horn' – listen to the huntsman), this is often very effective. It can be used to split the pack or to draw hounds off a scent. If the pack is split it may take the hunt a long time to reassemble the hounds. N.B. *See 'Warnings' no. 1.*

(5) Hunts often lose hounds. If you see one straying *take it to the local police station.* Allowing a dog to stray on to a road is an offence.

(6) In the exceptional case where hounds get close to their quarry, and the Sab can intervene, smoke bombs can be used between the quarry and the hounds. This should not be used unless necessary.

Warnings

(1) When drawing hounds over using holloas or hunting horns ensure:

(a) that there are no foxes about (not as stupid a suggestion as it seems).

(b) that you are not bringing the hounds near or over railway lines or busy roads.

(2) *Remember the 'Country Code'.* Don't antagonize farmers by trampling crops, etc.

(3) *Don't take any action that may harm horses, hounds or riders.* Be careful not to frighten the horses at a banner demo.

(4) Avoid tactics that don't directly help the hunted animal, such as interfering with supporters' cars, etc.

(5) If a hunted animal is heading towards you, stand perfectly still and quiet until it has passed. Any noise or movement may scare it back towards the hunt.

Confrontations

Violent hunt reactions seldom occur, so don't go out expecting them. But the following points should be noted:

(1) *Avoid if possible direct confrontations with riders and supporters.* Chat to the supporters – do not antagonize them. They can be of assistance if trouble starts. If you get hurt by a hunt member you can take the perpetrator to court, but in such cases the Sab nearly always ends up being bound over while the supporter gets a minimal fine; so *always* walk away if supporters get 'uptight'.

(2) If a rider is chasing you it helps to have a safe escape route planned, e.g. over a fence or into thick woods.

(3) It is nearly always fatal to run if being followed by hunt 'heavies'. They can go anywhere you can and running only encourages them (it probably reminds them of the chase!). In such cases Sabs should always keep together and should *walk* steadily back towards the cars.

(4) *If the police turn up, be polite to them.* Remember you need not give them your name and address (unless you are a car owner or are being arrested) – never admit to anything. Otherwise co-operate with them. Whilst they must officially remain neutral they are bound to have sympathies to one side or the other. Whichever side they're on, annoying them does not help. It's nice to have them around sometimes.

(5) *If there is a 'dust-up' take any injured Sabs to hospital for confirmation.* This is invaluable if there is to be a court case. Let H.Q. and the press know if there has been a great amount of violence from the hunt.

(6) If there are any violent incidents (being hit by a huntsman, etc.), even if not on a large scale, let H.Q. know immediately. Always note if incidents took place on private land/footpath/road.

(7) *Make written notes of any incidents as soon as possible after the event.* Get names and addresses of witnesses and photos where possible.

Elusive Hunts

Some hunts do not advertise and others go to great lengths to give Sabs the slip (in such cases they often give their own supporters the slip as well, so this in itself can be considered a victory for the Sabs). They may stop advertising their meets (this will lose them money) or even change the meet at the last moment (this will lose them supporters). In such cases tactics are as follows:

(1) Follow the hound van from the kennels (it is useful to know the registration number of the van). See also 3.

(2) If they were due to meet at a pub but are not there ask the publican where they have moved to. Alternatively ring the kennels or the hunt secretary. In both cases prepare a good story beforehand – they can often ask awkward questions. Telephone numbers can be obtained from H.Q., telephone books and *Baily's Hunting Directory.*

(3) If a number of Sabs are searching for the hunt, the first to find it can guide the others by chalking on the road the time and direction of the hunt (use a pre-arranged colour to prevent supporters tricking the Sabs). Alternatively, if the search is taking place over a wide area, arrange a central telephone number (this can be a call box) – when the hunt is discovered the first Sab car should phone information to the others via this number.

Trespass

You can go on to anyone's land providing you leave by the shortest route if ordered by the landowner/police/or official representative of the landowner (e.g. his gamekeeper). However they very rarely have with them the proof that they really *do* have the authority! If you refuse to leave (you must be given reasonable time to do so) the landowner etc. can use *reasonable force* to remove you. He can also take you to court but if you do no damage to crops or fences he will have an extremely weak case. 'No Trespassing' signs are only a warning not a law unto themselves.

Nobody but the aforementioned people can order you off land. *Nobody* can order you off a designated footpath.

Hints (TRANSPORT)

(1) If driving, make sure you have a full tank before you start.

(2) A locking petrol cap is an advantage.

(3) Take a tyre-pump if possible.

(4) Check that insurance, tax etc. is up to date (police sometimes spot-check Sabs' cars at hunts).

(5) Remove all 'give-away' car stickers that identify the car as that of a Sab.

(6) Have a whip-round for petrol (and, where applicable, van hire costs) if sharing transport.

(7) If possible, leave someone to look after cars. An unattended car may invite interference from supporters.

(8) If blocked in by supporters' cars, lock the doors, close the windows and keep your hand on the horn.

Hints (GENERAL)

(1) If the police turn up, make a note of their numbers.

(2) If you spot a fox, follow it and cover its scent with Antimate etc.

(3) When in woods keep an eye out for traps and snares (by fences, in drains etc.). Act accordingly!

(4) At the meet make a note of the registration numbers and car types of the supporters, horse boxes and hound van. Keep them handy for information next time you are trying to find the hunt.

(5) Opening meets (first Saturday in November) and Boxing Day meets attract large crowds, so deserve special attention. Always try and have a banner demo and sabotage. Invite the local news media along – they should be interested.

(6) When mingling as a supporter at the meet, remember to remove identity badges and use correct terminology (e.g. 'hounds' not 'dog'; 'Charlie' not 'the fox'; 'riding to hounds' not '. . . with hounds', etc.).

(7) Don't let the hunt get away while you argue with supporters.

(8) When following the hunt always stick with the hounds, *not* the horses.

(9) Always carry an Ordnance Survey map of the area. This shows footpaths and also gives an indication as to where the hunt is likely to go (they try to avoid main roads and railways).

(10) Always take a count of Sabs present so that none gets stranded. If there are enough cars, split forces but arrange rendezvous points and times.

(11) Have an alternative hunt lined up in case of cancellation.

After Each Hunt

At the end of each 'hit' send to H.Q.:

(1) A brief but full report of the day's proceedings.

(2) A list of hunt supporters' car registration numbers and any other information you may have picked up.

(3) If possible an account of the route the hunt took (coverts visited etc.).

(4) Numbers of Sab/riders, supporters/foxes killed (if verified).

Materials

(1) *Antimate etc.* – for covering up scents. Bob Martin's 'Antimate', Sherley's 'No Fol', etc. from pet shops or chemists; or 'Sab Special' (mix one tablespoon each of amyl acetate, from chemists, and Jeyes Fluid together, then add to a gallon of water). N.B. The initial mixture may cause red hands but is O.K. when added to the water. 'Special' is cheaper than Antimate etc. but less versatile. It is best used for pre-meet spraying of woods etc. Antimate can easily be carried in the pocket. Anything 'pongy' can be used as a scent-concealer as long as it is non-harmful to hounds or wildlife. Other ideas include strong cheese, goats' bedding, liquid garlic mixture. Remember, spray the ground, *never* the hounds.

(2) *False trails.* If you don't know a friendly fox-owner, try a smelly kipper on the end of a string. The Hound Trailing Association suggest soaking a rag or sock in aniseed, turps, best paraffin and heavy oil. Human urine can be included for added lustre! This mixture is used as a summer season drag for the Lakeland hounds.

(3) *Hunting horns* can be obtained from bric-à-brac and antique shops or Moss Bros. Make sure you can blow it before buying one – there are more bad ones than good. The best are about nine inches long, straight, and with a gradual taper giving a two-inch diameter aperture.

(4) *Smoke bombs* – marine distress flares from yacht suppliers, but not often needed and very expensive.

(5) *O.S. Maps*, 1:50,000 can be bought at stationers or borrowed from libraries. Vital for information. (Esso road maps contain a town index.)

(6) *Various* – home-made non-libellous banners; cameras; binoculars; whistles; chalk; tyre-pump; spare clothes; towel; string; sensible shoes/boots.

Finally, if at first you don't succeed . . . etc. The only way to sabotage hunts effectively is to have experience. The more you go out the easier it will become, so don't get discouraged if things don't go right the first time out. If necessary, ask H.Q. to get experienced Sabs out with you. The only good hunt is a drag-hunt.

Hunt Saboteurs Association – Rules

(1) Members shall not indulge in wanton or wilful damage to persons or property whilst acting or purporting to act in furtherance of the aims of the H.S.A.

(2) Members shall not strike or in any way cruelly treat any hunt animal.

(3) Members shall avoid swearing at or abusing hunters.

(4) Members shall not deliberately provoke hunters to violence and must make every effort to avoid any situation which is bound to lead to a violent reaction against themselves.

(5) Members shall not carry weapons.

(6) Comments to local press people may only be made by a recognized Group Officer or Representative. Official comments on H.S.A. policy should only be made by the Chairperson, Secretary, Treasurer, or Press Officer of the Executive Committee.

(7) Members should follow the Country Code as strictly as possible (see below).

Country Code

Guard against all risk of fire.
Fasten all gates.
Keep dogs under proper control.
Keep to the paths across farm land.
Avoid damaging fences, hedges and walls.
Leave no litter.
Safeguard water supplies.
Protect wild life, wild plants and trees.
Go carefully on country roads.
Respect the life of the countryside.

223

All across the town
All across the night
Everybody's driving with four headlights
Black or white, turn it on, force the new religion
Everybody's drowning in a sea of television
Up and down the Westway
In and out the lights
What a great traffic system
It's all so bright
I can't think of a better way to spend the night
Than speeding around underneath the yellow
lights
But now I'm in the subway looking for the flat
This one leads to this block and this one leads to
that
The wind howls through the empty blocks
looking for a home
But I run through the empty stone because I'm
all alone

FROM 'LONDON'S BURNING' BY THE CLASH

MOVING TO..

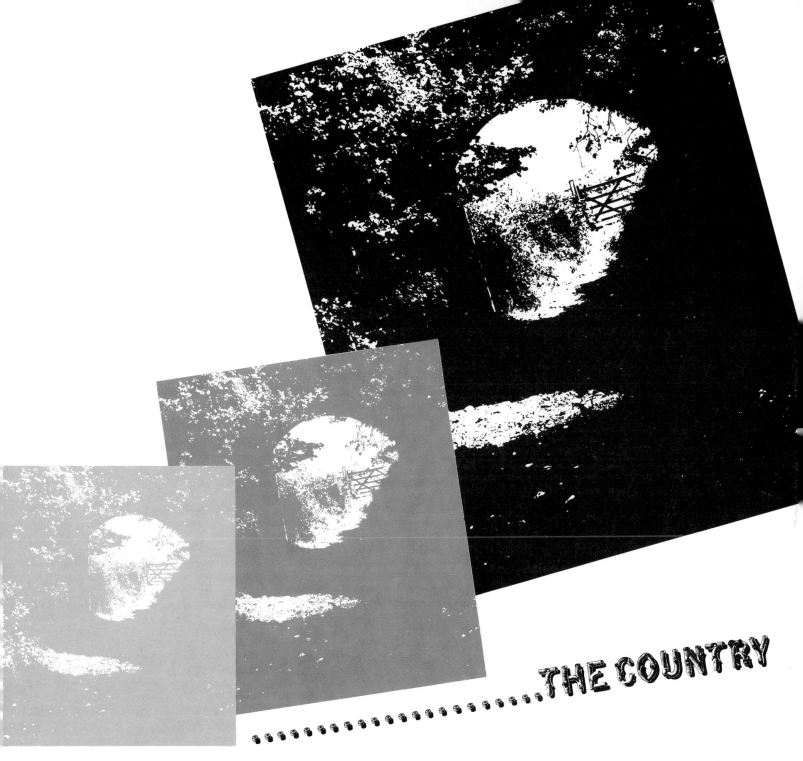

.............THE COUNTRY

The country is lyric, the town dramatic. When mingled, they make the most perfect musical drama.

LONGFELLOW

THIS last chapter is devoted to those of us who, despite the opportunities to change their lifestyle within the urban environment, are still hell-bent on moving out to the country – for there's no doubt about it, city life can be pretty awful. It's depressing to think of all those people, more by accident than design, who seem eternally shackled to the old perennial treadmill of the meaningless, going-nowhere, dead-end, 9–5 job (if they have a job at all, that is); commuting in appalling congestion every rush-hour, living like broiler hens in Orwellian concrete jungles suspended in the air, and risking life and limb every time they set one foot outside the door from hazardous traffic conditions and filthy air. So cut off from the very earth that sustains them, so far removed from any spiritual contentment that flowers with a natural relationship with the land, that it is hardly surprising the lure of 'moving to the country' becomes an overriding passion. When the pressures build up, it's a dream we all share.

We live, though, in strange times. For every fed-up-to-the-teeth-with-it-all city slicker who can hardly wait to uproot and flee from the city to take up country ways, there seems to be an equal number of fed-up-to-the-teeth-with-it-all country people who see the big city as their Mecca. It's a peculiar two-way exodus. The city person sees the country as a place of recreation where he can slow down, get back to nature, grow his own food, be self-sufficient, breathe clean air, lead a richer and more satisfying life. On the other hand the country person may see the city equally as a place of recreation – a source of secure and well-paid employment; better and more varied job opportunities, a richer cultural life, with excitement and lively people. So who is right?

Personally speaking (and I am living in London at the moment), I am addicted to both, for each environment offers riches galore and I don't think I could happily forsake one for the other. It's true I'm not living that awful zomboid existence mentioned above (the fact that I'm probably being stunted by polluted air is a risk I'm prepared to make), so I can reap the good things of the city. For all the talk now of moving to the country, the city *does* have a lot to offer. Is there anywhere in the world, for instance, with such a rich and varied cultural life as London? Even so, there is still a haunting

urge deep down inside which hankers after country life; the need to 'get away from it all', to be 'totally self-sufficient'. It's the townie's perpetual fantasy!

When You Gotta Go – You Gotta Go
So you really want to move to the country? You've thought it over and over and considered the idea a thousand times and it's no good – you've just got to go. O.K., then, what follows should be of some help to you. As testified by all my friends who finally made the break, the information is an exhaustive guideline to anyone whose *'sorely throbbing feet'*, as the poet Ada Smith once wistfully penned . . . *'tramp London's highways, through the endless streets, the gloomy squares and by-ways, homeless in the city, poor among the poor.'*

Employment
Any move to the countryside must involve the decision – what type of employment to pursue. Whatever you decide will inevitably fall into one of the following categories:

(a) Carrying on with your present trade or profession;
(b) Seeking local employment;
(c) Becoming self-sufficient.

Most people tend to fall within the first two categories, especially those with professional skills who are keen to continue their line of work. Self-sufficiency is the most radical choice with its complete change of lifestyle, but it does leave little time for anything else (*see below*). The ideal situation seems to be a combination of all three. Grow and provide for yourself as much as time will allow, hold down a local part-time job, and continue any professional skills that you possess (teaching, writing, etc.). Artistic people generally fare better, so learn to be creative. Learn new skills, crafts. Learn to paint, sculpt. Learn to write, illustrate. Grab every opportunity you can to increase your abilities.

The following list may help you to formalize ideas about rural employment. Experience proves that the more able and flexible you are in holding down varying types of employment and skilled work, the better your chances of survival. If one line of work fails, you will have the others to fall back on.

Collectives
The collective is a sensible and fair scheme whereby all expenditure and profit in a business is equally shared between a group of people. It cuts costs in the production of food, crafts, running a market stall, running a shop. With a shop, for instance, it will mean time off for members, thus enabling them to pursue other ventures. But first get to know who's who in your area and be sure they are sincere and trustworthy. Such schemes are liable to collapse if some fail to observe the rules and pull their own weight.

Crafts
Don't wait until you get into the country before learning a craft. With all the excellent facilities available in the big cities, it is far easier and cheaper to learn craft skills in an adult evening institute or part-time day course. For London, see *Floodlight* magazine for I.L.E.A. classes. These days you can learn literally anything, from wrought-iron work to lace-making. Bear in mind, though, the selling viability of the craft(s) you intend to study. Learning how to make stained glass windows may be all very well, but will it earn you a living? Visit the craft shops (if any) in the area you wish to go to and see what they sell. Ask the assistants what crafts sell better than others. Also, bear in mind costs of materials, transport costs, and the percentages shops take for selling your wares. With pottery, for instance, you may be able to dig your own clay and use the firing facilities of a local potter.

Always aim to be professional with your craftwork. The world is already full with enough machine-made junk without your adding to it with a pile of hand-made junk. You've a living to make, but try to combine craftsmanship, good design and aesthetic value with economic production. Consider the idea of attending college full-time to learn a craft properly. Government grants are available (see end of book). Grant schemes are also available for new craftsmen from both Cosira (Council for Small Industries in Rural Areas) and the Crafts Advisory Committee. You have to be professional and jolly good, though. They don't foster third-rate craftsmen.

Markets

Generally considered the most effective means of securing some sort of steady income. One way is to approach a stall-holder who is selling similar produce to your own and ask them to sell your goods for a percentage of the profit. This can provide a starting point from which you can become established. A stall of your own is the next step. There's no criterion as to what sells and how to sell it. If your produce is good and offered at a fair price you should have no trouble. Be prepared for competition – which makes a collective stall a good proposition.

If you join the Women's Institute, you may be able to sell your work or produce on their own stall for a small cut of the profits.

Part-time Work

First rule – be prepared to take *anything*. Even the most contrary of jobs may provide a contact for something better. Scour the local papers and notice boards. Ask around in the local pubs or the library.

Teachers have a better chance than most, especially if they teach a specialist subject. Approach the Workers' Educational Association or the local Adult Institute of Education. On the whole, part-time work is difficult to come by.

Seasonal Work

If you move near to the coast you should have little trouble in getting a summer job. Favourite seasonal work will be on the beach as a deckchair attendant, selling ice creams, taking the kids for donkey rides, in the hotels and restaurants as kitchen assistant, waitress/waiter, chambermaid or cleaner. Holiday camps provide numerous jobs and can be fun into the bargain. Other jobs include working on the boats or a fairground assistant.

Inland, there will be the farms at harvest time. Fruit farms will be the best bet, though as a form of piece work it can be quite poorly paid and unbearably back-breaking.

All these jobs would only be available in the summer, but should the winter be especially severe there may be work available on the roads clearing snow. At all times keep on friendly terms with your neighbours and locals. Many country jobs tend to go by word of mouth.

Shops

Of the many friends of mine who have moved to the country, the most successful have been a couple who started up a junk-cum-antique-cum-crafts-shop. Starting from absolutely nothing, they built up a thriving business. They first rented an old shop in a tiny village in north Devon and then set about attending all the local auctions and jumble sales, buying up anything that caught their eye and seemed like a bargain. In their beat-up old van they toured around other areas for junk and even made one or two forays up to London to buy from the antique markets. By a system of trial and error they ended up in business. The addition of crafts manufactured from the bits of junk they couldn't sell (hand-painted chamber pots, lamp shades, prints in old frames, etc.) has added a new dimension to the shop.

This is just one example of the sort of success a shop can bring. If the idea appeals to you, then take into consideration the following details. Does your village or area lack any particular type of shop? If so, could you provide that need? Look around and see whether there are other people like yourself trying to sell produce or crafts. If there are, they why not combine forces and start a co-operative? Chat up the local garden enthusiasts who may have a glut of fruit and vegetables they may need to get rid of. Chat up the local farmers, they may let you have produce at a fair price. Is there a wholefood and health shop in the area? If not, then form a food co-operative and buy cereals and grains in bulk from your nearest bulk merchants.

Training Courses

The government runs a training scheme for those anxious to learn essential trades such as carpentry, bricklaying, plumbing and electrical work. The training centres are situated all over the country; so the chances are there will be one within reasonable distance from you. Training varies between six months and one year, during which time you get paid a liveable wage. The waiting lists vary from area to area – some are hopelessly long, while others often have little delay. On average, be prepared for up to a year's waiting.

Unemployment

If you have rotten luck, then you will be able to claim unemployment benefit, provided you have paid adequate stamps. Failing that you will be eligible for supplementary benefits from the Department of Health and Social Security.

Only resort to State benefits as a last-ditch effort when all else has failed. It's so easy to slide into a mood of State dependence which does neither you nor the community any good whatsoever.

Self Sufficiency

With the open air and a leisurely life,
Homespun, and spaniels, and honey,
An eave-full of swallows, a sun-browned wife,
He's never a thought for money.

T. FARQUHARSON

Us townies must be forgiven for entertaining glossy, romantic ideas of living in the country-side. It's so easy to see it as one great big green oasis where the sun always shines and where the good life there is picturesquely full of contented cows, hens, ducks, goats, pigs, bees – with fresh milk, butter and cheese, fruit galore and organic vegetables, cottage flowers, and chestnuts on an open fire. This Hollywood conception of country life dies hard. Of course, such an abundant fulfilling life *is* there, *is* possible, and there are hundreds of New Age country settlers to prove it. But let's not forget that country life, self-sufficiently speaking, is damn hard work. Cows don't live daydream existences in buttercup meadows and produce milk of their own accord like an Ovaltine advertisement. They need intensive care, winter feeding, cleaning out. Fields don't seed, weed and harvest themselves. They need good soil husbandry, and this often means long hours of often boring, back-breaking physical labour. Being self-sufficient is a day-in day-out job and no messin'. It means no three-week holidays or days off when you feel like it. It often means getting up at all hours, rain or shine. And for townie people, country life can sometimes be disconcertingly lonely.

It is essential, then, to cast off all previously held romantic aspirations of what a self-sufficient country life will be like. It won't be. Prove it for yourself. Go on a self-sufficiency course and see what is involved. Stay on a farm

for a working holiday. Visit the country in the winter when it is at its 'worst' and see how you like it – it'll look and feel a whole lot different from those balmy summer days. Talk to country people. Hear what they have to say about where they live, what they like about it, what they don't like about it, what they do on cold winter nights.

From the experience of my friends who have moved away from the city and are practising varying degrees of self-sufficiency, it seems the rewards can be great, but the commitment must be total. Self-sufficiency is a full-time occupation and the decision to enter into it must mean turning your back on city ways for good. But then that's what it's all about!

FINDING A HOME – AN A TO Z

There are many ways of finding property and living in the country. Try the following suggestions – over and over again if need be. If you're *that* determined you will get there in the end. Whatever happens, don't give up or succumb to disappointment.

Boats
A romantic lifestyle not without possibilities. The trouble comes not so much in getting a boat (old hulls and vessels can be bought quite reasonably) but in finding a place to moor. Unless you are prepared to be constantly on the move, a sort of piratical existence, you can pay up to £10 a week mooring charges (even more in some places).

Buying
Perhaps the most secure and straightforward approach. You already own a house. You sell it. You buy another in the country. On the whole, houses in the country are cheaper than those in the city, which is an advantage to those moving out. The more remote a property, the cheaper it tends to be.

If you are at all handy with tools, especially if you happen to be a carpenter, it may be worth your while to buy a derelict property and renovate it yourself. Most 'derrys' can be bought for under £6,000.

Collective buying, or what is more commonly

230

known as a 'Housing Co-operative' is an excellent way of obtaining property. You find two or more other couples who have the same idea as yourself. You pool your capital and with the aggregate sum you purchase a large house, mansion, farm building network, etc. and convert the property into flats. All expenditure such as rates and repairs is split equally. Whether you run the house as a commune or as a segregated unit is a personal choice (*see under communes*).

The problem arises when one or more of the parties decides to split. Unless the money can be raised to buy them out, or a new party found to take their place, the whole collective could be in danger of being terminated. One way to solve this is to form a Housing Association, providing there are at least seven participants in the scheme. It costs £50 and the association becomes a non-profit Limited Company. There are set rules of conduct laid down by the National Federation of Housing Societies which, though not compulsory, help to bind the scheme together. Another advantage of a housing association is in the application to the local council for any conversion intended for the property.

Where mortgages are concerned, building societies are usually very cagey about lending money for the purchase of older property. Council mortgages are a better bet. In some areas, councils encourage the buying and restoration of semi-derelict property. Remember that any housing association must be registered with the local housing corporation before mortgages can be granted.

Caravans and Converted Vans

If there is any Romany in your soul, this may appeal to you. Where caravans are concerned, you will be able to pick up ancient models for very modest prices (see *Exchange & Mart*). Farmers quite often allow single caravans in their fields for a small rent as they don't need planning permission. One couple I know spent three years in the corner of a field half-way up one of the Brecon Beacons in Wales for just £1 a week. The farmer even provided the caravan!

Converted vans and caravanettes are good forms of mobile accommodation while you look around for something more permanent. You never know, you may even end up preferring a life on the move! Old vehicles with wooden-framed bodies are ideal for conversion, though I have seen some very natty conversion jobs on Vauxhalls, Volkswagens and Ford Transits. Unless you are made of money, avoid those big touring caravanettes that come from Bedford and Volkswagen. They may look spectacular but they cost thousands (literally) of pounds.

Colleges

Every college has a notice board. Walk in and look out all the accommodation advertisements. Excellent for rented rooms, bedsits and digs. Even a talk with the college accommodation officer or a students' union may prove fruitful.

Communes

You may want to change your lifestyle completely and share everything with others in what is commonly known as a commune. This is a radical approach and not one to be entered into lightly. Many, many communes (including two I lived in personally) have failed for innumerable reasons, not the least because living under one roof with your fellow man can be a trying and difficult experience. The rewards are great if it works and the experience itself immeasurably valuable, but remember that even your dearest and closest friends may have habits that drive you mad when you're under each other's nose for 24 hours a day!

Communes inevitably need fair-sized living quarters for their members, which makes co-operative buying such as the housing association scheme the logical answer. One word of advice, though. Never mention the word 'commune' to any solicitor, council bureaucrat, building society etc. It will hamper your chances of success in any purchase.

Read about other communes and if possible, try and arrange to stay at one for a working weekend or an extended stay. *Never* turn up out of the blue – always write and be prepared to be told to get lost. After all, communes are every bit as private as single families (how would you entertain the idea of complete strangers coming to stay?).

Council Swaps

If you are already living in council accommodation you will be eligible for a swap with another council tenant in the area of your choice provided both local authority housing departments agree to the move. Two of my friends have done this recently and are now living in a heavenly spot just outside Totnes in Devon, completely secluded, with a massive garden and glorious views.

Crofts

This will only apply to Scotland. The demand for crofts in recent years has rocketed and the department which handles all crofting tenures (The Crofters Commission) has become somewhat unhelpful to would-be crofters, especially those from outside Scotland. As the situation is constantly changing, all you can do is enquire regularly – you could be lucky.

Estate Agents

Many estate agents produce a regular listing of property for sale and, in some cases, furnished flats and rooms to let. Get yourself put on their mailing list.

Farmers

Many farmers own an empty cottage, barn or farm building. Most are unwilling to let them to strangers but if you manage to befriend one (e.g. if you stay at a farm for a holiday) you may be lucky in persuading them otherwise. Even more so if you are willing to renovate derelict property.

Friends

If you have any friends living in the country you could be laughing. Get them to ask around for you, or look in the local papers or on the notice boards. They will be the first to know of any property coming up for sale or rent in their area. Arrange to stay with them if you can and look around yourself.

Grants

Every council provides house improvement grants. Go to the local authority and ask for any leaflets on such schemes. In nearly every case, you will have to pay for any improvement yourself before receiving the grant.

Holidays

Go for a holiday in the area you want to live and spend as much time as possible looking around and getting acquainted with the people and the accommodation possibilities. Camping is a good idea – both cheap and flexible.

Employment Housing

Some employers provide an accommodation service for would-be employees moving into their area, and in some cases they even provide a house with the job (e.g. gardeners, nannies, home helps, and professional jobs). Check out any such possibilities at the local employment exchange and/or bureau.

Local Library

All libraries have a list of accommodation available for teachers, students and people in employment by the council.

Local Papers

Arrange to have the local papers sent to you, either direct from the publishers or by a friend in the area. You will have to be mighty efficient in answering any suitable ad, as they are generally snapped up the minute they come out.

Local People

Making friends in the community is one of the surest ways to success. If you are genuinely friendly and the locals take to you, they may be willing to ask around or keep their ears open for any suitable accommodation. But you *must* be 100 per cent keen. Many people get star-struck on holiday and enquire after property, but then forget the idea. If necessary, be persistent in your enquiries – go back as often as you can. The local pub is a good focal point for socializing and for village gossip.

Notice Boards

Speaks for itself. Arm yourself with a pocketful of two-penny pieces and ring around. Wholefood shops and alternative bookshops quite often have notice boards.

Ordnance Survey Maps

Buy an O.S. map of your intended area and check all the marked buildings in outlying districts. Even the most derelict will be shown

and will give you an intimate knowledge of all the property in the area.

Publications

Exchange & Mart and *Daltons Weekly* are both good for property for sale and to let. Try also *The Lady*, where gardening, nanny and home help jobs are advertised with accommodation thrown in with the employment. The parents of a good friend of mine spent most of their working lives in this form of employment and had the experience of living in some very beautiful houses in equally beautiful countryside.

Repairing Lease

This is an agreement entered into with a landlord whereby you agree to renovate his property in lieu of paying rent. In most cases the landlord provides the materials.

Roughing It

The most straightforward yet disarming approach of all. You simply get up and go. My friends with the junk shop did exactly that. They piled all they could into their van and headed west for the summer. For some weeks they camped around, living from the van but in that time they struck up a number of acquaintances and eventually something turned up.

Unfortunately this method is fraught with danger. In the unlikely event of failing to find a place you will be forced to go back to where you came from. It's a long shot which usually pays off, but . . .

Squatting

You should not take precedence over the people who are already homeless or in need of alternative housing in the area you want to live. This is unfair and will only cause bad feelings. If you must squat, contact the local squatting group *before* making any move and follow their advice implicitly. The advisory service for squatters will put you in touch with your nearest group.

Tied Cottages

As a temporary measure, tied cottages may be the answer. With more and more workers leaving the land, such accommodation becomes more available. The snag with tied cottages is

235

the farmer has every right to evict you if he takes on a new farm worker who needs accommodation.

Winter Lets and Holiday Cottages
Statistically the most successful way of making the break. I know plenty of people who initially took up a winter let (the rents are usually pretty reasonable) and during the period found alternative accommodation. In one case the landlord allowed them to stay on permanently at a fixed rent, though this is very rare. Winter lets can be found from notice boards, local papers and *Daltons Weekly*, or via the locals' grapevine.

And The Return?

Let them talk of lakes and mountains and romantic places – all that fantastic stuff, give me a ramble by night, in the winter nights in London – the lights lit – the pavements of the motley Strand crowded with to and fro passengers – the shops all brilliant, and stuffed with obliging customers and obliged tradesmen – give me the old bookstalls of London – a walk in the bright Piazzas of Covent Garden. I defy a man to be dull in such places! I have lent out my heart with usury to such scenes from my childhood up, and have cried with fullness of joy at the multitudinous scenes of life in the crowded streets of ever dear London.

I don't know if you quite comprehend my low Urban Taste; but depend upon it that a man of any feeling will have given his heart and his love in childhood and in boyhood to any scenes where he has been bred, as well to dirty streets (and smoky walls as they are called) as to green lanes, "where live nibbling sheep", and to the ever lasting hills and the lakes and ocean.

A mob of men is better than a flock of sheep, and a crowd of happy faces jostling into the playhouse at the hour of six is a more beautiful spectacle to man than the shepherd driving his "silly" sheep to fold.

FROM 'THE GLAMOUR OF THE TOWN' BY CHARLES LAMB

Getting Out and About

HITCH-HIKING

HITCHING out of the cities can sometimes mean a frustrating wait (I stood for a whole day at the Hatfield roundabout one time and came home again) yet it is still the cheapest and friendliest way to travel. Aim to travel along the motorways as far as possible on a journey where lifts are more easily come by, especially at the service areas (it is illegal to hitch on the motorway itself). As a general rule males are the least likely to be picked up, especially if travelling in twos. The best arrangement is to hitch with a girl if you are male, or girls together. **Single girls usually have little trouble getting a lift but it is very risky and they are advised to make a point of enquiring as to where the driver is going** *before* **getting into the vehicle, and** *never* **getting into one with two or more males. Wherever you hitch, always carry a clearly-written sign of the destination or route if possible.**

Here is a list of hitching points out of London:

TRAVELLING NORTH

A1 – Northern Line tube to Hendon Central, then a 113 bus to Northway Circus N.W.7. Alternatively, take the Northern Line to Burnt Oak and a 292 bus. Alternatively, hitch from Hendon Way.

M1 – Northern Line tube to Hendon. Travel to the North Circular by going down the Broadway and turning left, and then hitch from the roundabout just past the railway bridge ¾ mile on.

M6 – Hitch from the M1 starting point and

238

change at Watford Gap services after junction 16.

TRAVELLING EAST

A12 – Central Line tube to Gants Hill and hitch from the roundabout outside the station.

TRAVELLING WEST

M4 – The usual procedure on this, the most heavily hitched exit from London, is to take the tube to Hammersmith (District, Piccadilly, Metropolitan Lines) and travel from there to the slip-road alongside the flyover, or further on to the Hogarth roundabout. It is often better, however, to get off the tube earlier at Earls Court, take the Warwick Road exit and travel the ¼ mile to the Cromwell Road left-hand slip-road (you will need an 'M4' sign on this route).

A40 – As for M4. Use an 'A40' sign.

A30 – As for M4 and turn off at exit 3.

TRAVELLING SOUTH

A3 – District Line tube to Putney Bridge and hitch from the bridge. Alternatively, take an 85, 93 or 74 bus from the tube to the flyover 1½ miles up the hill. Make sure to use an 'A3' sign when hitching from the bridge.

A23 – Victoria Line tube to Brixton then travel the ¼ mile to Brixton Hill.

A20 – Metropolitan Line tube to New Cross and then a 21 bus to Sidcup Road.

A2 – Metropolitan Line tube to New Cross and then a 53 bus to the top of Blackheath Hill. Often better, though, to walk further along the Dover Road over the heath to the roundabout and hitch from there.

PUBLIC TRANSPORT

Coaches

Coach travel really is excellent value. At half to two-thirds the cost of the equivalent rail fare, you can journey to every major town and city in the country, as well as reaching a vast network of places that are not served by rail. There are express coaches between most of the cities and large towns, but the country-seeker will be more interested in slower journeys into more remote areas and these are cheaper during the week if going on a period return – cheaper still when travelling there and back the same day. Many private coach firms organize day and period excursions to beauty spots and places of interest which are normally excellent value. Check in Yellow Pages for your nearest coach operator.

Trains

Rail travel today is generally an expensive business but of course it does have the advantage of speed, which may be all-important on a day excursion.

British Rail operate four separate 'Fare Deal' schemes, as well as a number of other reduced fare schemes some of which are shown below:

Awayday Return – There and back on the same day, on any train Saturdays, Sundays, and Bank Holidays, and during the week except for rush hours. Cost – 45 per cent saving on the standard fare.

Weekend Return – Leave on Friday, Saturday or Sunday and return the same weekend on Saturday, Sunday or Monday. Cost – 35 per cent saving on the standard fare.

Monthly Return – Tickets must be booked at least seven days in advance and travel out must be on a Tuesday, Wednesday or Thursday. You must stay away over at least one weekend and return on any Tuesday, Wednesday or Thursday within one calendar month of the outward journey. There is a minimum fare of £6. Cost – a return for the price of the single fare.

RAILROVER TICKETS

There are ten separate Railrover schemes which give the traveller 7 or 14 days unlimited travel in the specific areas covered. These are: 1. *All Line Railrover* (7 days); this covers all stations on British Rail; Sealink shipping services to and from the Isle of Wight, on Lake Windermere and between Tilbury and Gravesend and Hull and New Holland; the Firth of Clyde and Loch Lomond sailings of Caledonian MacBrayne Ltd. 2. *Freedom of Scotland* (7 or 14 days) – anywhere in Scotland.. 3. *Freedom of Wales* (7 days) – anywhere in Wales. 4. *Eastern Railrover* (7 days) – anywhere in Lincolnshire, East Anglia, and other counties in the east of England. 5. *East Anglia Railrover* (7 days) – anywhere in East Anglia. 6. *London Midland Railrover* (7 days) – anywhere in the Midlands. 7. *Southern Railrover* (7 days) – anywhere in the southern counties. 8. *Western Railrover* (7 days) – anywhere in the western counties. 9. *West of England Railrover* (7 days) – anywhere in the West Country.

Runabout Seasons – for local areas in Scotland. Start on any day of the week and travel as often and as far as you like within the specified area.

Seaside Saver Tickets – Special reduced day return fares to the coast from specified stations. Each adult can take up to two children for 40p each.

Travelpass – A ticket valid for 8 or 12 consecutive days between March and October for the whole of the Scottish Highlands and Islands, including bus and ferry routes.

Buses

London's Green Line coaches and London Country buses penetrate many areas of beautiful countryside and travelling on the top deck the country-seeker is afforded the best views possible compared with other forms of transport. The central point for most Green Line services is near Victoria Coach Station, and behind the Railway Station just off Buckingham Palace Road, but ask at your local bus station (or the conductor on any bus) if there is a Green Line route near to where you live. Most city bus services operate special country services.

REFERENCE SECTION

THE SUBURBAN BUTTERFLY FARM

SOURCES OF SUPPLIES

Butterfly livestock and breeding equipment, as well as other sundries can be obtained from:
R. N. Baxter, 16 Bective Road, London, E.7. *Silkmoth livestock only.*
Beautiful Butterflies, Bourton-on-Water, Gloucestershire.
L. Christie, 137 Glenedon Road, Streatham, London, S.W.16.
T. A. Fox, 28 Boxwell Road, Berkhamsted, Hertfordshire. *Silkmoth livestock only.*
L. Hugh Newman, The Butterfly Farm Ltd, Bexley, Kent.
Lullingstone Silk Farm Ltd, Ayot House, Ayot St Lawrence, Hertfordshire. *Silkmoth livestock only.*
Saruman, High Street, Tunbridge Wells, Kent.
R. E. Stockley, 1 Marsh Street, Warminster, Wiltshire.
Worldwide Butterflies Ltd, Bilsington, Ashford, Kent.
Many wild flowers and cottage perennials available from:
Mr and Mrs Emmerson, Leeke, Limavady, Co. Derry, Ireland.
Mrs G. M. Millner, Brompton Regis, near Dulverton, Somerset.
John Scott & Co. Ltd, The Royal Nurseries, Merriott, Somerset.
Thompson & Morgan (Ipswich) Ltd, London Road, Ipswich, Suffolk. *Seed only.*
Worldwide Butterflies Ltd.

SOCIETIES

Amateur Entomologist Society, c/o 355 Hounslow Road, Hanworth, Feltham, Middlesex.
Commonwealth Institute of Entomology, 56 Queen's Gate, London, SW7 5JR.
British Butterfly Conservation Society, Tudor House, Quorn, Leicestershire, LE12 8AD.
British Trust for Entomology, Horticultural Laboratories, Shinfield Grange, Reading, Berkshire.
Royal Entomologist Society, 41 Queen's Gate, London, S.W.7.
South London Entomological Society, 14 Rochester Row, London, S.W.1.
Teen International Entomology Group, c/o Mr J. Wilson, 67 Harcourt Road, Thornton Heath, Surrey, CR4 6BS.

BIBLIOGRAPHY

Entomologist Gazette, 353 Hanworth Road, Hampton, Middlesex, *Journal.*
Entomologist Monthly Magazine, c/o Nathaniel Lloyd & Co Ltd, Burrell Stone Works, Blackfriars, London, S.E.1.
The Entomologist Record, c/o F. W. Buyers, 59 Gurney Court Road, St. Albans, Hertfordshire.
Bright Wings of Summer, by David Measures/ Cassell.
Butterflies, by Robert Gooden/Hamlyn Books. *Excellent instruction book on the techniques of breeding.*
Butterflies (New Naturalist Series), by E. B. Ford/Collins.
A Butterfly Book for the Pocket, by E. Sanders/ Oxford University Press.
Butterfly Culture, by J. L. S. Stone and H. J. Midwinter/Blandford Press.
Complete British Butterflies in Colour, by E. Mansell and L. Hugh Newman/Michael Joseph.
Concise Guide: Butterflies, by J. Moncha/ Hamlyn.
Create a Butterfly Garden, by L. Hugh Newman/World's Work. *Accepted classic of butterfly breeding.*
Living with Butterflies, by L. Hugh Newman/ John Baker.
The Observer's Book of Butterflies, by W. J. Stokoe/Warne.
The Young Specialist Looks at Butterflies, by G. Warnecke/Burke.

PLACES TO VISIT

Natural History Museum (British Museum). *Contains a complete collection of British butterflies.*
Bristol Museum.
City of Liverpool Museum.
Drusilla's Cottage, Polegate, Sussex. *A fine collection on view of butterflies and moths from all over the world.*
Exeter Museum.
Worldwide Butterflies Ltd.

THE NATURAL HEALTH GARDEN

SOURCES OF SUPPLIES

Most of the pesticides, fungicides, weedkillers and other treatments mentioned can be obtained from garden centres or chemists. Otherwise obtain from the following manufacturers:
Ammonium Sulphamate from:
Messrs Albright & Wilson, Knightsbridge Green, London S.W.1.
Boots Chemists, branches everywhere.
Bordeaux Mixture from:
May and Baker, Sales Division, Dagenham, Essex.
Murphy Chemical Co Ltd, Wheathampstead, Hertfordshire.
Burgundy Mixture from:
Copper sulphate and washing soda from **Boots Chemists.**
Derris Dust from:
Boots Pure Drug Co, Farms and Gardens Dept, Nottingham and branches.
International Toxin Products, Northwich, Cheshire.
P.B.I. Derris Dust, Pan Britannica Industries, Waltham Cross, Hertfordshire.
Derris Liquid from:
Abol Derris Spray: Messrs Plant Protection Ltd, Yalding, Kent.
Messrs Bugges Insecticides Ltd, London Road, Sittingbourne, Kent.
Shell Chemicals, Marlborough House, 15–17 Great Marlborough Street, London W.1.
Derris and Pyrethrum Mixtures from:
Bugges Insecticides Ltd
Cooper Garden Spray: Cooper, McDougall & Robertson Ltd, Berkhamsted, Hertfordshire. *Aerosol spray.*
Farm Disinfectant from:
Boots Chemists.
Fertosan and Safe Slug Killer from:
Fertosan Organic Products Ltd, Aberystwyth, Dyfed.
Henry Doubleday Research Association, Bocking, Braintree, Essex.
Pyrethrum from:
F. W. Berk & Co Ltd, Berk House, Portman Square, London W.1.
Grease Bands from:
Boltac Ready Prepared: Pan Britannica Industries.
Lime-Sulphur from:
Eclipse Lime-Sulphur, Bugges Insecticides Ltd.
Nicotine from:
E. J. Woodman, High Street, Pinner, Middlesex.
Quassia from:
Brome & Schimmer, 7 Leather Market, London S.E.1.
Henry Doubleday Research Association.
Predators, parasites and bacteria which are beneficial to the garden's ecosystem including Encarsia formosa, Phytoseiulus persimilis and Bacillus thuringiensis, can be obtained from:
Perifleur Ltd, Hangleton Lane, Ferring, Worthing, West Sussex, BN12 6PP.
Ryania from:
Bugges Insecticides Ltd.
W. J. Craven & Co Ltd, Port Street, Evesham, Hereford and Worcester.
S.M.134 from:
Chase Organics, Gibraltar House, Shepperton, Middlesex.
Sodium Chlorate from:
Boots Chemists.
Winter Wash from:
Mortlegg: Murphy Chemical Co.

SOCIETIES

Biodynamic Agricultural Association, Broome Farm, Clent, Nr Stourbridge, West Midlands.
Glass House Crops Research Institute, Entomology Section, Rustington, Littlehampton, West Sussex. *Researches and publishes growers bulletins on biological control.*
Good Gardeners Association, Arkley Manor, Arkley, Near Barnet, Hertfordshire.
Henry Doubleday Research Association, 20 Convent Lane, Bocking, Braintree, Essex. *Much of the information in this chapter has been standard knowledge in horticulture for years. However, renewed interest in natural pest control plus up-to-date research must be attributed to the H.D.R.A., a voluntary body whose members valuably assist in providing information from experiments in their own allotments and gardens. In their own words they are '. . . the keenest most practical and helpful compost gardeners association in the world'. A yearly subscription brings you up-to-date news on the society's work published in their newsletter. (Please enclose S.A.E. with all correspondence.)*
Mother Earth, P.O. Box 8, Malvern, Hereford and Worcester, WR14 2NG. *Incorporating the Organic Federation (Organic Research Assoc.; Bug Assoc.; Save Our Soil; Organic Farming Assoc.; Earthkeeping Ecology Group; Organic Architecture, and others).*
Soil Association, Walnut Tree Manor, Haughley, Stowmarket, Suffolk.

BIBLIOGRAPHY

The Henry Doubleday Association produces a series of publications concerning biodynamic gardening. Write for a complete list, enclosing an S.A.E.
The following publications are available from Her Majesty's Stationery Office:
Beneficial Insects. Agriculture Bulletin no. 20, by B. D. Morton.
Chemicals and the Gardener
Other Publications:
Be Nice to Nature, by Greet Buchner and Fieke Hoogvelt/Prism Press.
Bionomics of Six Species of Anthocoris in Britain, by N. H. Anderson/Transactions of the Royal Entomological Society, 114, 1962.
The Bug Book, by Helen and John Philbrick/ Thorsons Publishers.
Chemical Control of Insects, by T. F. West/J. E. Hardy.
Clubroot Disease of Crucifers, by John Colhoun/Commonwealth Mycological Institute, 1958.

Food Growing Without Poisons, by Meta Stanberg/Turnstone Books.
The Friendly Fungi, by C. L. Duddington/Faber & Faber.
Gardening Without Poisons, by Beatrice Trum Hunter/Berkley Medallion Books, New York.
Garden Success Without Poison Sprays, by J. I. Rodale/Rodale Press, U.S.A.
The Injurious Insects of the British Commonwealth, by J. W. Evans/Commonwealth Bureau of Entomology.
Insecticides from Plants, by Martin Jacobson/U.S.A. Dept of Agriculture, 1958.
Investigations into the Biological Activity of a Series of Butylene Polymers, by I. Greenfield/F. W. Berk.
The Natural Garden, by Roger Grounds/Davis Poynter.
Nature on Your Side, by G. Buchner and F. Hoogvelt/Pan.
Pests of Farm Crops, by S. H. Stapely/E. & F.

ALLOTMENT LIB

SOCIETIES

Friends of the Earth, 9 Poland Street, London W1V 3DG. *Please join if you haven't already done so. They really do a fantastic amount of good work on your behalf.*
The Gardeners Chronicle, Gillow House, 5 Winsley Street, London W1A 2HG. *Will give advice on any problem relating to seeds.*
E. F. Didcot Organic Garden Services, 117 Landseer Avenue, Bristol. *Advisory organisation on organic gardening as well as supplying sundries.*
National Allotments and Gardens Society, 22 High Street, Flitwick, Bedfordshire.

BIBLIOGRAPHY

Allotments/HMSO.
Allotments Campaign Manual/Friends of the Earth.
Crops and Shares: Manual for a Garden Sharing Scheme/Friends of the Earth.
The Law of Allotments, by Prof. J. H. Garner/Shaw and Sons.
Losing Ground, by M. Allaby, C. Hines and G. Blythe/Friends of the Earth.
Report of the Departmental Committee of Inquiry into Allotments, The Thorpe Report 1969/HMSO Command Paper no.4166.
Gardening Books:
Complete Urban Farmer, by David Wickers/Julian Friedman.
Compost Vegetable Growing, by B. G. Furner/Foulsham.
Down to Earth Gardening, by Lawrence Hills/Faber & Faber.
Grow Your Own Fruit and Vegetables, by Lawrence Hills/Faber & Faber.
Home Grown Food, by Roy Genders/Michael Joseph.
Organic Fertilizers/Rodale Press.

Organic Gardening, by Lawrence Hills/Penguin.
Practical Organic Gardening, by Ben East/Faber & Faber.
Step-by-Step to Organic Vegetable Growing, by Samuel Ogden/Rodale Press.

A GOURMET GUIDE TO WILD EATING

SOURCES OF MATERIALS

Wild flower seeds of many species can be obtained from:
Thompson & Morgan Ltd, London Road, Ipswich, Suffolk.

SOCIETIES

Wild Flower Society, c/o Mrs C. M. R. Schwerdt, Rams Hill House, Horse Moden, Tonbridge, Kent.

BIBLIOGRAPHY

All About Weeds, by Spencer/Dover Publications.
Eat The Weeds, by Ben Charles Harris/Keats Publishing Inc, Connecticut.
The Edible Ornamental Garden, by Brian Castle/Pitman.
The Englishman's Flora, by Geoffrey Grigson/Phoenix House.
Food for Free, by Richard Mabey/Collins/Fontana. *The 'bible' of wild foodophiles – excellent.*
Free for all, by Ceres/Thorsons Publishers.
How to Enjoy your Weeds, by Audrey Wynne Hatfield/Frederick Muller.
The Kindly Fruits, by F. Bianchini, F. Corbetta and M. Pistoia/Cassell.
Pick, Cook and Brew, by Suzanne Beedell/Mayflower. *Overflowing with wild food recipes.*
Plants that Feed and Serve us, by Else Hivass/Blandford.
The Wild Foods of Great Britain, by L. Cameron/Prism Press.
Wild Fruits and Nuts, by G. Ley/E. P. Publishing.
Wild Plants for Winemaking, by Belt/Amateur Winemaking.
Value of Weeds, by Joy Griffith-Jones/Soil Association.
Field Guides:
Collecting and Studying Mushrooms, Toadstools and Fungi, by Alan Major/Bartholomew.
Collins Guide to Mushrooms and Toadstools, by Morten Lange and F. Bayard Hora/Collins.
Collins Pocket Guide to Wild Flowers, by David McClintock and R. S. Fitter/Collins.
The Concise English Flora, by W. Keble Martin/Ebury Press.
Dangerous Plants, by Dr. Tampion/David & Charles.
The Friendly Fungi, by C. L. Doddington/Faber & Faber.

A Guide to Mushrooms, by Michael Jordan/Millington.
A Guide to Wild Plants, by Michael Jordan/Millington.
The Oxford Book of Food Plants, by G. B. Masefield, M. Wallis, S. G. Harrison and B. E. Nicholson/Oxford University Press.
Poisonous Plants and Fungi, by Pamela North/Blandford.
Wayside and Woodland Fungi, by W. D. K. Findlay/Frederick Warne. *Illustrated by Beatrix Potter.*
Wild Mushrooms, by Linus Zeitlmayr/Frederick Muller.

CYCLORAMA

SOURCES OF MATERIALS

Check the Yellow Pages for bicycle retailers in your area. The following shops are highly recommended by cycle buffs for their sales of high quality machines and service:
Fred Baker, 144 Cheltenham Road, Bristol 6.
Condor Cycles, 90 Gray's Inn Road, London W.C.1.
Excel Cycle Co, 26 Woolwich New Road, Woolwich, London, S.E.18.
Tommy Godwin, 10–12 Silver Street, Kings Heath, Birmingham 14.
W. F. Holdsworth Ltd, 132 Lower Richmond Road, Putney, London, S.W.15.
Bov Jackson, 148 Harehills Lane, Leeds LS8 5BD.
Harry Quin Ltd, 17–19 Walton Road, Liverpool 4.
David Rattray & Co Ltd, 261 Alexandra Parade, Glasgow, G31 3AD.
Jack Taylor Cycles, Church Road, Stockton-on-Tees, Cleveland.
Woodrup Cycles, 345 Kirkstall Road, Leeds 4.
Young's Lightweight Cycles, 290 Lee High Road, London, S.E.13.
Tandems available from:
The Tandem Centre, 281 Old Kent Road, London, S.E.1.
Jack Taylor Cycles.
Unicycles available from:
D.M. Engineering, 92 Hurn Road, Christchurch, Dorset.
Tricycles available from:
Jack Taylor Cycles.
Special cycling touring equipment available from:
Karrimor Products Ltd, Bell Street, Hastingden, Lancaster.
Youth Hostel Association, 29 John Adam Street, London, W.C.2.
Touring maps available from bookshops or from:
John Bartholomew, 12 Duncan Street, Edinburgh.
Director General, Ordnance Survey, Romsey Road, Maybush, Southampton, SO9 4DH. *For catalogue of all Ordnance Survey maps.*
For a list of Ordnance Survey Agents selling Ordnance Survey maps, write to:

Cook Hammond & Kell Ltd, 22–24 Caxton Street, London, S.W.1. – *for England and Wales.*
Thomas Nelson & Sons, 18 Dalkeith Road, Edinburgh EH16 5BS – *for Scotland.*

BICYCLES FOR HIRE

East Anglia and Midlands:
P. H. Allin & Sons, 189 Histon Road, Cambridge. Tel: 53431.
Denton's Cycles, 194 Banbury Road, Oxford. Tel: 53859.
Ben Hayward & Son, 69 Trumpington Street, Cambridge.
Peak Park Cycle Hire, Parsley Hay, Near Ashbourne, Derbyshire.
Robinson's Cycles, 46 Magdalen Road, Oxford.
Devon and Cornwall:
Plymtak Mini Coach Hire, 21 Chudleigh Road, Lipson Vale, Plymouth, Devon. Tel: 61283.
P. Taylor, John Langdon Ltd, 2 St Mary Street, Truro, Cornwall.
London:
Bell Street Bikes, 73 Bell Street, London, N.W.1. Tel: 01 724 0456.
Bicycle Revival, 11 Charleville Road, London, W.14. Tel: 01 385 1644.
Geoffrey Butler Cycles, 9 South End, Croydon. Tel: 01 688 5094.
F. W. Evans Cycles, 44/46 Kennington Road, London, S.E.1. Tel: 01 928 4785.
Rent-a-Bike, Kensington Student Centre, Kensington Church Street, London, W.8. Tel: 01 937 6089.
Savile's Cycle Stores Ltd, 97–99 Battersea Rise, Battersea, London, S.W.11. Tel: 01 228 4279.
North England:
Daisy Daisy, Springfield, Heslington, Near York, North Yorkshire.
Ghyll Side Cycle Shop, Ambleside, Cumbria.
Lake District Cycle Hire, Tithe Barn Street, Keswick, Cumbria; or South Henry Street, Botchergate, Carlisle.
Sander Bros, The Cycle Corner, Brighton Grove, Newcastle-upon-Tyne 4. Tel. 34045.

Scotland:
Mrs J. Anderson, Airlie, Brodick, Isle of Arran, Strathclyde. Tel: 2313.
J. Anderson, 46/52 Rosemount Viaduct, Aberdeen. Tel: 21520.
W. Band & Son, Crail Road, Montrose, Anstruther, Fife. Tel: 502.
James Benzie, 5 The Cross, Prestwick, Strathclyde. Tel: 77360.
Bremner's Store, 17 Cardiff Street, Millport, Isle of Cumbrae, Strathclyde. Tel: 521.
Eric Brown, Cycle Agents, 7 Commercial Road, Lerwick, Shetland. Tel: 433.
S. Buckeridge & Son, 5 Bishop Street, Rothesay, Strathclyde. Tel: 1279.
Messrs Calder Bros., 7 Bridge Street, Rothesay, Strathclyde.
Messrs. Chapells (Cycle Dealers), 17a Bridge Street, Berwick-Upon-Tweed. Tel: 6295.
W. Conroy, 17 Northesk Road, Montrose, Tayside.

The Cycle Shop, Main Street, Muir of Ord, Highland.
The Cycle Shop, Cromwell Street Pier, Stornoway, Isle of Lewis.
Dale's Cycles, 26/30 Maryhill Road, Glasgow. Tel: 041 332 2705.
Mrs A. Donaldson, 'Fairwinds', Torrin, Broadford, Isle of Skye. Tel: 270.
Halfords Ltd, 34 High Street, Elgin, Grampian. Tel: 2593.
Highland Guides, Aviemore, Highland. Tel: 729.
Mrs Hislop, Lilybank, Lamlash, Isle of Arran, Strathclyde. Tel: 230.
A. Howie, Roselyn, Brodick, Isle of Arran, Strathclyde. Tel: 2460.
Hughes (Cycles), Princes Street, Thurso, Highland. Tel: 2511.
Mr. Liddle, Marona, Orphir, Orkney.
D. MacLellan, Douthern Garage, Whiting Bay, Isle of Arran, Strathclyde. Tel: 293.
F. V. G. Mapes & Sons, 4 Guildford Street, Millport, Isle of Cumbrae, Strathclyde. Tel: 444.
A. McLean, 70 High Street, Fort William, Highland. Tel: 2157.
Hugh Morrison, The Post Office, Castlebay, Barra, Western Isles.
A. & W. Morton, 6 Mount Stuart Street, Millport, Isle of Cumbrae, Strathclyde.
Ian Patterson, Station Square, Ballater, Grampian. Tel: Aberdeen 343.
T. Piper, Prop: A. G. Smith, 41 Morningside Road, Edinburgh.
David Rattray & Co Ltd, 261 Alexander Parade, Glasgow. Tel: 041 554 3757.
W. Reid, 44 Broomhill Road, Aberdeen, Grampian. Tel: 26974.
H. Rodgers, Glenflorol, Brodick, Isle of Arran, Strathclyde. Tel: 2314.
A. Smith, Prop: Mrs. E. Smith, 32 High Street, Portobello, Edinburgh. Tel: 031 669 3518.
W. Stuart & Son, 30 High Street, Forres, Grampian. Tel: 2432.
R. G. Swan, 9 Bridge Street, Kelso, Borders. Tel: 2749.
Mr Vaughan, Docharn House, Boat of Garten, Highland. Tel: 617.
Mrs Work, Davaar Guest House, 6 Old Scapa Road, Kirkwall, Orkney. Tel: 2006.

South East England:
Cy Sales, 644 Wimborne Road, Winton, Bournemouth, Dorset. Tel: 55880.
Stubberfields, 12 South Street, Eastbourne, East Sussex. Tel: 70395.

West Country:
Haines & Son, 6–10 Water Lane, Salisbury, Wiltshire. Tel: 4915.

Wales:
Border Bicycle Hire, 36 Bellvue Road, Shrewsbury. Tel: 50562.
Reg. Braddick & Sons Ltd, 59/61 Broadway, Roath, Cardiff, South Glamorgan.
Cardiff Bicycle Hire and Tours, at 'Things Welsh', 5 Duke Street Arcade, Cardiff. Tel: 33445.

SOCIETIES

General:
All Change to Bikes, Greater London House, Hampstead Road, London, N.W.1.
Bicycle Polo Association of Great Britain, c/o Mrs D. Corby, 31 Shipman Road, London, S.E.22.
British Cycling Bureau, Greater London House, Hampstead Road, London, N.W.1.
British Cycling Federation, 70 Brompton Road, London, SW3 1EN.
Cyclist Touring Club, 69 Meadrow, Godalming, Surrey, GU7 3HS.
The Fell Club, 12 Ravenswood Crest, Stafford.
The 40-Plus Group, T. Wooder, 425 Upminster Road, North Rainham, Essex.
Lightweight Cycle Association of Great Britain, 25 Tanners Hill, Deptford Broadway, London SE8 4PJ.
Northern Ireland Cycling Federation, 144 Princes Way, Portadown, Co. Armagh, Northern Ireland.
Pennine Cycle Club, c/o Don Miles, Bradford. Tel: 614216.
The Rough Stuff Fellowship, H. G. Robson, 23 Spring Terrace, North Shields, Tyne and Wear.
Scottish Cyclists Union, 293 Rosemount Place, Aberdeen AB2 4YB.
South Eastern Road Club, Mrs J. Osborne, 13 Amherst Drive, St Mary, Kent.
Tandem Club, Hon. Secretary, 71 Exeter Road, Welling, Kent.
The Tricycle Association, Anvil Cottage, Sanrey, Ambleside, Cumbria.
The Vegetarian Cycling and Athletic Club, 18 Mill Lane, Kilburn, London, N.W.6.
Womens Tricycle Association, 92 Graham Gardens, Luton, Bedfordshire.

Veteran and Vintage:
Benson Veteran Cycle Club, C. N. Passey, 61 The Banglow, Brook Street, Benson, Oxfordshire.
Boston Veteran Cycle Club, P. Bates, 15 Rosebury Avenue, Boston, Lincolnshire.
Bygone Bikes Yorkshire Club, J. W. Auty, 85 Priory Road, Featherstone, Pontefract, West Yorkshire.
Long Sutton and District Veteran Cycle Club, P. Shirtcliffe, Hillcrest, Crowhall, Denver, Downham Market, Norfolk.
National Association of Veteran Cycle Clubs, Ray Hecley, 124 Southfields Avenue, Stanground, Peterborough.
Peterborough Vintage Cycle Club, Ms Young, 48 Newark Avenue, Peterborough.
Roadfarers Veteran Cycle Club, A. C. Mundy, 22 High Street, Caister, Peterborough.
Southern Veteran Cycle Club, I. Cowan, Woodbine Cottage, 8 Shrubbery Road, Gravesend, Kent.
Veteran Time Trials Association, 137 Glenwood Avenue, Westcliff-on-Sea, Essex.

Racing:
British Cycling Federation.
British Cyclo Cross Association, 5 Copstone Drive, Dorridge, Solihull, West Midlands.
British Professional Cycle Racing Association, Hebden Trowel, Lodge, Mill Lane, Hebden,

North Yorkshire.
Cycle Speedway Council, W. F. Gill, 67 St Francis Way, Chadwell St Mary, Grays, Essex, RM16 4RB.
Irish Cycling Federation, 155 Shanliss Road, Shantry, Dublin 9, Eire.
National Amateur Cycle Speedway Association, 50 Cromley Road, High Lane, Stockport.
Northern Ireland Cycling Federation, 144 Princes Way, Portadown, Co. Armagh, Northern Ireland.
Road Time Trials Council, 210 Devonshire Hill Lane, London, N.17.

Camping and Touring:
Association of Cycling and Lightweight Campers, 30 Napier Road, Wembley, Middlesex.
Camping Club of Great Britain and Ireland Ltd, 11 Lower Grosvenor Place, London, S.W.1.
Irish Youth Hostels Association, Dublin, Eire.
Ramblers Association, 1–4 Crawford Mews, York Street, London, W.1.
Scottish Youth Hostels Association, 7 Glebe Crescent, Stirling.
Youth Hostel Association, Trevelyan House, 8 St Stephen's Hill, St Albans, Hertfordshire.
Membership, Sales, Travel and Service Depts: 29 John Adam Street, London, W.C.2.
Youth Hostel Association of Northern Ireland, Bryson House, Belfast, BT2 7FE.

TOURIST INFORMATION SERVICES

Tourist information can be obtained in Britain from the following organisations:
British Tourist Authority, Tourist Information Centre, 64 St James's Street, London SW1A 1NF. Tel: 01 629 9191.
London Tourist Board, 4 Grosvenor Gardens, London SW1W 0DU. Tel: 01 730 0791.

England
English Tourist Board, 4 Grosvenor Gardens, London SW1W 0DU. Tel: 01 730 3400 (Administration) Tel: 01 730 0791 (Information).
East Anglia Tourist Board, 14 Museum Street, Ipswich IP1 1HU, Suffolk. Tel: 0473 214211.
East Midlands Tourist Board, Bailgate, Lincoln LN1 3AR. Tel: 0522 31521.
English Lakes Counties Tourist Board, Ellerthwaite, Windermere, Cumbria. Tel: Windermere 4444.
Isle of Wight Tourist Board, 21 High Street, Newport, Isle of Wight. Tel: 0983 81 4343.
Northumbria Tourist Board, Prudential Building, 140–150 Pilgrim Street, Newcastle upon Tyne NE1 6TH. Tel: Newcastle 28795.
North-West Tourist Board, 119 The Piazza, Piccadilly Plaza, Manchester M1 4AN. Tel: 061 236 0393.
South-East England Tourist Board, Cheviot House, 4–6 Monson Road, Tunbridge Wells, Kent. Tel: Tunbridge Wells 33066.
West Country Tourist Board, Trinity Court, Southernhay East, Exeter EX1 1QS, Devon. Tel: Exeter 76351.
West Midlands Tourist Board, P.O. Box 15, Worcester WR1 3QQ.
Yorkshire Tourist Board, 312 Tadcaster Road,

York YO2 2HF. Tel: 0904 67961
Scotland
Scottish Tourist Board, 23 Ravelston Terrace, Edinburgh EH4 3EU. Tel 031 332 2433.
The Borders Tourist Association, 66 Woodmarket, Kelso, Borders. Tel: Kelso 2125.
Clyde Tourist Association, c/o Information Centre, George Square, Glasgow G2 1ES. Tel: 041 221 9600.
Highlands and Islands Development Board, Bridge House, Bank Street, Inverness. Tel: Inverness 34171.
Grampian Tourist Association, 17 High Street, Elgin, Grampian IV30 1EG. Tel: Elgin 2666.
South West of Scotland Tourist Association, Douglas House, Newton Stewart, Dumfries and Galloway. Tel: Newton Stewart 549.
Wales
Wales Tourist Board, Welcome House, High Street, Llandaff, Cardiff CF5 2YZ. Tel: Cardiff 567701,
Mid Wales Tourism Council, 3 China Street, Llanidloes, Powys. Tel: Llanidloes 644.
North Wales Tourism Council, Civic Centre, Colwyn Bay, Clwyd. Tel: 0492 55222.
South Wales Tourism Council, Alexandra Buildings, Dark Gate, Carmarthen. Tel: Carmarthen 7557.
Northern Ireland
Northern Ireland Tourist Board, River House, 48 High Street, Belfast BT1 2DS. Tel: Belfast 31221.
Isle of Man
Isle of Man Tourist Board, 13 Victoria Street, Douglas, Isle of Man. Tel: Douglas 4323.
Channel Islands
The States of Guernsey Tourist Committee, P.O. Box 23, States Office, Guernsey, Channel Islands. Tel: Guernsey 24411.
The States of Jersey Tourism Committee, Weighbridge, St Helier, Jersey, Channel Islands. Tel: Central 21281.

BIBLIOGRAPHY

Journals:
Cycle Touring/Journal of the Cyclists' Tourist Club.
Cycling/IPC.
International Cycle Sport/Kennedy Brothers Publishing Ltd.
Books:
The Book of the Bicycle, by Roger St Prene/ Ward Lock.
Continental Cycle Racing, by N. G. Henderson/ Pelham Books.
Cycling Crazy, by Charles Messenger/Pelham Books.
Cycling is My Life, by Tommy Simpson/S. Paul.
Cyclists' Dictionary/F. C. Davis.
Discovering Old Bicycles, By T. E. Crowley/ Shire Publications.
England by Bicycle, by Frederick Alderson/ David & Charles.
Explore the Cotswolds by Bicycle, by The British Cycling Bureau/Ward Lock.
Give Way: A Report on Cycling in Britain, by Richard Feilden/Friends of the Earth.

Instead of Cars, by Terence Bendixson/Pelican.

The Pedal Power Book, by Phil Reardon/Friends of the Earth.

Richard's Bicycle Book, by Richard Ballantine/Pan Books.

The following publications are available from Selpress Books, 16 Berkeley Street, London W1X 6AP:

All About Bicycle Racing
American Bicycle Racing
Around Town Cycling
Bicycle Frames
Bicycle Track Racing
Bicycling: A History
Bicycling for Fun and Health
Bicycling Science
Bikes and Bicycling
Building Bicycle Wheels
Champion on Two Wheels
Complete Bicycle Time Trial Book
Cycle Racing and Touring
Cycle Racing: Training to Win
Cycle Touring in Europe
The Cyclists and The Postage Stamp
Fix Your Bicycle
It's Easy to Fix Your Bike
International Bicycle Training
King of The Road
A Man, A Bike, Alone Through Scotland
Leisureguide Cycling
The Raleigh Book of Cycling
Serious Cycling for the Beginner
Sting in the Tail
The Story of the Bicycle
The Story of The Raleigh Cycle
Sunbeam
Travelling By Bike
Two Wheels to the Top

CANALWAYS

CANAL COTTAGES

Those interested in taking a leasehold on a nationalized canal cottage should contact the following Regional Estate Offices of the British Waterways Board.
North: B.W.B., P.O. Box 9, 1 Dock Street, Leeds 1.
South East: B.W.B., Willow Grange, Church Road, Watford, Hertfordshire.
South West: B.W.B., Dock Office, Gloucester, GL1 2EJ.
Scotland: Estate Assistant, B.W.B., Old Basin Works, Applecross Street, Glasgow, C.4.

BOAT HIRE

Details of holidays and cruise firms can be obtained from:
British Waterways Board, Hire Cruiser Base, Chester Road, Nantwich, Chester (*see also Bibliography*).

BOAT BUYING

Details of craft for sale can be found in the trade journals (see Bibliography) or from:
Exchange & Mart
Before looking around it may be worthwhile consulting the following boatbuyers guides, published by Boat World Magazines:
No. 1 Sailing Dinghies
No. 2 Sailing Cruisers
No. 3 Motor Cruisers

MAPS

All maps and guides are available from the Inland Waterways Association *(see Societies), and in specific cases, the* British Waterways Board.
Imray's Maps:
Inland Waterways of England and Wales
Kennet and Avon Waterway – Eastern Section
Kennet and Avon Waterway – Western Section
Stanford Maps:
Canoeing Map of England and Wales
Inland Waterways
Others:
British Waterways Board Waterways/B.W.B.
Caledonian Canal/B.W.B.
Caledonian Canal/Inland Waterways Association (I.W.A.)
Inland Cruising Map/Motor Boat and Yachting Magazine
Kingston and Leominster Canal Map/Railway and Canal History Society
Waterways Atlas of the British Isles/I.W.A.

AUTHORITIES

British Waterways Board, Melbray House, Melbury Terrace, London, N.W.1. *Responsible for all nationalized river and canal navigations in England, Scotland and Wales. Sub offices include:*
B.W.B. – Licensing Office, Willow Grange, Church Road, Watford, Hertfordshire.
B.W.B. – Caledonian Canal Office, Clachnaharry, Highland.
B.W.B. – Crinan Canal Office, Ardrishaig, Strathclyde.
Basingstoke Canal Co Ltd, Trafford Works, North Road, Burnt Oak, Edgware, London.
Bridgewater Canal Dept, Manchester Ship Canal Co, Chester Road, Manchester.
Chichester Canal:
West Sussex County Council, County Hall, Chichester, West Sussex.
Exeter Ship Canal:
Exeter Corporation, The Guildhall, Exeter, Devon.
Rochdale Canal:
Rochdale Canal Co, 75 Dale Street, Manchester, M1 2HG.
Royal Military Canal – Seabrook Outfall to West Hythe administered by:
Hythe Corporation, Borough Treasurer, Municipal Offices, Stade Street, Hythe, Kent.
West Hythe Dam to Iden Lock administered by:

Kent River Authority, Rivers House, London Road, Maidstone, Kent.
Stratford-Upon-Avon Canal (Southern Section):
The National Trust, Southern Stratford Canal, Canal Office, Lapworth, Warwickshire.
Grand Canal and River Barrow Navigation:
Coras Iompair Eireann, Civil Engineering Dept, Pearse Station, Westland Row, Dublin 2.
Newry Ship Canal:
Newry Port and Harbour Trust, Harbour Office, Newry, Northern Ireland.

SOCIETIES

Ashby Canal Association, Brian Osbourne, 35 Westray Drive, Hinckley, Leicestershire.
Association of Pleasure Craft Operators, Harry Arnold, 26 Chaseview Road, Alrewas, Burton-on-Trent, Staffordshire.
Association of Water Cruising Clubs, C. F. Stevens, 38 Sandhurst Drive, Seven Kings, Ilford, Essex.
Birmingham Canal Navigations Society, J. B. Philips, 482 Sutton Road, Walsall, West Midlands.
The Broads Society, Pamela Oakes, 63 Whitehall Road, Norwich, Norfolk, NOR 9F.
Calder Navigation Society, Sowerby Bridge Wharf, Calder and Hebble Navigation, Sowerby Bridge, West Yorkshire.
Caldon Canal Society, R. Savage, 1 Cauldon Avenue, Cheddleton, Near Leek, Staffordshire.
Cambridge University Canal Club, c/o V. Hallet, Narrow Boat 'Phosphorus', Chesterton Road, Cambridge.
Coventry Canal Society, P. J. Williamson, 81 John Rons Avenue, Coventry.
Cromford Canal Society, c/o Dr A. D. Stoker, Bank House, Winster, Derbyshire.
Dolphin Sailing Barge Museum Trust, Dolphin Yard, Crown Quay Lane, Sittingbourne, Kent.
Driffield Navigation Amenities Association, c/o The County Stores, Brandesburton, Driffield, East Yorkshire.
Droitwich Junction Canal Trust, c/o I.W.A.
Dudley Canal Trust, J. E. Parkes, 58 Summer Road, Rowley Regis, Warley, West Midlands.
East Anglian Waterways Association Ltd, L. A. Edwards, Wych House, St Ives, Cambridgeshire.
Erewash Canal Preservation and Development Association, R. G. Goodwin, Lawn House, Main Street, Etwall, Derbyshire.
Grand Union Canal Society, Robert Hampson, Half-Way House, Cassio Bridge, Watford, Hertfordshire.
Grand Western Canal Preservation Committee, D. C. Harvard, Gotham House, Tiverton, Devon.
Grantham Canal Society, R. Sharman, 128 Kenrick Road, Mapperley, Nottingham, N.G.3.
Great Ouse Restoration Society, D. J. Kettle, 8 Manor Close, Kempston, Bedfordshire.
Inland Waterways Association, 114 Regent's Park Road, London, N.W.1. *The largest voluntary organization in the country to promote*

the use, maintenance and restoration of the inland waterways of the British Isles.
Inland Waterways Association of Ireland, Dr Alf Delany, Fourways, 58 Seafield Road, Clontarf, Dublin 3, Eire.
Inland Waterways Association of Scotland, Douglas Russell, 37 Ravelston Gardens, Edinburgh EH4 3LF.
Inland Waterways Protection Society, P. J. Bunker, Gorse-Side, Cartledge Lane, Holmesfield, Sheffield.
Kennet and Avon Canal Trust, D. D. Hutchings, The Coppice, Elm Lane, Lower Earley, Reading.
Lancaster Canal Trust, D. Slater, 163 St Alban's Road, St Annes-on-Sea, Lancashire.
Lower Avon Navigation Trust, c/o I. M. Beard, Gable End, The Holloway, Pershore, Hereford and Worcester.
Market Weighton Canal Restoration Committee, G. B. Miles, 47 Market Place, Market Weighton, Humberside.
Narrow Boat Trust, C. Johnstone, Willow Cottage, Timsway, Staines, Surrey.
National Association of Inland Waterways Carriers, Bridgewater Canal Offices, Chester Road, Manchester.
National Council on Inland Transport, c/o R. Calvert, 396 City Road, London, E.C.1.
Newport (Mon) Canal Preservation Society, c/o Secretary, 20 Coolgreany Close, Newport, Gwent.
Norfolk Wherry Trust, J. R. M. Bryce, 33 Brettingham Avenue, Cringleford, Norwich, Norfolk.
North Western Society for Industrial Archaeology and History, E. W. Paget-Tomlinson, Clifton House, Top Road, Kingsley, Near Warrington, Cheshire.
Old Union Canals Society, R. Wild, 61 Knights End Road, Great Bowden, Market Harborough, Leicestershire.
Oxford College Barges Preservation Trust, K. P. Gingell, Barclays Old Bank, High Street, Oxford.
Paddington Waterways Society, Col P. Flower, 20 Blomfield Road, Little Venice, London, W.9.
Peak Forest Canal Society, E. Keaveney, 35 Councillor Lane, Cheadle, Greater Manchester.
Pocklington Canal Amenity Society, S. M. Nix, 74 Westminster Road, York, YO3 6LY.
Railway and Canal Historical Society, J. R. Harding, 174 Station Road, Wylde Green, Sutton Coldfield, West Midlands.
Regent's Canal Group, C. Philips, 46 Noel Road, London, N.1.
Residential Boat Owners' Association, E. Fleming, MV 'Dorian', Ash Island, East Molesey, Surrey.
Risca Magor and St Mellons Canal Preservation Society, M. J. Bevan, 6 Gelli Unig Place, Pontywaun, Crosskeys, Newport, Gwent.

BIBLIOGRAPHY

Navigation Guides:
All available from the I.W.A., from large bookshops and the B.W.B.
Ladyline Guide Series:
1. Llangollen Canal
2. Oxford Canal
3. Shropshire Union Canal
4. Grand Union (North)
5. Grand Union (South)
6. Grand Union (Leicester Section)
Nicholson's Guides to the Waterways:
Part 1 – South-East
Part 2 – North-East
Part 3 – South-West
Part 4 – North-East
Part 5 – Midlands
Real Ale Guide to the Waterways
Inland Waterways Association Guides:
Brecon and Abergavenny, Cruising Map and Guide
Bridgewater Canal
Broads Book
Calder and Hebble Navigations and Huddersfield Broad Canal
Canals Book
Coventry's Waterway
Driffield Navigation Guide
Erewash Canal
Gateway to the Avon; Tewkesbury to Evesham
Grand Canal of Ireland
Stratford-upon-Avon Canal, Southern Section
Upper Avon
Towpath Guides:
No. 1 Staffordshire and Worcestershire Canal/Langford.
No. 2 Brecknock and Abergavenny and Monmouthshire/Stevens.
The Towpath Road: Guide to Liverpool and Leeds/I.W.A.
Other Guides:
The Shannon Guide, by J. K. Clear, 6 Waterloo Road, Dublin 4.
Boat Hire Guides and Magazines
Belmont Guide/I.W.A.
Getting Afloat (A Guide to Launching Sites)/I.W.A.
Inland Waterways Holiday Guide/I.W.A.
Lazy Man's Guide to Holidays Afloat/Boat Enquiries Ltd, 12 Western Road, Oxford.
Motor Boat and Yachting/I.P.C. Transport Press Ltd.
Small Boat/Link House, Dingwall Avenue, Croydon.
Waterways News/B.W.B.
Yachting and Boating Weekly/Pearce Publications Ltd.
Books
Boats:
Barges or Juggernauts?/Inland Shipping Group c/o I.W.A.
Boats and Boatmen, by D. D. Gladwin and J. M. White/Gladwin & White.
Canal and River Craft in Pictures, by Hugh McKnight/David & Charles.
The Canal Boatmen, by Harry Hanson/Manchester University Press.
Canals, Boats and Boaters, by D. J. Smith/

Hugh Evelyn.
Decorative Arts of the Mariner, by G. Frere-Cook/ Cassell.
English Canals Vol. 3, by D. D. Gladwin and J. M. White/Gladwin & White.
Fenland Barge Traffic, by J. K. Wilson and A. Faulkner/Robert Wilson.
Leeds and Liverpool Canal Craft, by G. Wheat/North Counties Carriers Ltd.
A Life on the Humber, by Harry Fletcher/Faber & Faber.
Mersey and Weaver Flats, by E. Paget-Tomlinson/Robert Wilson.
Narrow Boat Decoration/Birmingham Canal Navigation Society.
Narrow Boat Painting, by A. J. Lewery/David & Charles.
Sailing Barges, by F. Carr/Conway Maritime Press.
A Short History of the Narrow Boat, by T. Chaplin/Geoffrey Dibb.
Wherries and Waterways, by R. Malster/Terence Dalton.
Biography:
James Brindley, by H. Bode/Shire Publications.
James Brindley, Engineer, by C. T. G. Boucher/Goose & Son.
British Engineers, by M. Chappell/Collins.
The Canal Builders, by R. Payne/Macmillan.
The Canal Duke, by H. Malet/David & Charles.
Great Engineers and Their Works – Thomas Telford, by B. Bracegirdle and P. Miles/David & Charles.
Lives of the Engineers (1861) Vols 1 and 2, by S. Smiles/David & Charles (reprint 1968).
Newcomen, by L. T. C. Rolt/David & Charles.
John Rennie, by C. T. G. Boucher/Manchester University Press.
The Story of Telford, by Sir S. Gibb/Maclehose London.
Thomas Telford, by L. T. C. Rolt/Longmans.
James Watt, by L. T. C. Rolt/Batsford.
Cruising:
Beginners Guide to Motor Cruising, by C. Cove-Smith and R. E. Chase.
The Ben – A Cruising Guide to the Canals of Birmingham and The Black Country/Staffs and Worcs Canal Society.
Britain's Holiday Waterways, by R. J. Westlake/Bradford Barton.
Canal Cruising, by J. Hankinson/Ward Lock & Co.
Canal Enthusiasts' Handbook No. 2, by C. Hadfield (ed.)/David & Charles.
The Canals Book, by G. Dibb/Link House (annual).
Cruising along the Monmouth and Brecon, by J. Eyles/Starling Press.
Exploring Canals and Waterways, by G. Whittam/Odhams.
Holiday Cruising in Ireland, by P. J. G. Ransom/David & Charles.
Holiday Cruising on the Broads and Fens, by L. A. Edwards/David & Charles.
Holiday Cruising on Inland Waterways, by C. Hadfield and M. Streat/David & Charles.
Holiday Cruising on the Thames, by E. and

P. W. Ball/David & Charles.
Know Your Waterways – Holidays on Inland Waterways, by R. Aickman/Coram.
Narrow Boat Venture, by John Poole/Thornhill Press.
Pilotage on Inland Waterways, by C. Cove-Smith and R. E. Chase/Yachting and Boating Weekly.
Water Rallies, by D. E. Owen/J. M. Dent.
The Watney Book of Inland Cruising, by Viscount St Davids/Queen Anne Press.
Descriptive Cruises:
The Amateur Boatwoman, by E. Gayford/David & Charles.
5000 Miles 3000 Locks, by J. Gagg/Arthur Baker.
The Flower of Gloster (1911), by E. T. Thurston/David & Charles.
Green and Silver, by L. T. C. Rolt/Allen & Unwin.
Hold on a Minute, by T. Wilkinson/Allen & Unwin.
In the Wake of the Gods, by H. Mallet/Chatto & Windus.
Journey of the Swan, by J. Liley/Allen & Unwin.
Maidens' Trip, by E. Smith/MacGibbon & Kee.
My Holidays on Inland Waterways, by P. Bonthron/Thomas Murby & Co.
Narrow Boat, by L. T. C. Rolt/Eyre & Spottiswoode.
Sailing through England, by J. Seymour/Eyre & Spottiswoode.
Slow Boat through England, by F. Doerflinger/Wingate.
Slow Boat through Pennine Waters, by F. Doerflinger/Wingate.
Small Boat on the Thames, by R. Pilkington/Macmillan.
A Tour of the Grand Junction Canal in 1819, by J. Hassal/Cranfield & Bonfiel (reprint).
Voyage into England, by J. Seymour/David & Charles.
Water Byways, by D. E. Owen/David & Charles.
Children's Books:
Boats and Boating, by J. Gagg/Blackwell.
Britain's Inland Waterways, by R. Wickson/Methuen.
Canals, by Jane Dorner/Wayland.
Canals in Britain, by A. Ross/Blackwell.
Canoe Boy, by R. Bateman/Longmans Young Books.
Curlew on the Cut, by B. Lawrence/Geoffrey Dibb.
The Flower of Gloster, by B. Grundy/Rupert Hart-Davis.
Fun on the Waterways, by J. Banks and P. Hume/Penwork Ltd.
Getting to Know Boats, by D. Samson/Panda Publications.
History at Source – Canals 1720–1910, by R. Pearce/Evans Brothers.
Inland Waterways, by P. Thornhill/Methuen.
The Narrow Boat, by E. Harries/Macmillan.
River and Canal Transport, by J. Vince/Blandford.
Rivers and Canals, by R. W. Purton/Routledge

& Kegan Paul.
Rivers in Britain, by J. Gagg/Blackwell.
Saranne, by V. Bibby/Longmans.
The Story of our Canals, by C. Hutchings/Ladybird Books.
Your Book of Waterways, by E. De Mare/Faber & Faber.
General:
The Story of our Inland Waterways, by R. Aickman/George Dibb.
Canals in Town, by Lewis Braithwaite/Black.
A Handbook of Water Plants, by E. Bursche/Frederick Warne.
The Canal Builders, by A. Burton/Eyre Methuen.
Canals in Colour, by A. Burton and D. Pratt/Blandford.
Canals and Inland Waterways, by G. Cadbury and S. F. Dobbs/Pitman.
Grantham Canal Today, by C. Cove-Smith.
Canals Book, by D. Dalton (ed.)/Link House.
Canals and Rivers of Britain, by Andrew Darwin/Batsford.
The Canals of England, by E. De Mare/Architectural Press.
Exploring the Kennet and Avon, by Denyer.
Bradshaw's Canals and Navigable Rivers of England and Wales (1904), by H. R. De Salis/David & Charles (reprint).
Navigable Rivers of Yorkshire, by B. F. Duckham/Dalesman Publishing.
The Inland Waterways of Great Britain, by L. A. Edwards/Imray.
Wild Flowers of the Waterways and Marshes, by E. A. Ellis/Jarrold.
Morphological Studies of the English Canals, by J. H. Farringdon/University of Hull.
Our Waterways, by V. A. Forbes and W. H. R. Ashford/John Murray.
Canals in Camera Vols. 1 and 2, by J. Gagg/Ian Allan.
Book of Locks, by J. Gagg.
The Canaller's Bedside Book, by J. Gagg/David & Charles.
Book of Narrow Canals, by J. Gagg.
A Canal and Waterways Armchair Book, by J. Gagg/David & Charles.
Book of Tunnels, by J. Gagg.
The Canals of Britain, by D. D. Gladwin/Batsford.
Victorian and Edwardian Canals, by D. D. Gladwin/Batsford.
Introducing Canals, by C. Hadfield/Ernest Benn.
The Canal Age, by C. Hadfield/David & Charles.
Canals and Waterways, by C. Hadfield/David & Charles.
A Brief Guide to Canals and Waterways, by C. Hadfield/David & Charles.
British Canals, by C. Hadfield/David & Charles.
Introducing Inland Waterways, by C. Hadfield/David & Charles.
Canals and their Architecture, by R. Harris/Hugh Evelyn.
London's Canals/G.L.C.
London's Canals/Danetre Press.
The Unofficial Countryside, by R. Mabey/

Collins.

The Birmingham Canal Navigations, by R. May/C. R. Smith.

Canals, Locks and Canal Boats, by Hugh McKnight/Ward Lock.

Shell Book of Inland Waterways, by Hugh McKnight/David & Charles.

Canoe Cruising Manual (Guide to the Waterways of the British Isles), by Noel McNaught/British Canoeing Union/Kaye & Ward.

How Britain's Waterways are Used, by J. Merrett/Routledge & Kegan Paul.

Discovering Canals, by L. Metcalfe and J. Vince/Shire Publications.

Canals, Barges and People, by J. O'Connor/Art & Technics.

Water Highways, by D. E. Owen/Phoenix House.

Priestley's Navigable Rivers and Canals (1831), by J. Priestley/David & Charles (reprint).

Waterways Restored, by P. J. G. Ransom/Faber & Faber.

Regent's Canal – A policy for its Future, by Regent's Canal Group/Regent's Canal Group.

The Inland Waterways of England, by L. T. C. Rolt/Allen & Unwin.

Navigable Waterways, by L. T. C. Rolt/Longmans.

Inland Waterways, by L. T. C. Rolt/E.S.A.

Inland Sailors/Humber Keel and Sloop Preservation Society.

The Severn and its Bore, by F. R. Rowbotham/David & Charles.

Waterside Pubs, by R. Russell/David & Charles.

Discovering Lost Canals, by R. Russell/Shire Publications.

Canal Fishing, by K. Seaman/Barrie & Jenkins.

Our Canal Population, by G. Smith/E.P.

Waterways Heritage, by P. Smith/Luton Museum.

The Thames Highway: Vol. II Locks and Weirs, by F. S. Thacker/David & Charles.

Fenland River, by R. Tibbs/Lavenham Press.

Canals and Canal Architecture, by J. Vince/Shire Publications.

Thames and Severn Canal, by D. J. Viner/Hendon.

Finance of Canal Building in 18th Century England, by J. R. Ward/Oxford University Press.

A Canalside Camera, by M. E. Ware/David & Charles.

The Number Ones, by R. J. Wilson/Robert Wilson.

Roses and Castles, by R. J. Wilson.

Life Afloat, by R. J. Wilson.

Historical:

Leicestershire Canals, by John Anderson/J. D. Anderson, Leicester.

Ashby Canal, History and Facilities/Ashby Canal Association.

Canals and Waterways (It Happened Around Manchester), by A. H. Body/University of London Press.

The Canals of Eastern England, by J. H. Boyes/David & Charles.

The Birmingham Canal Navigations, by S. R. Broadbridge/David & Charles.

The Navigators, by Anthony Burton/Macdonald.

The Caledonian Canal, by A. D. Cameron/Terence Dalton.

The Chard Canal/Chard History Group.

Let's Explore Old Waterways in Devon, by A. L. Clamp/Westway Publications.

The Kennet and Avon Canal, by K. R. Clew/David & Charles.

The Somersetshire Coal Canal and Railways, by K. R. Clew/David & Charles.

The Dorset and Somerset Canal, by K. R. Clew/David & Charles.

The Wilts and Berks Canal, by L. J. Dalby/Oakwood Press.

Portrait of the Grand Canal (Eire), by G. D'Arcy/Transport Research Association.

Towpath Walks by the Basingstoke Canal, by G. David/Surrey and Hants Canal Society.

Canals of the South of Ireland, by V. T. H. and D. R. Delany/David & Charles.

The Grand Canal of Ireland, by D. R. Delany/David & Charles.

The Yorkshire Ouse, by B. F. Duckham/David & Charles.

The Inland Waterways of East Yorkshire (1700–1900), by B. F. Duckham/East Yorks History Society.

The Haytor Granite Tramway and Stover Canal, by M. C. Ewans/David & Charles.

English Rivers and Canals, by F. Eyre and C. Hadfield/Collins.

The Grand Junction Canal, by A. H. Faulkner/David & Charles.

George and Mary – A History of the Grand Union Canal Carrying Co, by A. H. Faulkner.

The Ballinamore and Ballyconnell Canal, by P. Flanagan/David & Charles.

Walton Summit and Branch Canal, by W. Gibbs/Preston Herald.

Victorian and Edwardian Canals, by D. D. Gladwin and J. M. White/Gladwin & White.

English Canals (In 3 vols.), by D. D. Gladwin and J. M. White/Gladwin & White.

Canals of Welsh Valley and Their Tramroads, by D. D. Gladwin and J. M. White/Oakwood Press.

Waterways – Yorkshire Canals, by J. Goodchild and W. J. Morrell/E.P.

Canals of the East Midlands (including part of London), C. Hadfield/David & Charles.

British Canals, by C. Hadfield/David & Charles.

Canals of the West Midlands, by C. Hadfield/David & Charles.

Canals of South Wales and the Border, by C. Hadfield/David & Charles.

Canals of South West England, by C. Hadfield/David & Charles.

Canals of South and South-East England, by C. Hadfield/David & Charles.

Canals of Yorkshire and North-East England, vols. 1 and 2, by C. Hadfield/David & Charles.

Waterways Sights to See, by C. Hadfield.

Canals of North-West England, vols. 1 and 2., by C. Hadfield and G. Biddle/David & Charles.

Waterways to Stratford, by C. Hadfield and J. Norris/David & Charles.

The Stroudwater Navigation, by M. A. Handford/David & Charles.

Boats from the Basingstoke's Past, by T. Harmsworth/Surrey and Hants Canal Society.

The Bude Canal, by H. Harris and M. Ellis/David & Charles.

The Grand Western Canal, by H. Harris/David & Charles.

The Thames and Severn Canal, by H. Household/David & Charles.

An Authentic Description of the Kennet and Avon Canal (1811)/Kennet and Avon Canal Trust.

Staffordshire and Worcestershire Canal, by Ian Langford/Goose & Son.

Clothes of the Cut, by Avril Lansdell/B.W.B.

History of the Manchester Ship Canal – 2 Vols, by Sir B. T. Leech/Sherratt & Hughes.

Canals of Scotland, by J. Lindsay/DAvid & Charles.

Portrait of the River Trent, by P. Lord/Robert Hale.

The Forth and Clyde Canal, by G. Matheson and D. Light/David & Charles.

The Canals of the North of Ireland, by W. A. McCutcheon/David & Charles.

Coastal Passenger Steamers and Inland Navigators of Ireland (N. & S.), by D. B. McNeil/Belfast Transport Museum.

A General History of Inland Navigation (1805), by J. Phillips/David & Charles.

A History of Inland Transport and Communications (1912), by E. A. Pratt/David & Charles (reprint).

British Canals – Is their Resuscitation Practicable?, by E. A. Pratt/John Murray.

Canal Architecture in Britain, by E. A. Pratt.

Lost Canals of England and Wales, by R. Russell/David & Charles.

The Sheffield Canal, an archive teaching unit, by R. Russell/Sheffield City Libraries.

The Upper Avon/Stratford-upon-Avon Canal Society.

BUILDING UP STEAM: BRITAIN'S ALTERNATIVE RAILWAYS

SOCIETIES

Many of the following societies own railway stock and operate steam-haul days at certain times during the year. Please send an S.A.E. if enquiring for membership and other details.

Aberdeen Gas Works Locomotive Preservation Trust Fund, c/o Alan Greig, 12 Cairnery Road, Aberdeen.

A4 Locomotive Society Ltd, G. R. Pope, 49a Townshend Road, St. John's Wood, London, NW8 6LJ.

Altrincham Electric Preservation Society, c/o D. Walton, 11 Laburnum Lane, Hale, Altrincham, WA15 0JR.

Association of Minor Railway Companies, Layerthorpe Station, North Yorkshire.

Association of Private Railway-Wagon Owners Ltd, 23 Bloomfield Street, London, E.C.2.

Association of Railway Preservation Societies, Chairman: Captain Peter Manisty, R.N. (Retd.), Gen. Secretary: M. D. Crew, 34 Templegate Road, Leeds, LS15 0H3.

Backworth Steam Locomotive Preservation Society, Backworth Colliery, Backworth, Tyne and Wear.

Bahamas Locomotive Society, Dinting Railway Centre, Dinting Lane, Glossop, Derbyshire.

Bala Lake Railway Society, c/o Mr. C. Bie, 28 Chestnut Close, Hoole, Chester, Cheshire.

Barnum Coach Trust, C. W. Wright, 140 Stokesley Crescent, Billingham, Cleveland.

Bath Railway Society, K. G. Payne, Long Dean, Chippenham, Wiltshire.

Battle of Britain Locomotive Preservation Society, c/o Association of Railway Preservation Societies. (*Please send S.A.E.*)

Bluebell Railway Preservation Society, Sheffield Park Station, Uckfield, East Sussex.

Blue Peter Locomotive Society, c/o A. M. Atkinson, 120 Holgate Road, York.

Bradford Railway Circle, The Centre, Girlington Baptist Church, Washington Street, Bradford 8.

Branch Line Society, N. J. Hill, 15 Springwood Hall Gardens, Gledholt, Huddersfield, HD1 4HA.

Breconshire Railway Society, G. S. Blackledge, 25 Adelaide Gardens, Llanfaes, Brecon, Powys, LD3 8DD.

Bristol LMS Club, D. L. Tudor, 16 Merrimans Road, Shirehampton, Bristol, BS11 0AG.

Bristol 7-4-2 Club, St. Michael's on the Mount Without, St. Michael's Hill.

Bristol Suburban Railway Society, c/o R. J. Marsh, 14 Dial Lane, Downend, Bristol, BS16 5UH.

Britannia Locomotive Society, c/o R. L. Kingston, 'Lysander', Merchant Land, Cranfield, Bedfordshire, MK43 0DA.

Bulleid Society Ltd, c/o A. P. Crotaz, 37 Hillside Road, Whyteleafe, Surrey.

Burton Transport Preservation Society, Nr. Nicholson, Yew Tree, Stubby Lane, Draycott-in-the-Clay, Staffordshire.

Caerphilly Railway Society, c/o South Wales Switchgear Ltd, Harold Wilson Industrial Estate, Van Road, Caerphilly, Mid Glamorgan.

Cambrian Railways Society, c/o Stephen C. Edwards, 'Sheldan', Chirk Road, Gobowen, Oswestry, Salop.

Cardiff and Avonside Railway Society, A. Skinner, 128 Livingstone Road, Gillingham, Kent, ME7 2EJ.

Chesterton Rail Society (Cambridge), I. K. Rolph, 47 Fen Road, Cambridge, CB4 1TU.

Coastal Cruising Association, 38 Noctorum Avenue, Birkenhead, L43 9SA.

Colne Valley Railway Preservation Society, c/o R. Hymas, St. James Street, Castle Hedingham, Halstead, Essex.

Continental Railway Circle, 25 Woodcock Dell Avenue, Kenton, Harrow, Middlesex.

Corby and District Model Railway Club, West Glebe, Corby, Northamptonshire.

Corris Railway Society, E. A. Meaden, 53 Main Street, East Leeke, Loughborough, Leicestershire.

Dalescroft Rail Fans Club, D. W. Fickes, 'Dalescroft', 3 Cranbourne Road, Chellow Dean, Bradford.

Dart Valley Railway Association, The Cyder Trees, Ashburton, Devon.

Dean Forest Railway Preservation Society, c/o C. A. Bladon, 'Highfields', Grange Road, Littledean, Gloucestershire.

Diesel and Electric Group, N. P. Ellis, 13 Upper Park, Harlow, Essex, CM20 1TN.

Dowty Railway Preservation Society, c/o Secretary, Dowty Sports and Social Society, Ashchurch, Near Tewkesbury, Gloucestershire.

'Earlestoke Manor' Fund, c/o R. H. Marrows, 32 Vincent Avenue, Tuffley, Gloucester.

East Lancashire Railway Preservation Society, Bury Transport Museum, Castlecroft Road, Bury, Greater Manchester.

East Somerset Railway, Cranmore, Somerset. David Shepherd, Winkworth Farm, Hascombe, Godalming, Surrey.

Electric Railway Society, 17 Catherine Drive, Sutton Coldfield, West Midlands.

Electric Transport Development Society, E. Relton, 37 Wellesley Road, Ilford, IG1 4JX.

Ffestiniog Railway Society, c/o Harbour Station, Porthmadog, Gwynedd.

Flint and Deeside Railway Preservation Society, c/o B. Chapple, 38 Hallfield Close, Flint, Clwyd.

Forest Prairie Fund, c/o P. Skinner, 16/18 Waverley Road, Redland, Bristol.

Foxcote Manor Society, D. Norman, 4 Yew Tree Court, Gresford, Near Wrexham, Clwyd, LL12 8ET.

Gainsborough and District Railway Society, T. J. Smithson, 4 Nelson Street, Gainsborough, Lincolnshire.

Glasgow and South Western Railway Association, W. H. Best, Pier Cottage, 1 Cairnlea Road, Strathaven, Strathclyde.

Gravesend Railway Enthusiasts Society, c/o D. G. Miall, 49 St. Gregory's Crescent, Gravesend, Kent.

Greenwich and District Narrow Gauge Railway Society, c/o West Greenwich House, 141 Greenwich High Road, Greenwich, London, S.E.10.

Great Central Railway Coach Group, c/o S. S. Parsons, 8 Grendon Way, Bierton, Aylesbury, Buckinghamshire, HPZZ 5DD.

Great Northern Railway (Ireland) Society, c/o P. G. McHugh, Priorland Road, Dundalk, Ireland.

Great North of Scotland Railway Association, N. Forrest, 14 Gordon Road, Bridge of Don, Aberdeen, AB2 8PT.

Great Western Railway, 813 Preservation Fund, c/o P. H. Goss, 15 Linnet Close, Patchway, Bristol, BS1Z 5RL.

Great Western (Severn Valley Railway) Association, c/o C. Howell, 63 Upper Street, Bewdley, Hereford and Worcester.

Great Western Society Ltd (South West Group), c/o Secretary, B. Murrish, 1 Goonvren Bungalows, St Agnes, Cornwall.

Great Western Society Ltd (Taunton Group), c/o T. J. Whitfield, 7 Upcott Hall, Bishops

Hull, Taunton, Somerset.

Gresley Society, P. Holmes, 9 Broadmead, Burton Joyce, Nottingham, NG14 5FL.

Groudle Glen Railway Association, H. L. Jones, 2 Oakhill Cottages, Oakhill, Braddan, Isle of Man.

Hallamshire Railway Preservation Society, c/o Association of Railway Preservation Societies. (Please send S.A.E.)

Hampshire Narrow Gauge Railway Society, c/o P. Hitchcock, 44 St. Thomas Avenue, Hayling Island, Hampshire.

'H' Class Trust, c/o E. R. C. Oades, 5 Senlac Way, St. Leonards-on-Sea, East Sussex.

Hull and Barnsley Railway Stock Fund, c/o N. P. Fleetwood, 36 St. Pauls Road, Thornton Heath, Surrey, CR4 8NB.

Humberside Locomotive Preservation Group, T. Tighe, 58 Church Balk, Thorne, Near Doncaster, DN8 5BY.

Ilford and West Essex MCR, 34 Abbotswood Gardens, Clayhall, Ilford, Essex.

Industrial Locomotive Society, Channings, Kettlewell Hill, Woking, GU21 4JA.

Industrial Locomotive Society, J. R. Rainbow, c/o 7 Gypsy Lane, Warminster, Wiltshire.

Industrial Railway Society (founded as the Birmingham Locomotive Club – Industrial Locomotive Information Section), T. Riddle, 14 Harcourt Street, Kettering, Northamptonshire, NN16 0RS.

Inter City Railway Society, 54 Hartland Avenue, Bradeley, Stoke-on-Trent, ST6 1NF.

Ipswich and District Historical Transport Society, D. J. Barton, 1 Sunningdale Avenue, Ipswich, IP4 5SH.

Ipswich Transport Society, J. L. Miles, 12 Quebec Drive, Kesgrave, Ipswich, IP5 7HP.

Irish Steam Preservation Society Ltd, c/o R. C. Flewitt, 6 Waterloo Avenue, Dublin 3, Eire.

Isle of Man Railway Society, c/o R. Powell Hendry, 4 Clifton Road, Rugby, Warwickshire.

Isle of Man Steam Railway Supporters' Association, c/o Association of Railway Preservation Societies. (Please send S.A.E.)

Ivatt Locomotive Trust, c/o R. B. Miller and P. I. Clarke, 'Ducal', 25 Loudham Road, Little Chalfont, Amersham, Buckinghamshire.

Keighley and Worth Valley Railway Preservation Society, Haworth Station, Keighley, West Yorkshire.

Kettering and District Locomotive Society, 84 Gypsy Lane, Kettering, Northamptonshire.

King Preservation Society, Quainton Road, Near Aylesbury, Buckinghamshire.

Lakeside Railway Society, c/o Haverthwaite Station, Near Newby Bridge, Ulverston, Cumbria.

Lambton No. 29 Locomotive Syndicate, c/o P. J. Brumby, 28 Laburnham Walk, Gilberdyke, Brough, Humberside HU15 2TU.

Lancashire and Yorkshire Saddletanks Fund, c/o G. Hallos, 9 Fairfield Close, Ossett, West Yorkshire.

Leamington Rail Society, Kingsway Community Centre, Leamington, Warwickshire.

Lee Moor Tramway Preservation Society, R. E. Taylor, 32 Honicknowle Lane, Pennycross,

Plymouth.

Leicester Railway Historical Society, H. W. Sadler, Ivinghoe, 76 Sandiacre Drive, Thurmaston, Leicestershire.

Leicester Railway Society, J. Williamson, 57 Greenhill Road, Leicester, LE2 3DN.

Leighton Buzzard Narrow Gauge Railway Society, The Railway Workshops, Mile Tree Road, Leighton Buzzard, Bedfordshire.

Light Railway Transport League, 4 Madge Hill, Church Road, Hanwell, London W7 3BW.

Liverpool Light Railway Society, c/o Association of Railway Preservation Societies. (Please send S.A.E.)

Liverpool Locomotive Preservation Group, c/o E. Wheelwright, 25 Glendevon Road, Childwall, Liverpool L16 7AE.

Liverpool University Public Transport Society, Students' Union, 2 Bedford Street North, Liverpool L7 7BD.

LMS and BR Coach Fund, D. J. Lacey, 9 Crantock Road, Perry Barr, Birmingham, 22B.

Locomotive Club of Great Britain, 8 Lovatt Close, Edgware, Greater London.

London and North Western Railway Society, c/o B. H. Morris, 1 Maxwell Close, Church Road, Buckley, Clwyd, CH7 3JE.

London Underground Railway Society, S. E. Jones, 113 Wandle Road, Morden, Surrey, SM4 6AD.

Lord Fisher Locomotive Group, c/o B. G. Buckfield, Cranmore Stations, West Cranmore, Shepton Mallet, Somerset.

Maid Marian Locomotive Fund, c/o D. C. Carrington, 223 Sunnybank Road, Unsworth, Bury, Greater Manchester, BL9 8JU.

Main Line Trust, c/o M. K. Law, 34 Deancourt Road, Leicester, LE2 6GH.

Manchester Rail Travel Society, c/o F. G. Cronin, 12 Chiltern Road, Ramsbottom, Greater Manchester.

M & GN Circle, I. R. Dack, 38 Holway Road, Sheringham, Norfolk.

Maunsell 'Q' Locomotive Preservation Society, c/o R. Hawker, 26 Columbia Close, Gloucester.

Merchant Navy Locomotive Preservation Society Ltd, c/o 32 Britten Road, Brighton Hill, Basingstoke, Hampshire.

Middleton Railway Trust, c/o M.R.T.L., Garnet Road, Leeds.

Mid-Hampshire Railway Preservation Society, c/o R. Haddock, Alresford Station, Alresford, Hampshire, SO24 9JG.

Midland and Great Northern Joint Railway Society, c/o M. D. Beckett, 17c Blackfriars Street, Kings Lynn, Norfolk, PE30 1NN.

Midland 4F Preservation Society, c/o Ian Johnson, 3 Meldon Avenue, Chase Park, Sherburn, Durham, DH6 1JX.

Midland Railway Company, c/o A. G. Doig, 6 South Street, Derby.

Monmouthshire Railway Society, J. D. Thorne, Lyn Orchard, Undy, Magor, Newport, NP6 3EN.

Narrow Gauge Railway Society, M. Swift, 47 Birchington Avenue, Birchencliffe, Huddersfield, HD3 3RD.

Nasmyth Wilson Locomotive Preservation

Group, A. Wakefield, 54 Gainsborough Road, Dronfield, Sheffield.

Newcastle Coach Group, G. J. Holt, 27 High Street, Carrville, Durham City.

Newcastle University Railway Society, Dr. A. E. Wraith, Department of Metallurgy, University of Newcastle-upon-Tyne.

Newcomen Society (The), The Science Museum, L. R. Day, Science Museum, London, S.W.7.

Norfolk Railway Society, S. C. Harvey, St Barbara Cottage, Great Walsingham, Norfolk.

Northamptonshire Ironstone Railway Trust Ltd, c/o Alan Clayton, 30 Fulford Drive, Northampton.

North Devon Railway Preservation Society, c/o Association of Railway Preservation Societies. (Please send S.A.E.)

North Eastern Locomotive Preservation Group, c/o D. Hanson, 'Dorville', Nevilles Cross Bank, Durham City, Co. Durham.

North Eastern Railway Coach Group, c/o P. J. Brumby, 48 Laburnham Walk, Gilberdyke, Brough, Humberside, HU15 2TU.

North Eastern Railway 1661 Coach Partnership, c/o J. B. Dawson, 20 Towton Avenue, York, YO2 2DW.

Northern Counties Transport Society, W. R. Hendry, 209 Warrington Road, Glazebury, Near Warrington, Cheshire.

Northern Railfans Club (1952), C. B. Brown, 17 Glenview Street, Cornholme, Todmorden, West Yorkshire, OL14 8LT.

North Staffordshire Society, c/o I. J. Bowland, 78 Belmont Avenue, Sandbach, Cheshire.

North-West of Ireland Railway Society, c/o D. E. Lloyd, 3 Knockwellan Park, Londonderry, BT47, Northern Ireland.

North York Moors Railway Locomotive Fund, c/o Pickering Station, Pickering, North Yorkshire.

Peterborough Railway Society, c/o J. H. Maddocks, 36 Sallows Road, Peterborough.

Plymouth Railway Circle, c/o R. E. Taylor, 32 Honicknowle Lane, Pennycross, Plymouth.

Princess Elizabeth Locomotive Society, c/o P. Walker, Flat 1, 34 Elmdeon Road, Acocks Green, Birmingham, B27 6LH.

Quainton Railway Society, c/o R. B. Miller, 25 Loudhams Road, Little Chalfont, Amersham, Buckinghamshire.

Railway and Canal Historical Society, Littlemoor, Puddington, Tiverton, Devon EX16 8LN.

The Railway Club, C. F. Wells, 112 High Holborn, London, WC1V 6JS.

Railway Correspondence and Travel Society, 95 Chestnut Avenue, London E7 0JF.

Railway Development Association (London Area), A. W. T. Daniel, 3 Hall Way, Purley, Surrey.

Railway Enthusiasts Club, H. Davies, 32 Charterhouse Road, Godalming, Surrey, GU7 2AQ.

Railway Photographic Society, 4 Beechwood Avenue, Tilehurst, Reading, Berkshire, RG3 5BJ.

Railway Preservation Society, Chasewater Light Railway, c/o B. J. Bull, 144 Freer Road,

Birchfields, Birmingham B6 6NB.

Railway Preservation Society of Ireland, 37 Westland Road, Portadown, Co. Armagh, Northern Ireland.

Railway Travel and Photography Group, 4 Spreadoaks Drive, Stafford, ST17 4RP.

Railway Vehicle Preservations, c/o G. E. Maslin, 33 Coleridge Avenue, Manor Park, London, E12 6RQ.

Ravenglass and Eskdale Railway Preservation Society, 'The Retreat', Ravenglass, Cumbria, CA18 1SW.

Red Rose Live Steam Group, c/o Association of Railway Preservation Societies. (*Please send S.A.E.*)

Rod Group, Quainton Road Station, Aylesbury, Buckinghamshire.

Romney, Hythe and Dymchurch Railway Association, New Romney Station, New Romney, Kent.

Rossendale Forest Railway Society, Haslingden, Lancashire.

Saffron Walden Model Railway Club, c/o Audley End House, Audley End, Essex.

St Andrews University Railway and Transport Society, c/o Students Union, St Andrews University, Fife.

Salisbury Steam Locomotive Preservation Trust, c/o E. J. Roper, 33 Victoria Road, Wilton, Near Salisbury, Wiltshire, SP2 0OZ.

Scottish Locomotive Owners' Group, c/o W. A. Peddie, 13 Royal Terrace, Linlithgow, Lothian.

Scottish Railway Preservation Society, 4 Beech Crescent, Larbert, Near Falkirk, FK5 3EY.

Scottish Society for the Preservation of Industrial Machinery, Prestongrange, Lothian.

Shackerstone Railway Society, c/o Secretary, 138 Sherwood Road, Stoke Golding, Nuneaton, Warwickshire.

Signalling Record Society, J. P. Morris, 37 Whitlow, Saundersfoot, Dyfed.

Somerset and Dorset Museum Trust, c/o M. E. Rimes, 2 Lower Bagborough Cottages, Pylle, Shepton Mallet, Somerset.

South-East Essex Railway Society, 8 Rayleigh Drive, Leigh-on-Sea, Essex.

Southern Coaching Stock Preservation Group, M. E. Sharland, 2 Station Cottages, Horsted Keynes, Near Haywards Heath, East Sussex.

Southern Coach Preservation Group, 32 Britten Road, Brighton Hill, Basingstoke, Hampshire.

Southern Counties Railway Society, c/o Department of Botany, University of Southampton.

Southern Electric Group, G. D. Beecroft, 2 Welldon Crescent, Harrow, Middlesex, HA1 1QT.

Southern Locomotive Preservation Company Ltd., c/o H. Frampton-Jones, 41 Harrow Road, Carshalton Beeches, Surrey.

Southern Mogul Preservation Society, c/o R. Packham, 132 Church Road, Swanscombe, Kent.

Southern Railway 'Q' Class Locomotive Fund, c/o D. Preece, 8 Podmead Place, Gloucester, GL1 5PD.

Southern Railways Group, P. Winchester, 68 Ridgeway, Edenbridge, Kent, TN8 6AP.

Southern Steam Group, 31 Waldeck Road,

London, W.13.

Southport Locomotive and Transport Museum Society, located at Derby Road, Southport, Merseyside.

Southport Railway and Omnibus Circle, N. R. Box, 89 Larkfield Lane, Churchtown, Southport, Merseyside, PR9 8NP.

South Tynedale Railway Preservation Society, c/o Secretary, 14 Westgate, Haltwhistle, Northumberland.

South Western Circle, 21 Cowley Crescent, Walton-on-Thames, Surrey, KT12 5RH.

Stanier Black Locomotive Preservation Society, c/o Secretary, 'Sheraton', 17 St. George's Road, Petts Wood, Kent, BR5 1JG.

Stanier 8F Locomotive Society, c/o A. Wilkinson, 42 Westlands Road, Middlewich, Cheshire.

Stanier Mogul Fund, 23 Garth Crescent, Ernsford Grange, Coventry.

Steam Power Trust 65, c/o A. Bowman, 'Evergreen', Durham Road, Stockton-on-Tees, Cleveland.

Stephenson Locomotive Society, G. K. J. Kerley, 34 Durley Avenue, Pinner, Greater London.

Stevenage Locomotive Society, A. P. Higgins, 'Mansfield', Potters Heath Road, Welwyn, Hertfordshire.

Stour Valley Railway Preservation Society, c/o R. G. Booth, 20 Wainfleet Avenue, Romford, Essex.

Strathspey Railway Association, Boat of Garten Station, Highland.

Swanage and Wareham Railway Group, 'Belvedere', Seymer Road, Swanage, Dorset.

Talyllyn Railway Preservation Society, c/o Wharf Station, Tywyn, Gwynedd, LL36 9EY.

Teifi Valley Railway Preservation Trust, c/o K. P. Mascetti, 34 Townhill Road, Swansea, West Glamorgan.

Tenterden Railway Co. Ltd., Tenterden Town Station, Tenterden, Kent.

Thompson BI Locomotive Society, c/o Dept. R.W., 14 Shepherds Way, Harpenden, Hertfordshire.

Tramway Museum Society, c/o D. J. H. Senior, 23 South Road, Twickenham, Greater London.

Transport Ticket Society, J. E. Shelbourn, 18 Villa Road, Luton, LU2 7NT.

Urie S15 Locomotive Preservation Group, Secretary, 29 Irwin Road, Guildford, Surrey, GU1 5PW.

Vale of Rheidol Supporters Association, Room 3, Divisional Manager's Office, British Rail, Station Road, Stoke-on-Trent, Staffordshire.

Vintage Carriages Trust, c/o M. J. Leving, 16 Buckstone Oval, Leeds, West Yorkshire, LS17 5HG.

Wainwright 'C' Class Preservation Society, c/o R. F. Stephens, 51 Dowas Avenue, Chislehurst, Kent.

Warwickshire Railway Society, c/o Severn Valley Railway, Bridgnorth Station, Salop.

Welshpool and Llanfair Light Railway Preservation Co, c/o Llanfair Caereinion Station, Powys.

West Lancashire Light Railway Group, Hesketh

Bank, Near Preston, Lancashire.

West Somerset Railway Association, Secretary, 4 Queensway, Galmington, Taunton, Somerset.

Wight Locomotive Society, c/o Secretary, Haven Street Station, Ryde, Isle of Wight.

Winchcombe Railway Museum Association, T. R. Petchey, 23 Gloucester Street, Winchcombe, Gloucestershire.

Wirral Railway Circle, c/o Box 74, Bebington, Wirral, Merseyside.

Witherslack Hall Society, 48 Holte Road, Atherstone, Warwickshire, CV9 1HN.

Worcester Locomotive Society, c/o R. G. Nowell, 1 Ronelagh Street, Hereford.

Worcester Locomotive Society, H. D. Wood, 24 Cecilia Avenue, Worcester, WR2 6EN.

Y Clwb Rheil Cymru, Rear of Swansea Museum, Victoria Road, Swansea. J. M. Evans, 2 Vicarage Lane, Cwmdu, Swansea, SA5 8EU.

Yorkshire Dales Railway Company, c/o Embsay Station, Embsay, Skipton, North Yorkshire.

Y7 Preservation Group, Priory Farm Thurgarton, Nottinghamshire.

The 6000 Locomotive Association, c/o D. C. Layton, 31 Blaydon Crescent, Hereford, HR1 2TX.

The 1708 Locomotive Preservation Trust, c/o G. S. Mimms, 64 Elmwood Crescent, Luton, Bedfordshire.

The 1338 Preservation Fund, c/o J. B. True, 119 The Avenue, Kennington, Oxford, OX1 5QZ.

The 9642 Preservation Group, c/o W. T. Jones, 'Bryn-Awelon', 55 Salisbury Road, Maesteg, Mid Glamorgan.

The 46464 Preservation Trust, c/o I. N. Fraser, Palace Gates, Arbroath, DD11 2BS.

The 45428 Stanier Black Five Preservation Society, c/o J. B. Hollingsworth, 'Creua', Llanfrothen, Penrhyndeudraeth, Gwynedd, LL48 6SH.

7597 Fund, G. E. Maslin, 33 Coleridge Avenue, Manor Park, London, E12 6RQ.

RAILWAY MODELLING SOCIETIES

The Americana Model Railway Club, c/o The Americana Restaurant, 39 Bondgate, Darlington.

Andover and District Model Engineering Society, J. Pemble, 18 Windsor Road, Andover, Hampshire.

Ashton Model Railway Club, 1st Floor, 3 Market Avenue, Ashton-under-Lyne, OL6 6AR.

Aylesbury and District Society of Model Engineers, E. H. Smith, Wheatsheaf Cottage, Coleshill, Amersham, Buckinghamshire.

Barnsley Model Engineering Society, R. Hawke, 29 Winter Road, Pogmoor, Barnsley, South Yorkshire.

Bedford and District Model Railway Society, Ampthill Road, Bedford. A. J. Winterson, 3 Emerton Way, Wootton, MK43 9DS, Bedfordshire.

Bedford Model Engineering Society, J. F.

Dawe, Lanka, Station Road, Turvey, Bedfordshire.

Blackburn Model Engineering Society, J. Chadwick, 29 Lyndale Avenue, Wilpshire, Blackburn.

Boston Model Engineering Society, A. C. Smith, The Low Road, Wyberton, Lincolnshire.

Bradford and Shipley Model Engineering Society, G. S. Dunn, 13 Daisy Hill Lane, Bradford, BD9 6BN, South Yorkshire.

Breconshire Railway Society (Model Section), G. S. Blackledge, 25 Adelaide Gardens, Llanfaes, Brecon, Powys.

Brentwood and District Model Engineering Society, R. Harrison, 133 Priests Lane, Brentwood, Essex.

Brighton, British Rail Staff Association Model Railway Club, 4 Belmont Close, Brighton, East Sussex.

Brighton and Hove Society of Model and Experimental Engineers, C. F. Collins, 10 Mardon Close, North Woodingdean, Brighton, East Sussex, BN2 6NJ.

Bristol East (Downend) Model Railway Club, K. White, 9 Baugh Gardens, Downend, Bristol, BS16 6PN.

Bristol Society of Model and Experimental Engineers, Unitarian Hall, Lewins Mead, Bristol 1.

Burton-on-Trent Model Engineering Society, B. Schofield, 52 Harbury Street, Burton-on-Trent, DE13 0RY.

Cambridge and District Model Engineering Society, J. V. Millburn, 51 Marks Avenue, Raffles, Cambridge.

Carlisle and District Model Engineering Society, 49 Green Lane, Bellvue, Carlisle.

Chelmsford Society of Model Engineers, Waterhouse Lane, Chelmsford, Essex.

Cheltenham Society of Model Engineers, R. Greiffenhagen, Grange Cottage, Malvern Lane, Cheltenham.

Chesterfield and District Model Engineering Society, A. Rutherford, 69 Cuttholme Road, Chesterfield.

Chingford and District Model Engineering Society, K. S. Lane, 342 Firs Lane, Palmers Green, London, N.13.

City of Leeds Society of Model and Experimental Engineers, J. M. Powell, 33 Birchwood Avenue, Leeds 17.

Colchester Society of Model Engineers, A. E. L. Morrison, 40 St. John's Street, Colchester, Essex.

Crewe Model Engineering Society, R. A. Hawkesford, 455 Newcastle Road, Shavington, Near Crewe, Cheshire, CW2 5JU.

Derby Locomotive Works Society of Model Engineers, I. Tricklebank, 29 Tudor Road, Chaddesden, Derby, DE1 1AA.

Derby Model Railway Society, A. Straw, 33 Briar Lea Close, Sinfin, Derby, DE2 9PB.

Dublin Society of Model and Experimental Engineers, G. Mooney, 16 Harmonstown Crescent, Artane, Dublin 5.

Durham Model Engineering Society, J. H. Routledge, 4 Dene Gardens, Houghton-le-Spring, Tyne and Wear.

East Sussex Model Engineers, R. Clothier, 'Grosvenor Bungalow', Beacon Road, Hastings, East Sussex.

Erith Model Railway Society, P. J. Walsh, 25 Barnehurst Avenue, Erith, Kent.

Fylde Society of Model Engineers, C. Brockbank, 31 Abbotts Walk, Fleetwood, Lancashire.

Grimsby and Cleethorpes Model Engineering Society, R. F. Jackson, 28 Woodsley Avenue, Cleethorpes, Humberside.

Harrow and Wembley Society of Model Engineers, P. W. Reade, 5 Rydal Gardens, Kingsbury, London, NW9 0DS.

Hastings and District Model Engineering Society, L. J. Harwick, 577 Bexhill Road, St Leonards-on-Sea, East Sussex.

Hatfield and District Society of Model Engineers, Breaks Youth Centre, Link Drive, Hatfield, Hertfordshire.

Hitchin and District Model Engineering Club, W. A. Cross, 26 Stirling Road, Shortstown, Bedfordshire.

Ickenham and District Society of Model Engineers, P. J. Morgan, 89 Elm Avenue, Eastcote, Ruislip, HA4 8PG.

Ilford Junior Model Railway Club, J. K. Nelson, 36 South Park Drive, Ilford, Essex, IG3 9AQ.

Isle of Wight Model Engineering Society, H. A. Spanner, 144 High Street, Newport, Isle of Wight.

Keighley and District Model Engineering Society, T. H. Brownless, 159 Redcliffe Street, Keighley, West Yorkshire.

Kinver and West Midlands Society of Model Engineers Ltd, R. Humphries, 71 Rosemary Crescent, Woodsetton, Dudley, West Midlands.

Leeds Model Railway Society, D. H. Townsley, 19 Baronscourt, Leeds 15.

Leicester Society of Model Engineers, C. R. Clarke, 30 The Osiers, Braunstone, Leicester, LE3 2NX.

Leyland and District Model Engineering Society, Mrs R. Simpson, 71 Fylde Road, Preston, Lancashire.

Lincoln Model Engineering Society, P. J. Layfield, Westgate, Old Lincoln Road, Caythorpe, Grantham, Lincolnshire.

Lucas Society of Model Engineers, W. H. Bennett, Joseph Lucas Ltd, Great King Street, Birmingham, B19 2XF.

Lune Valley Model Railway Club, 76 Fairhope Avenue, Bare, Morecambe, Lancashire.

Macclesfield and District Model Engineering Society, K. Walwyn, 11 Elm Drive, Macclesfield.

Maidstone Model Engineering Society, J. Revell, 187 Loose Road, Maidstone, Kent.

Malden and District Society of Model Engineers Ltd, 34 Elmwood Road, Chiswick, London, W.4.

Mid-Hants Model Railway Group, 3 Hinton Crescent, Thornhill, Southampton, SO2 6GS.

Midland and Southern Counties Joint Railway, Ross I. Mackie, 26 Surbiton Hill Park, Surbiton, Greater London.

Model Railway Club, Keen House, 4 Calshot Street, London, N.1.

Nonsuch Notebook and Model Railway Club, 24 Tyler's Acre Avenue, Edinburgh, EH12 7JE.

Northampton Society of Model Engineers, Kingsthorpe Community Centre, Mill Lane, Kingsthorpe, Northamptonshire.

North London Society of Model Engineers, 1 Farquhar Street, Bengeo, Hertfordshire.

North Staffordshire Model Engineers, W. Hutchings, 65 Caverswall Road, Blythe Bridge, Stoke-on-Trent.

Norwich and District Society of Model Engineers, A. W. E. Hoskins, 5 Hellesdon Road, Norwich, NOR 9LJ.

Pendle Forest Model Railway Society, 4 Fletcher Street, Nelson, Lancashire.

Peterborough Society of Model Engineers, S. Bates, 15 Briar Way, Peterborough, PE1 5HL.

Polegate and District Model Engineers, N. Cowtan, Nursery Cottage, Horsebridge, Hellingly, East Sussex.

Portsmouth Model Engineering Society, W. J. Edwards, 39 Lichfield Road, Copnor, Portsmouth.

Reading Society of Model and Experimental Engineers, J. Shayler, 14 Westwood Road, Tilehurst, Reading, Berkshire.

Rochdale Society of Model and Experimental Engineers, T. A. Whitley, 13 Haslam Street, Rochdale, Greater Manchester.

Romford Model Engineering Society, E. Shirley, 42 The Parade, Greatstone, Kent.

Romney Marsh Model Engineering Society, W. Jupe, 32 Coleridge Road, Gidea Park, Romford, Essex.

Rotherham College of Technology Engineering Society, H. Beacher, The Cottage, Guilthwaite, Whiston, Rotherham, S60 4NE.

St Martin's Model Railway Club, Mrs S. E. Thompson, 56 Warren Avenue, Sherwood, Nottingham.

St Mellons Model Engineering Society, H. C. Linck, 18 Heathwood Grove, Cardiff, CF4 3RD.

Sale Area Model Engineering Society, W. Auty, 25 Eden Avenue, Culcheth, Greater Manchester.

Salisbury and District Model Engineering Society, J. D. Ollywright, 52 Wyndham Road, Salisbury, Wiltshire.

Sheffield and District Model Engineering Society, D. Wright, 32 Thorpe House Rise, Sheffield 8.

Southampton Model Railway Society, B. Moody, 5 Avon Road, Bitterne Park, Southampton, SO2 4FR.

South Cheshire Model Engineering Society, B. Jenks, 62 Moreton Road, Crewe, Cheshire.

South Devon Model Railway Company (and Castle Railway Circle), M. Cook, 110 The Village, Strenshall, York, YO3 1XB.

Southend Model Railway Club, B. W. Page, 52 Templewood Court, Benfleet, Essex, SS7 2RH.

Stockport and District Model Engineering Society, M. S. Taylor, 66 Dean Drive, Wilmslow, Cheshire.

Sunderland Society of Model and Experimental Engineers, T. Richwood, 96 Coniston Avenue, Fulwell, Sunderland, Tyne and Wear.

Sussex Model Locomotive Society, G. C. Lavis, Ingleside, Ash Vale, Chiddingfold, Godalming, Surrey.

Sutton Coldfield and North Birmingham Model Engineering Society, D. Palmer, 77 Hartley Road, Kingstanding, Birmingham 22C.

Sutton Model Engineering Club Ltd, J. Merrett, The Lych, 199 Croydon Road, Wallington, Surrey.

Swansea Society of Model and Experimental Engineers, L. C. Turner, 24 Ashgrove, Killay, Swansea.

Urmston and District Model Engineering Society, G. H. Naylor, 16 Grammar School Road, Lymm, Cheshire.

Welling and District Model Engineering Society, F. E. C. Wood, 67 Picardy Road, Belvedere, Kent.

Westbury Society of Model Engineers, A. J. Savory, 45 Leigh Road, Westbury, Wiltshire.

Western Model Railway Society (Acton), D. F. B. Kevan, 35 Woodhall Gate, Pinner, HA5 4TN.

Weston-Super-Mare and West Huntspill Live Steam Society, K. J. Webber, 17 Kensington Road, Weston-Super-Mare, Avon.

Whitefield and District Model Engineers Society, A. F. Stevenson, 2 Newlands Drive, Prestwich, Greater Manchester.

Willesden and West London Society of Model Engineers, M. Saytch, 13 Brooksville Avenue, Kilburn, London, N.W.6.

Wimbledon Model Railway Club, R. W. Jebbitt, 39 Willows Avenue, Morden, Surrey, SM4 5SG.

Winchester Model Engineering Society, K. Barnes, 36 Bramshaw Close, Harestock, Winchester, Hampshire.

Wirral Model Engineering Society, Dr. D. Postlethwaite, 29 Wood Lane, Greasby, Wirral, Merseyside.

Worcester and District Society of Model Engineers, C. A. Castle, 29 Fort Royal Hill, Worcester.

Wrexham and District Model Engineers Society, P. G. Jesson, 19 Vicarage Fields, Ruabon, Near Wrexham, Clwyd.

York and District Society of Model Engineers, R. A. Douglas, 16 Lawson Road, York, YO2 2NE.

York Model Railway Society, P. A. Dew, c/o United Services Club, 61 Micklegate, York.

MODELLING ASSOCIATIONS

Association of Model Railway Clubs, 31 Fairfield Road, Lodge Farm Estate, Caerleon, Gwent.

Association of South Wales Railway Societies, B. Keitch, 129 Redlands Road, Penarth, South Glamorgan.

E.M. Gauge Society, D. J. Murrells, 428 Bedonwell Road, Abbey Wood, London, SE2 0SE.

Gauge 'O' Guild, Tony Watts, 62 Allingham Road, South Park, Reigate, Surrey.

Hornby Railway Collectors' Association, A. Brown, 7 Coleford Bridge Road, Mytchett, Camberley, Surrey.

MODEL RAILWAY CLUBS

South Hampshire Association of Railway Modellers, D. L. Mundy, 22 Maytree Road, Chandlers Ford, Hampshire.

Three Millimetre Society, J. McGarry, 12 East Rise, Lichfield Park, Sutton Coldfield, B75 7TH.

2 MM Scale Association, L. W. Little, 16 Springfield Road, Wilbarston, Market Harborough, Leicestershire.

MUSEUMS AND OTHER PLACES TO VISIT

Aberdeen Gasworks Locomotive Preservation Trust, c/o Alan Greig, 129 Cairncry Road, Aberdeen. *Locomotives in store.*

Albany Steam and Industrial Museum, Forest Road, Newport, Isle of Wight.

Albert Draper and Son Ltd, Dairycoates Depot, Hull. *Locomotive in store.*

Albright & Wilson Ltd, Portishead, Avon. *Locomotive on Exhibition.*

Aveling-Barford Ltd, Invicta Works, Grantham, Lincolnshire. *Locomotive on exhibition.*

Aylesbury British Rail Goods Yard. *Locomotives in store.*

L. Bamford Ltd, Rochester, Near Uttoxeter, Staffordshire. *Locomotives in store.*

Belfast Transport Museum, Witham Street, Belfast 4, Northern Ireland.

Birmingham Museum of Science and Technology, Newhall Street, Birmingham.

Birmingham Railway Museum, Tyseley Motive Power Depot, Warwick Road, Birmingham.

Blackburn Brothers (Haulage) Ltd, Cateshall Road, Cotterstock, Surrey.

Blists Hill Industrial Museum, Ironbridge, Telford, Salop.

Bressingham Steam Museum, Bressingham Hall, Diss, Norfolk.

Brighton Belle Inn, Winsford, Cheshire. *Converted Pullman coach from the Brighton Belle now used as a restaurant.*

Bristol City Museum, Queens Road, Bristol.

British Celanese Ltd, Spondon, Derby. *Locomotive on display.*

British Rail, Newton Abbot. *Locomotive on display.*

British Sugar Corporation, Wissington Factory, Norfolk.

Brockham Museum, Brockham, Near Dorking, Surrey.

Bulmer Railway Centre, H. P. Bulmer Ltd, Whitecross Road, Hereford. *Locomotives on display.*

Burnham Market, Norfolk. *Locomotives in store.*

J. Butler, 5 Heath Rise, Grove Heath, Surrey. *Locomotives on display.*

Cambridge Museum of Technology, Chedders Lane, Cambridge.

Carnegie Trust, Pittencrieffe Park, Dunfermline, Fife. *Locomotive on display.*

Cheadle Moseley Grammar School for Boys, Cheadle, Greater Manchester. *Locomotives on display.*

China Clay Industrial Museum, Wheal Martyn, Trenance Valley, St Austell, Cornwall.

City Industrial Ltd, Finsbury Park, London. *S.R. Pullman coach from the Brighton Belle on display.*

City of Aberdeen District Council, Parks Department, Aberdeen. *Locomotive in store.*

City of Birmingham Corporation, St Francis Street Road, Aston, Birmingham. *Locomotive on display.*

Coalbrookdale Works Museum, Ironbridge Gorge Museum Trust Ltd, Coalbrookdale, Salop.

Collection 'X', Burgate Farm, Loxhill, Surrey. *Locomotives in store.*

T. Collings, Trehedyn, Tynewydd. *Locomotive on display.*

Conway Valley Railway Museum, Old Goods Yard, Bettws-y-Coed, Gwynedd.

Corby Urban District Council, West Glebe Park, Cottingham Road, Corby. *Locomotive on display.*

Courtaulds Ltd, Coventry. *Locomotive in store.*

Crewe and Nantwich Borough Council, Crewe Shopping Centre. *Locomotive on display.*

Cusworth Hall Museum, Doncaster Rural District Council, Doncaster. *Locomotive on display.*

Dane John Gardens, Canterbury, Kent. *Locomotive on display.*

Darlington North Road Museum, North Road Station, Darlington, Co Durham.

Delph Station, Oldham, Lancashire. *Locomotives on display.*

Dinsdale Park Residential School, Near Darlington, Co Durham. *Locomotive on display.*

Dinting Railway Centre, Dinting, Glossop, Derbyshire.

East Anglia Transport Museum, Chapel Road, Carlton Colville, Lowestoft, Suffolk.

W. Elliott & Son (York) Ltd, Rufforth Airfield, North Yorkshire. *Locomotive in store.*

P. Elms, 73 Crow Lane, Romford, Essex. *Locomotives in store.*

J. A. Farr, Fox Covert Drive, Edinburgh 12. *Locomotive on display.*

Glasgow Museum of Transport, Coplawhill Works, 25 Albert Drive, Glasgow.

Glenrothes Council, Muir's Yard, Kirkcaldy, Fife. *Locomotive in store.*

A. Guinness Son & Company (Dublin) Ltd, St James Gate Brewery, Dublin 8. *Locomotive on display.*

S. Harrison & Sons (Transport) Ltd, Sheffield Road, Tinsley, South Yorkshire. *Locomotive in store.*

George Hastwell Training Centre, Abgey Road, Barrow-in-Furness. *Locomotive on display.*

'Hayling Billy', Brickwoods Ltd, Hayling Island, Hampshire.

Head Wrightson & Co Ltd, Teesdale Ironworks, Thornaby-on-Tees. *Locomotives on display.*

R. Hilton, 'Poplars', North Moreton, Didcot, Oxfordshire. *Locomotives in store.*

J. Hirst & Sons, Bank Top, St Mary Bourne, Near Andover, Hampshire. *Locomotives in store.*

Hunslet Engine Company, Jack Lane, Leeds. *Locomotive on display.*

Hunt & Co (Hinckley) Ltd, London Road, Hinckley, Leicestershire. *Locomotives in store.*

Ian Allan Ltd, Shepperton, Middlesex. *Locomotive on display.*

Dr. R. P. Jack, Station House, Eddleston, Peebles. *Locomotives in store.*

Jubilee Park, Ashby, Scunthorpe, Lincolnshire. *Locomotive on display.*

Mr A. M. Keef, Cote Farm, Bampton, Oxfordshire. *Locomotives in store.*

Kettering Museum, Manor House Gardens, Sheep Street, Kettering. *Locomotives on display.*

Kingston-upon-Hull Corporation Transport Museum, 36 High Street, Kingston-upon-Hull, Humberside.

Mr M. Knight, Ibornden Farm, Biddenden, Kent. *Locomotive in store.*

J. B. Latham, 'Channings', Kettlewell Hill, Woking, Surrey. *Locomotives in store.*

Leeds City Museum, Copley Mill Motive Power Depot, Leeds. *Locomotives in store.*

Leicester Corporation Museum, Abbey Lane Pumping Station, Corporation Road, Leicester.

Leonard Fairclough Ltd, Adlington, Lancashire. *Locomotive in store.*

Liverpool Museum, Land Transport Gallery, William Brown Street, Liverpool, L3 8EN.

London Transport Museum, Syon Park, Brentford, Greater London.

Longfield Collection, 'The Sidings', 193 Main Road, Longfield, Kent. *Locomotives on display.*

Long Marston Ministry of Defence Central Engineering Park, Long Marston, Warwickshire. *Locomotives in store.*

Longmoor Camp, Ministry of Defence (Army Department), Longmoor, Hampshire. *Locomotives on display.*

Lound Hall Mining Museum, Berescotes, Near Retford, Nottinghamshire.

Lower Meadow Play Centre, off Paringdon Road, Southern Way, Harlow, Essex.

Lytham Motive Power Museum, Helical Springs Ltd, Dock Road, Lytham, Lancashire.

Molewood Railway Museum, Molewood, Near Hereford.

Monkwearmouth Station Museum, North Bridge Street, Sunderland.

Narrow Gauge Railway Museum, Tywyn, Gwynedd.

National Railway Museum, Leeman Road, York.

New Church Farm Play Area, Skelmersdale New Town, Lancashire.

New Street Childrens Playground, Daventry. *Locomotive on display.*

P. D. Nicholson, 17 Crossland Road, West Ewell, Surrey. *Locomotive in store.*

North of England Open Air Museum, Beamish, Durham.

Nottingham Industrial Museum, The Eastcroft, London Road, Nottingham.

Pembrokeshire County Museum, Scotton House, Scotton, Dyfed.

Penrhyn Castle Museum, Llandegai, Near Bangor, Gwynedd.

Port Erin Railway Museum, Port Erin, Isle of Man.

Portsmouth City Museum, British Gas Corporation Works, Eastney, Southsea, Hampshire. *Locomotive in store.*

Preston Park Museum, Yarm Road, Eaglescliffe, Stockton-on-Tees, Cleveland.

Railwayana Ltd, 745 Abbeydale Road, Sheffield 7.

Reid Kerr Technical College, Yoker Power Station, Glasgow. *Locomotive in store.*

Riber Castle Wild Life Park, Near Matlock, Derbyshire. *Locomotive on display.*

C. Roads, Hillside, Wimpole. *Locomotive in store.*

Royal Scottish Museum, Chambers Street, Edinburgh 1.

M. Saul, Wengeo Lane, Ware, Hertfordshire. *Locomotive on display.*

Science Museum, South Kensington, London, S.W.7.

Sharpe Brothers, Gables Service Station, Rayleigh Spur Road, Rayleigh, Essex. *Locomotives on display.*

Somerset Railway Museum, Bleadon and Uphill Station, Near Weston-super-Mare, Avon.

South Cambridgeshire Rural and Industrial Museum, Heydon, Cambridgeshire.

South Devon Railway Museum, Dawlish Warren Station, Dawlish, Devon.

Southport Locomotive and Transport Museum, Derby Road, Southport, Lancashire.

South Wales Industrial Museum, Swansea, Glamorgan.

Splotts Park, Cardiff, Newport. *Locomotive on display.*

Stafford British Railways Station, Victoria Gardens, Stafford. *Locomotive on display.*

Staffordshire County Council Industrial Museum, Great Haywood, Staffordshire.

Steam Centre, Kirkmichael, Isle of Man.

Steam Enterprises Ltd, Steamtown, Carnforth, Lancashire. *Locomotives in store.*

Steamtown, Lakeside Railway Estates Co Ltd, Carnforth Motive Power Depot, Warton Road, Carnforth, Lancashire.

Stone Cross Special School, Ulverston, Lancashire. *Locomotive in store.*

Tasker Museum Trust, The Castle, Winchester.

Tewin Primary School, Collins Meadow, Near Hertford. *Locomotive on display.*

Tiverton Museum, Blundells Road, Tiverton, Devon.

Tyne and Wear County Museum of Science and Engineering, Exhibition Park, Great North Road, Newcastle-upon-Tyne.

Ulster Folk Museum, Cultra Manor, Holywood.

Walsh Transport Services, Darwen, Lancashire. *Locomotive in store.*

A. J. Wilson, 6 Trentdale Road, Carlton, Nottingham. *Locomotive in store.*

Winchcombe Railway Museum, 23 Gloucester Street, Winchcombe, Gloucestershire.

Wollaston Road Recreation Ground, Irchester, Northamptonshire. *Locomotive on display.*

BIBLIOGRAPHY

Magazines:

Airfix Magazine/PSL Publications Ltd, 9 Ely Place, London, EC1N 6SQ.

European Railways Magazine/Robert Spark, Evelyn Way, Cobham, Surrey, KT11 2SJ.

International Railway Journal/899 Clerkenwell Green, London, E.C.1.

Meccano Magazine, Model & Allied Publications/13–35 Bridge Street, Hemel Hempstead, Hertfordshire.

Model Railway Constructor/Ian Allan Ltd, Terminal House, Shepperton, Middlesex, TW17 8AS.

Model Railways/Model and Allied Publications.

Modelworld/49 Malden Way, New Malden, Surrey, KT3 6EA.

Modern Railways/Ian Allan Ltd.

Modern Tramway/Ian Allan Ltd and Light Railway Transport League.

Railway Forum Steam Journal/ARPS Year Book.

Railway Gazette International/IPC Transport Press, Dorset House, Stamford Street, London, SE1 9LU.

Railway Magazine/IPC Transport Press.

Railway Modeller/Pecoway, Seaton, Devon, EX12 2LU.

Railway World/Ian Allan.

Steam Sphere, 6 Victoria Square, Portland, Dorset.

Books:
The following publishers specialize in railway books:

D. Bradford Barton Ltd.

Ian Allan Ltd.

David & Charles Ltd.

SKYWORKS

SOURCES OF MATERIALS

Fabrics of all kinds from departmental stores, etc.
Cotton cambric available from:
Louis Mankin Ltd, 20 Charlotte Street, London, W1P 1HJ.

Ripstock spinnaker nylon available from:
Barnes (HG), Hawkesfield, Fernhurst, Haslemere, Surrey.

Bowker & Budd Ltd, Bosham, West Sussex.

W. G. Lucas & Son, Broad Street, Portsmouth, Hampshire, PO1 2JF.

Tyvek available from:
Sean Rawnsley, Top Cottage, Willersley, Broadway, Hereford and Worcester.

Tissue, crêpe and kraft papers available from:
Paperchase, 216 Tottenham Court Road, London, W.1.

Bamboo available from:
Bethell Brothers Ltd, 87–89 St Pauls Street, London, E.C.2.

Eaton, 16 Manette Street, London, W1V 5LB.

Aluminium rod available from:
John Smith & Sons (Clerkenwell) Ltd, 53–54 St Johns Square, London, E.C.1.

Balsa wood from modelmaking shops, or:
Balsa Wood Supplies Ltd, Commerce Way, Lancing, West Sussex, BN15 8TE.
Rattan cane available from:
Eaton, 16 Manette Street, London, W1V 5LB.
Nylon line from fishing tackle shops, or:
Barnes (HG), Hawkesfield, Fernhurst, Haslemere, Surrey.
Arthur Beale Ltd, 194 Shaftesbury Avenue, London, WC2H 8JP.
Monofilament line available from:
F. A. Sharp & Sons, 162 Malden Road, London, N.W.5.
Kites, accessories (and in some cases construction materials) available from:
Beatties, 112 High Holborn, London, W.C.1.
R. & R. Beckley, 228 Navestock Crescent, Woodford Green, Essex.
Brookite Ltd, Francis Terrace, Junction Road, London, N.19.
Collets Chinese Gallery, 40 Great Russell Street, London, W.C.1.
Conran, 77 Fulham Road, London, S.W.3.
Graham & Green, 7 Elgin Crescent, London, W.11.
Habitat; most branches.
Hamleys, 200 Regent Street, London, W.1.
The Kite Shop, 29 Neal Street, London, W.C.2.
Paperchase, 216 Tottenham Court Road, London, W.1.
Peter Powell Kites Ltd, 2 Robertson Road, Shurdington, Cheltenham, Gloucestershire.
Raggity Ann's, 26 Tranquil Vale, Blackheath, London, S.E.3.
D. A. Rice (Engineering) Ltd, 62 Orchard Road, Burgess Hill, West Sussex.
Warehouse, 39 Neal Street, London, W.C.2.
Yachtmail Company Ltd, 7 Cornwell Crescent, London, W11 1PH.

SOCIETIES

American Kite Flyers Association, P.O. Box 1511, Silver City, New Mexico 88061. *A non-profitmaking worldwide organization.*
British Hang Gliding Association, Monksilver, Taunton, Somerset.
British Kite Flyers Association, M.A.P. Ltd, P.O. Box 35, Hemel Hempstead, Hertfordshire. *The newly formed K.F.A. was resurrected from the old Kite and Model Aircraft Association originally founded by Marconi, Baden-Powell and Cody in 1902.*

BIBLIOGRAPHY

Magazines:
Kite Lines. British Kite Flyers Association.
Kite Tails. American Kite Flyers Association.
Books:
The Aeropleustic Art, or Navigation in the Air by the Use of Kites, or Buoyant Sails, by George Pocock, 1851.
The Art of the Japanese Kite, by Tal Streeter/John Weatherhill, New York.
Chinese Kites, by David Jue/Charles E. Tuttle, Rutland, Vermont.
Colourful Kites from Japan, by Tadao Saito/Ward Lock.
The Complete Book of Kites and Kite Flying, by Will Yolen/Thomas Nelson.
The Dream of Flight, by Clive Hart/Faber & Faber.
The Flying Cathedral: The Story of Samuel Franklin Cody, by Lee Arthur Gould/Methuen.
Flying Kites, by James Wagenvoord/Macmillan.
Fun With Kites, by John and Kate Dyson/Angus & Robertson.
Hang Gliding, by Dan Poynter/Daniel F. Poynter, Massachusetts.
How to Make and Fly Kites, by Eve Barwell and Conrad Bailey/Studio Vista.
Kite Craft, by Lea Scott Newman and Jay Hartley Newman/Crown Publishers, New York.
Kite Folio, by Timothy Burkhart/Wildwood House.
Kite Making and Flying, by Harold Ridgeway/Arco Mayflower.
Kites, by Jean-Paul Mouvier/Collins.
Kites, by Wyatt Brummitt/Golden Press, New York.
Kites, by Tsutomo Hiroi/Mainichi Newspapers, Tokyo.
Kites: An Historical Survey, by Harold Ridgeway/Arco Mayflower.
Kites: A Practical Guide to Kite Making and Flying/Ronald Press, New York.
Making and Flying Kites, by Lloyd, Mitchell and Thomas/John Murray.
Parakites, by Gilbert T. Woglom/G. P. Putnam, New York, 1896.
The Penguin Book of Kites, by David Pelham/Penguin. *A truly fabulous book, not only for its content but its superb design. Solid information on the history, construction and flying techniques of kites, as well as detailed plans for bridles, tails, reels, etc.*
Practical Kites and Aeroplanes, by Frederick Walker/Guilbert Pitman, 1903.
Tako, by Tatsue Miyawaki/Biken-Sua, Tokyo.
The Young Sportsman's Guide to Kite Flying, by Will Yolen/Thomas Nelson.
Your Book of Kites, by Clive Hart/Faber & Faber.

THE STRANGE WORLD OF TOPIARY

SOURCES OF MATERIALS

The most extensive and amazing selection of shrubs and trees is available from:
Hillier & Sons Ltd, Winchester.
Seeds of many shrubs and trees available from:
Thompson & Morgan (Ipswich) Ltd, London Road, Ipswich, Suffolk.

BIBLIOGRAPHY

The Book of Topiary, by John Lane/Nathaniel Lloyd, 1904.
Discovering Topiary, by Margaret Baker/Shire Publications.
Garden Craftsmanship in Box and Yew, by Ernest Benn, 1925.
Green Animals and Other Things, by Susie Slack and Martin Poole/First Edition.
Topiary and Ornamental Hedges, by Miles Hadfield/Adam & Charles Black.

SOME PLACES TO VISIT

Many great and many humble gardens have topiary and the reader is advised to refer to the various garden scheme brochures which give details of the various gardens they cover:
Eire Gardens Scheme/c/o The Superintendent, Queen's Institute of District Nursing, 19 Pembroke Park, Dublin 4.
Gardens of England and Wales open to the Public under the National Gardens Scheme/c/o The Secretary, The National Gardens Scheme, 57 Lower Belgrave Street, London, S.W.1.
Gardens Open to the Public (In Aid of the Gardeners Royal Benevolent Society and The Royal Gardeners Orphan Fund)/c/o The Gardeners Sunday Organisation, White Witches, Claygate Road, Dorking, Surrey.
Historic Houses, Castles and Gardens in Great Britain and Northern Ireland/Index Publishers Ltd.
Metropolitan Public Gardens Association, 4 Carlos Place, London, W1Y 5AE.
The National Trust List of Properties/c/o The Secretary, 42 Queen Anne's Gate, London, S.W.1.
Scotland's Gardens Scheme/c/o The General Organizer, 26 Castle Terrace, Edinburgh 1.
Ulster Gardens Scheme/c/o The Public Secretary, The National Trust, 82 Dublin Road, Belfast, Northern Ireland.

TREASURE ISLAND

SOURCE OF MATERIALS

Metal detectors can be obtained from:
John Allen Electronics Ltd, 184 Main Road, Biggin Hill, Kent.
Branches at:
35 Craven Street, London, W.C.2.
9 High Street, Totnes, Devon.
M. L. Beach (Products) Ltd, 41 Church Street, Twickenham, Middlesex.
Also at:
7 Kings Parade, Ditchling Road, Brighton.
C-Scope Metal Detectors, 62 Castle Street, Canterbury, Kent.
Midas Instruments Ltd, 26 Cottam Crescent, Marple Bridge, Greater Manchester.
Pulse Inductions Ltd, Greencoat House, Francis Street, London, S.W.1.
Savo Electronics Ltd, Longman Road Industrial Estate, Inverness, Highland.
Treasure Hunting Supplies, 175 Church Road, Willesden, London, S.W.1.
Branches at:
71 Caledonian Road, London, N.1.
139 Witton Street, Northwich, Cheshire.
68 Gillygate, York.
Underground Exploration, Faraday House, P.O. Box 1, Hailsham, East Sussex.

SOCIETIES

Bottles and Relics Book Club, c/o Chris Morris, 6 The Causeway, Oxney Green, Chelmsford, Essex.
The British Amateur Treasure Hunting Club, The Secretary, 27 Pangbourne, William Road, London, N.W.1.
The British Bottle Collectors Club, 19 Hambro Avenue, Rayleigh, Essex, SS6 9NJ.
Treasure Hunters Association, 71 Caledonian Road, London, N.1.

BIBLIOGRAPHY

Journals:
Bottles and Relics News – now defunct. Back copies available from 'The Gatehouse', Station Lane, Ingatestone, Essex. *Also from:* S. F. Barker, 19 Hambro Avenue, Rayleigh, Essex, SS6 9NJ.
Bottles and Relics, c/o S. F. Barker (*address above*).
Bottles and Relics Quarterly, c/o S. F. Barker (*address above*).
True Treasure, c/o F. Mellish, 2 Lidell Close, Kenton, Harrow.
The following books are by Edward Fletcher:
Bottle Collecting/Blandford.
A Bottle Collector's Guide to European Seals, Case Gins and Bitters/Latimer.
Collecting Potlids/Pitman.
Digging Up Antiques/Pitman.
International Bottle Collecting/Blandford.
Non Dating Price Guide to Bottles, Pipes and Doll's Heads/Blandford.
A Treasure Hunter's Guide/Blandford.
Treasure Hunting For All/Blandford.
Where to Dig Up Antiques/S.C.P.
Other authors:
Anchovy Paste – By Appointment, by Frank George/Frank George, Orpington.
Bottle Collector's Dictionary, by Adams and Payne/S.C.P.
Bottle Digger's Site Finding Guide, by John Webb/B.R.P.
British Bottle Collecting Review/c/o British Bottle Collectors Club.
Clay Tobacco Pipes in Cambridgeshire, by R. J. Flood/Oleander.
Collector's Book of Ink Bottles, nos 1, 2, and 3, by June Tansley/Barker (*address above*).
The Fortune Hunter's Guide, by Peter Haining/Sidgwick & Jackson.
Ginger Beer Collecting, by Adams and Payne/S.C.P.
Mainly Codds Wallop, by Roy Morgan, c/o S. F. Barker (*address above*).
Pot Lid Booklet, c/o F. Mellish, 2 Lidell Close, Kenton, Harrow, HA3 9EP.
Prospecting and Collecting Clay Pipes, by John Webb and Alec Childs/B.R.P.

Sealed Bottles, by Roy Morgan/M.A.B.

Sussex Bottle Collector's Guide, by D. Askey, c/o S. F. Barker (address above).

The Toothpaste Potlid Book, by Ben Swanson/B.R.P.

Treasure Hunting Tools You Can Make, c/o F. Mellish (address above).

ROCKS AROUND THE CLOCK

SOURCES OF MATERIALS

Tumble polishing machines, trimsaws, grinding units, grits, polishes, rough rock specimens and other lapidary equipment and supplies available from:

Avon Gems, Strathaven, Boon Street, Eckington, Pershore, Hereford and Worcester.

Bains Orr Ltd, 1–5 Garlands Road, Redhill, Surrey.

M. L. Beach (Products) Ltd, 41 Church Street, Twickenham, Middlesex.

W. A. Bolton, 19 Lynwood Road, Liverpool 9.

G. & B. Butler, 186 The Pantiles, Tunbridge Wells, Kent.

Caverswall Minerals, The Dams, Caverswall, Stoke-on-Trent.

Cornerstones, 2 North Parade, Matlock Bath, Derby.

The Craft Centre, Chart Sutton, Maidstone, Kent.

Craftorama, 14 Endell Street, London, W.C.2.

Crystal Tips Lapidary, 25a Linaker Street, Southport, Merseyside.

Fidra Stone Shop, 47 Meeting House Lane, Brighton, East Sussex.

Fife Stone Craft, 3 Edison House, Fullerton Road, Glenrothes, Fife.

Gallery Gems, 31 Fore Street, Kingsbridge, Devon.

Galloway Gems, 26 Oakwell Road, Castle Douglas, Dumfries and Galloway.

Gemlines, 10 Victoria Crescent, London, S.W.19.

Gemlode, 35 Bolton Road, Chessington, Surrey.

Gemma, 494 Notlingham Road, Chaddesden, Derby.

The Gem Rock and Lapidary Centre, 41 Fore Street, St Just, Penzance, Cornwall.

Gemrocks Ltd, 7 Brunswick Shopping Centre, London, W.C.1.

Gemset of Broadstairs Ltd, 31 Albion Street, Broadstairs, Kent.

Gemstones, 44 Walmsley Street, Hull, Humberside.

Gemtree, 8 Dingle Bank, Sandbach, Cheshire.

Geobright, 28 Queens Road, Brighton, East Sussex.

Glenjoy Lapidary Supplies, 19–20 Sun Lane, Wakefield, West Yorkshire.

H. & T. Gems, 31 Rosebury Road, Hartlepool, Cleveland.

Harrisons, 174 Woodlands Road, Glasgow, C.3.

Hillside Gems, Wylde Green, Sutton Coldfield, West Midlands.

Hirsch Jacobson, 91 Marylebone High Street, London, W.1.

Howard Minerals Ltd, 27 Heddon Street, London, W.1.

A. & D. Hughes Ltd, Popes Lane, Oldbury, Warley, West Midlands.

International Crafts, P.O. Box 73, Hemel Hempstead, Hertfordshire.

Jacinth Gems, 10 Highfield Crescent, Southampton, Hampshire.

The Jam Pot, Slaidburn, Clitheroe, Lancashire.

Kernowcraft Rocks and Gems Ltd, 44 Lemon Street, Truro, Cornwall.

Key Minerals, Brienz, Hendra Road, St Dennis, Cornwall.

Keystones, 1 Local Board Road, Watford, Hertfordshire.

C. Kilpatrick, 27 Colsea Road, Cove Bay, Grampian.

Lakeland Rockshop, Packhorse Yard, Main Street, Keswick, Cumbria.

J. Lane, The Haven, Danes Road, Awbridge, Romsey, Hampshire.

Little Rocks, 36 Oakwood Avenue, Cardiff, South Glamorgan.

Love-Rocks, 56/58 North Street, Bedminster, Bristol.

L.W.S. Ltd, 46 Walmsley Street, Hull, Humberside.

Manchester Minerals, 33 School Lane, Heaton Chapel, Stockport, Greater Manchester.

Marbleshop, Portsoy, Grampian.

Marcross Gems, 13 Market Place, Shepton Mallet, Somerset.

A. Massie & Son, 158 Burgoyne Road, Sheffield 6, South Yorkshire.

Merritt, Eastleigh Road, Devizes, Wiltshire.

Mineralcraft (North), 192 Barnsley Road, Cadworth, Barnsley, South Yorkshire.

Mineral Imports, 72 Netheravon Road, London, W4 2NB.

C. & N. Mineral Supplies, Adelphi Chambers, Shakespeare Street, Newcastle-on-Tyne, Tyne and Wear.

Natural Gems Ltd, Kingsbury Square, Aylesbury, Buckinghamshire.

D. M. Naylor, 1 The Knoll, Crown Hill, Rayleigh, Essex.

J. L. Newbigin, 13 Narrowgate, Alnwick, Northumberland.

Norgems, 4 Front Street, Sandbach, Cheshire.

Opie Gems, 13 Gilbert Close, Hempstead, Gillingham, Kent.

Opie Gems, 57 East Street, Ilminster, Somerset.

Pebblegem, 88a Wallis Road, London, E9 5LN.

Pebblegem, 71 St Marks Road, Bush Hill Park, Enfield, London.

P.M.R. Lapidary Equipment, Pitlochry, Tayside.

Port Beag Pebblecraft, Albany Street, Oban, Strathclyde.

Quercus Gems, Lindisfarne House, Rucklers Lane, King's Langley, Hertfordshire.

Rockhaven Gem Company, 125a Clephington Road, Dundee, Tayside.

Rockhound, Greenacres, Church Road, Black Notley, Braintree, Essex.

The Rockhound Shop, Newbiggin, Northumberland.

Rose Gems, 637 Lord Street, Southport, Merseyside.

Rough and Tumble Ltd, 3 Tyne Street, North Shields, Tyne and Wear.

Scotrocks Partners, 48 Park Road, Glasgow, C.4.

Seaway, Perranporth, Cornwall.

J. Simble & Sons, 76 Queens Road, Watford, Hertfordshire.

Solent Lapidary, 145 Highlaw Road, Southsea, Hampshire.

The Stone Corner, 21 High Street, Hastings, East Sussex.

Stones and Settings, 54 Main Street, Prestwich, Greater Manchester.

Tideswell Dale Bookshop, Tideswell, Derbyshire.

Tim Gems, The Old Shop, Ludham, Great Yarmouth, Norfolk.

Tor Minerals, 2 The Orchard, Trevanson, Wadebridge, Cornwall.

Trilobite, 11 Chester Road, Northwich, Cheshire.

Tudor Amethyst, 24 West Street, Exeter, Devon.

Wee Gem Shop, 18 Cathcart Street, Ayr, Strathclyde.

Westcott Antiques, 2 The Green, Westcott, Dorking, Surrey.

Whithear Lapidary Co, 35 Ballards Lane, London, N.3.

Worldwide Mineralogical Co, Great Shelford, Cambridge.

Geological Survey maps available from:

Edward Stanford Ltd, 12 Long Acre, London, W.C.2.

Regional Geological Handbooks available from:

H.M. Stationery Office, 49 High Holborn, London, W.C.1.

SOCIETIES

Amateur Geological Society, Hampstead Garden Suburb Institute, Central Square, London, N.W.11.

Bath Lapidary Society, 10 Pulteney Street, Bath, Avon.

Borders Lapidary Club, 47 Albert Place, Galashiels, Borders.

Bristol Lapidary Society, 10 Grove Park, Redland, Bristol.

Cambridge Lapidary Club, 93 Queen Edith's Way, Cambridge.

Cardiff Lapidary Society, 36 Oakwood Avenue, Cardiff.

Cheltenham Mineral Society, 2 Westcote Road, Tuffley, Gloucestershire.

Danum Lapidary Society, 39 St Augustines Road, Bressacarr, Doncaster, South Yorkshire.

Dartford Lapidary Society, 45a Elmdene Road, London, S.E.18.

Dorset Mineral Club, 70 Manor Road, Dorchester, Dorset.

Essex Rock and Mineral Society, 176 Wanstead Park Avenue, Ilford, Essex.

Exeter Gem and Mineral Society, High Barn, Kenton, Exeter.

Golspie Lapidary Club, The Wee Shop, Golspie, Highland.

Harrogate Lapidary Society, 71 Wetherby Road, Harrogate, North Yorkshire.

Huddersfield Mineralogical Society, 25 Branch Street, Paddock, Huddersfield, West Yorkshire.

Irish Lapidary Society, Grafton Court, Grafton Street, Dublin 2.

Kingston Lapidary Society, 219 Summergangs Road, Hull, Humberside.

Leeds Lapidary Society, 2 Earlswood Avenue, Leeds, LS8 2BR.

Mid-Cornwall Rocks and Mineral Club, 91 Queens Crescent, Bodmin, Cornwall.

New Forest Lapidary Society, 30 Denham Drive, Highcliff, Christchurch, Dorset.

Norfolk Lapidary Society, St Mary's, New Buckenham, Norwich.

North Surrey Lapidary Society, 28 The Causeway, Carshalton, Surrey.

Northumbrian Lapidary Teachers Association, 17 Westhill, Kirkhall, Morpeth, Northumberland.

Peak District Rock and Mineral Society, Youth Centre, Tideswell, Derbyshire.

Pentland Lapidary Society, 12 Kirkgate, Currie, Lothian.

Plymouth Mineral and Mining Club, 36 Ponsonby Road, Milehouse, Plymouth, Devon.

Scottish Mineral and Lapidary Club, 22b St Giles Street, Edinburgh.

Sheffield Amateur Geological Society, 5 Hutcliffe Wood Road, Sheffield, South Yorkshire.

Southampton Lapidary Society, 52 Kinross Road, Totton, Southampton.

Stanley Rockhound Club, 24 Cecil Street, East Stanley, Durham.

Sutherland Rockhounds, Lonemore, Dornoch, Highland.

Tees-side Lapidary Society, 65 Staindrop Drive, Acklam, Middlesbrough, Cleveland.

Thanet Mineral Society, 5 Maisons Rise, Broadstairs, Kent.

Warrington Lapidary Society, 28 Thelwall New Road, Thelwall, Warrington, Cheshire.

Wessex Lapidary Society, 1 Avenue Road, Winchester, Hampshire.

West Midlands Lapidary Society, 148 Foleshill Road, Coventry, Warwickshire.

West Scotland Mineral and Lapidary Society, 82 Dumbreck Road, Glasgow.

West Surrey Lapidary Society, 10 Whitemore Green, Hale, Farnham, Surrey.

Whitehaven Lapidary Society, 110 Tomlin Avenue, Mirehouse, Whitehaven, Cumbria.

BIBLIOGRAPHY

Magazines:

Gems/29 Ludgate Hill, London, E.C.4.

Rockhound/24–9 Trellick Tower, 5 Golbourne Road, London, W.10.

Books:

Geology

Agate Collecting in Britain, by Peter R.

Rodgers/Batsford.

Collecting Gems and Ornamental Stones, by K. Blakemore and G. Andrews/Foyles Handbook.
Gems and Jewels, by Ned Seidler/Hamlyn.
The Mineral Kingdom, by Paul Desautels/Hamlyn.
Mineralogy for Amateurs, by J. Sinkankas/Van Nostrand Reinhold, New York.
Minerals, Rocks and Fossils, by W. R. Hamilton/Hamlyn.
Pebbles on the Beach, by C. Ellis/Faber & Faber.
The Physical Basis of Geography: An Outline of Geomorphology, by S. W. Wooldridge and R. S. Morgan/Longmans.
Precious Stones and Pearls, by Hermann Bank/Pinguin Verlag, Innsbruck.
The Rock Book, by C. L. and M. A. Fenton/Doubleday, New York.
Rocks and Minerals, by H. Zim and P. R. Schaffer/Hamlyn.
Rocks and Minerals, by Paul E. Desautels/Ridge Press.
Rocks and Minerals, by Cedric Rogers/Ward Lock.
Rocks, Minerals and Gemstones, by I. O. Evans/Hamlyn.
Stones and Minerals, by W. Schumann/Lutterworth Press.
Van Nostrand's Standard Catalogue of Gems, by J. Sinkankas/Van Nostrand Reinhold, New York.
Lapidary
Collecting and Polishing Stones, by Herbert Scarfe/Batsford.
Gemcutting, by J. Sinkankas/Van Nostrand Reinhold, New York.
Gem Tumbling and Baroque Jewelry, by 'The Victors'/Victor Agate Shop, Spokane, Washington, U.S.A.
Pebble Polishing, by Edward Fletcher/Blandford.
Pebble Polishing and Pebble Jewelry, by Cedric Rogers/Hamlyn.
Rock and Gem Polishing, by Edward Fletcher/Blandford.
Stone Grinding and Polishing, by David F. Olsen/Little Craft Books.

MUSEUMS

British Museum (Natural History Section), Cromwell Road, South Kensington, London, SW7 5BD.
*There are many other museums throughout the country with geological collections and the reader is advised to refer to the guide **Museums and Galleries**, available from most bookstalls and shops, or direct from ABC Travel Guides, Oldhill, London Road, Dunstable, Bedfordshire.*

THE ART OF DOWSING

SOURCES OF MATERIALS

Most of the instruments used in dowsing can easily be home-made, as they have been throughout history. However, there are now one or two manufacturers who specialize in dowsing equipment:
Metaphysical Research Group, Archer's Court, Stonestile Lane, Hastings, East Sussex. *Manufacturers of a wide range of rods and pendulums and other 'occult' equipment.*
Omni-Detector Company, 27 Latham Road, Twickenham, Greater London. *They produce a dowsing 'kit' which includes angle rods, pendulum, spring rod and manual.*
De La Warr Laboratories, Raleigh Park Road, Oxford. *Manufacturers of Radionic equipment including a Radionic Camera.*
The British Society of Dowsers, 19 High Street, Eydon, Daventry, Northamptonshire. *The society manufactures and sells equipment to members.*

SOCIETIES

The British Society of Dowsers, 19 High Street, Eydon, Daventry, Northamptonshire.
Psionic Medical Society, Hindhead, Surrey. *Researches the application of dowsing to agriculture and medicine.*
Radionic Association, The Secretary, Field House, Peaslake, Guildford, Surrey. *A society devoted to the aims of medical dowsing.*
Research into Lost Knowledge Organisation, 36 College Court, Hammersmith, London, W.6.
Independent local dowsing groups:
Bristol Dowsers, c/o Mrs Dalby, Grange Fell, Leigh Woods, Bristol 8.
East Anglian Dowsing Society, Miss F. M. Freestone, 7 Mill Road, Loddon, Norfolk.
East Kent Group, Sir Charles Jessel, Bt, South Hill Farm, Hastingleigh, near Ashford, Kent.
Essex Dowsers, F. B. Dineen, 4 Brentwood Road, Ingrave, Essex CM13 3QH.
North West London Group, Mrs A. Heron, 89 Highfield Avenue, London NW11 9TU.
Southport Group, G. H. Newton, 9 Weld Road, Southport, Lancashire PR8 2BX.
Warwickshire Group, David Haffner, 560 Binley Road, Coventry.
Worcester Dowsers, R. A. Homer, 22 Lansdowne Road, Worcester WR1 1SP.

COURSES

The Radionic Association *holds courses on handling radionic equipment which lead up to the Association's examination.*
Psionic Medical Society *holds courses on dowsing in connection with medicine and agriculture.*
Inner London Education Authority. *Tom Graves, author of 'Dowsing', is currently teaching dowsing at an I.L.E.A. adult evening class. Check times and location in* **Floodlight** *magazine.*

BIBLIOGRAPHY

The Divining Rod, by Sir William Barrett and Theodore Besterman/University Books.
Dowsing, by Tom Graves/Turnstone Books.
Dowsing, by Robert H. Leftwich/Aquarian Press.
Dowsing for You, by Bruce Copen/Academic Publications.
Elements of Dowsing, by Henry de France/Bell.
Ghost and Divining Rod, by T. C. Lethbridge/Routledge & Kegan Paul.
An Introduction to Medical Radiesthesia, by Vernon D. Wethered/C. W. Daniel.
Patterns of the Past, by Guy Underwood/Pitman.
Pendulum Diagnosis, by C. Dietrich/Academic Publications.
Practical Dowsing, by A. H. Bell/Bell.
Radiesthesia, by Abbé Mermet/Vincent Stuart.
Radionics, by Vernon D. Wethered/C. W. Daniel.
Journals:
Journal of the British Society of Dowsers.
Journal of the Radionic Association.

BREADLINES

SOURCES OF SUPPLIES

Flour in small quantities is not an economical buy. Why not join or form a food co-op and buy in bulk? Flour in bulk can be obtained from:
Cann Mills, Shaftesbury, Dorset.
Harmony, 1 Earl Cottages, Earl Road, S.E.1.
Harvest, 31 Belvedere Lansdown Road, Bath.
Horsefield's Stoneground Products, Water Mill, Pentrefoelas, Clwyd.
Jordans, Holme Mills, Biggleswade.
D. & M. Lickley & Sons, The Mill, Whitemill, Nantgaredig, Dyfed.
Mayall, Led Hall, Harmer Hill, Shrewsbury.
Grain mills for grinding flour can be obtained from:
Seed, 269 Portobello Road, London, W.11.
The Self-sufficiency and Small Holding Supplies, Priory Road, Wells, Somerset.

SOCIETIES

CAMREB – The Campaign for Real Bread, c/o Vegetarian Society, 53 Marloes Road, Kensington, W.8.

BIBLIOGRAPHY

Breadmaking: Its Principles and Practice, by Edmund B. Bennian/O.U.P.
The Bread Tray, by Louis P. DeGouy/Dover.
Food in England, by Dorothy Hartley/Macdonald & Jane's.
Home Baked, by George and Cecilia Scurfield/Faber & Faber.
Home Baker, by Super Cooks/Golden Hands.
Making Breads with Home-grown Yeast and Home-grown Grains, by Phyllis Hobson/Thorson.
Recipes from an Old Farmhouse, by Alison Uttley/Faber & Faber.
Use Your Loaf, by Ursel Norman/Fontana/Collins.
Wholegrain Baking Sampler, by Beatrice Trum Hunter/Pivot Paperbacks.

HOME AND DRY

BIBLIOGRAPHY

The Complete Book of Preserving, by Marye Cameron-Smith/Marshall Cavendish.
Complete Guide to Home Canning, Preserving and Freezing, by U.S.A. Department of Agriculture/Dover.
The Cordon Bleu Book of Jams, Preserves and Pickles, by R. Hume/Pan.
Food in England, by Dorothy Hartley/Macdonald & Janes.
Food Storage in the Home, by R. C. Hutchinson/Arnold.
Home Preservation of Fruit and Vegetables/H.M.S.O.
Jams and Jellies, by W. St Peter/101 Productions.
Jams and Preserves, by Good Housekeeping/Sphere Books.
Jams, Jellies and Preserves, by Ethelind Fearon/Barrie & Jenkins.
Jams, Pickles and Chutneys, by David and Rose Mabey/Penguin.
Keeping the Harvest, by Nancy Thurber and Gretchen Mead/Thorson.
Let's Preserve It, by Beryl Wood/Mayflower.
Making Your Own Preserves, by Robin Howe/Barrie & Jenkins.
Pickles and Chutneys, by Frances Carmichael/Barrie & Jenkins.
Preserves, by Beryl Gould-Marks/Faber & Faber.
Putting Food By, by Beatrice Vaughn and Janet Green/Bantam.
The Right Way to Make Jams, by Cyril Grange/Elliot Right Way Books.
Stocking Up, by Organic Gardening and Farming Magazine, U.S.A./Rodale Press.
Deep Freeze Books:
The Complete Home Freezer, by Mary Nowak/Ward Lock.
Deep Freezing, by Morag Williams/Hamlyn.
Deep Freezing, by Mary Nowak/Sphere.
Fresh From the Freezer, by Marye Cameron-Smith/Penguin.
Home Freezing Through the Year, by Audrey Ellis/Hamlyn.
The Manual of Home Freezing, by Rena Cross/Foulsham.
Step by Step Guide to Home Freezing, by Audrey Ellis/Hamlyn.

THE MINIATURE GARDEN

SOURCES OF MATERIALS

Hanging baskets, stone troughs, compost and most of the other materials mentioned can be obtained from any reputable garden centre. Sphagnum moss can be obtained from florist

shops. Many of the plants mentioned can be obtained from:
John Scott & Son, The Royal Nurseries, Merriott, Somerset.
Hillier & Sons, Winchester, *for dwarf conifers.*

SOCIETIES

Alpine Garden Association, Lye Endlink, St John's, Woking, Surrey.

BIBLIOGRAPHY

General:
Alpines, by Lionel Bacon/David & Charles.
Bottle Gardens, by Roger Grounds/David & Charles.
Collins Guide to Alpines and Rock Garden Plants, by Anna N. Griffith/Collins.
Gardening in Miniature, by Roy Genders/Hale.
Gardening with Alpines, by Stanley B. Whitehead/John Gifford.
Japanese and Miniature Gardens, by Leslie Woollard/Foyles Handbooks.
Miniature Gardens, by Anne Ashbury/David & Charles.
Plants in Tubs, Pots, Boxes and Baskets, by Leslie Johns/David & Charles.
Pots and Pot Gardens, by Mary Grant White/Abelard Schuman.
Rock Gardening, by Roy Genders/John Gifford.
Bonsai:
Bonsai, by Linda M. Walker/John Gifford.
Bonsai for Beginners, by H. J. Larkin/Angus & Robertson.
The Mini-Bonsai Hobby, by Tei Ichi Katayama/Japan Publications.
Step-by-Step Guide to Growing Bonsai Trees, by Joan Melville/Pelham Books.

THE JUVENILE THEATRE

SOURCE OF MATERIALS

Pollocks Toy Theatre Museum, Scala Street, London, W.1. *A magic world of toy theatres past and present. The place is always filled with kids who can hardly believe their eyes. They sell theatres and plays and props and dolls and all sorts of other bits and pieces. They also give theatrical performances.*

SOCIETIES

British Puppet and Model Theatre Guild, c/o G. Shapley, 18 Maple Road, Yeading, Near Hayes, Middlesex.

BIBLIOGRAPHY

Characters and Scenes, by Edward Draper/The Savage Club Papers, 1868.
Childhood's Drama, by John Ashton/Ward & Downey, 1894.
Chinese Children/Pollocks Toy Theatre Museum.
The Drama in Pasteboard, by William Archer/The Art Journal, April and May 1887.
Every Little Boy's Book/Routledge, 1886.
The Evolution of the Baby Doll and The Human Nursery/Pollocks Toy Theatre Museum.
The Glamour of a Toy Shop, by Francis Eagle/published by the author, 1919.
How to Make Dolls Houses, by Audrey Johnson/Blandford.
Juvenile Drama – The History of the English Toy Theatre/George Speaight/Macdonald & Co., 1946.
The Juvenile Theatres, by Frank Jay/The London Journal, 1921.
The Last of the Toy Theatre Makers, by Louise Morgan/John O'London's Weekly, October 30, 1936.
Our Model Theatre, by Samuel Highley/Routledge – published in Every Boy's Annual, 1874.
Penny Plain Two Pence Coloured. A History of the Juvenile Drama/Harrap, 1932.
A Penny Plain; Twopence Coloured, by Godfrey Turner/The Theatre, 1886.
Pollocks Shakespearian Theatrical Portraits/Pollocks Toy Theatre Museum.
The Victorian Parlour – A Cut and Colour Book, by Theodore Menton/Dover Colouring Book.
The Webb Juvenile Drama, by Francis Eagle/The Mask, April 1913.

PLACES TO VISIT

The British Museum (Print Room), Great Russell Street, WC1B 3DG.
Edinburgh Public Library.
The Hinkins Collection, 45 St Giles, Oxford.
The Lanchester Marionette Theatre, Malvern.
The London Museum.
Pollocks Toy Theatre Museum.
The Public Library, Birmingham.
The Robert Louis Stevenson Birthplace and Museum, Howard Place, Edinburgh.
The Victoria and Albert Museum, Cromwell Road, South Kensington, London, S.W.7.

HOUNDS OFF OUR WILDLIFE

SOURCES OF MATERIALS

The H.S.A. recommend Tuf 'Hippo' waterproof rubber boots for anti-hunt activities. They are totally free of animal produce.

SOCIETIES

British Deer Society, Forge Cottage, Askham, Penrith, Cumbria.
Crusade Against All Cruelty to Animals, Avenue Lodge, Bounds Green Road, London, N22E 4EU.
Frodsham Badger Group, 4 Middle Walk, Frodsham, Warrington, Cheshire.
Hunt Saboteurs Association, P.O. Box 19, Tonbridge, Kent.
Irish Council Against Blood Sports, 67 Newtown Avenue, Blackrock, Co Dublin.
League Against Cruel Sports, 1 Reform Row, London, N17 9TW.
National Society Against Cruel Sports, 8 Elsworthy Road, London, N.W.3.
New Sanctuary Animal Welfare Group, 47 Chudleigh Road, London, SE4 1JX.
Red Deer Commission, Elm Park, Island Bank Road, Inverness.
Royal Society for the Prevention of Cruelty to Animals, The Causeway, Horsham, Sussex.
Save Our Seals, 65 Lower Thrift Street, Northampton.
Seal Preservation Action Group, 2 The Cottages, Mesnington Grange Farm, Spennymoor; Durham.
Wild Animal Protection Society, The Lee Centre, 1 Aislibie Road, Lee Green, London, S.E.12.

BIBLIOGRAPHY

After Their Blood, by Leslie Pine/Kimber.
Against Hunting, by Patrick Moore/Gollancz.
Animal Rights, by Andrew Linzey/SCM.
The Ballad of the Belstone Fox, by Roger Burrows/David & Charles.
The Declining Otter, by Angela King, John Ottaway and Angela Potter/Friends of the Earth Campaign, Yew Tree Cottage, Chaffcombe, Chard, Somerset.
The Leading Hare, by George Ewart Evans and David Thompson/Faber & Faber.
Man's Dominion, by Monica Hutchings/Hart-Davis.
Town Fox/Country Fox, by Brian Vesey-Fitzgerald/André Deutsch.
Wild Fox, by Roger Burrows/David & Charles.

MOVING TO THE COUNTRY

SOCIETIES

BIT, 146 Great Western Road, London, W.11.
Commune Movement, c/o BIT, 146 Great Western Road, London, W.11.
Commune Network, 76 New North Road, Huddersfield. *A radical offshoot of the Commune Movement.*
Crofters Commission, 4–6 Castle Wynd, Inverness, Scotland.
Farmers and Smallholders Association, 25 Austin Friars, London, E.C.2.
Housing Centre Trust, 13 Suffolk Street, London S.W.1. *Provides information to house builders.*
National Federation of Housing Societies, 86 Strand, London, W.C.2.
National Federation of Owner Occupiers and Owner Residents Association Ltd, 29 Norview Drive, East Didsbury, Manchester.
National House Owners Society, 19 Sheepcote Road, Harrow, Greater London.
National Trust. *Write to Stourhead Estate Office, Stourton, Warminster, Wiltshire, for places to let in Dorset. Write to The Friaries, Bodmin, Cornwall, for places to let in Cornwall.*
People In Common, c/o Derek Goffin, 51 Hurst Street, Burnley. *An organisation which often helps residents in housing co-ops.*
Rural Survey of Empty or Derelict Buildings and Cottages, Fir Tree Cottage, Bisley, New Stroud, Gloucestershire.
Self Sufficiency Centre, Broadleys, Widdington, Saffron Walden, Essex.

BIBLIOGRAPHY

Magazines:
Homesteading Journal, c/o Mother Earth.
Mother Earth, P.O. Box 8, Malvern, Hereford and Worcester.
Natural Life Styles, Gordon & Breach Science Publishers, 41–42 William IV Street, London, W.C.2.
Practical Self Sufficiency, Self Sufficiency Centre, Broadleys, Widdington, Saffron Walden, Essex.
Resurgence, 275 Kings Road, Kingston, Surrey.
Seed, 8a All Saints Road, London, W.11.
Undercurrents, 275, Finchley Road, London, N.W.3.
The Village, c/o National Council of Social Service, 26 Bedford Square, London, W.C.1.
Whole Earth, 54 Queens Park Road, Brighton, East Sussex.
Books:
A Way of Living as a Means of Survival, by Michael Wheatley/Corgi.
Alternative England and Wales, by Nicholas Saunders, 65 Edith Grove, London, S.W.10.
Alternative Scotland, by Barry Wright and Chris Worsley/Wildwood House.
The Backyard Beekeeping Book, by William Scott/Prism Press.
The Backyard Dairybook, by Andrew Sinclair/Prism Press.
The Backyard Pig and Sheep Book, by Ann Williams/Prism Press.
The Backyard Poultry Book, by Andrew Sinclair/Prism Press.
The Complete Book of Self Sufficiency, by John Seymour/Faber & Faber.
The Complete Farmer, by John Murray/Main Street Press.
The Complete Urban Farmer, by David Wickers/Julian Friedman.
The Cottage Life, by Fred Archer/Arrow.
Country Bazaar, by Andy Pittaway and Bernard Schofield/Fontana Paperbacks.
Learning to Live In The Country, by Kathy Jones/Wildwood House.
On Next To Nothing – A Guide To Survival Today, by Thomas and Susan Hinde/Weidenfeld & Nicolson.
The Outdoor Handyman, by Adrienne and Peter Oldale/Collins.

SUNSET